Fundamentals of
Human Performance

Fundamentals of Human Performance

George A. Brooks
University of California—Berkeley

Thomas D. Fahey
California State University—Chico

Macmillan Publishing Company
New York

Collier Macmillan Publishers
London

Copyright © 1987, Macmillan Publishing Company,
a division of Macmillan, Inc.

Printed in the United States of America

Portions of this work were originally published under the title,
Exercise Physiology: Human Bioenergetics and Its Applications,
copyright © 1984 by John Wiley & Sons, Inc.

Macmillan Publishing Company
866 Third Avenue, New York, New York 10022

Collier Macmillan Canada, Inc.

Library of Congress Cataloging-in-Publication Data

Brooks, George A.
  Fundamentals of human performance.

  Includes index.
  1. Exercise—Physiological aspects.   I. Fahey,
Thomas D.   II. Title.
QP301.B8854   1987   612′.044   86-8393
ISBN 0-02-315150-1

Printing: 2 3 4 5 6 7   Year: 7 8 9 0 1 2 3

ISBN   0-02-315150-1

Preface

Fundamentals of Human Performance is aimed at physical education, nursing, nutrition, and physical therapy students who need an up-to-date, practical introduction to exercise physiology. We have attempted to include the essence of our more in-depth work, *Exercise Physiology: Human Bioenergetics and Its Applications,* but have eliminated much of the detail and the treatment of less essential topics. In addition, we have included a thorough discussion of exercise prescription and exercise stress testing for students interested in clinical exercise physiology.

The theme of our text is that exercise is basically an energetics event and that both the theoretical basis and practical applications of physical activity can be explained through an understanding of metabolic phenomena. Although the study of exercise bioenergetics is sometimes difficult, we believe the essence of the material is relatively simple. We have attempted to present an overview of exercise physiology in a simple, concise, easy-to-understand manner. Although we have eliminated much of the detail from our discussion, our presentation is based on the results of thousands of research studies and considerable practical experience. *Fundamentals of Human Performance* represents a state-of-the-art synopsis of the field.

Although this text has summarized the results of complicated research in a manner suitable to the beginning student with minimal scientific background, our presentation helps the student to understand *why* something happens during exercise. Exercise physiology is a science in rapid transition, moving from the point of simply describing phenomena to understanding fundamental mechanisms. This process allows practitioners to be more systematic and effective in measuring physical fitness and prescribing exercise programs. In the past, coaching techniques have usually been based on methods of successful coaches and athletes. Often, little thought was given to why something happened. Likewise, in the clinical environment, exercise was often prescribed with little thought given to individual differences or its actual effects on the patient. During the past 50 years, extensive research conducted in exercise physiology and sports medicine has provided a rational basis for various practices. Sophisticated research has provided the theoretical underpinnings for practical application. It is our hope that this text will provide the beginning student with a good background in exercise physiology and stimulate further study.

V

A book such as this would not have been possible without the help of many people. First and foremost is the support and understanding of our wives, Kilty and Suzanne, and our children, Daniel, Tommy, Timmy, and Mikey. We would like to thank our professors who instilled in us a love and respect for the sports sciences, including W.D. McArdle, J.A. Faulkner, R.E. Beyer, K.J. Hittelman, F.M. Henry, Frank Verducci, G.L. Rarick, and J.H. Wilmore. We would also like to thank friends who constructively reviewed the text, including Jim Gale, Rich Schroeder, and Martha Rowe.

Finally, a word to the student is in order. Most of you are interested in this field because of your love of sport. A practical knowledge of the sports sciences will help you to better enjoy your own physical fitness program as well as to help others do so. Both of us started out as athletes who eventually hoped to become coaches. In becoming students of our sport, we found that we could maximize our potential and the potential of others through an understanding of the process by which we improved performance through training. The manner in which the body's systems perform during exercise is truly elegant, and an understanding of them will only enhance your enjoyment of physical activity. In a way, we both ended up as coaches, because our work with students hopefully will help them enhance the performance of athletes and the health of the average person.

George A. Brooks
Thomas D. Fahey

Contents

CHAPTER 3
Nonoxidative Energy Sources for Human Movement:
Anaerobic Glycogenolysis and Glycolysis   33

CHAPTER 4
Oxidative Energy Sources for Human Movement   57

CHAPTER 5
Ventilation and Respiratory Gas Exchange　　89

CHAPTER 6
Control of Ventilation during Exercise   115

CHAPTER 7
Cardiovascular System Responses to Exercise   *135*

CHAPTER 8
Oxygen Transport Dynamics during Exercise   *159*

CHAPTER 9
Neuromuscular Structures and Functions   *179*

CHAPTER 10
Muscle Function during Exercise   199

CHAPTER 11
Exercise, Body Composition, and Nutrition   215

CHAPTER 12
Environmental Stress and Exercise: Altitude, Cold, Heat, Polluted Air, and Travel 253

CHAPTER 13
Athletic Training of Men and Women 287

CHAPTER 14
Ergogenic Aids and Human Performance 323

CHAPTER 15
Exercise, Growth, and Aging 351

CHAPTER 16
Exercise and Disease 379

CHAPTER 17
Exercise Testing and Prescription   405

APPENDIX I: *List of Symbols and Abbreviations*   441

APPENDIX II: *Units and Measures*   445

APPENDIX III: *Cardiac Drugs and Their Effects*   451

Index   455

1

Introduction: The Limits Of Human Performance

What are the limits of physical performance? Is it possible to run the 100 m dash in 9 sec (Figure 1-1)? Can the discus be hurled 300 ft (Figure 1-2)? Can the mile be run in less than 3 min (Figure 1-3), or is it possible to swim 100 m in less than 40 sec (Figure 1-4)? Can the routines of Olympic gymnasts become more complex and better executed than they are now (Figure 1-5)? Can exercise training be used to retard the advance of coronary heart disease, and can paraplegics be exercised to maintain the status of paralyzed limbs (Figure 1-6)? Are these goals unrealistic, or do they underestimate the limits of human performance? These are important questions of interest not only to physical educators and athletics coaches but also to a variety of others including physicians, nurses, physical therapists, human factors engineers, physical anthropologists, and zoologists.

The answers are somewhat predictable. The shot-putter who achieves the distance of 80 ft will have to generate the necessary force to propel the implement that distance. An athlete with insufficient muscle mass, less than optimal leverage, and inadequate metabolic capability will simply be incapable of this feat. Similarly, individuals with poor cardiovascular capacity, muscular strength, and coordination will lead physically restricted lives. The study of exercise physiology can lead to a better understanding of the physical capacity and limitations of the human body, as well at its underlying mechanisms.

The Scientific Basis of Exercise Physiology: Some Definitions

The scientific method involves the systematic solution of problems. The scientific approach to solving a problem involves the development and presentation of ideas (hypotheses), the collection of information (data) relevant to those hypotheses, and the acceptance or rejection of the hypotheses based on evaluation of the data (conclusions). Although the scientific method appears to be straightforward, the process of deriving appropriate hypotheses and systematically testing them can be complex. It is nevertheless evident that, in our increasingly technological society, those who systematically analyze their problems and take appropriate steps to solve them are most likely to acquire satisfactory answers to their questions. Individuals who make the best use of the scientific method will be the most successful scientists, educators, coaches, and health professionals.

Physiology is a branch of biological science concerned with the function of organisms and their parts. The study of physiology is dependent on and intertwined with other disciplines such as anatomy, biochemistry, and biophysics. The reason for this interdependence is that the function of the hu-

Figure 1-1
Carl Lewis hits the tape in the 1984 Olympic 100-m dash, the premier sprint event in international competition.

(SOURCE: Photo courtesy of Allsport/Steve Powell.)

Figure 1-2
Al Oerter has won four Olympic gold medals in the discus. Throwing the discus over 200 ft requires enormous power, coordination, and technique.

(SOURCE: Photo courtesy of Wayne Glusker.)

3

Figure 1-3
Sebastian Coe wins the 1984 Olympic 1500-m run. Athletic feats such as this represent possibly the supreme example of speed, power, and endurance in human endeavor.

(SOURCE: Photo courtesy of Allsport/Steve Powell.)

Figure 1-4
Steve Linquist reaches for the wall and an Olympic medal in the 100-m breast-stroke. In internationally recognized swim competition there is no pure sprint event, but athletes rely on muscular endurance, aerobic endurance, and technique.

Figure 1-5
Mary Lou Retton completes a floor exercise routine. Coordination, strength, and balance are premier attributes of athletes such as Mary Lou.

(SOURCE: Photo courtesy of UPI/Bettmann Newsphotos.)

man body must follow the natural laws of structure and function, which fall within the domain of these other disciplines.

Exercise physiology is a branch of physiology that deals with the function of the body during exercise. As will be seen, definite physiological responses to exercise occur that depend on its intensity, duration, and frequency, the environmental circumstances, and the physiological status of the individual.

Figure 1-6
Nan Davis suffered three transections of her spinal cord in an automobile accident. She now pedals a cycle around the Wright State University campus by means of computer-controlled contractions of her paralyzed leg muscles.

(SOURCE: Courtesy of Wright State University Communications.)

Science in Physical Education, Athletics, and Allied Health Professions

One might ask, Are physical educators and coaches scientists? The answer lies in their approach to problem solving. Many teachers and coaches systematically evaluate their selection and training of individuals, so they can be considered scientists. The scientist-coach introduces an exercise stimulus and systematically evaluates the response. The nonscientist-coach, in contrast, administers the training program according to whim and the dictates of tradition. This method relies on either mimicking the techniques of successful athletes or conforming tenaciously to traditional practices. Although nonscientist-coaches are sometimes successful, they are rarely innovative and seldom help an individual perform optimally. For progress to occur, systematic innovation is absolutely essential in any field.

Exercise and sport, particularly individual sports that demand extremes of strength, coordination, speed, or power, lend themselves to scientific analysis because the measures of success are easily quantified. If a weightlifting coach attempts to improve a particular athlete's performance with a specific training technique, the results can be evaluated objectively—the athlete either improves or fails to do so. Likewise, the distance a discus is thrown can be measured, the duration of a 100-m run can be timed, the number of baskets sunk in a game can be counted, and the distance an amputee can walk can be measured. The scientist-coach and health science professional observes and quantifies the factors affecting human performance and systematically varies them to achieve success. Admittedly, it is easier to predict performance in individual sports than in team sports or activities in which group interactions and extremes in environment operate to influence the outcome. It is not beyond the scope of our imagination, however, that, with continued development of exercise physiology and other branches of exercise science, it may be as possible to predict outcomes in team sports as in individual endeavors.

The Relevance of Physiology for Physical Education, Athletics, and the Allied Health Professions

Understanding the body during exercise is a primary responsibility of each physical educator, coach, and health science professional. Maximizing performance requires a knowledge of physiological processes. As competition becomes more intense, continued improvement will be attained only by careful consideration of the most efficient means of attaining biological adaptation.

Physical educators and health science professionals are increasingly working with a more heterogeneous population. New populations are interested in assuming an active life-style and even participating in competitive sports. Older adults are flocking to masters' sporting events, heart attack patients are resuming physical activity earlier than ever, and people with diseases such as asthma and diabetes are using exercise to reduce the effects of their disabilities. These people need guidance by trained professionals who understand the responses to exercise in a variety of circumstances. Knowledge of exercise responses in these diverse populations requires a thorough understanding of both normal and abnormal physiology.

Degenerative diseases such as coronary heart disease and osteoarthritis have replaced infectious diseases as primary health problems. Many of these degenerative disorders are amenable to change through modification of lifestyle, such as participating in regular exercise. The importance of exercise in a program of preventive medicine has reinforced the role of the physical educator as part of the interdisciplinary team concerned with health care and maintenance. The physical educator must speak the "language of the science" to become a true professional and interact with the other professionals of the health care team.

The Body as a Machine

In many ways the exercising human can be compared to a machine, such as an automobile. The machine converts one form of energy into another in performing work; likewise, the athlete converts chemical energy to mechanical energy in the process of running, throwing, and jumping. The athlete, like the machine, can increase exercise intensity by increasing the rate at which energy is converted from one form to another. The athlete goes faster by increasing the metabolic rate and speeding the breakdown of fuels, which provides more energy for muscular work.

At their roots, motor activities are based on bioenergetics, which control and limit the performance of physical activities. In this sense, the body is a machine. The reasons for exercising can be quite varied, but when the exercise starts, the mechanisms of performance are determined by physical and chemical factors. Understanding how to select and prepare the biological apparatus for exercise, and how the exercise affects the machine over both the short and the long term is important in exercise physiology and other fields.

This book emphasizes understanding the individual during exercise from the standpoint of the energetics that support the various activities. The discussion begins with energy and its importance to living organisms, emphasizing how we acquire, conserve, store, and release energy for everyday life. The functions of various physiological systems (ventilatory, circulatory, endocrine, etc.) are examined from the perspective of their function in supporting physical performance and their place in the process of energy conversion. Discussion of immediate as well as the long-term effects of exercise is integrated into this text. Some background information on general principles of physiological response and the field of exercise physiology is offered next.

The Rate-Limiting Factor

In a complex biological machine such as an exercising human, many physiological processes are occurring simultaneously. For example, when a person runs a mile, the heart's contractility and beating frequency increase, hormones are mobilized, the metabolic rate is raised, and body temperature is elevated. Despite the vast number of events occurring simultaneously, usually only a few control and limit the overall performance of the activity. Many scientists approach the understanding of physiological systems by studying the rate-limiting processes. Let us imagine an assembly line that manufactures a commodity such as an automobile. Although there are many steps in the manufacturing process, let us assume that one step—installing the engine—is the slowest. If we want to increase production, it will do us little good to increase the speed of the other steps, such as assembling the chassis. Rather, we should focus our attention on speeding up the process of installing the engine. For instance, we might hire some extra people to do that task, or we might remove some impediment to the process so that the workers can perform more rapidly. As will be seen, the body is controlled by and adjusts to exercise in a similar fashion.

In athletics, successful coaches are those who can identify the rate-limiting factor, sometimes called a weakness, and improve the individual's capacity to perform that process. Let us assume, for instance, we are coaching a novice wrestler who has been a successful competitive weight lifter. It makes no sense to emphasize strength training. Rather, we should emphasize technique development and other aspects of fitness, such as endurance. We would strive to maintain strength while concentrating on the performance-limiting factors. Similarly, we would be ill-advised to have a 400-m runner do 100 miles of road running a week, because this type of fitness is of minimal use to this athlete and may even interfere with the required fitness.

Maximal Oxygen Consumption ($\dot{V}O_{2max}$) and Physical Fitness

The ability to supply energy for activities lasting more than 30 sec depends on the consumption and use of oxygen (O_2). Because most physical activities in daily life, in athletics, and in physical medicine require more than 90 sec, consumption of O_2 provides the energetic basis of our existence. The rate of consumption of a given volume of O_2 (abbreviated $\dot{V}O_2$) increases from rest to easy, to difficult, and finally to maximal work loads (Figure 1-7). The maximum rate at which an individual can consume oxygen ($\dot{V}O_{2max}$) is an important determinant of the peak power output and the maximal sustained power output or physical work capacity of which an individual is capable.

As will be shown in later chapters, the capacity for $\dot{V}O_{2max}$ depends on the capacity of the cardiovascular system. This realization that physical work capacity, $\dot{V}O_{2max}$, and cardiovascular fitness are interrelated has resulted in a convergence of physical education (athletic performance) and medical (clinical) definitions of fitness. From the physical education–athletics perspective, cardiovascular function determines $\dot{V}O_{2max}$, which in turn determines physical work capacity, or fitness (Figure 1-8). From the medicoclinical perspective, fitness involves, minimally, freedom from disease. Because cardiovascular disease represents the greatest threat to the health of individuals in contemporary Western society, medical fitness is largely cardiovascular fitness. One of the major ways of determining cardiovascular fitness is measuring $\dot{V}O_{2max}$. $\dot{V}O_2$ is therefore not only an important parameter of metabolism but also a good measure of fitness for life in contemporary society. Because the measurement of $\dot{V}O_{2max}$ is so important from the medicoclinical and physical education–athletics perspectives, $\dot{V}O_{2max}$ has emerged as the single most important criterion of physical fitness.

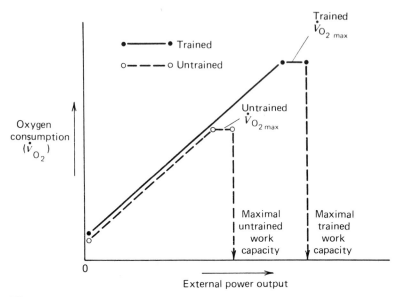

Figure 1-7

Relationship between oxygen consumption ($\dot{V}_{O_2}$) and external work rate (power output). In response to increments in power output, both trained and untrained individuals respond with an increase in $\dot{V}_{O_2}$. The greater ability of trained individuals to sustain a high power output is largely due to a greater maximal O_2 consumption ($\dot{V}_{O_2max}$).

Factors Affecting the Performance of the Biological Machine

Although the body can be compared to a machine, it would be simplistic, and indeed dehumanizing, to leave it at that. Unlike a machine, the body can adapt to physical stresses and improve its function. Likewise, in the absence of appropriate stress, functional capacity deteriorates. In addition, whereas the functions of particular types of machines are set at the time of manufacture, the performances of human machines are quite variable. Performance capabilities change continuously throughout life according to several time-honored principles that account for much of the observed individual differences. These principles are examined next.

Stress and Response

Physiological systems respond to appropriate stimuli. Sometimes the stimulus is called "stress," and the response is called "strain." Repeated stresses on physical systems frequently lead to adaptations, resulting in an increase in functional capacity. Enlargement (hypertrophy) in skeletal muscle occurs as

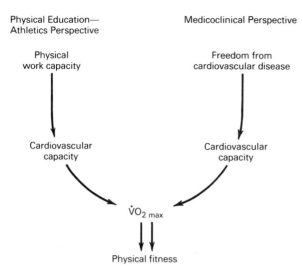

Figure 1-8
Because maximal oxygen consumption ($\dot{V}_{O_2max}$) is dependent on a high degree of cardiovascular health, and because it is very important in aerobic (endurance) exercise, maximal $\dot{V}_{O_2max}$ is becoming recognized as the most important index of physical fitness.

a result of the stress of weight training. However, not all stresses are appropriate to enhance the functioning of physiological systems. For instance, although cigarette smoking is a stress, it is not going to improve lung function. Smoking is an example of an inappropriate stimulus.

Physiologically, the purpose of any training session is to stress the body so that adaptation results. Physical training is beneficial only as long as it forces the the body to adapt to the stress of physical effort. If the stress is not sufficient to overload the body, then no adaptation occurs. If a stress is so great that it cannot be tolerated, then injury or overtraining result. The greatest improvements in performance will occur when the appropriate exercise stresses are introduced into the individual's training program.

Dr. Hans Selye has done much to make us aware of the phenomenon of the stress-response-adaptation process, which he called the general adaptation sydrome (GAS). Selye described three stages involved in response to a stressor: alarm reaction, resistance development, and exhaustion. Each of these stages should be extremely familiar to every physical educator, athlete, coach, physician, nurse, physical therapist, and other health professional who uses exercise to improve physical capacity.

Alarm Reaction　　The alarm reaction, the initial response to the stressor, involves the mobilization of systems and process within the organism. During exercise, for example, the stress of running is supported by the strain of increasing oxygen transport through an augmentation of cardiac output and a redistribution of blood flow to active muscle. The body has a limited capacity to adjust to various stressors; thus, it must adapt its capacity so that the stressor is less of a threat to its homeostasis in the future.

Resistance Development   The body improves its capacity or builds its reserves during the resistance stage of the GAS. This stage represents the goal of physical conditioning. Unfortunately, the attainment of optimal physiological resistance (or, the term more commonly used in athletics, physical fitness) does not occur in response to every random stressor. During physical training, for example, no training effect occurs if the stress is below a critical threshold. At the other extreme, if the stimulus cannot be tolerated, injury results.

The effectiveness of a stressor in creating an adaptive response is specific to an individual and relative to any given point in time and place. For example, running a 10-min mile may be exhausting to a sedentary 40-year-old man but would cause essentially no adaptive response in a world-class runner. Likewise, a training run that could easily be tolerated one day may be completely inappropriate following a prolonged illness. Environment can also introduce intraindividual variability in performance. An athlete will typically experience decreased performance in extreme heat and cold, at high altitudes, and in polluted air.

Exhaustion   When the chronic stress becomes intolerable, the organism enters the third stage of GAS, exhaustion (or distress). The stresses that result in exhaustion can be either acute or chronic. Examples of acute exhaustion include fractures, sprains, and strains. Chronic exhaustion (overtraining) is more subtle and includes stress fractures, emotional problems, and a variety of soft-tissue injuries. Again, the resistance development stage of the GAS may require considerable time. It may therefore be inadvisable to frequently elicit the alarm reaction through severe training because the exhaustion stage of the GAS may result. Periodization of training, involving training to a peak, and then at a reduced load before attempting a new peak, is discussed in Chapter 15.

The Overload Principle

Application of the appropriate stress is sometimes referred to as overloading the system. The "principle of overload" states that habitually overloading a system will cause it to respond and adapt. Overload is a positive stressor that can be quantified according to load (intensity and duration), repetition, rest, and frequency.

Load refers to the intensity of the exercise stressor. In strength training, the load refers to the amount of resistance, whereas in running or swimming, it refers to speed. In general, the greater the load, the greater the fatigue and recovery time required.

Repetition refers to the number of times a load is administered. More favorable adaptation tends to occur (up to a point) when the load is administered more than once. In general, there is little agreement on the ideal number of repetitions in a given sport. The empirical maxims of sports training are in a constant state of flux as athletes become successful using overload combinations different from the norm. In middle-distance running and swimming, for example, interval training workouts have become extremely demanding as a result of the success of athletes who employed repetitions far in excess of those practiced only a few years ago.

Rest refers to the time interval between repetitions. Rest is vitally important for obtaining an adaptation and should be applied according to the nature of the desired physiological outcome. For example, a weight lifter who desires maximal strength would be more concerned with load and less concerned with rest interval. Too short a rest interval would impair the weight lifter's strength gain because inadequate recovery would make it impossible to exert maximal tension. Mountain climbers, by contrast, are more concerned with muscular endurance than peak strength, so they would use short rest intervals to maximize this fitness characteristic. Rest also refers to the interval between training sessions. Because some responses to stress are prolonged, adaptation to stress requires adequate rest and recovery. Resting is a necessary part of training.

Frequency refers to the number of training sessions per week. In some sports, such as distance running, the tendency has been toward more frequent training sessions. Unfortunately, this often leads to increases in overuse injuries due to overtraining. Although more severe training regimens have resulted in improved performance in many sports, these workouts must be tempered with proper recovery periods or injury may result.

Specificity

It has repeatedly been observed that stressing a particular system or body part does little to affect other systems or body parts. For example, doing repeated biceps curls with the right arm may cause the right biceps to hypertrophy, but the right triceps or left biceps will be little affected. Any training program should reflect the desired adaptation. The closer the training routine is to the requirements of competition, the better the outcome will be.

Reversibility

In a way, this is a restatement of the principle of overload and emphasizes that, whereas training may enhance performance, inactivity will lead to a performance decrement. For example, someone who built a robust circulatory system in college as a runner should expect little or no residual capacity at 40 years of age following 20 years of inactivity.

Individuality

It is wise to note that we are all individuals and that, whereas physiological responses to particular stimuli are largely predictable, the precise response and adaptations to those stimuli are largely unpredictable and will vary among individuals. The same training regimen therefore may not equally benefit everyone who participates.

Development of the Field of Exercise Physiology

Many researchers, too numerous to mention here, have contributed the groundwork to the study of exercise physiology. Today, knowledge in this field is obtained from a wide range of types of studies. This book elaborates on these studies, but some of them deserve particular mention. The testing of physical work capacities of athletes, laborers, and a variety of people to determine their metabolic responses to exercise remains an important area of interest. Questions relating to the caloric cost of exercise, the efficiency of exercise, and the fuels used to support the exercise are addressed. In addition to traditional methods of respiratory determination, more recent techniques using muscle sampling (biopsy), light and electron microscopy, enzymology, nuclear magnetic resonance (NMR) and radioactive tracers have contributed to our understanding of the metabolic responses to exercise.

Along these lines, research has been carried out and is under way to determine the optimal training techniques to use for particular activities. The training regimens to improve such qualities as muscular strength and running endurance are vastly different.

When exercise tests are performed in a clinical setting, the term *stress test* is often used. Under controlled exercise conditions cardiac and blood constituent responses are useful in determining the presence of underlying disease. Following an exercise stress test, an exercise prescription can be written to improve functional capacity.

Recent advances at Wright State University in Dayton, Ohio, in computerized control of paralyzed muscles now allow paraplegic and quadriplegic individuals to use their own muscle power to provide locomotion (See Figure 1-6). As with nonparalyzed muscles, repeated overload of paralyzed muscles by computer-controlled electrical stimulation results in significant improvements in strength and endurance. Consequently, some muscles paralyzed for years can be trained and restored to near-normal strength.

The effects of environment on physical performance have long been a concern in exercise physiology. Environmental studies may have reached their peak of interest during preparations for the high-altitude Olympics held in Mexico in 1968. Similarly, the factors of heat and air pollution that could have been, but fortunately were not, factors in the Los Angeles Olympics, stimulated research into the effects of these factors on human performance. At present, the physiological stress of work in the heat and in polluted environments remains a particularly active area of research.

Summary

Although the study of exercise physiology is in its infancy compared with other sciences such as chemistry and physics, it is bustling with activity. This area of research has a great deal of appeal because it concerns the limits of human potential. The results of these studies affect us all, whether we jog three times a week to improve our health, are concerned with the health of others, or are concerned with the training of world-class performers.

Selected Readings

ASMUSSEN, E. Muscle metabolism during exercise in man: A historical survey. In: Pernow, B. and B. Saltin (eds). Muscle Metabolism During Exercise. New York: Plenum Press, 1971, pp. 1–12.

BROOKS, G.A. (ed.). Perspectives on the Academic Discipline of Physical Education. Champaign, Ill.: Human Kinetics, 1981.

BROOKS, G.A., and T.D. FAHEY. Exercise Physiology: Human Bioenergetics and Its Applications. New York: Macmillan, 1984.

FAHEY, T. Getting into Olympic Form. New York: Butterick Publishing, 1980.

FENN, W.O. History of the American Physiological Society: The Third Quarter Century 1937–1962. Washington, D.C.: The American Physiological Society, 1963.

GLASER, R.M., J.S. PETROFSKY, J.A. GRUNER, and B.A. GREEN. Isometric strength and endurance of electrically stimulated leg muscles of quadriplegics. Physiologist. 25:253, 1982.

HENRY, F.M. Physical education: An academic discipline. J. Health Phys. Ed. Recreation. 35:32–33, 1964.

HILL, A.V., C.N.H. LONG, and H. LUPTON. Muscular exercise, lactic acid, and the supply and utilization of oxygen (Pt. I–III). Proceedings of the Royal Society of London, Series B, 96:438–475. 1924.

HILL, A.V., C.N.H. LONG, and H. LUPTON. Muscular exercise, lactic acid, and the supply and utilization of oxygen (Pt. IV–VI). Proceedings of the Royal Society of London, Series B, 97:84–138, 1924.

HILL, A.V., C.N.H. LONG, and H. LUPTON. Muscular exercise, lactic acid, and the supply and utilization of oxygen (Pt. VI–VIII). Proceedings of the Royal Society of London, Series B, 97:155–176, 1924.

LEHNINGER, A.L. Biochemistry. New York: Worth Publishing, 1970.

MARGARIA, R., H.T. EDWARDS, and D.B. DILL. Possible mechanisms of contracting and paying oxygen debt and the role of lactic acid in muscular contraction. Am. J. Physiol. 106:689–715, 1933.

SEYLE, H. The Stress of Life. New York: McGraw-Hill, 1976.

2

Exercise Energetics: Energy Sources for Human Movement

(AP/Wide World Photos)

Exercise and Laws of Energetics

Physical activities are energetic events. How the body utilizes energy determines success in athletic, recreational, occupational, and rehabilitative activities. Thus, to understand how the body functions during physical activity requires an understanding of how the potential chemical energy in foodstuffs is captured and converted into chemical energy forms that can provide energy to power events of cellular work.

In almost all of the body's cells, particularly in skeletal muscle cells, energy conversions can be divided into two general categories. The first of these involves chemical reactions in which the chemical energy present in products of digested foodstuffs is converted to a usable high-energy substance, usually adenosine triphosphate (ATP). The second major category of energy transductions involves the conversion of ATP chemical energy into cell work. Several forms of cell work exist, including muscle contraction, protein synthesis, and ion pumping. As we shall see, these three forms of cell work are particularly important in understanding the immediate and long-term effects of exercise on the body.

It is beyond the scope of this book to describe in detail the physical–chemical factors that govern interconversions of one energy form to another. It is important to realize, however, that all energy interconversions (transductions) are governed by two basic laws of energetics (thermodynamics). The first law is that during their interconversions, energy and matter can neither be created nor destroyed. Rather, the total amount of energy and matter is constant but changes from one form to another. The second law is that energy transductions take place with less than perfect efficiency. In other words, when energy of one form is converted to another form, some of the energy is not available and will be lost in the conversion process. In biological systems, this unavailable ("lost") energy usually appears as heat. For example, in human exercise the process of muscle contraction is at most 30% efficient. This is because only 30% of the energy released appears as external work; therefore, 70% of the energy released appears as heat.

The following equation describes energy balance in a healthy, young adult. The equation is a statement of neither the first nor the second law of energetics as just described, but it conforms to the two laws:

$$\text{Energy in (food)} = \text{Energy out (heat)} + \text{Energy out (work)} \pm \text{Energy stored (fat)} \tag{2-1}$$

This equation conforms to the first law of energetics because we have accounted for all the energy and matter involved in the energy conversion. The equation also conforms to the second law because it indicates that a significant amount of the energy released will appear as heat.

Energetics and Athletics

Physical activities can be classified into three groups, based on the energy systems that support them. Particularly in athletic activities, we see examples of **power, speed,** and **endurance** events. Examples of these are the shot put, the 400 m sprint, and the marathon run, respectively. In each of these activities, success depends on energetics and on a highly developed but different cellular energy system. In power events, in which the activity lasts a few seconds or less, the muscle has several immediate energy sources (Figure 2-1). For rapid, forceful exercises lasting from a few seconds to approximately

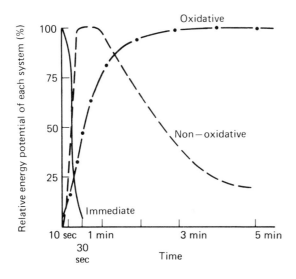

Figure 2-1

Energy sources for muscle as a function of activity duration. Schematic presentation showing how long each of the major energy systems can endure in supporting all-out work.

(SOURCE: From D. W. Edington and V. R. Edgerton, 1976. Used with permission.)

1 min, muscle can depend on nonoxidative, or glycolytic, energy sources as well as immediate energy sources. For activities lasting 90 sec or more, oxidative mechanisms become increasingly important. Before describing these three basic muscle energy sources, we need to describe the chemical-mechanical energy transduction that occurs during muscle contraction, as depicted in the following reaction:

$$ATP + Actin + Myosin \xrightarrow{Ca^{++}} Actomyosin + P_i + ADP + Work + Heat \qquad (2\text{-}2)$$

In this reaction, which is triggered by the appearance of calcium ion (Ca^{++}, released within a muscle when it is excited by a nerve impulse), ATP is the high-energy chemical intermediate, actin and myosin are the two contractile proteins of muscle, actomyosin represents combined (contracted) protein, and

19

adenosine diphosphate (ADP) and inorganic phosphate (P_i) are products of ATP utilization.

Muscle as a Chemical–Mechanical Energy Transducer

A transducer is a device that converts one energy form into another. In the body, muscles convert chemical energy into mechanical energy (external work). Thus, the process of muscle contraction represents a chemical to mechanical energy transduction.

Figure 2-2*A* depicts the structure of skeletal muscle, from total muscle tissue through the ultrastructure of the contractile proteins, actin and myosin. Figure 2-2*B* is a diagrammatic rendering of the process of the interactions between actin and myosin that produce muscle shortening (contraction). The thick myosin filament possess protrusions (heads) that contain enzymes (ATPases). On the thin actin filaments is bound ATP. Through the process of excitation–contraction coupling (which will be explained in more detail in Chapter 9), Ca^{++} is released from holding sites within the muscle cell. The

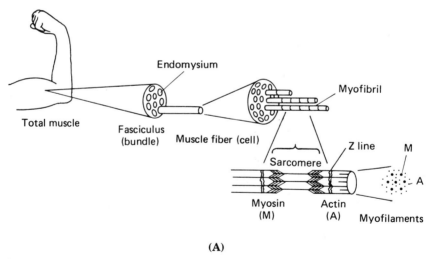

(A)

Figure 2-2*A*

Muscle tissue is composed of muscle bundles (fasciculi), muscle fibers (cells), myofibrils, and myofilaments (actin and myosin). Actin filaments are connected to the Z-disk which, viewed from the side, yields the Z-line. The distance from Z-line to Z-line is termed a sarcomere and is the basic contractile element in muscle.

(SOURCE: Modified from D. W. Edington and V. R. Edgerton, 1976, p. 16. Used with permission of the authors.)

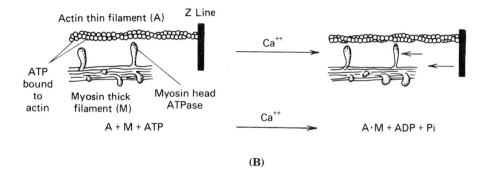

(B)

The shortening (contraction) of muscle involves the interaction of myosin heads with actin to form actomyosin. Calcium ion (Ca^{++}) triggers this reaction. This process involves utilization of ATP. Not shown are the events of muscle relaxation, which are detailed in Chapter 8.

free Ca^{++} then allows myosin to interact with actin and produce muscle shortening. This shortening is due to the release of potential chemical energy supplied to the contraction process by ATP.

Immediate Energy Sources

Each of the three main energy sources in muscle is mediated by specific enzymes or enzyme systems, as described in Table 2-1. In any muscle contraction, whether the activity is primarily one of power or endurance, the degradation of ATP supplies the chemical energy to power muscle contraction (Eq. 2-2).

The immediate energy source in muscle, as in most other cells, is composed of three components. First, there is ATP itself. ATP is degraded by enzymes that are generally called ATPases. Because the reaction involves combination with H$_2$O, the splitting of ATP is called hydrolysis.

$$\text{ATP} + \text{H}_2\text{O} \xrightarrow{\text{ATPase}} \text{ADP} + \text{P}_i \qquad (2\text{-}3)$$

The chemical products of ATP hydrolysis are adenosine diphosphate (ADP) and inorganic phosphate (P$_i$). In the cyclic process of muscle contraction and recovery from contraction, ATP is continually being hydrolyzed to ADP, and ADP is continually being reenergized by phosphorylation back to ATP.

The structure of ATP is given in Figure 2-3. One of the group of compounds called nucleotides, ATP contains the nitrogenous base (adenine), a five-carbon sugar (ribose), and three phosphates. Removal of the terminal phosphate results in ADP; and cleaving off two phosphates gives adenosine monophosphate (AMP). In the cell ATP is negatively charged, and the terminal phosphates of each molecule are associated with a magnesium ion (Mg^{++}), which is required for enzymatic activity.

The standard free energy of hydrolysis ($\Delta G^{o'}$) measured under test-tube conditions is 7.3 kcal/mol. In the body, however, the actual free energy of hydrolysis of ATP (i.e., the ΔG) is probably closer to 10 kcal/mol. This is because conditions in the living cell are somewhat different from standard test-tube conditions.

The second cellular source of immediate energy is creatine phosphate (CP). This high-energy phosphorylated compound exists in five to six times greater concentration in resting muscle than does ATP. Creatine phosphate provides a reserve of phosphate energy to regenerate ATP, which is consumed as the result of muscle contraction. The interaction of CP and ADP (degraded ATP) is catalyzed by the enzyme creatine kinase.

$$CP + ADP \xrightarrow{\hspace{3cm}} C + ATP \qquad\qquad (2\text{-}4)$$
$$\text{Creatine kinase}$$

TABLE 2-1 Energy Sources of Muscular Work for Different Types of Activities

	Power	Speed	Endurance
Duration of event	0 to 3 sec	4 to 50 sec	>2 min
Example of event	Shot put, discus, weight lifting	100 to 400-m run	≥1500-m run
Enzyme system	Single enzyme	One complex pathway	Several complex pathways
Enzyme location	Cytosol	Cytosol	Cytosol and mitochondria
Fuel storage site	Cytosol	Cytosol	Cytosol, blood, liver, adipose tissue
Rate of process	Immediate, very rapid	Rapid	Slower but prolonged
Storage form	ATP, CP	Muscle glycogen and glucose	Muscle and liver glycogen, glucose; muscle, blood, and adipose tissue lipids; muscle, blood, and liver amino acids
Oxygen involved	No	No	Yes

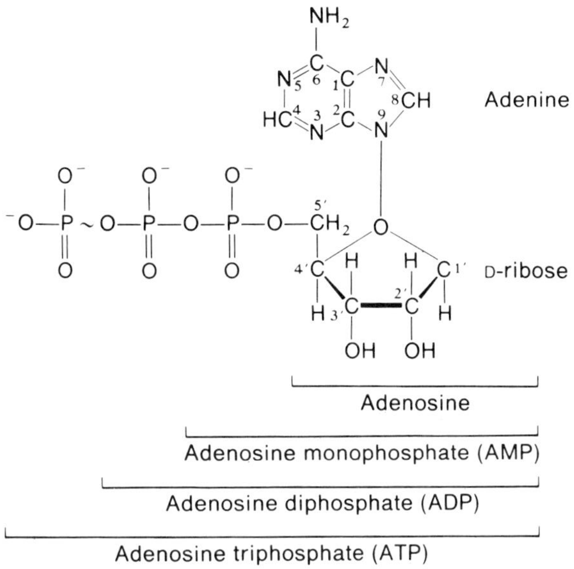

Figure 2-3

The structure of ATP. At pH 7 the molecule is ionized. Usually, the terminal phosphate (bond) is hydrolyzed to provide energy. In the body, the energy available to do work (free energy, ΔG) when the terminal phosphate is split is about 10 kcal/mol of ATP.

Thus, in the muscle, ATP that is hydrolyzed to ADP during muscle contraction is rephosphorylated by CP. Seen in this role, CP is particularly important as an intracellular energy shuttle. (This will be discussed more in Chapter 4.)

The third immediate energy source in muscle involves an enzyme called myokinase. The enzyme has the ability to generate one ATP from two ADPs.

$$\text{ADP} + \text{ADP} \xrightarrow{\hspace{2cm}} \text{ATP} + \text{AMP} \qquad (2\text{-}5)$$
$$\text{Myokinase}$$

The three components of the immediate energy system in muscle are all H_2O soluble. Therefore, they exist throughout the aqueous part of the cell, from near the cell's inner boundary to deep within it, surrounding the contractile elements, actin and myosin and other important parts of the cell. The immediate energy sources are so named because they are immediately available to support muscle contraction.

Quantitatively, ATP and CP (which, together, are called phosphagen) make up a critical and important energy reserve. The amount of ATP on hand, however, cannot sustain maximal muscle contraction for more than a few seconds (Table 2-2). Even when ATP is augmented by both CP and the myokinase enzyme system, activities that must be sustained for more than a fraction of a minute (i.e., 5–15 sec) require the assistance of other energy sources.

TABLE 2-2 Estimation of the Energy Available in the Body Through Immediate Energy Sources

	ATP	CP	Myokinase ATP Equivalent	Total Phosphagen (ATP + CP)
Muscular concentration				
mMol/kg muscle[a]	6	28		34
mMol total muscle				
mass[b]	180	840	90	1110
Useful energy[c]				
kcal/kg muscle	0.06	0.28		0.34
kcal total muscle mass	1.8	8.4	0.9	11.1

[a] Based on data from Edwards et al., 1982.
[b] Assuming 30 kg of muscle in a 70-kg man.
[c] Assuming 10 kcal/mol ATP.

Nonoxidative Energy Sources

The nonoxidative energy source in muscle involves the breakdown of glucose (a simple sugar) and glycogen (stored carbohydrate made up of many glucose subunits). These processes are specifically termed glycolysis and glycogenolysis, respectively. Muscle tissue is densely packed with glycolytic and glycogenolytic enzymes; therefore, muscle is specialized in these processes and can break down glucose and glycogen rapidly. The nonoxidative energy source in muscle (glycosis) can be summarized as follows:

$$\text{Glucose} \xrightarrow[\substack{\text{Nonoxidative} \\ \text{rapid glycolysis}}]{} 2\ \text{ATP} + 2\ \text{Lactate} \qquad (2\text{-}6)$$

In skeletal muscle, the concentration of free glucose is very low, so most of the potential energy available from nonoxidative energy sources comes from the breakdown of glycogen (Table 2-3).

Like the immediate energy system, the nonoxidative energy system is composed of elements that are H_2O soluble. The apparatus for nonoxidative energy metabolism therefore exists in immediate proximity to the contractile elements in muscle. Nonoxidative energy sources are called upon when muscle contraction lasts more than a few seconds.

Quantitatively, the energy available through nonoxidative metabolism (Table 2-3) is significantly greater than that available through immediate energy sources (Table 2-2). However, the immediate and nonoxidative energy sources combined provide only a small fraction of the energy available through oxidative metabolism. Therefore, intense muscular activities lasting longer

24

TABLE 2-3 Estimation of the Energy Available in the Body Through Nonoxidative Metabolism (Anaerobic Glycolysis)

	Per Kilogram Muscle	Total Muscle Mass[a]
Maximal lactic acid tolerance (g)	3.0	90
ATP formation (mmol)	50.0	1500
Useful energy (kcal)	0.5	15

[a] Assumptions if all muscle were activated simultaneously.

SOURCE: Based on data from Karlsson.

than approximately 30 sec cannot be sustained without the benefit of oxidative metabolism (Figure 2-1).

Oxidative Energy Sources

Potential oxidative energy sources for muscle include sugars, carbohydrates, fats, and amino acids. As just noted, muscle tissue in healthy, fed individuals has significant reserves of glycogen. This fuel source can be supplemented by glucose supplied from the blood, liver glycogen which can be broken down to glucose and delivered to muscle through the circulation, and fats and amino acids which exist in muscle as well as other depots around the body. Further, whereas the sugar glucose can be metabolized to an extent by glycolytic mechanisms (Eq. 2-6), oxidative mechanisms allow far more energy to be liberated from a glucose molecule (Table 2-4).

$$\text{Glucose} + O_2 \xrightarrow[\text{Oxidative metabolism}]{} 36 \text{ ATP} + H_2O + CO_2 \qquad (2\text{-}7)$$

TABLE 2-4 Estimation of Energy Available from Muscle and Liver Glycogen, Fat (Adipose Triglyceride), and Body Proteins

	Energy Equivalent (kcal)
Glycogen in muscle	480
Glycogen in liver	280
Fat (triglyceride in adipose)	141,000
Body proteins	24,000

SOURCE: Based on data from Young and Scrimshaw, 1971.

Far more energy is available when glucose undergoes oxidative catabolism (breakdown) than when it undergoes nonoxidative catabolism because the oxidative pathways of metabolism carry on the process of glucose catabolism to a far greater extent. Because the oxidative breakdown of glucose is longer and more involved, there is a greater opportunity for energy transduction and capture of glucose chemical energy in the form of ATP. The details of oxidative metabolism will be explained in more detail in Chapter 4.

Fats can be catabolized by oxidative mechanisms only, but the energy yield is very large. For palmitate, an average-sized and commonly occurring fatty acid:

$$\text{Palmitate} + O_2 \xrightarrow{\text{Oxidative metabolism}} 129 \text{ ATP} + CO_2 + H_2O \qquad (2\text{-}8)$$

Amino acids, like fats, can be catabolized only by oxidative mechanisms. Before an amino acid can be oxidized, the nitrogen residue must be removed. This is generally done by switching the nitrogen to some other compound (a process called transamination) or by a unique process of nitrogen removal in the liver (oxidative deamination). Examples for alanine, a three-carbon amino acid, are given in the following:

$$\text{Alanine} + \alpha\text{-Ketoglutarate} \xrightarrow[\substack{\text{Glutamate} \\ \text{pyruvate transaminase}}]{} \text{Pyruvate} + \text{Glutamate} \qquad (2\text{-}9)$$

$$\text{Pyruvate} + O_2 \xrightarrow{\text{Oxidative metabolism}} 15 \text{ ATP} + CO_2 + H_2O \qquad (2\text{-}10)$$

In Table 2-4 the significance of oxidative metabolism for energy production in the body is illustrated. In comparison with the energy potential form the immediate energy system (Table 2-2), and the nonoxidative metabolism of glycogen (Table 2-3), the energy available from oxidative energy sources is far greater. Also, the energy available from the combustion of muscle glycogen is small compared with the much larger potential energy reserves in fat and body protein.

Aerobic and Anaerobic Metabolism

Of the body's three energy systems, two systems (the immediate and nonoxidative) do not require oxygen for their operation. Consequently, these systems are referred to as anaerobic, meaning not dependent on O_2. The third, the oxidative energy system, is referred to as the aerobic energy system. Energy transduction in this system is dependent on the presence of O_2.

Power and Capacity of Muscle Energy Systems

Although the maximal energy capacity of immediate (See Table 2-2) and non-oxidative (See Table 2-3) energy systems is small compared with that of the oxidative energy system (See Table 2-4), immediate and nonoxidative energy systems are important because they are activated very rapidly when muscles start to contract. By comparison, the oxidative energy system is slower to be activated and also produces energy at a lower rate even when fully activated. In Table 2-5 the maximal rates (power) at which the various systems provide energy for muscle contraction are contrasted with the maximal capacities (total contribution available) for energy release. In such a comparison, the immediate and nonoxidative energy systems are revealed to possess superior, though short-lived, power capacities. Thus, the three energy systems in muscle together provide a means to sustain short, intense bursts of activity as well as more sustained activities of lesser intensity.

Energetics and Athletic Performance

Our interpretation that energy for the human engine comes from three sets of enzyme systems (Table 2-1) is supported by an analysis of the world's running records (Figure 2-4). A plot or running speed versus time reveals three distinct curve components. Thus, it appears that the selection and training of athletes for athletic events requires knowledge of both the metabolic requirements of the activity and the metabolic characteristics of the individual. Because many athletic events and most of life's other activities require longer than 90 sec, the primary importance of oxidative energy metabolism is obvious.

TABLE 2-5   Maximal Power and Capacity of the Three Energy Systems

System	Maximal Power (kcal/min)	Maximal Capacity (Total kcal Available)
Immediate energy sources (ATP + CP)	36	11.1
Nonoxidative energy sources (anaerobic glycolysis)	16	15.0
Oxidative energy sources (from muscle glycogen only)	10	480

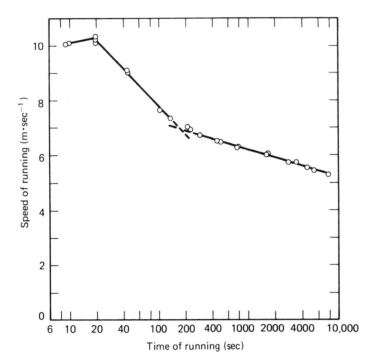

Figure 2-4
Logarithmic plot of average speed maintained versus time to event for men's world running records. Note the presence of three curve components that suggest the presence of three energy systems.

(SOURCE: Modified from R. W. McGilvery, 1975. Used with permission.)

Training the Immediate Energy System

Activities that last only a few seconds are those which depend on the immediate energy system. For instance, throwing the discus is one example of an athletics activity that requires the generation of maximal muscle power and depends on immediate energy sources. Although the maximal (total) energy capacity of the immediate energy system is relatively small, these sources provide energy at the greatest possible rate (See Table 2-5).

The design of a training regimen to improve performance in any physical activity should begin with an evaluation of which energy system or systems are involved. Assuming that maximal performance is desired, consulting Figure 2-1 reveals that for activities lasting a few seconds it is the immediate energy system that is of primary importance.

In training for an athletics event such as the discus throw, the training principles of overload and specificity require consideration. In training for the discus throw, the immediate energy system in the throwing muscles must be developed by progressive overload. Additionally, for reasons to be explained later, strength training and skill development are very important.

Investigations into the effects of training on the relative concentrations of enzymes (eg., creatine kinase, myokinase) and ATP and CP of the immediate energy system indicate very little effect of heavy strength training and of throwing the discus. Rather, training for the discus results in marked muscle enlargement (hypertrophy), which increases the absolute levels of ATP and CP and enzymes of the immediate energy system present in muscle.

That strength training and throwing the discus do not increase the muscular concentrations of ATP and CP should be understood in terms of the roles of ATP and CP on metabolic regulation. These factors will be explained in more detail later in Chapters 3, 4, and 7. For the present, it is helpful to know that ATP and CP inhibit some of the key processes of intermediary metabolism that regenerate ATP and CP. It is an advantage, in terms of metabolic regulation, to have sufficient but still rather low levels of ATP and CP on hand. This is because when exercise starts, the conversion of ATP and CP to their catabolic products (ADP, AMP, and creatine) results in the stimulation of intermediary metabolism. Theoretically, having large stores of ATP and CP on hand in resting muscle would result in metabolism responding more slowly to an energy need.

Strength training is important for activities such as throwing the discus because an increase in strength allows a muscle to accelerate more rapidly a given mass (in this case the discus). The greater the speed of the discus on release, the greater the potential for flight. Progressive resistance (overload) training to improve strength will be discussed in Chapter 13. For the present, it should be emphasized that the lifting of heavier and heavier weights (over a period of months and years), utilizing the muscles of the thighs, back, chest, shoulders, and arms, will improve strength and the potential to throw the discus.

The discus throw is also an example of highly skilled motor activity in which technique is tremendously important. An athlete simply must have mastered the skill to have the the proper pattern of nerve and muscle cell recruitment so that maximal force can be provided by the contractile elements and the immediate energy sources.

In very short duration activities, such as the discus throw, maximal strength will determine, to a large extent, the maximal power output (work accomplished per unit of time). In activities of slightly longer duration, however, muscular power will depend on both strength and the metabolic capacity to regenerate ATP for muscle contraction (See Eq. 2-2).

Summary

Performance in muscular activity depends on energetics. The use of energy by machines, both mechanical and biological, can be precisely defined. Basically two considerations govern physical and biological reactions involving energy exchanges: (1) energy is not created but is acquired in one form and converted to another; and (2) the interconversion of energy between forms is inefficient, and a large fraction of the energy released will appear in an unusable form, usually as heat. Muscles utilize three different systems of energy release during exercise. These are the (1) immediate, (2) nonoxidative, and (3) oxidative energy stores. Each of these differs in mechanism, capacity, and power. Consequently, muscular capacity is limited by these three systems of energy release.

Throwing the discus is an example of an activity that depends on skill, muscular power, and the immediate energy system. Training to improve performance in throwing the discus should emphasize technique as well as building the metabolic apparatus. Progressive resistance (heavy weight) training will improve muscle size and strength. Increases in muscle size will improve muscle content of actin, myosin, ATP, CP, and the enzymes creatine kinase and myokinase. These training adaptations will improve the ability to generate muscle power for short periods.

Selected Readings

Bray, H.G., and K. White. Kinetics and Thermodynamics in Biochemistry. New York: Academic Press, 1966.

Brooks, G.A., and T.D. Fahey. Exercise Physiology: Human Bioenergetics and Its Applications. New York: Macmillan, 1984, pp. 17–66.

Edington, D.W., and V.R. Edgerton. The Biology of Physical Activity. Boston: Houghton Mifflin, 1976, pp. 3–11.

Edwards, R.H.T., D.R. Wilkie, M.J. Dawson, R.E. Gordon, and D. Shaw. Clinical use of nuclear magnetic resonance in the investigation of myopathy. Lancet i: 725–731, 1982.

Gibbs, C.L., and W.R. Gibson. Energy production of rat soleus muscle. Am. J. Physiol. 223:864–871, 1972.

Helmholtz, H. Uber die Erhaltung der Kraft. Berlin (1847). Reprinted in Ostwald's Klassiker, No. 1, Leipzig, 1902.

Hill, T.L. Free Energy Transductions in Biology. New York: Academic Press, 1977.

Karlsson, J. Lactate and phosphagen concentrations in working muscle of man. Acta Physiol. Scand. (Suppl.) 358:1–72, 1971.

Kleiber, M. The Fire of Life. New York: John Wiley, 1961, pp. 105–124.

Krebs, H.A., and H.L. Kornberg. Energy Transformations in Living Matter. Berlin: Springer-Verlag OHG, 1957.

Lehninger, A.L. Biochemistry. New York: Worth Publishing, 1970, pp. 289–312.

Lehninger, A.L. Bioenergetics. Menlo Park, CA: W. A. Benjamin, 1973, pp. 2–34.

McGilvery, R.W. Biochemical Concepts. Philadelphia: W. B. Saunders, 1975.

Merowitz, H.J. Entropy for Biologists. New York: Academic Press, 1970.

Mommaerts, W.F.H.M. Energetics at muscle contraction. Physiol. Rev. 49:427–508, 1969.

Wendt, I.R., and C.L. Gibbs. Energy production of rat extensor digitorum longus muscle. Am. J. Physiol. 224:1081–1086, 1973.

WILKIE, D.R. Heat work and phosphorylcreatine breakdown in muscle. J. Physiol. London 195:157–183, 1968.

WILKIE, D.R. The efficiency of muscular contraction. J. Mechanochem. Cell Motility 2:257–267, 1974.

YOUNG, V.R., and N.S. SCRIMSHAW. The physiology of starvation. Sci. American. 225:14–22, 1971.

3

Nonoxidative Energy Sources for Human Movement: Anaerobic Glycogenolysis and Glycolysis

(AP/Wide World Photos)

Of the three main energy fuels (carbohydrates, fats, proteins) only carbohydrates can be catabolized within the cell to provide energy without the benefit of oxygen (see Table 2-1). The simple sugar glucose, and its intracellular storage form glycogen, can be rapidly broken down to provide a limited amount of energy. The first stage in glucose catabolism is called glycolysis. The first stage in glycogen catabolism is called glycogenolysis. Together, glycogenolysis and glycolysis make up the cell's nonoxidative, or anaerobic, glycolytic energy system. The nonoxidative energy system can provide energy to sustain powerful muscle contractions for a period of a few seconds to about a minute (see Figure 2-1). However, the maximal energy capacity of nonoxidative mechanisms is limited (see Table 2-5) and becomes exhausted if not supplemented by the oxidative energy system. Exercises that rely on nonoxidative energy sources (e.g., the 400-m sprint in track, and Olympic wrestling) are among the most fatiguing of all activities. This is because the glycogenolytic energy reserves are depleted, and acidic products (mainly lactic acid) of glycogenolysis and glycolysis also accumulate. Lactic acid accumulation indicates that nonoxidative energy mechanisms have been called into play and that the mechanisms of lactic acid removal (mainly through oxidative metabolism) are inadequate. Lactic acid accumulation means that an individual is under stress and continued activity is becoming very difficult.

Dietary Sources of Glucose

The dietary sources of glucose are numerous. After their digestion and assimilation from the small intestine, the products of most starches and sugars reach the blood in the form of glucose (Figure 3-1). This is because the enzymes of digestion and of absorption through the intestinal wall reduce and convert most dietary carbohydrate forms to a common sugar glucose on which most of the body's cells depend. Additionally, after digestion occurs and the products are assimilated into the blood, the first organ that encounters the products of digestion is the liver. As part of its function, the liver takes up large quantities of different kinds of substrates (fuels) from both the digestive (portal) circulation and the main (systematic) circulation, but the liver releases relatively few substrates. The sugar released by the liver is glucose.

Glucose and Body Metabolism

The uptake of glucose by cells depends on several factors including the type of tissue, the levels of glucose and glycogen in the blood and tissue, the presence of the hormone insulin, and the physiological status of the tissue. Most

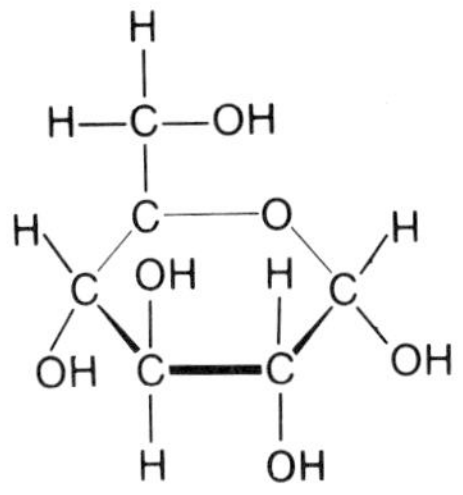

Figure 3-1

Structure of glucose, a simple sugar. Five carbons and an oxygen atom serve to create a hexagonal ring conformation. Shaded lines represent the three-dimensional platelike structure.

cells, with the possible exception of contracting muscle and heart, require insulin for glucose uptake. The central and peripheral nerve cells as well as kidney and red blood cells depend heavily on glucose as a fuel source. In fact, if blood glucose levels fall too low during exercise, brain and nerve function will be so impaired as to cause exercise to stop. Heart and skeletal muscle can use alternative fuels (mainly fatty acids), but the heart and muscle also appear to require glucose or stored glycogen for high rates of energy output.

The liver uses mainly fatty acids as its fuel source, but it can also utilize glucose. Following a carbohydrate-rich meal, the liver will take up large amounts of fats released into the circulation by the digestive system. It has recently been found, however, that most of the glucose released into the circulation from the digestive system bypasses the liver (Figure 3-2). In the peripheral musculature, glucose is taken up and stored as glycogen or released mainly as lactate, but also as pyruvate and alanine. These substances then circulate to the liver where they are converted to glucose 6-phosphate and released into the blood as glucose or stored as glycogen. Fat cells in adipose tissue also consume glucose. In adipose tissue, glucose serves to stimulate fat (triglyceride) synthesis.

Glycolysis

The metabolic pathway of glucose breakdown in mammalian cells is termed glycolysis. The process is frequently referred to as a metabolic pathway because it proceeds by a specific route, involving specific steps (intermediate products), in which each step is catalyzed and regulated by a specific enzyme.

Aerobic (Slow) and Anaerobic (Fast) Glycolysis

There are two general ways to describe glycolysis—fast and slow glycolysis. Alternatively, the terms anaerobic (for fast) and aerobic (for slow) glycolysis are used. The terms *aerobic* (meaning with air, air contains O_2), and *anaerobic* (meaning without O_2) were developed by pioneer biochemists such as Louis Pasteur.

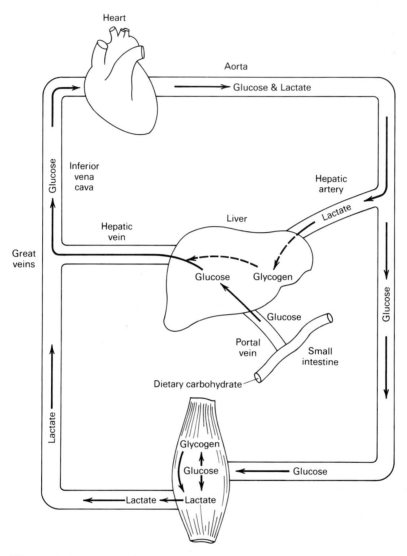

Figure 3-2
Diagram of the new glucose to hepatic glycogen pathway ("glucose paradox") by which the liver prefers to make glycogen from lactate as opposed to glucose. Glucose released into the blood from the digestion of dietary carbohydrate bypasses the liver and is taken up by skeletal muscle. The muscle can either synthesize glycogen or produce lactate. The lactate then recirculates to the liver and stimulates glucose and glycogen formation. See Foster, 1984.

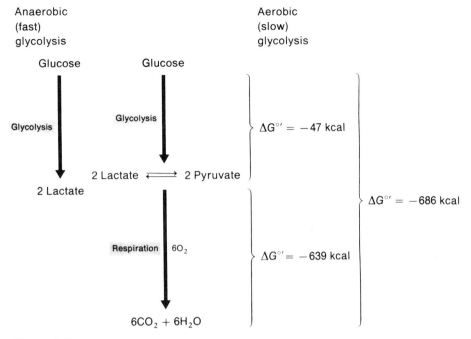

Figure 3-3

In anaerobic (fast) glycolysis, lactic acid is the product. In aerobic (slow glycolysis, pyruvic acid is the main product. The terms *aerobic* (with O_2) and *anaerobic* (without O_2) refer to the test-tube conditions used by early researchers to speed up or slow down glycolysis. In real life, pyruvate and lactate pools are in equilibrium, and the rapidity of glycolysis largely determines the product formed. Note the far greater energy released under aerobic conditions.

The processes of fast (anaerobic) and slow (aerobic) glycolysis are diagrammed in Figure 3-3. Pyruvic and lactic acids each possess a carboxyl (-COOH) group (Figure 3-4). At physiological pH, these molecules dissociate a hydrogen ion (or proton, H^+) and, therefore, are acids:

$$R\text{-}COOH \rightarrow R\text{-}COO^- + H^+ \tag{3-1}$$

where R is the remainder of the lactate or pyruvate molecule.

The terms *lactate* and *pyruvate,* properly meaning salts of the respective acids, are generally used interchangeably with lactic and pyruvic acid.

If glucose is catabolized to pyruvic or lactic acids, a net of two ATPs will be formed for each glucose utilized. However, if glycolysis proceeds slowly enough so that the lactic and pyruvic acids formed can be combusted in the process of cellular respiration (oxidative energy system; see Chapter 4), much more energy is released and much more ATP is formed. Therefore, if a cell can meet its energy needs through oxidative mechanisms, it will consume

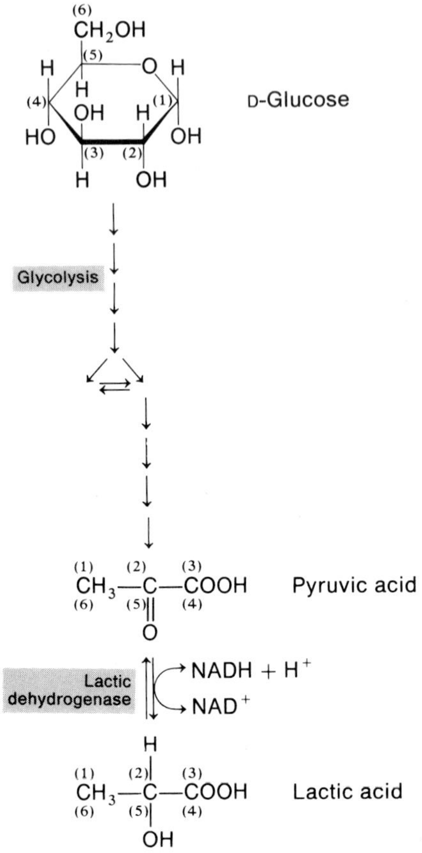

Figure 3-4
Chemical structures of glucose and pyruvic and lactic acids. The small numbers in parentheses identify the carbon atoms in the original glucose structure. At physiological pH, lactic and pyruvic acids dissociate a hydrogen ion.

(SOURCE: Modified from A. L. Lehninger, 1971. Used with permission.)

glucose (and glycogen) at a much slower rate. If oxidative metabolism is inadequate to meet energy demands, however, glycolysis will have to proceed much more rapidly (approximately 20 times faster) to supply the difference between the ATP supplied through oxidative metabolism and that required by the contractile apparatus (actin and myosin; see Figure 2-2*B*).

As we shall see when describing the factors that regulate entry of glucose into the cell and the intracellular catabolism of glycogen, glycogenolysis and glycolysis can sometimes occur faster than oxidative mechanisms can accept the products of glycolysis for combustion. Ordinarily, the oxygenation of cells indirectly determines the rates of glycogenolysis and glycolysis. It is possible, however, that a cell can have sufficient O_2 while glycolysis still produces pyruvic and lactic acids faster than they can be removed through oxidative metabolism. In such cases, the cells involved release lactic acid into the bloodstream.

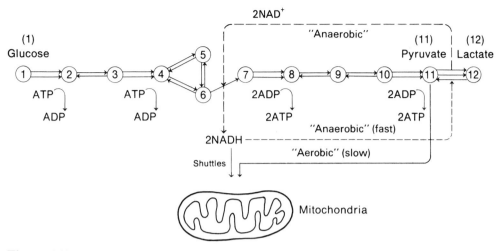

Figure 3-5
Simplified portrayal of glycolysis showing the beginning and ending substances, the sites of ATP utilization and production, and the sites of NADH formation and utilization. When glycolysis is slow, mitochondria can accept the NADH and pyruvate formed. When mitochondrial function is inadequate because of low enzymatic activity or insufficient O_2 supply, glycolysis is rapid.

Pyruvate and Lactate as Products of Glycogenolysis and Glycolysis

Figure 3-5 is a simplified flow chart of the glycolytic pathway. In this flow chart, each of the numbered intermediates represents a different substance, the first of which is glucose (No. 1) and the last of which is lactate (No. 12). To understand why glycolysis goes slowly and produces pyruvate under aerobic conditions, and why it progresses rapidly under anaerobic conditions, we must know that glycolysis reduces (adds a hydrogen and electron) to the substance nicotinamide adenine dinucleotide. As a result, nicotinamide adenine dinucleotide-reduced (NADH) is a by-product of glycolysis.

$$NAD^+ + 2H^{\cdot} \rightarrow NADH + H^+ \tag{3-2}$$

The hydrogens (H) and electrons ($\cdot$) added to NAD^+ during glycolysis represent potential energy for the formation of ATP in mitochondria. Mitochondria are those cellular organelles (microstructures) in which O_2 is used and most ATP is formed. Mitochondria are the cellular sites of the oxidative energy system and are described in more detail in Chapter 4. Under circumstances in which mitochondria are functional and well oxygenated, the pyruvate and high-energy hydrogens and electrons of glycolysis (captured in

NADH) are shuttled into mitochondria. Thus, under aerobic conditions, the carbon products of glucose are directed to combustion in mitochondria. However, when mitochondrial function is inadequate, or inadequate to handle the glycolytic production of pyruvate and NADH, then lactate will be formed. As indicated in Figure 3-4, the formation of lactate from pyruvate and NADH is catalyzed by the enzyme lactate dehydrogenase (LDH):

$$\text{Pyruvate} + \text{NADH}^+ \ \text{H}^+ \xrightarrow{\text{LDH}} \text{Lactate} + \text{NAD}^+ \tag{3-3}$$

The formation of lactate or pyruvate, then, depends on a balance of glycolytic and mitochondrial activities, and not on the presence or absence of oxygen.

Control of Glycolysis

Phosphofructokinase

Several mechanisms serve to regulate the rate of glycolysis. Usually the dominant factor is the activity of the glycolytic enzyme phosphofructokinase (PFK). PFK, which catalyzes the third step of glycolysis, is the slowest, or rate-limiting, enzyme of glycolysis. PFK is also an enzyme whose activity is affected by a number of factors. Some of the known modulators (regulators) of PFK are listed in Table 3-1. In effect, PFK acts like a dam in the flow of material down the glycolytic pathway (Figure 3-6). The height of the dam can be raised or lowered to regulate the rate of glycolysis. In the resting muscle cell, factors that inhibit PFK (and therefore glycolysis) are in relatively high concentration. When a muscle starts to contract, inhibitory factors of PFK, such as ATP, are consumed, and factors such as ADP, which stimulate PFK, increase in concentration. Thus, when exercise starts, glycolysis occurs more rapidly because the restraint on glycolysis by PFK is reduced. Consequently, the concentration of reactants in front of the PFK reaction decreases and the concentration of products behind the reaction increases. Of the several factors that regulate the activity of PFK, the concentration of ADP appears to be most

TABLE 3-1 Control Enzymes of Glycolysis

Enzyme	Stimulators	Inhibitors
Phosphofructokinase	ADP, P_i, AMP, $\uparrow$ pH, NH_4^+	ATP, CP, citrate
Pyruvate kinase		ATP, CP
Hexokinase		Glucose 6-phosphate
Lactate dehydrogenase		ATP

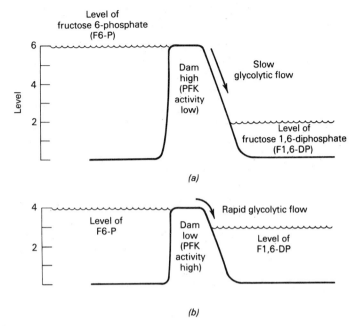

Figure 3-6

Phosphofructokinase (PFK) is the rate-limiting enzyme in glycolysis. PFK functions like a dam on a river. When PFK activity is low (**A**), the level of PFK reactant (fructose 6-phosphate) backs up and is high. When PFK is stimulated (**B**), in effect the height of water (F6P level) behind the dam is lowered, compared to the before, and the level of product, fructose 1,6-diphosphate (F1,6DP), is raised. Thus, glycolytic flow is increased like when water goes over a dam.

(SOURCE: From L. Opie. Used with permission.)

important (see Chapters 4 and 7). In addition to PFK, other glycolytic enzymes whose activity is regulated include hexokinase, pyruvate kinase, and lactate dehydrogenase. The activities of these enzymes are coordinated with that of PFK (Table 3-1).

Insulin

Insulin is a pancreatic hormone that promotes the entry of glucose into cells. As noted previously, most cells require insulin for glucose uptake. On the outer surface of most cells, insulin binds to a specific (receptor) site. The binding of insulin facilitates the binding of glucose to a carrier, (transporter) also on the cell's surface. The complex of insulin, carrier, and glucose is then transported across the cell membrane and internalized within the cell. Inside the cell, glucose and insulin are metabolized separately and the carrier is returned to the cell's surface. Contracting skeletal muscle and perhaps heart do not require insulin for glucose uptake, but insulin appears to facilitate the uptake of glucose in working muscle. By allowing, or promoting, glucose entry into cells, insulin makes possible the processes of glycolysis, glycogen synthesis, and, ultimately, glycogenolysis.

Glycogenolysis and Glycogen Synthesis— The Metabolism of Glucose 6-Phosphate

Skeletal muscle glycolysis depends heavily on the intracellular carbohydrate storage form, glycogen. During heavy muscular exercise, glycogen may supply most of the glucosyl (coming from glucose) residues for nonoxidative as well as oxidative metabolism. In its structure, glycogen (Figure 3-7) consists mostly of end-to-end (carbon-1 to carbon-6, C1–C6) linkages, with a few (C1–C4) branching linkages.

Glycogen Synthesis

The synthesis of glycogen depends on several factors. In resting muscle, glucose uptake depends on high circulating levels of glucose and insulin. Because glucose taken up by muscle and liver are rapidly converted to glucose 6-phosphate (G6P) by the enzymes hexokinase and glucokinase, respectively (see Figure 3-6), high levels of G6P in resting muscle promote the formation of glycogen by increasing the availability of the precursor (G6P). In addition, insulin and G6P promote glycogen synthesis by stimulating glycogen synthase enzyme activity.

Glycogenolysis

Glycogenolysis (meaning the dissolution of glycogen) is the process of glycogen breakdown. The process involves action of the enzyme phosphorylase. As noted previously, in muscle, glycogenolysis supplies most of the glucosyl residues for the glycolytic pathway in muscle during heavy exercise. In the liver of a well-fed individual, glycogenolysis supplies most of the glucose released into the blood. The activity of phosphorylase appears to be controlled by two mechanisms. One system is hormonally mediated and involves the actions of epinephrine (in muscle) and glucagon (in liver). The other system, which operates in both liver and muscle, is calcium ion (Ca^{++}) mediated. When exercise starts, Ca^{++} is released as part of the excitation-contraction coupling process in muscle (Chapter 8). The release of Ca^{++} from the sarcoplasmic reticulum in muscle is responsible for initiating glycogenolysis and supplying substrate for the nonoxidative energy system. In prolonged, exhaustive exercise, when blood glucose levels fall as a result of consumption of glucose by muscle for glycolysis, circulating levels of insulin decline while epinephrine

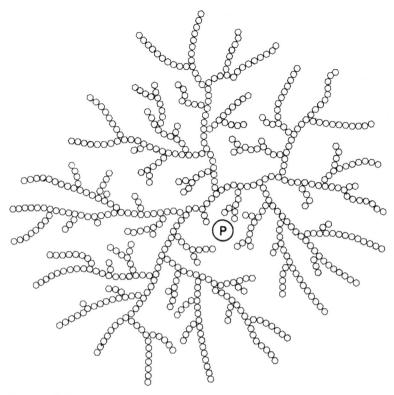

Figure 3-7
The structure of glycogen is seen to be a polymer of glucose units.
The linkages exist mainly end to end (carbon-1 to carbon-4 linkages),
but there is also some cross-bonding (carbon-1 to carbon-6 linkages).
A pinwheel-like structure results from C1–C4 and C1–C6 linkages.
The hexagons represent glucosyl units. Under high magnification in
the electron microscope (e.g., Figure 3-9) the pinwheel-like structures
of glycogen appear as dark granules. Glycogen forms around a "foundation" protein Ⓟ.

and glucagon levels rise. Under these circumstances, glycogenolysis is stimulated by hormonal mechanisms.

In skeletal muscle and most other types of cells, the rate of metabolite
flow down the glycolytic pathway depends on the combined rates of glucose
and glycogen utilization. Therefore, control of glucose 6-phosphate metabolism is central in the regulation of overall muscle intermediary metabolism
(Figure 3-8). G6P represents a branch point where the processes of glycolysis
(pyruvate and lactate production), glycogen synthesis, and glycogenolysis are
regulated. Additionally, in liver and kidney, G6P represents a site that determines the release of glucose into the blood (Figure 3-8).

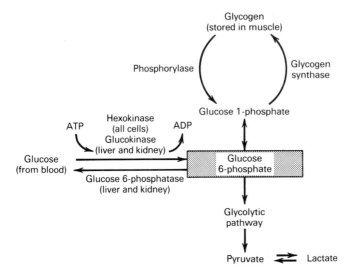

Figure 3-8

Illustration of the central role of glucose 6-phosphate in determining the direction of carbon flow in glycolysis (catabolism of glucose), glycogenolysis, glycogen synthesis, lactate and pyruvate production, and glucose release.

Glycogenolysis and Glycolysis in Muscle

Glycolysis is a very active process in skeletal muscle, which is often termed a *glycolytic tissue*. In particular, fast-contracting (fast-twitch) white skeletal muscles contain large quantities of glycolytic enzymes (Figure 3-9). In addition, fast-twitch but oxidative muscle cells contain large amounts of glycolytic enzymes. Thus, when fast-twitch muscle fibers are contracted during exercise (see Figure 2-2A), significant glycolytic carbon flow will occur.

As mentioned in Chapter 2, the enzymes of glycolysis are distributed throughout the cytoplasm of the muscle cell (Figure 3-10). The glycolytic, nonoxidative energy system is ideally located to provide energy for bursts of muscular activity. However, as also described previously (see Table 2-5), although the rate of energy output from glycolysis can be high, the total energy capacity of the nonoxidative (anaerobic glycolytic) energy system is limited.

Glycogen Depletion and Fatigue

During hard, prolonged exercise the body's carbohydrate reserves (blood glucose, liver, and muscle glycogen) can be consumed. Muscle glycogenolysis to support both oxidative and nonoxidative metabolism (Figure 3-10) is augmented by the uptake of glucose from the blood. In turn, blood glucose level is maintained by glucose released from the liver. Although skeletal muscle can oxidize fuels other than carbohydrate (Chapter 4), high rates of exercise

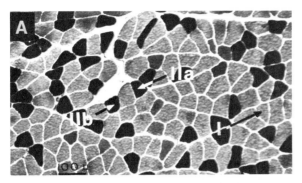

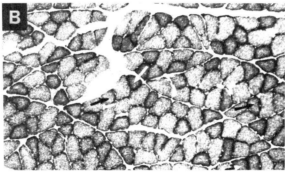

Figure 3-9

Serial transverse sections of rodent hind limb skeletal muscle incubated as follows:
(A) myofibrillar ATPase, pH 9.4; **(B)** succinate dehydrogenase (SDH). Type II fibers
are further classified as Types IIa and IIb based on high or low activity, respectively,
of SDH. Type I fibers are sometimes also called "slow-oxidative" (SO) fibers; Type IIa
fibers are sometimes also called "fast-oxidative glycolytic" (FOG) fibers; and Type IIb
fibers are sometimes also called "fast-glycolytic" (FG) fibers. Types I and IIa fibers
are red, whereas Type IIb is white.

(SOURCE: Micrographs courtesy of T. P. White.)

power output appear to require a significant contribution of carbohydrate fuel
reserves. In the heart, also, glucose metabolism appears to assist in both contraction and relaxation. Additionally, if blood glucose falls too low, the function of the brain and nerve cells will be seriously affected. If exercise results
in depletion of carbohydrate reserves, therefore, both nonoxidative and oxidative energy systems in muscle, as well as nerve and brain metabolism, are
impaired. Consequently, glycogen depletion is a cause of muscle fatigue.

Glycogen depletion occurs not only during prolonged exercise, such as in
marathons in which the phenomenon of "hitting the wall" is reached by many
competitors, but also in shorter, intermittent activities involving bursts of
muscle power that require fast-glycolytic (Type IIb) muscle fibers (see Figure
3-9). Recruitment (use) of these fibers can result in glycogen depletion and
fiber fatigue.

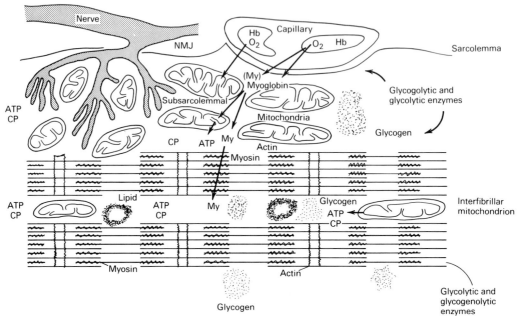

Figure 3-10

Schematic drawing of a longitudinal section of a muscle fiber, showing the relationship between the neuromyojunction (NMJ), the vascular myojunction, and the subcellular components of the muscle fiber. The enzymes of glycogenolysis and glycolysis (nonoxidative energy system) are distributed throughout the cytoplasmic parts of the muscle cell as are the enzymes of the immediate energy system. The enzymes of the oxidative energy system are compartmentalized in mitochondria. These "powerhouses of the cell" are distributed immediately below the cell membrane (subsarcolemmal mitochondria) and deep within the fiber (interfibrillar mitochondria).

(SOURCE: Modified from D. W. Edington and V. R. Edgerton, 1976, p. 16. Used with permission of the authors.)

Through wise practices of training and nutrition, glycogen storage can be increased. Therefore, an individual's susceptibility to glycogen depletion can be reduced. Exercise nutrition is discussed in more detail (Chapter 14).

Gluconeogenesis

Cori Cycle

Gluconeogenesis is the making of new glucose. Gluconeogenesis is a specialized function of the liver and the kidneys. When glycogenolysis and glycolysis in muscle produce more lactate and pyruvate than can be combusted (Figure 3-11), these 3-carbon molecules appear in the blood and circulate to the glu-

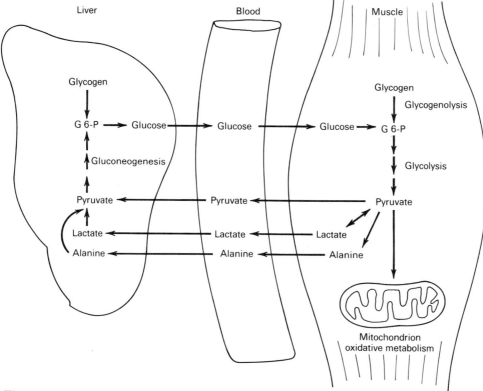

Figure 3-11

Interrelationships among glycogenolytic, glycolytic function in muscle and liver and glyconeogenic function in liver and kidney (not shown). Recycling of glycogenolytic and glycolytic carbon is possible because of the Cori and glucose–alanine cycles. See the text for details.

coneogenic organs (liver and kidney). These organs have a significant capacity to convert lactate and pyruvate to glucose, a 6-carbon molecule ($2 \times 3C = 6C$). This synthesized glucose can be released into the circulation to support glycolytic function in tissues such as muscle and brain. The recirculation of glycolytic intermediates to gluconeogenic organs for glucose synthesis is termed the *Cori cycle,* after the husband-wife team of scientists who discovered the sites of gluconeogenesis.

Glucose–Alanine Cycle

In addition to releasing pyruvate and lactate, skeletal muscle releases a third 3-carbon gluconeogenic precursor. This is the amino acid alanine that is formed from the action of the enzyme glutamate pyruvate transaminase (GPT) in muscle:

$$\text{Pyruvate} + \text{Glutamate} \xrightarrow{\hspace{1cm}} \text{Alanine} + \alpha\text{-Ketoglutarate} \qquad (3\text{-}4)$$
$$\text{GPT}$$

Alanine recirculates to the liver to undergo gluconeogenesis in a process called the glucose–alanine cycle. This recycling of carbon-containing molecules is very important in maintaining blood glucose levels during starvation because the amino acid glutamate is derived largely from muscle protein stores. The glucose–alanine cycle is also thought to help maintain blood glucose levels in prolonged exercise.

During exercise approximately 20% of the glucose released from the gluconeogenic organs results from substrate recycling (i.e., the Cori and glucose–alanine cycles). Glycogenolysis in liver supplies the remaining 80% of glucose released into the circulation during prolonged exercise. Therefore, preexercise nutrition by raising muscle and liver glycogen reserves, can be very important for maintaining glucose homeostasis during exercise (Chapter 14).

The Lactate Shuttle

Recently, isotope tracer studies have allowed precise estimation of the rates of lactate and glucose production and oxidation during sustained, submaximal exercise. The results indicate that lactate is actively oxidized, and may be a preferred fuel in heart and red skeletal muscle fibers. Within a muscle tissue during sustained exercise, lactate produced at some sites, such as Type IIb (FG) fibers, diffuses or is transported into Type I (SO) fibers (Figure 3-12). Some of the lactate produced in Type IIb fibers shuttles directly to adjacent Type I fibers. Alternatively, other lactate produced in Type IIb fibers can reach Type I fibers by recirculation through the blood. Thus, by this mechanism of shuttling lactate between cells, glycogenolysis in one cell can supply a fuel for oxidation to another cell. Skeletal muscle tissue then becomes not only the major site of lactate production but also the major site of removal. In addition, much of the lactate produced in a working muscle is consumed within the same tissue and never reaches the venous blood.

Lactate–Glycogen–Glucose Interrelationships in the Body

On the basis of contemporary radiotracer studies as well as the classic studies of the Coris, a different, but more unified view of carbohydrate metabolism in the body is emerging. As suggested in Figure 3-2, dietary carbohydrate enters the blood as glucose. However, some of this glucose bypasses the liver and gets metabolized to lactate in the musculature. The lactate released from

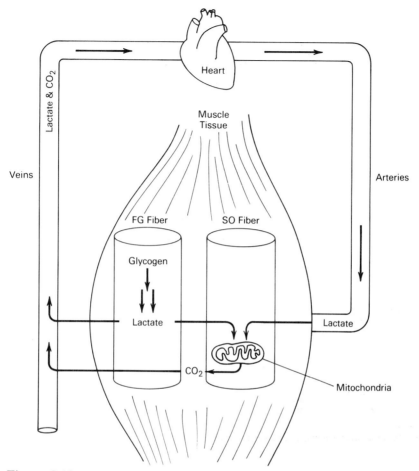

Figure 3-12

Diagram of the lactate shuttle. Lactate produced in some cells [eg., fast-glycolytic (FG, Type IIb) muscle cells] can shuttle to other cells [eg., slow-oxidative (SO, Type 1) fibers] and be oxidized. Also, lactate released into the venous blood can recirculate to the active muscle tissue bed and be oxidized. During exercise the lactate shuttle can provide significant amounts of fuel. See Brooks, 1985.

muscle recirculates to the liver, where it can stimulate glucose production and release as well as glycogen synthesis. In the contemporary literature, this process is called the "glucose paradox" (referring to the liver's preference to make glycogen from lactate rather than glucose).

During sustained exercise, a similar thing happens. Glycogenolysis in muscle, particularly FG muscle, results in the release of pyruvate, lactate, and alanine into the circulation. When these substances reach the liver, they can be taken up and converted to glucose and released back into the circulation. The recycling of pyruvate and lactate carbon atoms to glucose has been termed the *Cori cycle,* whereas the recycling of alanine carbon has been termed the *glucose–alanine cycle.* As pointed out earlier, during sustained exercise only a minor fraction (20%) of the lactate formed is reconverted to glucose whereas most of it is combusted within the active muscle bed. This process has been termed the *lactate shuttle. Therefore, in actuality, the Cori and glucose–alanine cycles as well as the lactate shuttle are parts of an integrated process by which the body deals with carbohydrates.*

Training of the Nonoxidative Energy System

In training for a particular athletic, recreational, occupational, or rehabilitative activity, the exercise duration and intensity are of primary concern. Assuming that the intention is to improve the capacity for maximal effort or to reduce the stress of a given effort, planning the training regimen should begin with consulting Figure 2-1. If the duration of maximal effort ranges between a few seconds and a minute, then the nonoxidative energy system will be of primary importance. The nonoxidative energy system should therefore be improved in its capacity by training. In addition, because the oxidative energy system possesses so much greater an energy potential than does the nonoxidative system, consideration should also be given to improving the oxidative energy system, particularly if the duration of activity approximates a minute (as opposed to a few seconds) or if repeated bouts of high exertion are called for. This is because the recovery process between activity bursts is an oxidative (aerobic) process. The procedures to improve the oxidative energy system will be discussed in Chapter 4.

As discussed previously with regard to improving capacity of the immediate energy system (Chapter 2), the design of a training regimen should consider the training principles of overload and specificity. If the activity of interest requires maximal effort for approximately a few seconds to a minute, then the duration of training exercises (intervals) should usually fall within that range.

Interval Training

In interval training, periods of high-intensity exercise are alternated with periods of rest. The intensity of exercise usually approximates that to be used during the criterion task (i.e., competition for the athlete, or occupational or recreational activity for the rehabilitation patient); the duration of exercise ranges from half to two-thirds of the criterion performance duration; the rest interval between training exercises is one to five times the exercise interval, and the number of exercise intervals ranges from 4 to 20.

Because intense exercise bouts of short duration result in fatigue, the interval training regimen has been developed. Interval training allows an individual to do the following:

- practice important motor skills,
- specifically overload the nonoxidative energy system,
- minimize the fatigue associated with a single (maximal) exercise bout, and
- increase the total volume of high-intensity training far above that possible with a single continuous bout of exercise training.

Given the numbers of permutations and combinations of training possibilities in the interval training system, it is possible to vary the workouts given to an athlete or rehabilitation patient while at the same time maintaining a high intensity of exercise and minimizing the boredom frequently associated with training. Given the numbers of combinations and permutations of training possibilities in the interval training system, it is also possible to become confused and lose sight of the specific purposes for training. Therefore, an example is given for one athletic event, the 400-m run. In Chapter 13 training procedures will be described in more detail.

Training for the 400-m Run

For a male, an excellent time for the 400-m run is 45 sec. For a female, an excellent time is 50 sec. Consulting Figure 2-1 reveals that all energy systems will be used by both sexes to support performance of the 400-m run, but the nonoxidative energy system will be the most important. The training employed should therefore emphasize the nonoxidative energy system.

Early Season Training Successful participation in this athletic event carries the prerequisite of excellent leg speed. Therefore, the young or untrained individual who can run 100 m in 12 sec (men) or 13 sec (women) or better should become interested in the 400-m event. If, after some training, the individual cannot come close to running 200 m in less than 24 sec (men) or 26 sec (women), then participation in some other event should be considered.

In the early season, the athlete who wants to run 45 sec (men) or 50 sec (women) for 400 m should focus on building the endurance necessary for the event. In the fall, the athlete should participate in cross-country or over-distance training. This will build the apparatus of oxidative metabolism, help maintain body weight, and provide a break from competition and high-intensity training. In the winter and early spring, the athlete's attention should be directed to the track, and the training workouts should be designed with the 400-m competition specifically in mind. With the criterion performance goals specified, a minimum running speed of 12 sec/100 m (men) and 13 sec/100 m (women) is indicated. Therefore, an early season workout after a thorough warm-up would consist of the following:

Men—10 intervals, 200-m run in 24 sec with 2- to 4-min rest intervals.
Women—10 intervals, 200-m run in 26 sec, with 2- to 4-min rest intervals.

Because of the high intensity of this workout for the early season, the next training day should be different and easier. For example, an easy 2-mile run might be followed by several 400-m runs in 60 sec (men) or 65 sec (women), each with a 4-min rest interval in between. Such an off-day training program would allow for recovery from intense training as well as preserve the training base of the oxidative energy system.

Competitive Season Training Given the indicated criterion performance times specified, the race pace should be the cornerstone of the competitive season training. Therefore, competitive season workouts could be as follows:

Men—10 intervals, 200-m run in 22 to 24 sec, with 2-min rest intervals.
Women—10 intervals, 200-m run in 24 to 26 sec, with 2-min rest intervals.

Again, as in the early season, the next training day should be easier.

As the season progresses, both the coach and the performer should be aware of problems associated with both mental and physical fatigue. Therefore, while the intensity of training will become greater, rest days between intense training or competition should become more frequent and the interval training procedures followed should be varied.

Effects of Training on Glycogenolysis and Glycolysis

Although sprint-interval training, as described previously, results in significant improvements in performance, the known effects of training on the muscle enzymes of glycolysis and glycogenolysis are few. This contrasts starkly with the well-documented effects of endurance training on enzymes of the oxidative energy system (see Chapter 4).

Sprint-interval training results in some increase in muscle size (hypertrophy); therefore it results in an increase in the absolute amount of glycolytic and glycogenolytic enzymes contained in muscle. Some studies indicate that training results in an increase in muscle hexokinase activity. This adaptation would be important for improving the rate of glycolysis (i.e., the rate of glucose utilization). Interestingly, in response to training, the concentration of LDH in muscle has been reported to decrease slightly. This adaptation would tend to decrease the rate of lactate production. The concentration of PFK has not been observed to respond consistently to training.

The apparent lack of effect of interval-sprint training on enzymes of glycolysis and glycogenolysis may result because untrained muscle is already loaded with glycolytic enzymes. The effect of training may then be attributed to better regulation of the glycolytic pathway in trained individuals. Alternatively, it may be that scientists have not yet identified the major effects of training on muscle glycogenolysis and glycolysis, or may not even fully understand what limits this type of performance. Under investigation are the possibilities that training increases the ability to buffer lactic acid present in muscle and that muscles of trained individuals are better able to eliminate lactic acid by emptying it into the blood. *Thus, high-intensity training may not greatly improve the capacity for glycogenolysis and glycolysis but rather enable muscle to better resist the effects of rapid glycogenolysis and glycolysis.*

Summary

Of the three main groups of energy substrates (carbohydrates, fats, and proteins), only carbohydrates can be catabolized without the participation of oxygen (see Table 2-1). Thus, the production of energy without the benefit of oxygen involves the catabolism of carbohydrate within the cell. The main product of dietary sugar and starch digestion is glucose, which is released into the blood from the gastrointestinal (GI) tract. The simple sugar glucose enters cells, including muscle and liver, and is either used directly or stored for later use.

The first stage in cellular glucose catabolism is a process called glycolysis. Glycolysis is a process involving 10 or 11 linked, enzymatically catalyzed and regulated reactions. Glycolysis produces a small amount of energy (ATP), and the products of glycolysis can be used as oxidative fuels, either immediately or later.

Glucose molecules not undergoing glycolysis can be linked together to form the carbohydrate storage form called glycogen. Glycogen stored in muscle is broken down in a process called glycogenolysis. Both glycogen storage and glycogenolysis are enzymatically mediated processes. These processes of glycolysis and glycogenolysis occur in most all cells, but they are highly developed in skeletal muscle cells. Glycogenolysis and glycolysis can provide the energy to sustain powerful muscle contractions for a period of a few seconds to about a minute (see Figure 2-1). Because their function does not directly and immediately involve oxygen, glycolysis and glycogenolysis, together are referred to as the "nonoxidative energy sources." Of the two muscular carbohydrates for nonoxidative, glycogen is far more important than glucose.

In prolonged exercise, glycogenolysis in muscle still provides a large part of the fuel used to sustain contractions; however, the products of glycolysis and glycogenolysis are oxidized to produce approximately 20 times more ATP per glucose unit than when nonoxidative energy pathways are used exclusively. During prolonged exercise, also, the liver releases glucose into the circulation. This glucose can circulate through the bloodstream to working muscle and other tissues that require glucose.

The liver possesses two mechanisms by which to supply glucose for release into the blood: glycogen breakdown (liver glycogenolysis) and formation of glucose out of simpler molecules. This synthesis of glucose by the liver (and to a lesser extent, the kidneys) is termed gluconeogenesis.

During exercise it is possible to exhaust glycogen reserves. Fatigue during prolonged exercise (the phenomenon of "hitting the wall") results from running out of glycogen in the active, oxidative (Types I and IIa) muscle fibers. During intense, powerful exercises, fatigue can result from glycogen depletion in the fast-glycolytic (Type IIb) fibers.

In contracting muscle, regulation of the rate of oxygen consumption is more tightly coupled to the power output than are the rates of glycogenolysis and glycolysis. Consequently, in Type IIb muscle fibers and in other fibers under the influence of epinephrine, the rate of pyruvate formation can exceed the rate of pyruvate oxidation. Consequently, lactate will be formed and released from particular muscle fibers. This lactate can then be taken up from the interstitium and plasma by adjacent cells, or even cells anatomically far removed form the site of lactate formation. This shuttling of oxidizable fuel in the form of lactate (i.e., the lactate shuttle) represents an important means of supplying energy needs during exercise.

The principles of specificity and overload (Chapter 1) apply to the training procedures used to improve the capacity for nonoxidative metabolism. Thus, in preparing for activities lasting from a few seconds to about a minute, athletes must train at high intensities. The fatigue that results from such training exercises requires that rest intervals be imposed in the training. During a workout, brief periods of activity (a few seconds to a minute) should be interspersed with rest intervals at least as long as the active period. Further, days of intense training should be interspersed with days of reduced training intensity.

Selected Readings

BALDWIN, K.M., W.W. WINDER, R.L. TERJUNG, and J.O. HOLLOSZY. Glycolytic enzyme in different types of skeletal muscle: adaptation to exercise. Am. J. Physiol. 225:962–966, 1973.

BARNARD, R.J., V.R. EDGETON, T. FIRUKAWA, and J.B. PETER. Histochemical, biochemical and contractile properties of red, white, and intermediate fibers. Am. J. Physiol. 220:410–414, 1971.

BARNARD, R.J., and J.B. PETER. Effect of training and exhaustion on hexokinase activity of skeletal muscle. J. Appl. Physiol. 27:691–695, 1969.

BROOKS, G.A. Lactate: Glycolytic end product and oxidative substrate during sustained exercise in mammals—The "Lactate Shuttle." In Circulation, Respiration, and Metabolism: Current Comparative Approaches, R. Gillis (Ed.), Springer-Verlag, Berlin, 1985, pp. 208–218.

BROOKS, G.A., and T.D. FAHEY. Exercise Physiology: Human Bioenergetics and Its Applications. New York: Macmillan, 1984, pp. 67–95.

CORI, C.F. Mammalian carbohydrate metabolism. Physiol. Rev. 11:143–275, 1931.

DAVIES, K.J.A., L. PACKER, and G.A. BROOKS. Exercise bioenergetics following spring training. Arch. Biochem. Biophys. 215:260–265, 1982.

DONOVAN, C.M., and G.A. BROOKS. Endurance training affects lactate clearance, not lactate production. Am. J. Physiol. 244 (Endocrinol. Metab. 7):E83–E92, 1983.

FOSTER, D.W. From glycogen to ketones and back. Diabetes. 33:1188–1199, 1984.

GOLLNICK, P.D., R. ARMSTRONG, C. SAUBERT, W. SEMBROWICH, R. SHEPHERD, and B. SALTIN. Glycogen depletion patterns in human skeletal muscle fibers during prolonged work. Pflugers Arch. 344:1–12, 1973.

GOLLNICK, P.D., and L. HERMANSEN. Biochemical adaptations to exercise: anaerobic metabolism. In Wilmore, J.H., (ed.). Exercise and Sport Sciences Reviews, Vol. 1. New York: Academic Press, 1973, pp. 1–43.

GOLLNICK, P.D., K. PIEHL, and B. SALTIN. Selective glycogen depletion pattern in human muscle fibers after exercise of varying intensity and various pedaling rates. J. Physiol. London 241:45–57, 1974.

HICKSON, R.C., W.W. HEUSNER, and W.D. VAN HUSS. Skeletal muscle enzyme alterations after sprint and endurance training. J. Appl. Physiol. 40:868–872, 1976.

KREBS, H.A., and M. WOODFORD. Fructose 1,6-diphosphatase in striated muscle. Biochem. J. 94:436–445, 1965.

LEHNINGER, A.L., Biochemistry. New York: Worth Publishing, 1971, pp. 313–335.

McGILVERY, R.W. Biochemical Concepts. Philadelphia: W.B. Saunders, 1975, pp. 230–266.

SCRUTTON, M.C., and M.F. UTTER. The regulation of glycolysis and gluconeogenesis in animal tissues. Annu. Rev. Biochem. 37:269–302, 1968.

VANDER, A.J., J.H. SHERMAN, and D.S. LUCIANO. Human Physiology, 3rd Ed. New York: McGraw-Hill, 1980.

YORK, J., L.B. OSCAI, and D.G. PENNY. Alterations in skeletal muscle lactic dehydrogenase isozymes following exercise training. Biochem. Biophys. Res. Commun. 61:387–1393, 1974.

4

Oxidative Energy Sources for Human Movement

Physical activities lasting a minute or more absolutely require the presence and use of oxygen in active muscle. Far more energy can be realized through oxidative metabolism than through glycolytic processes alone. Within muscle cells are specialized structures called mitochondria, which link the breakdown of foodstuffs, the consumption of oxygen, and the production of ATP. In contrast with glycolysis, which involves carbohydrate-derived substrates exclusively, cellular oxidative mechanisms allow for the continued metabolism of carbohydrates as well as for the breakdown of derivatives of fats and proteins. Even though the processes of cellular oxidation are far removed from the anatomical sites of breathing and pumping of blood, it is the process of cellular oxidation that the lungs and heart serve. Seen in their proper perspective, the two most familiar physiological processes (ventilation and circulation) play a key role in energy transduction.

Mitochondrial Structure

Cellular oxidation takes place in organelles called mitochondria (mitochondrion, singular). Pyruvate (a product of glycolysis) and also products of lipid (fat) and amino acid metabolism are metabolized to carbon dioxide and water (CO_2 and H_2O) within mitochondria. Mitochondria are the cellular sites where the vast majority of ADP is phosphorylated to ATP. For this reason, mitochondria are called "powerhouses of the cell," Consequently, those activities that last longer than about 1 min are powered by mitochondria (See Figure 2-1). As suggested earlier in Figure 3-10, mitochondria appear in two places in skeletal muscle cells. A significant population of mitochondria exists immediately beneath the cell membrane (sarcolemma), and these are called subsarcolemmal mitochondria. Subsarcolemmal mitochondria are in a position to receive O_2 provided by capillaries and the arterial circulation (Figure 4-1). Subsarcolemmal mitochondria are believed to provide the energy for transport processes, such as the pumping of ions and metabolites across the sarcolemma. Deeper within muscle cells are the interfibrillar mitochondria. As the name implies, these mitochondria exist among the contractile elements (myofibrils). The interfibrillar mitochondria probably provide most of the ATP for contraction.

Because of their capsule-shaped appearance in electron micrographs of muscle, as well as their appearance in tissue homogenates, mitochondria have long been believed to exist as discrete capsule-shaped organelles. Recent research however, indicates that mitochondria are interconnected in a network called the mitochondrial reticulum (Figure 4-2). Some of the interconnections can be seen in Figure 4-1. Thus, *instead of thousands of mitochondria, a muscle cell may contain relatively few mitochondria, with each mitochondrion giving rise to thousands of branches.*

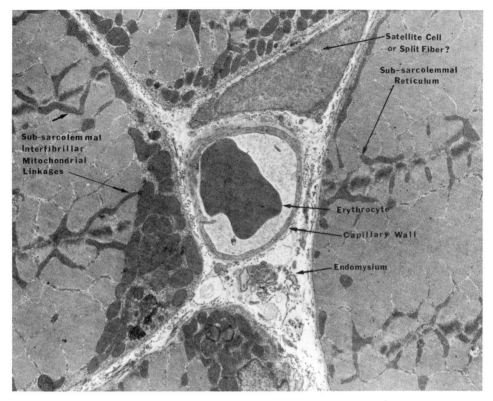

Figure 4-1
Electron micrograph of rat deep (red) vastus thigh muscle showing linkages between subsarcolemmal and interfibrillar mitochondria.

(SOURCE: Micrograph courtesy of S. P. Kirkwood, E. A. Munn, L. Packer, and G. A. Brooks.)

It is now well established that mitochondrial content varies greatly among cells of different tissues; among skeletal muscle fiber types, mitochondrial content also varies. Red pigmented (dark) skeletal muscle fibers (see Figure 3-9) obtain their color from iron-containing compounds, which are red when combined with O_2. Among these compounds are hemoglobin (in red blood cells), myoglobin (a cytoplasmic hemeprotein), which functions to attract O_2 from the blood and to transport it within muscle cells, and mitochondrial cytochromes. In addition to red skeletal muscle, other tissues such as heart and liver are pigmented because of high mitochondrial content. By comparison, white (pale) muscle fibers contain few mitochondria (Figure 3-8). Therefore, in general *the darker in color a muscle is, the greater is its ability to obtain and use oxygen.*

Figure 4-3 provides a schematic representation of a mitochondrion. Area

Figure 4-2
A model of the mitochondrial reticulum in rat skeletal muscle. In all probability, "mitochondria" do not exist as separate, individual entities within muscle cells but rather as parts of a network, or "reticulum." Evidence for the mitochondrial reticulum in limb skeletal muscles was obtained by modeling of mitochondria seen in electron micrographs of serial cross sections through rat soleus muscles. The process of modeling involves reconstruction (stacking) of individual mitochondria seen in serial electronmicrographs (e.g., Figure 4-1). The resulting model is pictured.

(SOURCE: Model courtesy of E. A. Munn and C. Greenwood, Babraham, England.)

1, the outer membrane, functions as a barrier to maintain important internal constituents (e.g., NADH) and to exclude exterior factors. The outer membrane does contain specific transport mechanisms to regulate the influx and efflux of various materials such as pyruvate and activated fatty acids. Area 2, the intermembrane space, also contains enzymes for exchange and transport. Area 3, the inner membrane, contains many folds, or cristae (crista, singular). The inner mitochondrial membrane is the site where electron transport, O_2 consumption, and ATP production take place.

The precise mitochondrial site of phosphorylation has been found to be the F complex, which appears as a ball on a stalk on the mitochondrial inner membrane. The F complex, alternatively termed the elementary particle, is made up of two subunits, the stalk (F_0), and the ball (F_1), which is the site of the mitochondrial ATPase enzyme.

Area 4, the matrix, is not simply a space but contains nearly half the mitochondrial protein. In the matrix are located enzymes, such as those of the "Krebs cycle." We will discuss them in detail next.

Krebs Cycle

The mitochondrial Krebs cycle begins what is called the final common pathway for the catabolism of oxidizable substrates. Because we have been dis-

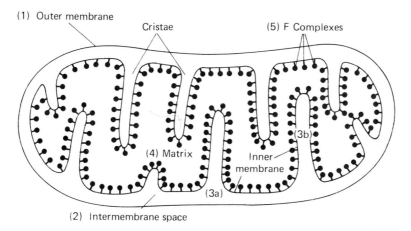

(1) Outer membrane

Cristae

(5) F Complexes

(3b)

(4) Matrix

Inner membrane

(3a)

(2) Intermembrane space

Figure 4-3

Schematic representation of a mitochondrion (reticulum fragment). Areas indicated are (1) the outer membrane, (2) the intermembrane space, (3) the inner membrane, and (4) the matrix. The inner membrane is diagrammed as existing in either of two orientations, either juxtaposed to the outer membrane (3a) or protruding into the matrix (3b). F complexes (5) protrude from the inner membrane, which is a mobile phospholipid structure. Inward folds of the inner membrane form the cristae. See the text for a description of the functions of each area.

cussing the catabolism of carbohydrates, we shall begin describing mitochondrial function by following pyruvate metabolism. Later in this chapter, we shall also describe how products of fat and protein catabolism enter the Krebs cycle and are used to produce energy.

Pyruvate is formed in the cytoplasm (Chapter 3) and gains entry into the mitochondrial matrix by a carrier mechanism located in the outer membrane. After entry into the matrix, pyruvate is acted on by an enzyme called pyruvate dehydrogenase (PDH), with CO_2 and acetylcoenzyme A (acetyl-CoA) being the carbon-containing products. Acetyl-CoA is then acted on by the Krebs cycle enzymes. The series of enzymes depicted in Figure 4-4 were named the Krebs cycle after Sir Hans Krebs, who did much of the work elaborating the pathway. The Krebs cycle is alternatively termed the citric acid cycle (the first constituent is citric acid) and the tricarboxylic acid (TCA) cycle (the initial constituents have three carboxyl groups).

Figure 4-4 reveals the purposes of PDH and the TCA cycle—decarboxylation (CO_2 formation), ATP production, and, most important, NADH production. As we shall see, NADH is energetically equivalent to three ATP, and Flavin-adenine dinucleotide, reduced (FADH) is equivalent to two ATP when processed by the electron transport chain (ETC). Thus, in the TCA cycle, the continued metabolism of pyruvate from glucose (as well as the products of

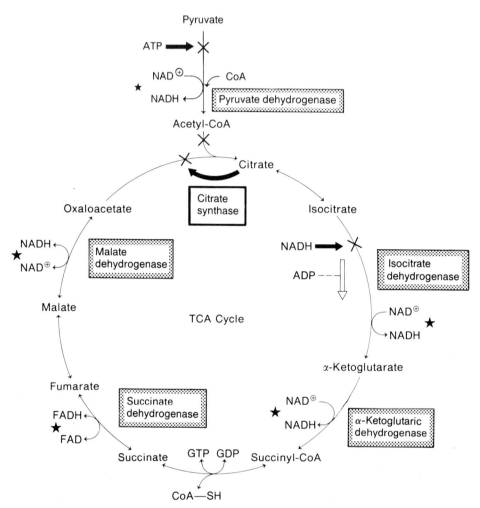

Figure 4-4

Regulation of the tricarboxylic acid (TCA) cycle. The starred dehydrogenase reactions require oxidized coenzymes; in resting muscle the dehydrogenases are inhibited by coenzyme (NADH and FADH) reduction. During exercise, the coenzymes are oxidized (to NAD⁺ and FAD) and the dehydrogenases are activated. In resting tissue, high levels of mitochondrial ATP inhibit pyruvate dehydrogenase (PDH), and in mitochondria of active tissues ADP stimulates isocitrate dehydrogenase (IDH). The first TCA cycle enzyme, citrate synthases, is inhibited by its product, but the inhibition is removed when IDH is activated. Thus, the levels of ADP and ATP as well as the mitochondrial NADH/NAD⁺ control TCA cycle activity.

lipid and protein catabolism) results in the trapping of energy in the form of guanosine triphosphate (GTP; equivalent to ATP) and high-energy-reduced compounds (NADH and FADH).

The control of the TCA cycle is such that the cycle is inhibited in resting tissues, where ATP and NADH concentrations are relatively high, and the concentrations of ADP and NAD$^+$ are low. The TCA cycle enzymes that reduce NAD$^+$ and FAD to NADH and FADH are called *dehydrogenases*. These enzymes are inhibited by their products. When the mitochondrial redox (reduction–oxidation potential, NADH/NAD$^+$) is high, as it is in resting tissues, TCA cycle activity is low. Inversely, the dehydrogenases are stimulated when the mitochondrial redox potential declines (i.e., becomes more oxidized), as is active muscle. Additionally, two dehydrogenases—PDH, which functions on pyruvate before entry into the TCA cycle, and isocitrate dehydrogenase (IDH), which catalyzes the conversion of isocitrate to α-ketoglutarate—are modulated by the levels of ADP and ATP. In mitochondria, PDH is inhibited by ATP and, most important, IDH is stimulated by ADP. Thus, when exercise starts, the inhibitory effect of ATP is removed as ATP is hydrolyzed and a stimulus is provided by the increased levels of ADP. In the TCA cycle, IDH is the major control point and its function is analogous to that of PFK in glycolysis.

Oxidative Phosphorylation

The term *oxidative phosphorylation* is used to describe the overall process by which the energy provided from use of O_2 allows for the addition of phosphate to ADP to form ATP. In reality, oxidative phosphorylation is composed of two separate but linked processes, oxidation and phosphorylation. Mitochondria are structured to link the processes of oxygen consumption and ATP production.

The Electron Transport Chain—
Oxygen, the Final Electron Acceptor

Components of the ETC are arranged in respiratory assemblies located on the mitochondrial inner membrane (Figure 4-5). The ETC functions as follows. Reducing equivalents (hydrogens and electrons) from NADH and FADH gain entry at or near the beginning of the ETC. Along the ETC, electrons move from areas of electronegativity (NADH) toward electropositivity (atomic oxygen). Along the ETC, electrons are stripped off the hydrogens, and the resulting protons (H$^+$) are pumped out of the mitochondrion; the electrons continue along the ETC toward oxygen. For each NADH entering the ETC, three pairs of protons are pumped out of the mitochondrion; for each FADH entering, two pairs of protons are extruded. This pumping process of electron transport creates a gradient of protons across the mitochondrial membrane (Figure 4-5).

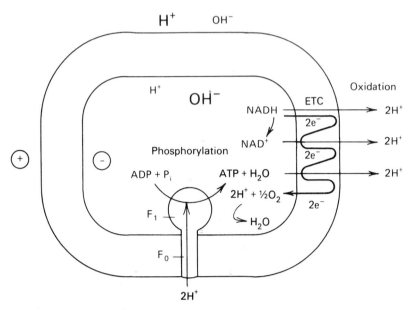

Figure 4-5
Orientation of components of the electron transport chain (ETC) within
the mitochondrial inner membrane. Entry of hydride ions (H) from
high-energy reduced compounds (e.g., NADH) into the ETC results in
the oxidation of those compounds, electron transport, and the expulsion
of protons (H$^+$). This creates a chemical and electrical gradient across
the membrane. Entry of protons through specific portals into the F_0–F_1
complex (elementary particle or stalk and ball) provides the energy for
the phosphorylation of ADP to ATP.

    Figure 4-5 depicts oxygen's role as the "final electron acceptor." As the
result of mitochondrial electron transport, a region of increased proton concentration (decreased pH) is created outside the mitochondria relative to that
inside the mitochondria. Some of these protons are exchanged for other charged
particles, with the result being a transmembrane chemical-electrical and osmotic potential that supplies the energy to join ADP and P_i, forming ATP.

    According to the "chemiosmotic" theory of oxidative phosphorylation, pairs
of protons enter mitochondria and are directed through the stalk or F_0 part
of the elementary particle. The proton motive force (derived from the difference in concentration of H$^+$ ions inside to outside) allows for the combination
of ADP and P_i, which were previously bound to the ball (F_1) part of the elementary particle.

    The formation of ATP according the chemiosmotic theory represents a
reversal of the hydrolysis of ATP (See Eq. 2-3). The hydrolysis and formation
of ATP can be written as:

$$ATP + H_2O \quad \xrightarrow{\text{Hydrolysis}} \atop \xleftarrow[\text{Phosphorylation}]{} \quad \text{Mitochondrial ATPase} \quad ADP + P_i + 2H^+ \qquad (4\text{-}1)$$

The Role of Oxygen in Cellular Respiration

From the beginning of this text (Chapter 1), the importance of O_2 consumption, $\dot{V}O_{2max}$, and the circulatory delivery of O_2 in understanding exercise performance and the basic life processes has been emphasized. We now address why O_2 is so critically important. *The presence of oxygen is critical for mitochondrial function because oxygen is the final electron acceptor at the end of the ETC.* The consumption of oxygen in mitochondria is sometimes termed mitochondrial, or cellular, *respiration*. By accepting electrons from the ETC, and by combining with protons to form water, oxygen utilization results in the formation of H_2O:

$$\tfrac{1}{2} O_2 + 2 \ e^- + 2 \ H^+ \rightarrow H_2O \qquad (4\text{-}2)$$

Ultimately, therefore, electron and proton flow toward O_2 provides the energy to support exercise and other life processes.

Control of the Electron Transport Chain

The rate of electron transfer along the ETC is controlled by a number of substances. These are the availability of substrate (e.g., the H^- in NADH), the presence of O_2, and the concentrations of P_i, and ADP. In terms of performance of the intact individual functioning in exercise, several of these factors are important. We have seen that the rate at which substrate can be supplied is greater from carbohydrate sources (glycolysis and glycogenolysis) than from fat or protein sources (Chapter 2). Therefore, if carbohydrate reserves are depleted during prolonged exercise, the sources of high-energy-reducing equivalents (NADH and FADH) will be limited to those supplied from lipid and protein. Consequently, the rates of mitochondrial electron transport and ATP supply will be reduced when the supply of oxidizable substrate is reduced as the result of glycogen depletion.

The rate of ATP supply and exercise power output can be limited by the availability of O_2. Therefore, the maximal rate at which O_2 can be consumed from the atmosphere and delivered to active muscle through the arterial circulation sets the upper limit of O_2 consumption (i.e., $\dot{V}O_{2max}$).

The most important factor that regulates the mitochondrial rates of O_2 consumption and ATP production is the mitochondrial concentration of ADP. This, in turn, is related to the cytoplasmic concentration of creatine phosphate (CP) and the rate of ATP utilization. The relationship between ATP use in the cytoplasm to sustain muscle cell work and the regulation of mitochondrial respiration is illustrated in Figure 4-6. Basically, ATP hydrolyzed by the interaction of actin and myosin in the contraction process is regenerated by cytoplasmic creatine phosphate. Cytoplasmic creatine is regenerated to CP by interaction with enzymes in the mitochondrial membrane. These are mitochondrial creatine kinase and adenine nucleotide translocase. The resulting mitochondrial ADP is rephosphorylated by the mitochondrial ATPase (F_1).

The Oxidative ATP Yield from Glucose

Under aerobic (slow) glycolysis, for each glucose a net of two ATPs are formed in the cytoplasm and the reducing equivalents of two NADHs can be shuttled into mitochondria producing four to six ATPs. The two pyruvate formed from a glucose each produces the equivalent of 15 ATPs as the result of TCA cycle and ETC activity. Thus, from a glucose molecule, 36 to 38 ATPs will be formed depending on the cytoplasmic-mitochondrial NADH shuttle used.

Fats as Fuels during Exercise

As described earlier (Table 2-4), the energy reserves stored in fat (lipid) are vast compared with other fuel reserves. Although fats provide an almost inexhaustible fuel supply for any single bout of muscular exercise, the processes of fat utilization are activated slowly and proceed at significantly lower rates than those processes controlling sugar and carbohydrate metabolism. Despite these limitations, fats constitute an important segment of the fuel used during prolonged exercise, and significant increases in the ability to use fats as fuel during exercise can effectively slow glycogen metabolism. The sparing of glycogen catabolism by substituting fats during prolonged exercise in endurance-trained individuals slows the depletion of this essential metabolite. Thus, increased fat oxidation capability due to genetic endowment and training greatly enhances endurance capacity.

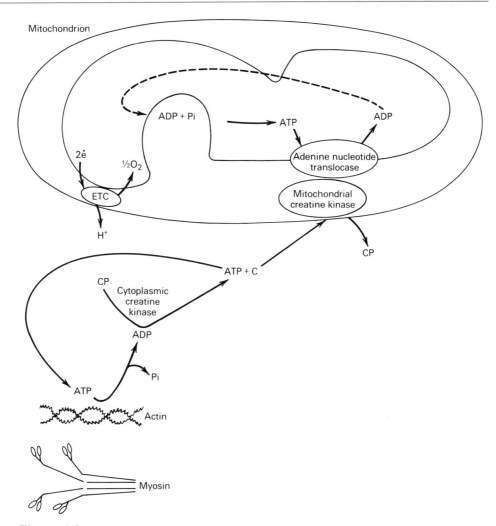

Figure 4-6

A model of the control of cellular respiration by creatine phosphate and ADP. The model begins at the lower left, where the contractile proteins actin and myosin hydrolyze ATP. The resulting ADP is phosphorylated by cytoplasmic creatine kinase with CP serving as the phosphate donor. The resulting cytoplasmic creatine is rephosphorylated by mitochondrial creatine kinase. Thus, ATP hydrolysis in the cytoplasm results in ADP formation in mitochondria. The rates of electron transport and O_2 consumption in mitochondria respond to the presence of ADP, phosphorylating it to ATP.

The Nature of Lipids

There are many kinds of lipids, but they all possess the characteristics of high solubility in organic solvents and low solubility in H_2O. Triglycerides are the most common form of dietary fat and the major form of fat storage in the body. The synthesis of triglycerides involves esterification, whereas lipolysis is the process of triglyceride breakdown into free fatty acids (FFA) and glycerol. Triglycerides synthesized in plants and animals are consumed by humans. Digestion involves the lipolysis of triglycerides, whereas fat deposition involves the reesterification of fatty acids delivered to adipose (body fat) tissue. The mobilization of triglycerides stored in adipose for utilization involves another lipolysis. Synthesis, digestion, storage, and mobilization can be simply diagrammed as a series of reversal reactions.

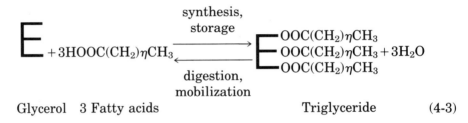

$$\text{Glycerol} \quad \text{3 Fatty acids} \qquad\qquad\qquad \text{Triglyceride} \qquad (4\text{-}3)$$

Mobilization of Fatty Acids during Exercise

Half or more of the fat combusted during prolonged exercise comes from adipose (fat) tissue. Triglyceride in adipose must therefore be mobilized (hydrolyzed) to fatty acids, released into the blood, circulated to active muscle, taken up, and oxidized. These processes are illustrated in Figure 4-7. Lipolysis in adipose is under the control of an enzyme, hormone-sensitive lipase (HSL). The hormones that activate HSL are catecholamines (epinephrine and norepinephrine), growth hormone, and cortisol. These hormones reach adipocytes (fat cells) through the circulation, and, in addition, sympathetic nerve endings release norepinephrine within the adipose. The hormone that inhibits HSL is insulin, which is released after a high-carbohydrate meal. Compared with the release of growth hormone and cortisol, which is slow during exercise, the release of catecholamines is relatively rapid. Therefore, the catecholamines are thought to be responsible for initiating substrate mobilization at the beginning of exercise, whereas growth hormone and cortisol help to maintain adipose triglyceride lipolysis during prolonged exercise. Because of their low solubility in water, the fatty acids released from adipose must be transported in combination with the blood protein albumin.

Glycerol released into the circulation from adipose as the result of lipolysis in soluble in the blood. It has only a minor role, however, as a substrate

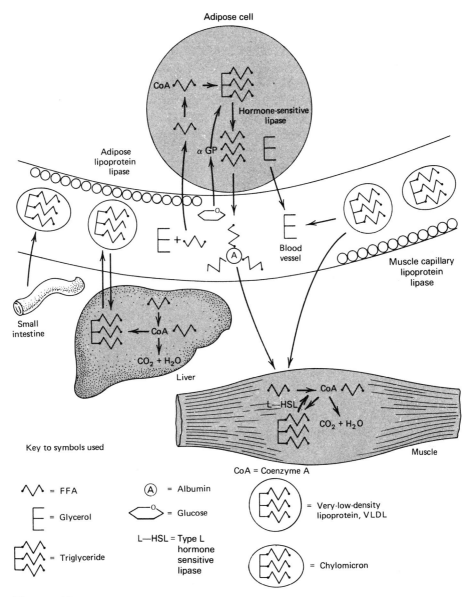

Figure 4-7

Mobilization and circulation. Most of the lipid oxidized in muscle during exercise is delivered by the circulating blood. The blood contains free fatty acids (FFA) that are released from adipose tissue after mobilization of triglyceride stores by activation of the hormone-sensitive lipase. The blood also contains lipoproteins [both chylomicrons from the GI tract and very low density lipids (VLDL) from the liver] that deliver a much smaller quantity of lipid to muscle during exercise. Thus, the ability to use fat as a fuel during exercise depends on the arterial blood level (a function of mobilization) and muscle blood flow (a function of circulation).

(SOURCE: Modified from R. J. Havel. Used with permission.)

in muscle during exercise; rather, glycerol is a gluconeogenic precursor during exercise.

Triglyceride synthesis in adipose is controlled by the activity of lipoprotein lipase enzyme. This enzyme is stimulated by insulin and glucose. As a result, triglyceride synthesis in adipose cells is stimulated after a meal when blood levels of chylomicrons, glucose, and insulin are high.

Circulation and Uptake of Fatty Acids

Approximately half the fatty acids contained in a volume of arterial blood are taken up in passing through the capillary bed in active muscle. Therefore, the rate of blood flow and the arterial concentration of fatty acids are important determinants of fat utilization during exercise. Endurance-trained individuals possess several advantages over the untrained for fat utilization during exercise. They possess a greater cardiac output and ability to circulate fuel substances such as fatty acids. In addition, trained individuals clear lactic acid from the blood better during exercise; consequently, their circulating levels of lactate are lower. *This is important because lactic acid inhibits fatty acid mobilization from adipose.* Thus, untrained individuals engaged in heavy exercise will suffer in at least two ways. High levels of lactate are distressing to the athletes' perception of their performance and to muscle function. Further, high levels of lactate, which inhibit fat utilization, result in increased reliance on muscle glycogen as a fuel, resulting, in turn, in glycogen depletion and muscle fatigue.

Activation, Translocation, and β-Oxidation of Fatty Acids

The fates of fatty acids taken up by muscle are illustrated in Figure 4-8. Fatty acid–albumin complexes bind to a receptor site on the muscle membrane. The fatty acids are then internalized and the albumin remains in the blood. Fatty acid catabolism begins with an activation step involving ATP and CoA. The result is fatty acyl-CoA (a molecule like a very large acetyl-CoA), an adenosine monophosphate (AMP), and a pyrophosphate (PP_i). There fatty acyl-CoA continues to be catabolized whereas the AMP and PP_i activate metabolic processes. Recall that a similar activation occurs at the beginning of glycolysis with the hexokinase step in which an ATP is used.

Fatty acyl-CoA gains entry into the mitochondrial matrix by combining with a carrier substance, carnitine, which exists in the mitochondrial membrane. An enzyme, carnitine transferase, facilitates the movement of fatty

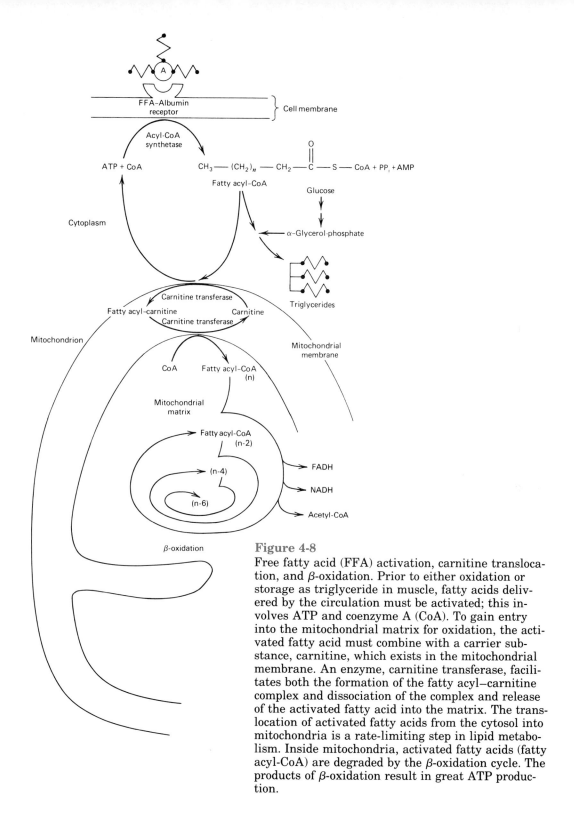

Figure 4-8

Free fatty acid (FFA) activation, carnitine transloca-
tion, and β-oxidation. Prior to either oxidation or
storage as triglyceride in muscle, fatty acids delivered by the circulation must be activated; this involves ATP and coenzyme A (CoA). To gain entry
into the mitochondrial matrix for oxidation, the activated fatty acid must combine with a carrier substance, carnitine, which exists in the mitochondrial
membrane. An enzyme, carnitine transferase, facilitates both the formation of the fatty acyl–carnitine
complex and dissociation of the complex and release
of the activated fatty acid into the matrix. The trans-
location of activated fatty acids from the cytosol into
mitochondria is a rate-limiting step in lipid metabolism. Inside mitochondria, activated fatty acids (fatty
acyl-CoA) are degraded by the β-oxidation cycle. The
products of β-oxidation result in great ATP production.

acyl–carnitine across the mitochondrial membrane where it reacts with CoA from the matrix to form fatty acyl-CoA in the matrix.

In the matrix, fatty acyl-CoA is catabolized by an enzyme system called the beta (β)-oxidation cycle. Each time fatty acyl-CoA traverses the β-oxidation cycle, a 2-carbon unit is cleaved off to form acetyl-CoA. In addition, an NADH and an FADH are formed in each revolution of the cycle.

Number of ATPs from Oxidation of a Fatty Acid

As seen in Figure 4-8, each time a fatty acyl-CoA traverses the β-oxidation cycle, a 2-carbon acetyl-CoA is cleaved off. For palmitate, a 16-carbon fatty acid, eight acetyl-CoAs will be formed, but only seven cycles of the β-oxidation pathway will occur. This is because the products of the seventh cycle are two acetyl-CoAs, the acetyl-CoA produced during the seventh pass and the 2-carbon acyl-CoA that is left.

Each acetyl-CoA that enters the TCA cycle from β-oxidation will eventually yield 12 ATPs. Additionally, each cycle of the β-oxidation pathway will yield one NADH (equivalent to three ATPs), and one FADH (worth two ATPs). Therefore, from a palmitate molecule (a 16-carbon fatty acid) a net gain of 129 ATPs will be formed if the initial ATP hydrolyzed to AMP is taken into account. This AMP has to be rephosphorylated twice to be returned to ATP.

Control of Fatty Acid Utilization

As already mentioned, the rate of fatty acid utilization will depend on the circulating level of fatty acids and the rate of blood flow. Enzymatically, the activity of mitochondrial carnitine transferase enzyme is thought to limit the maximal rate of fatty acid oxidation. Modulation of fatty acid oxidation is accomplished by regulation of the last enzyme in the β-oxidation cycle. This enzyme is β-keto thiolase, an enzyme that is inhibited by its product, acetyl-CoA. Thus, when acetyl-CoA levels are high, such as after a high-carbohydrate meal, fat catabolism is slowed. During prolonged, moderate-intensity exercise, when acetyl-CoA levels are reduced as a result of increased TCA cycle activity, fat utilization is promoted.

As noted previously in this chapter, entry of acetyl-CoA into the TCA begins the final common pathway of intermediary metabolism. Therefore, regulation of β-oxidation products in the TCA cycle and electron transport chain is the same as for carbohydrate-derived products.

Intramuscular Triglycerides and Blood Lipoproteins as Fuel Sources

Although fatty acids provide most of the lipid material for oxidation, triglyceride reserves in muscle provide a significant reserve of oxidizable substrate. Muscle tissue contains two lipolytic enzymes which, unfortunately, have the same name, *lipoprotein lipase* (LPL). Lipoprotein lipase in the muscle capillary wall hydrolyzes triglycerides in blood lipoproteins and makes the resulting fatty acids available in muscle. Also, a form of lipoprotein lipase that exists within muscle cells is responsible for hydrolyzing triglycerides in circulating lipoproteins as well as the triglyceride stores within muscle cells. This form of LPL is termed Type L-HSL (lipoprotein hormone-sensitive lipase).

Both LPLs in muscle are hormonally regulated. Type L-HSL is inhibited by high levels of insulin and stimulated by glucagon. Thus, regulation of the muscle L-HSL is similar to that of adipose HSL but opposite that of capillary bed LPL. This antagonistic regulation of triglyceride lipases within the body allows for triglyceride synthesis after eating and triglyceride mobilization during exercise and starvation. Additionally, growth hormone release activates L-HSL during prolonged exercise and helps to supply fat for combustion in muscle.

Endurance training has the effect of increasing muscle L-HSL activity. For this reason, lipid reserves within muscle cells are more available as fuel sources in muscles of trained individuals.

Tissue Specificity and Lipid Utilization

Various tissues in the body such as heart and liver are highly adapted for lipid utilization. Other cells, such as the brain and red blood cells, rely almost exclusively on glycolysis for energy supply. Among skeletal muscle cells, the ability to utilize fats as an energy source varies greatly. Fast-contracting, white (Type IIb) fibers depend on glycogenolysis for energy. In contrast, red skeletal muscle fibers, rich in blood supply with high mitochondrial contents, are well adapted for fat utilization. As we shall see, endurance training can greatly improve the capacity to use fats as a fuel.

Amino Acids as Fuel Sources

Although amino acids and proteins were long believed to have played no significant role in supplying fuels for muscular exercise, it now appears that

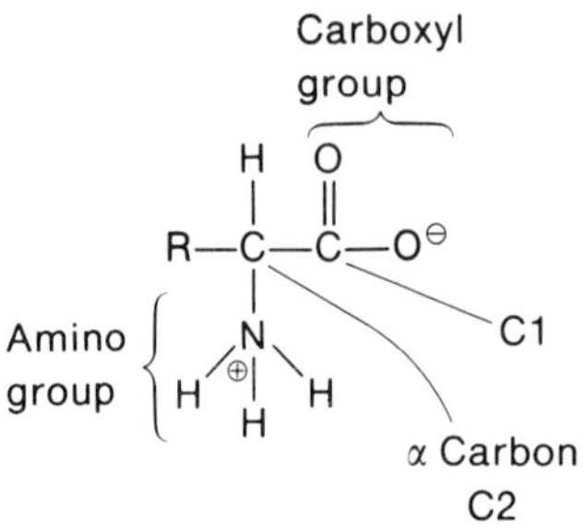

Carboxyl
group

$$R—\underset{\underset{\underset{H}{\overset{\oplus}{\underset{|}{N}}}{\diagup}\diagdown H}{\overset{\overset{H}{|}}{C}}—\overset{\overset{O}{\parallel}}{C}—O^{\ominus}$$

Amino group

C1

α Carbon
C2

Figure 4-9

General structure of an amino acid, an α-amino carboxylic acid. At physiological pH, most amino acids carry a negative ($-$) charge, and usually a positive ($+$) charge as well. Note: R groups are side chains.

they do participate in the metabolic adjustments to exercise. Significant amounts of amino acids exist free in muscle, liver, and blood. Also, proteolytic (protein-dissolving) enzymes in liver and muscle can be activated during exercise and other stress conditions by the hormone cortisol.

Amino acids are distinguished from carbohydrates and fats in their nitrogen content (Figure 4-9). The free amino acids used to support the metabolic adjustments to exercise exist in muscle, blood, and the liver. Amino acids are also provided by the breakdown of proteins in liver and skeletal muscle. The nitrogen-containing group of amino acids can be removed by switching the nitrogen to another compound (transamination) or by removing the nitrogen group to form ammonia (oxidative deamination). After the nitrogen is removed, the carbon residue of the original amino acid can be catabolized in a number of ways. Depending on its structure, the molecule can gain entry into the TCA cycle at a number of steps. In addition, the carbon residue can be converted to glucose, and then be oxidized. Results of recent isotope tracer investigations reveal that approximately 5 to 10% of the energy supplied during exercise comes from the combustion of amino acids. Of the more than 20 amino acids in the body, one (leucine) is particularly important as an oxidizable substrate in muscle. Leucine can also provide nitrogen groups that make their way to the amino acid alanine.

By means of the glucose–alanine cycle (Chapter 3), the amino acid alanine helps to maintain glucose homeostasis during prolonged exercise. In active muscle, the carbon structure of alanine is formed from pyruvate. The nitrogen group of alanine comes from the amino acid glutamate, which receives its nitrogen from leucine. Along with lactate, pyruvate, and glycerol, alanine is a 3-carbon gluconeogenic precursor of significance during prolonged exercise. Moreover, radiotracer studies have demonstrated that alanine can be oxidized during exercise without conversion to glucose.

In addition to providing oxidizable substrates and gluconeogenic precursors, amino acids help sustain prolonged exercise in another way. Besides its central role in energy metabolism, the TCA cycle has a number of other functions. Therefore, various of the TCA cycle intermediates become depleted, and the TCA cycle's function can be compromised. The TCA cycle must therefore be filled back up if it is to continue functioning. During times of rapid TCA cycle turnover, the carbon residues of amino acids play important roles as anaplerotic substances to replenish the lost intermediates from the TCA cycle.

One example of an anaplerotic process is the conversion of aspartate to oxaloacetate (OAA, the last TCA cycle intermediate) by action the enzyme glutamate-oxaloacetate transaminase (GOT):

$$\text{Aspartate} + \alpha\text{-ketoglutarate} \xrightarrow[\text{GOT}]{} \text{Oxaloacetate} + \text{Glutamate}$$

An explanation of how an anaplerotic process could postpone glycogen depletion and muscle fatigue is given later.

Caloric Equivalents of Combusted Foodstuffs

Table 4-1 presents the relationships among caloric equivalents for combustion of various foodstuffs in the body. These values are based on direct measurements of the heat released, O_2 consumed, and CO_2 produced in resting individuals. On a gram-weight basis, the combustion of carbohydrates and proteins produce about the same amount of energy (i.e., about 4 kcal/g). In comparison, on a weight basis, the combustion of fat produces more than twice (over 9 kcal/g) the energy of carbohydrate and fat.

On the other hand, Table 4-1 also indicates that for a given O_2 utilization, the combustion of carbohydrate provides the greatest amount of energy. Thus, when an individual is engaged in very hard exercise, approximately 7% more energy per liter of O_2 consumed will be produced from the combustion of carbohydrate than from fat. During very hard exercise most of the substrate oxidized is derived from carbohydrate (Figure 4-10). This selection is made because of the enzymatic mechanisms described earlier. The body's selection of carbohydrate as the major oxidizable substrate during very hard

TABLE 4-1 Caloric Equivalents of Foodstuffs Combusted Inside the Body

Food	kcal·liter O_2^{-1}	RQ ($\dot{V}_{CO_2}/\dot{V}_{O_2}$)	Inside Body (kcal·g^{-1})
Carbohydrate	5.05	1.00	4.2
Fat	4.70	0.70	9.5
Protein	4.5	0.80	4.2
Mixed diet	4.82	0.82	
Starving individual	4.70	0.70	

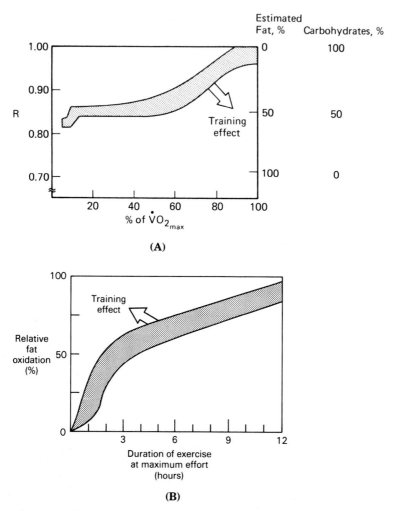

Figure 4-10

(A) Relationship between the ventilatory respiratory exchange ratio $(R = \dot{V}_{CO_2}/\dot{V}_{O_2})$ and relative exercise intensity in well-nourished individuals. Utilization of fat and carbohydrate can be estimated from the R. As relative exercise intensity increases, the proportional use of carbohydrate increases. Training shifts the curve to the right. (Based on tables of Zuntz and Schumberg and other sources.) **(B)** Relationship between the relative utilization of fat and the duration of exercise. The utilization of fat was estimated from the R. As exercise duration increases, the relative utilization of fat increases. Training shifts the curve to the left.

exercise makes good sense because, in this way, the greatest amount of energy is made available.

The ratio of CO_2 produced to O_2 consumed is termed the respiratory quotient (RQ). When individuals are studied under the steady-state conditon of rest, measurement of the RQ provides a means to determine which fuel is being combusted (see Table 4-1). These differences result from the different proportions of carbon (C), hydrogen (H), nitrogen (N), and oxygen (O) in their structures. Of the three different fuels, carbohydrate contains the most oxygen, fats contain the most hydrogen, and proteins contain the only nitrogen. For example, when the sugar glucose, a simple carbohydrate, is combusted, the ratio of CO_2 produced to O_2 consumed will be 1.0.

$$C_6H_{12}O_6 + 6\ O_2 \rightarrow 6\ CO_2 + 6\ H_2O \qquad (4\text{-}4)$$

Similarly, when fat is combusted, the ratio of CO_2 to O_2 will approximate 0.7. For example, for trioleate, a common triglyceride:

$$C_{57}H_{104}O_6 + 80\ O_2 \rightarrow 57\ CO_2 + 52\ H_2O \qquad (4\text{-}5)$$

Whenever the rates of CO_2 production ($\dot{V}_{CO_2}$) and oxygen consumption ($\dot{V}_{O_2}$) are measured at the mouth, the ratio of these values is termed the respiratory exchange ratio ($R = \dot{V}_{CO_2}/\dot{V}_{O_2}$). During steady-state conditions, such as during rest and prolonged exercise when body CO_2 stores are not changing, measurement of the whole body $\dot{V}_{CO_2}$ and $\dot{V}_{O_2}$ can reliably be used to predict the respiratory quotient of cellular combustion. Therefore, under steady-state conditions measurement of the $\dot{V}_{CO_2}$ and $\dot{V}_{O_2}$ can provide a good estimate of the fuel or mixture of fuels combusted (Figure 4-10).

During prolonged submaximal exercise, the mechanisms of fatty acid mobilization and oxidation function to supply a greater proportion of energy than during high-intensity, short-duration exercise. This conclusion is based mainly on the observation that the R is lower during sustained exercise than it is during exercise of high intensity. Table 4-1 indicates that fat is a very efficient energy storage form containing more than twice the energy per unit weight of other foodstuffs. Utilization of fat as a fuel during prolonged exercise therefore, makes available a nearly inexhaustable energy source.

Glycogen Depletion and Muscle Fatigue

It has been well documented that exhaustion of glycogen reserves in muscle during exercise results in a reduction or cessation of muscle activity. Why this occurs when large fat reserves exist is a question of major interest. It is apparent, however, that fat utilization depends on the presence of carbohydrate. One way in which carbohydrates, and to some extent amino acids, could allow fat oxidation is diagrammed in Figure 4-11. During high rates of me-

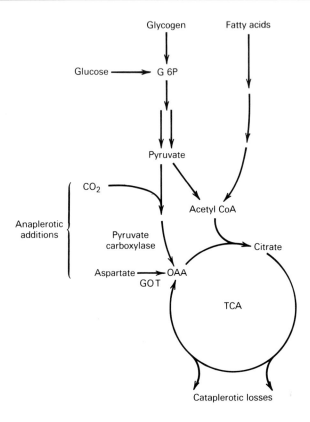

Figure 4-11
A mechanism by which the carbohydrates glucose and glycogen, as well as amino acids (to a lesser extent), support the combustion of fats. The anaplerotic addition of carbon to the TCA cycle balances cataplerotic losses. This mechanism would explain why glycogen depletion results in muscle fatigue.

tabolism, TCA cycle intermediate compounds are siphoned off to perform various (cataplerotic) functions. Therefore, for adequate levels of OAA to remain to combine with acetyl-CoA to form citrate, material must reenter into the TCA cycle at or close before the OAA level. Although muscle has been thought not to contain the enzyme pyruvate carboxylase, it now appears that low levels of this enzyme are present in muscle. Further, it appears that muscle pyruvate carboxylase activity increases in response to endurance training.

Another reason why muscle glycogen is needed to sustain exercise has to do with the fact that in humans fat cannot be utilized rapidly enough to sustain high power outputs.

Metabolic Effects of Hormones

Hormones are chemical substances secreted in very small amounts into body fluids, usually by the endocrine glands. The target tissues of hormones can be anatomically close to or quite far removed from the glands of secretion, and the targets can be one of several tissues. At the targets of their action, hormones powerfully affect metabolism. In the resting person, metabolism is largely controlled by hormones. In general, hormonal secretion is controlled by a negative-feedback system in which changing levels of the hormone, itself, or the substance affected as a result of hormone action, affect secretion of the hormone. For example, following a substantial carbohydrate meal, the blood glucose level rises. The increase in blood glucose stimulates the secretion of insulin, which increases glucose uptake from the blood. When blood glucose falls during exercise, so does insulin secretion. The falling insulin level slows the rate of glucose removal from the blood and helps maintain a "normal" blood glucose level.

A primary consideration during the stress of exercise is the maintenance of nearly "normal resting" levels of blood and cellular metabolites. During exercise, the blood glucose level can be maintained at about 4 mM (90 mg/100 ml) by increased release into the blood of glucose as well as fuels that may serve as alternatives. The coordinated physiological response to maintain homeostasis of glucose and alternative fuels to glucose is governed by hormones.

Throughout this and the previous chapter, the metabolic effects of several hormones have been discussed. The metabolic effects of hormones are summarized in Table 4-2.

Effects of Training on Skeletal Muscle Mitochondria

One of the most significant of all physiological adaptations that have been discovered is the increase in amount of muscle mitochondrial material because of endurance training. This adaptation affects the ability to use O_2 at high rates over time. In response to training, the mitochondrial activity in all types of skeletal muscle has been observed to approximately double (Table 4-3). Constituents of the TCA cycle (e.g., citrate synthase), components of the ETC (e.g., cytochrome c), and enzymes of fatty acid oxidation (e.g., carnitine palmityl transferase) all increase (Table 4-3). Interestingly, mitochondrial activity in heart muscle does not increase in response to endurance training. This is probably because the heart is very high in oxidative capacity to begin with.

For several years an important question for scientists has been whether the increase in mitochondrial biochemical activity in trained skeletal muscle is due to an increase in the size or the number of mitochondria. Results of electron microscopic examination of trained versus sedentary muscle clearly show more mitochondria in the trained tissue (Figure 4-12). However, it is now believed probably that training results in the budding and branching of the mitochondrial reticulum (see Figure 4-2).

TABLE 4-2 Summary of Metabolic Effects of Hormones

Metabolic Effect	Hormone(s)
Cellular glucose uptake	Insulin
Glycolysis and glycogen synthesis	Insulin
Triglyceride synthesis	Insulin
Decrease in blood glucose level	Insulin
Liver glycogenolysis	Epinephrine (nonspecific)
	Glucagon (specific)
	Norepinephrine (?)[a]
Liver gluconeogenesis	Glucagon
Muscle glycogenolysis	Epinephrine
	Norepinephrine (?)
Adipose lipolysis	Cortisol
	Epinephrine
	Growth hormone
Muscle lipolysis	Glucagon
Protein synthesis	Growth hormone
	Insulin
Protein catabolism	Cortisol
Increase in blood glucose level	Epinephrine
Direct effect	Glucagon
Indirect effect	Cortisol
	Epinephrine
	Glucagon
Increased metabolic rate	Epinephrine
	Norepinephrine
	Thyroxine

[a] Question mark indicates that specificity of effect is unknown.

The increase in mitochondrial material in muscle from endurance training results in an increase in exercise endurance capacity. As determined in laboratory animals, muscle mitochondrial capacity is significantly better correlated with running endurance than is $\dot{V}_{O_{2max}}$ (Table 4-4). The increase in exercise endurance associated with an increase in muscle mitochondrial mass is probably due to a number of factors:

- Increased mitochondrial mass and activity provide an increased capacity to oxidize all substrates.
- Increased mitochondrial mass specifically allows for greater fat oxidation capacity, thereby sparing glycogen reserves.
- Increased mitochondrial mass allows for a greater clearance of lactic acid formed during exercise. Thus, trained individuals can tolerate greater rates of glycolysis and lactic acid production while at the same time maintaining low circulating lactic acid levels. Lactic acid is a stressor that, among other effects, inhibits fat mobilization.

TABLE 4-3 Effect of Endurance Training on Respiratory Capacity of Rat Skeletal Muscle Mitochondria[a]

Muscle	Group	Citrate Synthase ($\mu mol \cdot min^{-1} \cdot g^{-1}$) Muscle	Carnitine Palmityl Transferase	Cytochrome c ($nmol \cdot g^{-1}$)
Fast-twitch white	Exercised	18 ± 1	0.20 ± 0.02	6.3 ± 0.7
	Sedentary	10 ± 1	0.11 ± 0.01	3.2 ± 0.3
Fast-twitch red	Exercised	70 ± 4	1.20 ± 0.09	28.4 ± 2.1
	Sedentary	36 ± 3	0.72 ± 0.06	16.5 ± 1.6
Slow-twitch red	Exercised	41 ± 3	1.20 ± 0.05	——
	Sedentary	24 ± 2	0.63 ± 0.07	——
Heart	Exercised	160 ± 4	——	46.6 ± 0.9
	Sedentary	158 ± 1	——	47.1 ± 1.0

[a] In response to endurance training, mitochondrial components in different types of rat skeletal muscles double in concentration. The heart does not change.

SOURCE: Data from Baldwin et al., Oscai et al., and Holloszy.

- Increased mitochondrial mass provides for a greater capacity to withstand mitochondrial damage during exercise. Although not a great deal of research has yet been performed on mitochondrial damage during exercise, it is apparent that oxygen reacts in nonenzymatically mediated

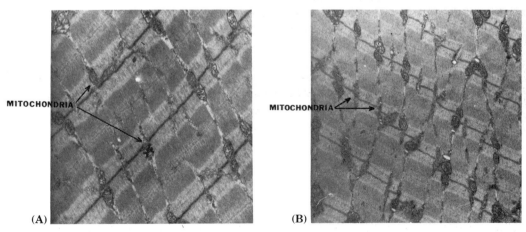

(A)   (B)

Figure 4-12

Electron micrographs of mitochondria in tissues of **(A)** untrained and **(B)** trained rats. Mitochondria in trained animals appear to be more numerous, probably because there is a more elaborate mitochondrial reticulum.

(SOURCE: Micrographs courtesy of P. D. Gollnick.)

TABLE 4-4 Correlation Matrix for Muscle Oxidases, $\dot{V}_{O_2max}$, and Maximal Endurance in Rats on a Treadmill[a,b]

	Pyruvate- Malate Oxidase	Palmityl Carnitine Oxidase	$\dot{V}_{O_2max}$ (weight normalized)	Maximal Endurance
Cytochrome oxidase	0.95	0.93	0.74	0.92
Pyruvate-malate oxidase	———	0.89	0.68	0.89
Palmityl carnitine oxidase	———	———	0.71	0.91
$\dot{V}_{O_2max}$ (weight normalized)	———	———	———	0.70

[a] All correlations reported were statistically significant ($P < 0.01$).

[b] Running endurance of rats as measured on a standardized treadmill test correlates significantly better with skeletal muscle mitochondrial activity (i.e., cytochrome oxidase activity) than with maximal O_2 consumption ($\dot{V}_{O_2max}$).

SOURCE: Data from Davies et al.

ways (e.g., as superoxide free radical) with cellular membranes, including mitochondrial membranes. By increasing the mitochondrial mass, endurance training reduces the impact of oxidative damage. In addition, training induces an increase in the amount of enzymes (e.g., superoxide dismutase, SOD) that protect against oxidative damage.

Other Intramuscular Biochemical Adaptations to Endurance Training

In addition to increasing the mitochondrial mass, endurance training results in several other biochemical adaptations within muscle. These adaptations function to improve the supply of O_2 and substrates to mitochondria.

Endurance training greatly increases the concentration of myoglobin in the cytoplasm of muscle cells. This adaptation facilitates the movement of O_2 from areas of higher oxygen partial pressure (P_{O_2}) within and near capillaries to areas of lower P_{O_2} deep within the cell.

Endurance training increases the sensitivity of muscle to insulin. Working muscle of trained individuals can therefore take up glucose from the blood even though glucose and insulin levels may be low.

Endurance training increases the amount of the glycolytic enzyme hexokinase in skeletal muscle. Selectively increasing the amount of hexokinase, a large fraction of which is bound to the outer mitochondrial membrane, allows for greater utilization of blood glucose and lesser use of muscle glycogen during exercise. This adaptation is possibly one of the reasons that exercise training improves the utilization of glucose in Type 2, insulin-insensitive diabetes.

Endurance training improves the amount of Type L hormone-sensitive lipase in muscle. This adaptation allows for greater use of triglyceride contained in circulating lipoproteins and intramuscular fat during exercise.

Endurance training also increases the involvement of amino acids in the metabolic adjustments sustaining prolonged exercise. Increased amounts of glutamate-pyruvate transaminase (GPT) allow for more pyruvate to be converted to alanine (and less to lactate) during exercise. Consequently, glucose–alanine cycle activity and blood glucose homeostasis are improved with endurance training. And, finally, training increases the ability to use leucine and alanine as oxidizable substrates during exercise.

Cardiovascular Capacity Increased by Endurance Training

No discussion of the aerobic adaptations to endurance training can be complete without mentioning that training increases the volume of blood that can be ejected from the heart on each beat. Endurance training therefore improves stroke volume, cardiac output, O_2 transport capacity, and $\dot{V}_{O_2max}$. These adaptations are discussed in Chapters 7 and 8.

Training to Increase the Mitochondrial Mass

Over the last several decades, athletes' maximal oxygen consumption capacity ($\dot{V}_{O_2max}$) has not greatly changed, but their capacity for endurance performance has drastically improved. This is probable because $\dot{V}_{O_2max}$ is determined by circulatory oxygen transport capacity:

$$\dot{T}_{O_2} = \dot{Q}(C_{aO_2}) \tag{4-5}$$

where $\dot{Q}$ is the cardiac output, and C_{aO_2} is the oxygen content of arterial blood. As just noted, these factors will be discussed more in following chapters. However, it appears that the limit to cardiac output is set by heart volume, a parameter that changes little (10–20%) with training. The important endurance training adaptations are therefore central (cardiovascular) as well as peripheral. The peripheral adaptations likely include the mitochondrial adaptations described earlier.

The precise cellular stimulus that causes an elaboration of the mitochondrial reticulum with endurance training is unknown. Perhaps oxidative damage induces the mitochondrial adaptation. However, it is known that this type of cellular adaptation results from long-distance training. Consequently, successful endurance athletes today are required to spend many hours practicing at distances in excess of their competitive distance.

We illustrate the selection and training of an endurance athlete by describing the preparation of a marathon runner. This is because the marathon is the longest competitive distance in Olympic competition. Successful competition in the marathon depends almost completely on the oxidative energy system. Two components of this system are the circulatory system (for the consumption of atmospheric O_2 and its circulation to active muscles) and skeletal muscle mitochondrial mass. A high circulatory capacity is necessary to supply O_2 and to distribute metabolic wastes (heat, CO_2, lactic acid) for removal. As was already mentioned, through training $\dot{V}O_{2max}$ can improve only 10 to 20%, and muscle mitochondrial density can increase 100% (see Table 4-3). In healthy young untrained adults, however, $\dot{V}O_{2max}$ can vary between 40 and 70 ml of oxygen per kilogram of body weight per minute (ml/kg/min), and mitochondrial activity can vary three- to fourfold in untrained muscle (see Table 4-3). To be very successful at a competitive level, therefore, a marathoner must be genetically endowed with prerequisites of a high cardiac output and oxidative types of muscle fibers.

The ability to transport O_2 can be assessed by means of a $\dot{V}O_{2max}$ test on a treadmill or bicycle ergometer (Figure 4-13). To be ultimately successful in marathon competition, a young, untrained male would require a $\dot{V}O_{2max}$ of at least 60 ml/kg/min, and a woman would require a $\dot{V}O_{2max}$ of 50 ml/kg/min. Preferably, the starting values would be closer to 70 and 60 ml/kg/min, respectively. Assuming the outer limit of 20% improvement through years of dedicated training, the requisite competitive $\dot{V}O_{2max}$ levels for O_2 transport and utilization could be achieved. The determination of $\dot{V}O_{2max}$ is now a fairly standard laboratory procedure; most college and university physical education departments possess the necessary equipment, as do many cardiology and pulmonary function departments in hospitals. In this instance, estimations of $\dot{V}O_{2max}$ on the basis of submaximal exercise heart rate response to ergometer work are inappropriate.

Compared with assessment of $\dot{V}O_{2max}$, the assessment of muscle mitochondrial capacity is more difficult. At present such an assessment would require a muscle biopsy (Chapter 8). Biopsy is not a routine procedure, and sampling problems occur, as well as ethical questions about performing the procedure on young, untrained adults. Perhaps in the future nuclear magnetic resonance (NMR) technique will allow a noninvasive assessment of muscle respiratory capacity? For the present, the best predictor of exercise endurance capacity remains exercise performance itself.

In Chapter 15, specifics of preparing for competition in various sports and activities are described in greater detail.

Summary

Physical activities lasting more than approximately 90 sec are mainly supported by oxidative metabolism. Oxygen supplied to active muscle by the lungs,

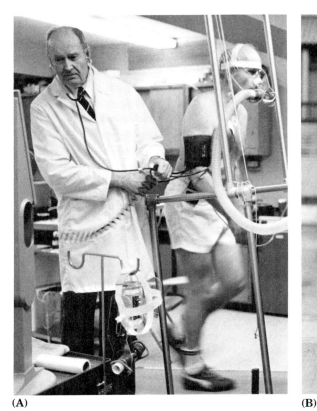 

(A)   **(B)**

Figure 4-13

(A) Treadmills are frequently used in the laboratory as a means to apply exercise stress and to record physiological responses on relatively stationary subjects during exercise. Compared to the bicycle ergometer, it is difficult to quantitate external work on the treadmill. However, the treadmill does allow subjects to walk or to run, which are perhaps more common modes of locomotion than is bicycling. **(B)** Bicycle ergometers are convenient, stationary laboratory devices to control the external work rate (power output) while physiological responses are observed.

(SOURCE: Photo courtesy of Wayne Glusker.)

heart, and blood serves to support cellular production of ATP. High-energy-reducing equivalents from the catabolism of carbohydrates, fats, and proteins supply the potential energy to support oxidative phosphorylation. Of the three types of skeletal muscle fibers, the pigmented (Types I and IIa) fibers are the sites of oxidative energy metabolism. Endurance training improves the capacity for O_2 transport and $\dot{V}O_{2max}$ by 10 to 20%. Endurance also has a dramatic effect on improving the mitochondrial content of skeletal muscle by approximately 100%. This adaptation improves the ability to oxidize all substrates, but enhancement of the ability to oxidize lipids is perhaps most important in terms of improving endurance at a given submaximal workload.

The coordination of physiological responses during exercise allows for the maintenance of near-"normal" blood glucose levels and for the provision of glucose as well as alternative fuels to glucose. The regulation of metabolism during rest and exercise depends on hormonal as well as local muscle factors. These responses hydrolyze muscle and liver glycogen, mobilize adipose and intramuscular triglyceride, and break down liver and muscle proteins to amino acids. All of these substances are important in supporting the energy requirements for endurance exercise.

Selected Readings

BAKEEVA, L.E., Y.S. CHENTSOV, and V.P. SKULACHEV. Mitochondrial framework (reticulum mitochondriale) in rat diaphragm muscle. Biochim. Biophys. Acta. 501:349–369, 1978.

BALDWIN, D., G. KLINKERFUSS, F. TERJUNG, P.A. MOLÉ, and J.O. HOLLOSZY. Respiratory capacity of white, red, and intermediate muscle: adaptive response to exercise. Am. J. Physiol. 22:373–378, 1972.

BARNARD, R., V.R. EDGERTON, T. FURUKAWA, and J.B. PETER. Histochemical, biochemical and contractile properties of red, white, and intermediate fibers. Am. J. Physiol. 220:410–414, 1971.

BROOKS, G.A., and T.D. FAHEY. Exercise Physiology: Human Bioenergetics and Its Applications. New York: Macmillan, 1984, pp. 97–188.

BUSE, M.G., J. BIGGERS, C. DRIER, and J. BUSE. The effect of epinepherine, glucagon, and the nutritional state on the oxidation of branched chain amino acids and pyruvate by isolated hearts and diaphragms of the rat. J. Biol. Chem. 248:697–786, 1971.

CALLOWAY, D.H., and H. SPECTOR. Nitrogen balance as related to caloric and protein intake in active young men. Am. J. Clin. Nutr. 2:405–411, 1954.

CHANCE, B., and C.R. WILLIAMS. The respiratory chain and oxidative phosphorylation. In Advances in Enzymology, Vol. 17. New York: Interscience, 1956, pp. 65–134.

COSTILL, D.L., J. DANIELS, W. EVANS, W. FINK, G. KRAHENBUHL, and B. SALTIN. Skeletal muscle enzymes and fiber composition in male and female track athletes. J. Appl. Physiol. 40:149–154, 1976.

DAVIES, K.J.A., L. PACKER, and G.A. BROOKS. Biochemical adaptations of mitochondria, muscle, and whole-animal respiration to endurance training. Arch. Biochem. Biophys. 209:538–553, 1981.

DOHM, G.L., A.L. HECKER, W.E. BROWN, G.J. KLAIN, F.R. PUENTE, E.W. ASKEW, and G.R. BEECHER. Adaptation of protein metabolism to endurance training: increased amino acid oxidation in response to training. Biochem. J. 164:705–708, 1977.

DONOVAN, C.M., and G.A. BROOKS. Training affects lactate clearance, not lactate production. Am. J. Physiol. 244(Endocrinol. Metab. 7):E83–E92, 1983.

GOLLNICK, P.D., and D.W. KING. Effect of exercise and training on mitochondria of rat skeletal muscle. Am. J. Physiol. 216:1502–1509, 1969.

GOLLNICK, P.D., and B. SALTIN. Hypothesis: significance of skeletal muscle oxidative enzyme enhancement with endurance training. Clin. Physiol. 2:1–12, 1983.

HAVEL, R.J. Lipid as an energy source. In Biskey, E.J. (ed.). Physiology and Biochemistry of Muscle as a Food. Madison: University of Wisconsin Press, 1970, pp. 109–622.

HENDERSON, S.A., A.L. BLACK, and G.A. BROOKS. Leucine turnover and oxidation on trained and untrained rats during exercise. Am. J. Physiol. 249 (Endocrinol. Metab. 12):E137–E144, 1985.

HICKSON, R., M. RENNIE, R. CONLEE, W. WINDER, and J. HOLLOSZY. Effects of increased plasma FFA on glycogen utilization and endurance. J. Appl. Physiol. 43:829–833, 1977.

HOLLOSZY, J.O. Adaptation of skeletal muscle to endurance exercise. Med. Sci. Sports. 7:155–164, 1975.

ISSEKUTZ, B. JR., W.A.S. SHAW, and A.C. ISSEKUTZ. Lactate metabolism in resting and exercising dogs. J. Appl. Physiol. 40:312–319, 1976.

LEMON, P.W., and J.P. MULLIN. Effect of initial muscle glycogen levels on protein catabolism during exercise. J. Appl. Physiol.: Respirat. Environ. Exercise Physiol. 48:624–629, 1980.

MOLÉ, P., L. OSCAI, and J. HOLLOSZY. Adaptations in muscle to exercise. J. Clin. Invest. 50:2323–2330, 1971.

MUNN, E.A. The Structure of Mitochondria. London: Academic Press, 1974.

ODESSEY, R., and A.L. GOLDBERG. Oxidation of leucine by rat skeletal muscle. Am. J. Physiol. 223:1376–1383, 1972.

PAUL, P. FFA metabolism in normal dogs during steady-state exercise at different work loads. J. Appl. Physiol. 28:127–132, 1970.

RUDERMAN, N.B. Amino acid metabolism and gluconeogenesis. Annu. Rev. Med. 26:245–258, 1975.

TERBLANCHE, S.E. Endurance training increases muscle pyruvate carboxylase activity (personal communication).

TERBLANCHE, S.E., R.D. FELL, A.C. JUHLIN-DANNFELT, B.W. CRAIG, and J.O. HOLLOSZY. Effects of glycerol feeding before and after exercise. J. Appl. Physiol.: Respirat. Environ. Exercise Physiol. 50:94–101, 1981.

TERJUNG, R.L., K.M. BALDWIN, W.W. WINDER, and J.O. HOLLOSZY. Glycogen repletion in different types of muscle and in liver after exhaustive exercise. Am. J. Physiol. 226:1387–1391, 1974.

WHITE, T.P., and G.A. BROOKS. [U-^{14}C]glucose, -alanine, and -leucine oxidation in rats at rest and two intensities of running. Am. J. Physiol. 240(Endocrinol. Metab. 3):E155–E165, 1981.

WINDER, W., K. BALDWIN, and J. HOLLOSZY. Exercise-induced increase in the capacity of rat skeletal muscle to oxidize ketones. Can. J. Physiol. Pharmacol. 53:86–91, 1974.

WOLFE, R.R., R.D. GOODENOUGH, M.H. WOLFE, G.T. ROYLE, and E.R. NADEL. Isotopic analysis of leucine and area metabolism in exercising humans. J. Appl. Physiol. 52:458–466, 1982.

5

Ventilation and Respiratory Gas Exchange

(AP/Wide World Photos)

The movement of air in and out of the pulmonary system is called breathing or ventilation. Four specific purposes are accomplished by breathing: (1) the exchange of O_2, (2) the exchange of CO_2, (3) the control of blood acidity, and (4) oral communications. In general, breathing is essential to the cellular bioenergetic processes of life. This is because O_2 (the final electron acceptor) is made available to cells of the body.

Gases such as O_2 and CO_2 move from areas of high concentration or pressure to areas of lower concentration or pressure. Because it is in the alveoli (air sacs) of the lung that O_2 and CO_2 are exchanged between the atmosphere and the blood, the process of ventilation results in a relatively higher partial pressure of O_2 in the lungs' alveoli (P_AO_2) than in the metabolizing tissues or the venous blood draining those tissues. Therefore, by keeping the alveolar partial pressure of O_2 at about 105 mm Hg, ventilation results in a positive pressure gradient whereby O_2 moves from alveoli into the blood, which then circulates around the body to deliver O_2 to metabolizing tissues.

Through the action of ventilation, the partial pressure of the metabolic waste CO_2 is kept relatively low in the alveoli (P_ACO_2). This creates a negative pressure gradient for CO_2 to move from tissues, through blood and alveoli, to the atmosphere. The rapidity and depth of breathing affects the amount of O_2 and CO_2 exchanged between body and atmosphere. Metabolic CO_2 dissolved in the body fluid forms carbonic acid, which then dissociates a proton or H^+ ($CO_2 + H_2O \leftrightarrow H_2CO_3 \leftrightarrow H^+ + HCO_3^-$). Because ventilation affects CO_2 exchange and storage, and because CO_2 affects H^+ concentration (pH), ventilation affects the blood acid–base balance (i.e., the balance of acids and bases in the blood).

Rhythmicity in Ventilation

We breath continually by means of a complex neural control mechanism. Sometimes, such as during heavy exercise, the vigor of ventilation makes breathing noticeable; usually, however, breathing goes on unnoticed. Breathing is usually controlled at an unconscious level, but sometimes we can modify the pattern of breathing volitionally. The trumpeter and the opera singer must breathe continually, but they coordinate ventilation with the musical requirements. Similarly, the swimmer must coordinate breathing with complex stroke mechanics. With practice, complex conscious breathing patterns can be learned and precisely integrated into motor performance. Breathing then becomes automatic and unconscious.

The movement of air into the pulmonary system (inspiration) and the movement out of previously inhaled air (expiration) are regulated in two basic ways, by frequency and by amount or volume. Within seconds after an inhalation, the partial pressure of O_2 in alveoli falls below its optimum, and the partial pressure of CO_2 becomes greater than optimal. Very shortly after beginning to hold a breath, the sensation to breathe again becomes very strong. This sensation is delayed only slightly if we take a large breath and hold it. It is a good thing that we ventilate so frequently, because the O_2 content of our lungs, inflated to maximum, can sustain us for only a few minutes even at rest.

Pulmonary Minute Volume

The rate of pulmonary ventilation is usually expressed in terms of volume (liters) per minute. The abbreviation for pulmonary ventilation per minute (pulmonary minute volume) is ($\dot{V}$), where the $\dot{V}$ refers to volume per minute. Pulmonary ventilation can be measured either as volume expired per minute ($\dot{V}_E$), or volume inspired per minute ($\dot{V}_I$). Because the respiratory exchange ratio (R) is not necessarily 1.0 (i.e., CO_2 production/ $= O_2$ consumption) and H_2O vapor is added to inspired air during ventilation, $\dot{V}_I$ and $\dot{V}_E$ are not necessarily equal.

Pulmonary minute volume is equal to the product of frequency of breathing during a minute *(f)* and the average volume of air moved on each ventilatory excursion (V_T), or tidal volume:

$$\dot{V}_E = (f)(V_T) \tag{5-1}$$

Environmental Influences on Pulmonary Gas Volumes

Environmental conditions have significant effects on pulmonary gas volumes. At this point, the reader is referred to Appendix I for a review of pulmonary symbols and terminology. In addition, it is necessary to mention that there are three sets of conditions, or standards, by which pulmonary gas volumes can be defined. The first of these is the STPD volume, where ST = standard temperature = 0°C; P = standard pressure = 760 mm Hg [1 atmosphere (atm)]; and D = dry = 0.0 mm Hg H_2O vapor pressure. Clearly, the STPD condition is nonphysiological, but it is a norm by which results obtained under different environmental conditions, on different occasions, and at different places can be compared.

The second pulmonary gas condition is the BTPS volume, where BT = body temperture (37°C); P = ambient pressure; and S = saturated with H_2O. At approximately 1 atm pressure, the PH_2O depends on temperature; for 37°C, the $PH_2O = 47$ mm Hg. The BTPS volume is the volume that a subject actually holds in his or her lungs.

The third pulmonary gas condition of measurement is the ATPS volume, where AT = the ambient temperature in degrees Celsius; P = the ambient pressure; and S = the ambient PH_2O, which is a result of the relative humidity. The ATPS volume is the volume that a subject actually inhales.

In expressing pulmonary gas volumes, $\dot{V}O_2$ will usually be given in liters · min^{-1} (STPD), $\dot{V}_E$ and lung volumes will usually be given in liters · min^{-1} (BTPS), and $\dot{V}_I$ will usually be given in liters · min^{-1} (ATPS).

Pulmonary Anatomy

Gross anatomy of the pulmonary system is diagrammed in Figure 5-1*A*, and the terminal anatomy is diagrammed in Figure 5-1*B*. Although O_2 and CO_2 are exchanged only in the alveolar air sacs, the remaining upper respiratory tract (nose, mouth, trachea) performs important functions, including adding H_2O vapor to inspired air, warming (usually, or sometimes cooling) it to body temperature, and trapping particulate material (e.g., dust, yeast, and bacteria) as well as noxious chemical fumes (e.g., ozone). The upper respiratory tract is extremely efficient in performing these tasks and is adequate to prevent all but the most overwhelming invasions from reaching the delicate alveolar membranes.

As suggested in Figure 5-1, the lower end of the pulmonary tree anatomy provides a large surface area for respiratory gas exchange between air (alveoli) and blood (pulmonary capillaries). The exchange diffusion of O_2 and CO_2 between an alveolus and one of its surrounding capillaries is illustrated in Figure 5-2. Because the cross-sectional area of the capillary is barely adequate to allow for passage of red blood cells (erythrocytes), and because no other structure intervenes between the outer walls of the alveolus and capillary, the diffusion distance is held to a minimum. This short distance facilitates the exchange of O_2 and CO_2. The exchange of respiratory gases, particularly O_2, is further facilitated by the large lipid content of the alveolar and capillary membrane walls, in which O_2 has a greater solubility than in H_2O.

Mechanics of Ventilation

Movement of air into and out of the lungs is caused by changes in thoracic volume, which result in intrapulmonary pressure changes. The structures responsible for this bellowslike action are diagrammed in Figure 5-3. During rest, an inspiration begins with contraction of the diaphragm and external intercostal muscles. These actions "lower the floor" of the thorax and lift the ribs up and out. The volume of the thorax increases and the intrapulmonary

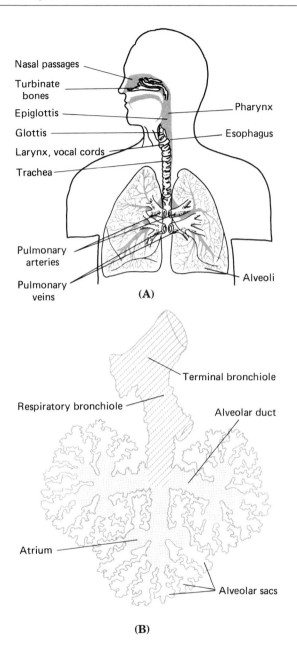

Nasal passages
Turbinate bones
Epiglottis
Glottis
Larynx, vocal cords
Trachea
Pharynx
Esophagus
Pulmonary arteries
Pulmonary veins
Alveoli

(A)

Terminal bronchiole
Respiratory bronchiole
Alveolar duct
Atrium
Alveolar sacs

(B)

Figure 5-1

Structure of the ventilatory (respiratory) passages. **(A)** The gross anatomy; **(B)** the respiratory lobule including the alveolar sites of gas exchange.

(SOURCE: **(A)** From A. C. Guyton, Textbook of Medical Physiology. Copyright W. B. Saunders Co., Philadelphia, 1976, p. 526. Used with permission. **(B)** From W. S. Miller, The Lung, 1947, p. 42. Used with permission.)

pressure momentarily decreases. Atmospheric air moves into the pulmonary system to equilibrate the pressure gradient between lung and atmosphere.

During rest, expiration is a passive action wherein the diaphragm and external intercostals relax. The diaphragm recoils, moving up and "raising

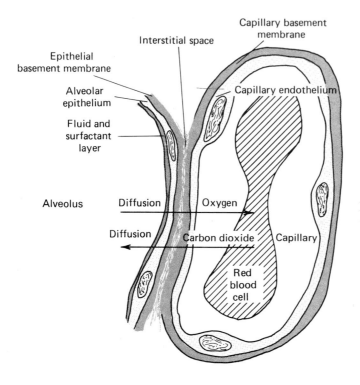

Figure 5-2

The ultrastructure of the alveolar capillary provides a minimum distance and mass of tissue between "alveolar air" and red blood cells in the pulmonary circulation.

(SOURCE: Modified from A. C. Guyton, *Textbook of Medical Physiology.* Copyright W. B. Saunders Co., Philadelphia, 1976, p. 539. Used with permission.)

the floor" of the thorax, and the lung and ribs recoil to their original positions. The movements decrease the volume of the thorax, transiently increasing intrapulmonary pressure and forcing pulmonary air out.

During exercise, inspiratory movements are assisted by accessory inspiratory muscles, which include the scalene, sternocleidomastoid, and trapezius muscles. These muscles lift the ribs and clavicles vertically and transversely, allowing for large increases in tidal volume (V_T) during exercise.

Expiration becomes an active (forced) movement during exercise. Contractions of the internal intercostals pull the ribs down and in, and contraction of abdominal muscles increases abdominal pressure, forcing the diaphragm up into the thorax. The rapid and forceful movements of accessory ventilatory muscles during exercise greatly increase the maximal rate of ventilatory air flow. Consequently, pulmonary minute flow ($\dot{V}_E$) can increase tremendously without a dramatic increase in breathing frequence (*f*). Typical changes in pulmonary minute volume, tidal volume, and breathing frequency during the transition from rest to exercise are given in Table 5-1. Note that by a relatively greater expansion in V_T than in *f*, sufficient time is allowed for efficient gas exchange in the alveoli, and ventilation of respiratory dead space is minimized.

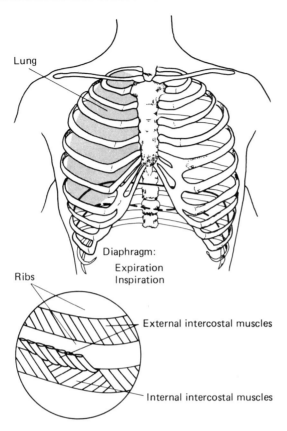

Lung

Diaphragm:
Expiration
Inspiration

Ribs

External intercostal muscles

Internal intercostal muscles

Figure 5-3
The major ventilatory muscles for breathing at rest include the diaphragm and external intercostal muscles. During the elevated breathing accompanying exercise (hyperpnea), other thoracic muscles including the sternocleidomastoid, scalene, and trapezius assist in ventilatory movements.

Dead Space and Alveolar Ventilation

Because of the anatomy of the pulmonary system (see Figure 5-1), not all the inspired air reaches the alveoli where O_2 and CO_2 are exchanged. Therefore, the alveolar minute ventilation ($\dot{V}_A$) will be less than the pulmonary minute ventilation ($\dot{V}_E$). The part of each breath that remains in the upper respiratory tract is not exchanged; this is called anatomical dead space (DS). Air in the dead space is warmed and humidified, but the relative concentrations of O_2 and CO_2 are between those in atmospheric air and those in the alveoli. As Figure 5-4 indicates, the fractions of O_2 and CO_2 expired from the mouth during a breath change continuously until the alveolar air streams out. The last air out during a tidal volume (i.e., the end-tidal air) has the highest P_{CO_2} and the lowest P_{O_2} of gas moved during a breath. This air reflects the alveolar composition. Recall Eq. 5-1, that

$$\dot{V}_E = (f)(V_T)$$

Condition	$\dot{V}_E$ (liters·min^{-1})	V_T (liters·breath^{-1})	f (breath·min^{-1})
Rest	6	0.5	12
Maximal exercise	192	4.00	48
Relative increase from rest to exercise	$32 \times$ Rest	$8 \times$ Rest	$4 \times$ Rest

However, as just described, not all of the tidal volume will represent air entering the alveoli. The difference between tidal volume and alveolar volume ventilated is the dead space (Figure 5-4).

$$\dot{V}_A = (V_T - DS)(f) \qquad (5\text{-}2)$$

The anatomical dead space is not a fixed volume but increases slightly during exercise as tidal volume increases. Bronchiolar dilation and greater

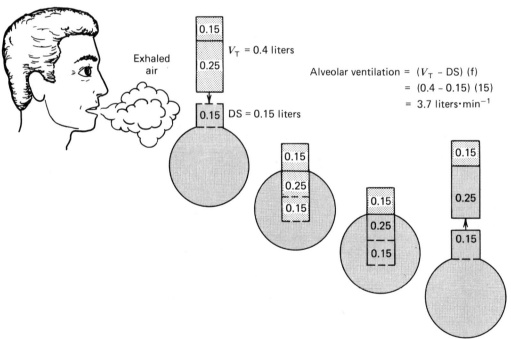

V_T = 0.4 liters

Alveolar ventilation = $(V_T - DS)\,(f)$
= $(0.4 - 0.15)\,(15)$
= 3.7 liters·min^{-1}

DS = 0.15 liters

Figure 5-4
During each breath (tidal volume, V_T), inspired air enters structures in which no exchange of ventilatory gas is possible. This dead space volume (DS) constitutes part of each tidal volume. Consequently, the alveolar minute ventilation equals the pulmonary minute ventilation less the minute dead space ventilation.

96

distances for air to flow within the lung before it reaches newly ventilated and more distant alveoli increase the DS volume during exercise. Compared with the rather small effect of increasing V_T on DS, the effect of increasing f on alveolar ventilation is relatively greater. This is illustrated in Table 5-2 for a resting individual. Clearly the effects of rapid, shallow breathing (panting) is to cause $\dot{V}_A$ to be much less than $\dot{V}_E$.

In addition to the anatomical dead space, where respiratory gas exchange is not possible, there exists some "physiological dead space." This space is represented by alveoli that receive inadequate blood flow to effect an equilibration of alveolar and pulmonary capillary blood. In the seated resting person, not all the alveoli are open—particularly those at the top of the lung. Similarly, because blood reaching the lung tends to flow to the bottom of the lung under the influence of gravity, the lower lung tends to be better perfused than the top. Consequently, alveoli can exist that are ventilated but not circulated. Such areas constitute the physiological dead space.

The pulmonary volumes measured during exercise (i.e., $\dot{V}_E$ and V_T) are called dynamic lung volumes. These are opposed to the "static" lung volumes, which describe the pulmonary dimensions in resting individuals.

Static Lung Volumes—Physical Dimensions of the Lungs

Static lung volumes (Figure 5-5A) are measured with a device called a spirometer (Figure 5-5B). To use the device illustrated in Figure 5-5B, called a displacement spirometer, a person breathes into and out of a chamber that consists of a counterbalanced cylinder suspended over a water seal. On exhalation, the person's breath raises the cylinder. On inhalation the cylinder falls. By means of a pen attached to the cylinder, a written record of ventilatory movements and volumes is obtained. The older displacement-type spirometer illustrated in Figure 5-5B is gradually being replaced with electronic devices called pneumotachometers.

In general, lung volumes are correlated with body size; lung volumes

TABLE 5-2　Effect of Panting on Alveolar Ventilation ($\dot{V}_A$) in a Resting Individual (Ventilatory Volumes in BTPS)

Value	Breathing Normally	Panting
$\dot{V}_E$	6 liters·min^{-1}	6 liters·min^{-1}
V_T	0.4 liters·min^{-1}	0.2 liters·min^{-1}
f	15 breaths·min^{-1}	30 breaths·min^{-1}
$\dot{V}_A$	3.7 liters·min^{-1}	1.5 liters·min^{-1}

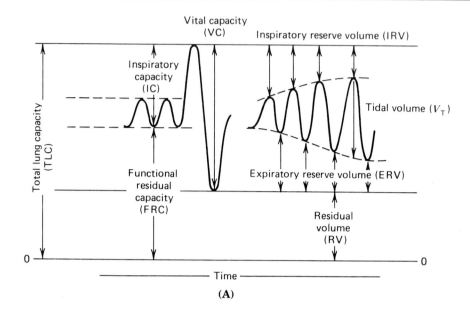

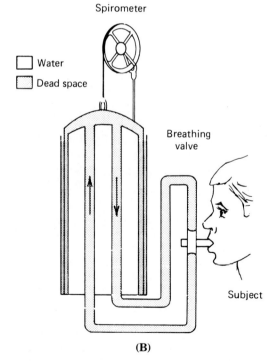

Figure 5-5
Lung volumes and capacities (**A**) can be measured during rest and exercise on
devices called displacement spirometers (**B**). Both tidal volume and ventilatory
frequency can range from rest to exercise.

tend to be larger in tall people than in short people and larger in males than in females. Figure 5-5A illustrates that the normal resting tidal volume can be increased or decreased in size by inspiring a bit more or less. This has the effect of decreasing or increasing, respectively, the inspiratory reserve volume (IRV) or the expiratory reserve volume (ERV). When tidal volume is maximal, it is termed vital capacity (VC).

Even after a maximal respiration, some part of the air in the lungs cannot be forced out. This volume is termed the residual volume (RV). The VC and RV together make up the total lung capacity (TLC).

Vital capacity is a commonly measured pulmonary parameter of static lung volume. Similarly, the 1-sec timed vital capacity is a commonly measured parameter of dynamic lung volume change. In some types of pulmonary problems (e.g., emphysema), distensibility of the lungs is reduced, but the total volume is unaffected. The VC is therefore normal, but the timed VC, or the percentage of VC achieved in 1 sec, is greatly reduced. In this case, the dynamic lung volume (timed vital capacity) is more reflective of the pathological condition than is the measure of static lung volume (vital capacity).

By means of a much larger spirometer than that illustrated in Figure 5-5B, which has been filled with a mixture of 95% O_2 and 5% CO_2, the maximum amount of air a subject can ventilate in 1 min can be measured. This volume is termed maximum voluntary ventilation (MVV). To perform the MVV test, a subject wears a special breathing valve or mask to inspire from the spirometer and expire into the atmosphere. The MVV is measured by emptying the spirometer. The high O_2 during the MVV test is to supply O_2 for respiration, and the high CO_2 is to prevent dizziness from a decrease in the P_{CO_2} during rapid ventilation. In most individuals the MVV is much greater than the $\dot{V}_E$ observed during maximal exercise at sea level altitudes. In other words, even during maximal exercise, a ventilatory reserve exists. This ventilatory reserve allows people to exercise intensely and for prolonged periods, to inhabit very high altitudes (14,000 ft), occasionally to sojourn at altitudes exceeding 20,000 ft, and even to abuse their pulmonary systems through habits such as smoking without immediate effects.

Physics of Ventilatory Gases

Partial Pressures

The purpose of ventilating the pulmonary alveoli is to provide a place where the partial pressure of O_2 can be kept relatively high and the partial pressure of CO_2 can be kept low, so that these respiratory gases are exchanged with the blood. We have previously defined the partial pressure of a gas as the pressure exerted by that species of gas. The partial pressure of a dry gas depends on the total barometric pressure (P_b) and the fractional composition (F_{O_2}) of that gas.

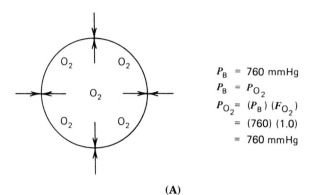

$$P_B = 760 \text{ mmHg}$$
$$P_B = P_{O_2}$$
$$P_{O_2} = (P_B)(F_{O_2})$$
$$= (760)(1.0)$$
$$= 760 \text{ mmHg}$$

(A)

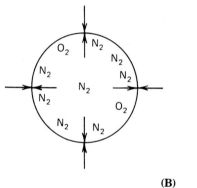

$$P_{O_2} = (P_B)(F_{O_2})$$
$$= (760)(.21)$$
$$= 160 \text{ mmHg}$$

$$P_{N_2} = (P_B)(F_{N_2})$$
$$= (760)(.79)$$
$$= 600 \text{ mmHg}$$

(B)

Figure 5-6
In a gas mixture, the total pressure is equal to the total of partial pressures exerted by the individual gases. For dry environments, the partial pressure exerted by a gas equals the total pressure times the fractional concentration of that gas. In environment **A,** the partial pressure of O_2 equals the total pressure. In environment **B,** the total pressure equals the total of the partial pressures exerted by O_2 and N_2.

Partial pressure of gas *a* in a dry environment $= (P_b \text{ mm Hg})$ (fractional composition of gas *X*) (5-3)

For oxygen:

$$P_{O_2} = (P_b \text{ mm Hg})(F_{O_2})$$
$$= 760 \text{ mm Hg } (0.21)$$
$$= 159.6 \text{ mm Hg}$$

This is illustrated in Figure 5-6. In a dry container at 1 atm pressure (760 mm Hg) containing 100% O_2, the P_{O_2} will be 760 mm Hg (Figure 5-6*A*). In a container containing 21% O_2 and 79% N_2, the partial pressures of O_2 and N_2 will approximate 160 and 600 mm Hg, respectively (Figure 5-6*B*).

Water Vapor

In studying the movement of gas around the body, it is important to realize that the body is not a dry environment; water is always present, and respiratory gases will exist either dissolved or in a gaseous environment saturated with H_2O vapor.

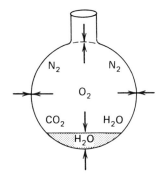

Figure 5-7
In a warm, moist environment (such as the alveolus), H_2O vapor saturates the environment, contributing significantly to the total pressure and diluting the relative fractional concentrations of O_2 and the other ventilatory gases. At a body temperature of 37°C, H_2O exerts a pressure of 47 mm Hg. Carbon dioxide delivered to the alveolus from the venous circulation also dilutes the concentration of O_2.

The partial pressure exerted by water is somewhat different from the partial pressure exerted by other ventilatory gases, in that the P_{H_2O} depends on environmental temperature. At body temperature (37°C), the P_{H_2O} is 47 mm Hg. Therefore, as illustrated in Figure 5-7, if gas from a tank containing dry 100% O_2 is allowed to flush through and fill a wet container warmed to 37°C, then 47 mm Hg of the 760 mm Hg total pressure will be occupied by H_2O vapor. The diluting effect of water vapor will be to reduce the partial pressures of other gases present. Therefore, Eq. 5-3 must be rewritten to include H_2O vapor.

$$\text{Partial pressure of gas } X \text{ in a wet environment} = (P_b - P_{H_2O}) \quad (5\text{-}4)$$
$$\text{(fractional composition of gas } X)$$

The effect of H_2O vapor on the P_{O_2} of inspired air in the trachea (tracheal air) reaching the alveoli is

$$P_{O_2} = (P_b - 47 \text{ mm Hg}) (F_{IO_2})$$
$$P_{CO_2} = (760 - 47 \text{ mm Hg})(0.0003)$$
$$= 0.2 \text{ mm Hg}$$

Similarly, for CO_2, which is 0.03% of the inspired air, the tracheal P_{CO_2} will be

$$P_{CO_2} = (760 - 47 \text{ mm Hg})(0.0003)$$
$$= 0.2 \text{ mm Hg}$$

In the alveolus itself, the partial pressure of O_2 will be decreased as a result of the ongoing consumption of O_2 and the diluting effect of CO_2, and the P_{CO_2} will be higher because of diffusion into the alveolus from the blood. In healthy resting individuals at sea level altitudes, the alveolar partial pressure of O_2 (P_{AO_2}) is about 105 mm Hg, and the P_{ACO_2} is about 40 mm Hg (Figure 5-7). As we will see, ventilation is controlled to maintain these partial pressures.

In the pulmonary system, not only does H_2O move into the gas phase but

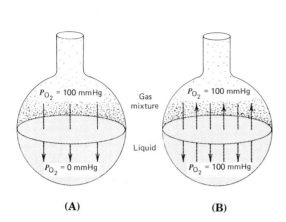

Figure 5-8
Given sufficient time, a gas in a closed environment will equilibrate across the gas–liquid interface. The partial pressure of the gas will then be equal in gaseous and liquid phases. O_2 admitted to a closed environment (**A**) will equilibrate in the liquid phase (**B**). By analogy, the sphere represents an alveolus, the O_2 is from inspired air, and the water represents body fluids.

(SOURCE: Modified from A. C. Guyton, Textbook of Medical Physiology. Copyright W. B. Saunders Co., Philadelphia, 1976, p. 531. Used with permission.)

the respiratory gases O_2 and CO_2 also dissolve in the aqueous phases of fluids lining the alveoli and into the plasma (see Figure 5-2). For movement of respiratory gases, it is important that the partial pressures of O_2 and CO_2 in the gas (alveolar) phase equilibrate with pressures in the aqueous (blood) phase. As illustrated in Figure 5-8, the molecules of a gas continuously move in all directions. Some of the molecules of a gas in contact with water will penetrate the surface and occupy spaces between the molecules as well as (in the case of CO_2) react chemically with the water. Those gas molecules entering the fluid phase dissolve in the fluid. Gas molecules dissolved in a fluid are not trapped there but can move around within the fluid or leave it. The gas therefore exerts a partial pressure both within and around the fluid. Given enough time at a particular temperature and pressure, the gas molecule in liquid and gas phases will come to equilibrium. At that point, the same number of molecules will be entering and leaving each phase for the other. At equilibrium, then, the partial pressures of the gas in liquid and gas phases will be equal. By this means, O_2 in alveolar gas can move through the body fluids to cellular mitochondria, and the reverse pathway for CO_2 is possible.

In the pulmonary capillaries, the equilibration of O_2 and CO_2 with alveolar air depends on the pressure gradient and the time the blood is in the capillary. During rest, red blood cells (erythrocytes) are in the pulmonary capillary an average of 0.75 sec. This time period is referred to as the capillary transit time (Figure 5-9). This is adequate time for O_2 and CO_2 to equilibrate between the pulmonary capillary and alveoli. During maximal exercise, capillary transit time has been estimated to decrease to 0.25 to 0.5 sec. At sea level altitudes, this is still adequate time for equilibration of CO_2 and marginally adequate time for equilibration of O_2. At higher altitudes, where the P_b decreases, and with it also the $P_{I_{O_2}}$ and $P_{A_{O_2}}$, the $P_{a_{O_2}}$ will necessarily decrease from sea level values of about 100 mm Hg.

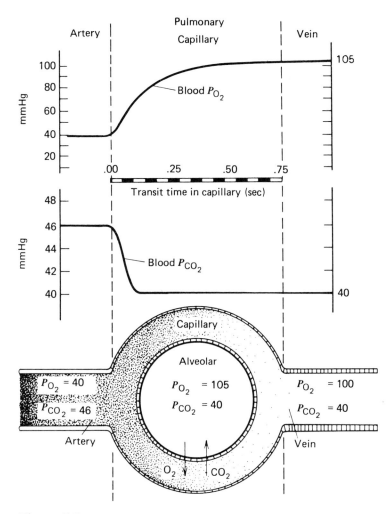

Figure 5-9
The exchange of O_2 and CO_2 in alveolar capillaries depends on time as well as partial pressure. Note in the figure that CO_2 equilibrates faster than O_2. During hard exercise at sea level altitudes there is usually sufficient time (0.5 sec) to complete the exchange.

(SOURCE: From P.-O. Åstrand and K. Rodahl, 1970. Used with permission.)

Pulmonary Diffusing Capacity

The amount of O_2 [in ml of O_2 and STPD] diffusing across the pulmonary membranes per minute per mm Hg pressure difference between alveolar air

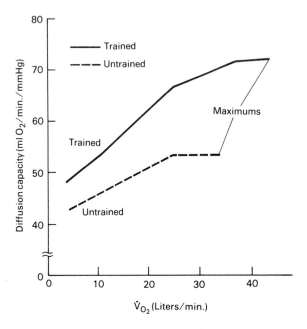

Figure 5-10
Pulmonary diffusing capacity (D_L) increases in both trained and untrained subjects. Diffusing capacity is greater in trained subjects because of greater lung size and $\dot{V}_{O_2max}$.

(SOURCE: Modified from Magel and Andersen, 1969.)

and pulmonary capillary blood is defined as the lung diffusing capacity (D_L). Diffusing capacity increases from rest to exercise and as the result of endurance training (Figure 5-10). However, the acute effect of altitude hypobaria (low pressure) on sea level residents is to decrease D_L. With chronic exposure to high altitude, however, D_L increases.

Entry of O_2 into Blood

We ventilate to keep the partial pressure of O_2 in the alveoli ($P_{A}O_2$) at about 105 mm Hg. From the alveoli, the diffusion distance for O_2 into erythrocytes in the blood perfusing the alveolar walls is relatively short (Figure 5-11). This is necessary because the solubility of O_2 in body water at 37°C is low; only 0.3 ml $O_2 \cdot dl^{-1}$ blood is physically dissolved. Fortunately, erythrocytes contain the heme–iron compound hemoglobin, which can bind O_2 according to its partial pressure (Figure 5-12). At an O_2 partial pressure of 100 mm Hg, as exists in alveolar capillaries at sea level, hemoglobin is nearly 100% saturated with O_2. Because a very small percentage of blood passing through the lungs passes through alveoli that are not ventilated (physiological dead space), the saturation of blood returning to the left heart from the lungs is about 96%. This impressive figure is maintained not only in the individual

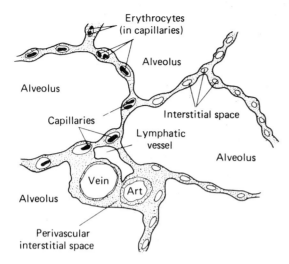

Figure 5-11

Schematic of a cross-sectional view through alveolar walls showing the relationship between the "alveolar air" and the blood supply.

(SOURCE: Modified from A. C. Guyton, Textbook of Medical Physiology. Copyright W. B. Saunders Co., Philadelphia, 1976, p. 538. Used with permission.)

resting at a sea level altitude, but also during maximal exercise (Figure 5-13).

Quantitatively, normal hemoglobin can bind about 1.34 ml of $O_2 \cdot g^{-1}$. In the average male, blood hemoglobin is about 15 g $\cdot$ dl^{-1} blood. Arterial O_2 content (Ca_{O_2} is then equal to the sum of the dissolved O_2 plus that combined with hemoglobin:

$$\text{Arterial } O_2 \text{ content} = O_2 \text{ physically dissolved} + \text{product of } O_2 \quad (5\text{-}7)$$
$$\text{carrying capacity of hemoglobin and the arterial hemoglobin}$$

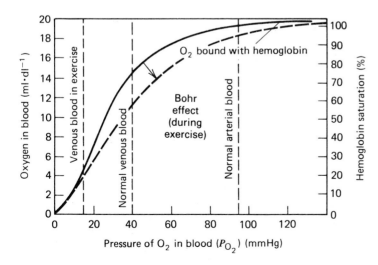

Figure 5-12

According to the oxygen–hemoglobin dissociation curve, the O_2 carried in blood in combination with hemoglobin depends mainly on the partial pressure of O_2. At normal arterial partial pressure of O_2 (P_{O_2} approximately 95 mm Hg), hemoglobin is 95 to 98% saturated with O_2.

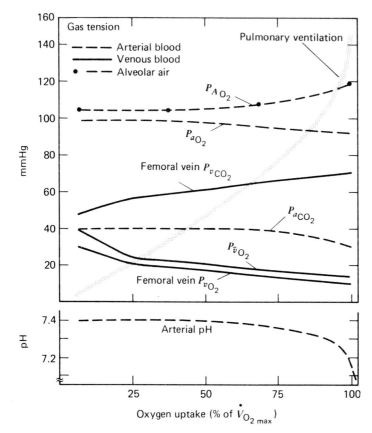

Figure 5-13

Oxygen and carbon dioxide partial pressures in alveolar air (P_A) arterial blood (P_a) and mixed venous blood (P_V) during rest and graded exercise. Note that as relative effort increases, the partial pressure of O_2 in arterial blood (P_{aO_2}) remains constant or falls only slightly. Because of the shape of the oxyhemoglobin dissociation curve (Figure 11-2), arterial O_2 content remains close to resting levels of approximately 95 to 98% saturation.

(SOURCE: Modified from P.-O. Åstrand and K. Rodahl, 1977. Used with permission.)

$$Ca_{O_2} = 0.3 \text{ ml } O_2 \cdot dl^{-1} \text{ blood} + (1.34 \text{ ml } O_2 \cdot g^{-1} \text{ Hb})(15 \text{ g Hb} \cdot dl^{-1} \text{ blood}) = 20.4 \text{ ml } O_2 \cdot dl^{-1} \text{ blood}$$

(By convention, this figure can also be referred to as 20.4 vol %, or 20.4 ml O_2/100 ml; note that 1 dl = 100 ml, and vol % = vol/100 ml.)

In females, in whom the blood hemoglobin concentration is less than that in males (about 13 g · dl^{-1} in females), the Ca_{O_2} = 17.7 vol %.

Oxygen Transport

As we have just seen, if one knows the partial pressure of O_2 in arterial blood (P_aO_2) and the concentration of hemoglobin in the blood, then barring any unusual circumstances, the arterial O_2 content can be calculated. Further, knowing the cardiac output (Q, the volume of blood ejected from the left ventricle each minute) the maximum O_2 transport capacity ($\dot{T}_{O_2}$) from heart (or lungs) to the rest of the body can be calculated:

For example, during rest,

$$\dot{T}O_2 = (Ca_{O_2})\,(\dot{Q}) \tag{5-8}$$

O_2 transport $= (20 \text{ ml } O_2 \cdot dl^{-1} \text{ blood}) (50 \text{ dl blood} \cdot min^{-1}) = 1000 \text{ ml } O_2 \cdot min^{-1}$

During maximal exercise in a young fit individual, O_2 transport can be much greater, for example,

$$= (20 \text{ ml } O_2 \cdot dl^{-1} \text{ blood})(300 \text{ dl blood} \cdot min^{-1})$$
$$= 6000 \text{ ml } O_2 \cdot min^{-1}$$

During rest, the actual whole-body O_2 consumption will be much less than the O_2 transport capacity, because mixed venous blood returning to the right heart will contain substantial amounts of O_2. During maximal exercise, as just illustrated for a very fit male, the actual O_2 consumption will approach the limits of the O_2 transport capacity. This is because most of the O_2 present in arterial blood is removed during each circulatory passage.

Effects of the Internal Environment on O_2 Transport (the Bohr Effect)

In addition to the partial pressure of O_2, other factors can affect the combination of O_2 with hemoglobin. These factors include temperature, pH, and concentration of 2,3-diphosphoglycerate (2,3-DPG).

The effects of elevated temperature and H^+ (lower pH) on the O_2 dissociation curve are given by the dashed line in Figure 5-12. This shifting of the dissociation curve down and to the right during exercise is termed the Bohr effect, and it facilitates the unloading of O_2 from hemoglobin of blood passing through active muscle beds.

As the result of their metabolism, erythrocytes produce the substance 2,3-DPG. Levels of 2,3-DPG are elevated during exercise, particularly during exercise at high altitude. The binding of 2,3-DPG to hemoglobin occurs at a site that negatively affects the binding of O_2. Consequently, increased levels of 2,3-DPG cause a rightward shift in the oxyhemoglobin dissociation curve.

Because of the sigmoidal (S) shape of the O_2 dissociation curve (see Figure 5-12), the Bohr effect during exercise will have a minimal impact on the combination of O_2 with hemoglobin in the lung. In active tissues, however, where the P_{O_2} is below 40 mm Hg, the binding of O_2 to hemoglobin can be reduced to 10 to 15% as a result of the Bohr effect. This difference represents a small additional amount of O_2 available in tissues to support metabolism.

Red Blood Cells and Hemoglobin in CO_2 Transport

In almost everyone's mind erythrocytes (red blood cells) and hemoglobin are synonymous with oxygen transport. As described previously, O_2 transport is a paramount role for the erythrocyte. In addition, the erythrocyte, which contains hemoglobin, and the enzyme carbonic anhydrase, is crucial for CO_2 transport in the blood.

Carbon dioxide is a by-product of cellular respiration. Because the respiration quotient of metablism ($R = \dot{V}_{CO_2}/\dot{V}_{O_2}$) approximates unity, quantitatively the problem of CO_2 transport from cells to lungs is as great as transporting O_2 from lungs to body cells. The cellular formation and accumulation of CO_2 results in diffusion out of the cell, mostly in the gaseous form. As the CO_2 reaches the capillary blood, the reactions diagrammed in Figure 5-14 occur rapidly. In relation to O_2, CO_2 is more soluble in the aqueous phase of the blood; still, only about 5 to 7% of CO_2 is carried in dissolved form.

The CO_2 that diffuses from plasma into red blood cells reacts with water in the erythrocyte to form carbonic acid. In the red blood cell this reaction is catalyzed by the enzyme carbonic anhydrase.

$$CO_2 + H_2O \xrightarrow{\hspace{3cm}} H_2CO_3 \qquad (5\text{-}9)$$
$$\text{Carbonic anhydrase}$$

Carbonic anhydrase, the enzyme that hydrates (wets) CO_2, is not present in plasma, so although carbonic acid is also formed there from the physical interaction of CO_2 and H_2O, it is formed at a rate several thousand times slower than in the erythrocytes.

Although the formation of carbonic acid ($H_2CO_3{}^-$) is slow and enzyme limited, the dissociation of carbonic acid to bicarbonate ion ($HCO_3{}^-$) and a proton (H^+) is not enzyme catalyzed and proceeds spontaneously.

$$H_2CO_3 \xrightarrow{\hspace{2cm}} HCO_3{}^- + H^+ \qquad (5\text{-}10)$$

The $HCO_3{}^-$ so formed diffuses from the erythrocyte into the plasma. The resulting chemical–electrical gradient causes a shift of chloride ion (Cl^-) into the erythrocyte. About 70% of all CO_2 transported from tissues to lungs is carried in the form of $HCO_3{}^-$.

The H^+ formed as the result of carbonic acid dissociation reacts rapidly with reduced hemoglobin (i.e., hemoglobin that has dissociated its O_2 molecule). The stoichiometry of hemoglobin O_2 and H^+ binding is interesting in that there is almost a one-to-one exchange of H^+ for O_2. In fact, hemoglobin that has lost its O_2 (reduced hemoglobin, Hb) is such a strong buffer that it can take up almost all the H^+ formed as the result of CO_2 transport.

$$Hb^- + H^+ \rightleftarrows HHb \qquad (5\text{-}11)$$

The reaction goes to the right, as presented here, when the P_{O_2} is low (hemoglobin dissociates O_2) and when the P_{CO_2} and H^+ are high. In fact,

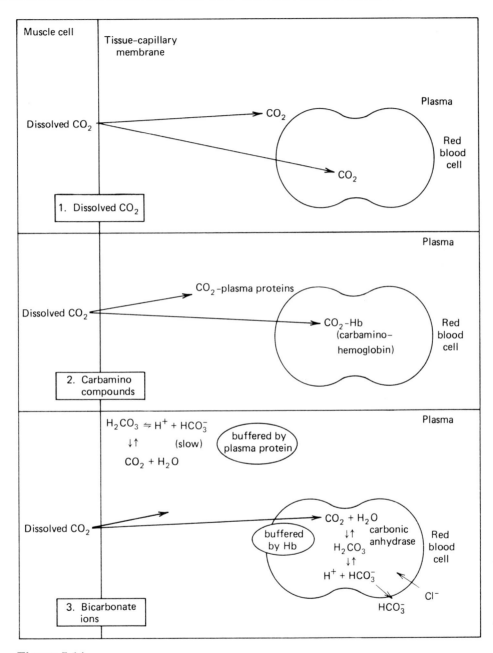

Figure 5-14

Carbon dioxide is transported in the blood by three mechanisms: (1) in dissolved CO_2, (2) in carbamino compounds, and (3) as bicarbonate ion. Hemoglobin and carbonic anhydrase enzyme in red blood cells are essential in the transport of CO_2 from sites of tissue formation to elimination in the lung.

elevated CO_2 and H^+ concentrations help to dissociate the oxyhemoglobin complex as part of the Bohr effect. In the lung, where P_{CO_2} is low and P_{O_2} is high, the reactions proceed from right to left.

Figure 5-14 also illustrates that CO_2 is carried in a third way in the blood. Some of the CO_2 entering the erythrocyte reacts directly with hemoglobin to form carbaminohemoglobin. Carbon dioxide reacts more readily with reduced hemoglobin than with oxyhemoglobin, although both reactions are possible. Some CO_2 also combines with plasma proteins. Together the carbamino compounds account for approximately 25% of CO_2 transported.

CO_2 Content of Blood Dependence on the P_{CO_2}

Just as the combination of O_2 with hemoglobin can be expressed as a function of the P_{O_2} (see Figure 5-12), the CO_2 content of blood can be described as a function of the P_{CO_2} (Figure 5-15). The normal resting arterial partial pressure of CO_2 (Pa_{CO_2}) of 40 mm Hg corresponds to an arterial CO_2 content (Ca_{CO_2}) of about 48 vol %. During rest the mixed venous partial pressure of CO_2 (P_{CO_2}) rises to about 45 mm Hg, and the venous concentration of CO_2 (Cv_{CO_2}) rises to about 52 vol %.

During rest the C_{aO_2} is about 20 vol %, and mixed venous O_2 content is about 16 vol %. Therefore, the arterial-venous O_2 difference [(a-v)O_2] is about 4 vol %. During maximal exercise the C_{aO_2} remains about constant, but the C_{vO_2} falls to about 4 vol %, so the (a-v)O_2 rises to about 16 vol %. During heavy exercise the respiratory exchange ratio ($R = \dot{V}_{CO_2}/\dot{V}_{O_2}$) reaches values of 1.0 or greater. This means that the (v-a)CO_2 reaches >16 vol %. As we will see, addition of acid to blood (e.g., a metabolic acid such as lactic acid) causes the Pa_{CO_2} to decrease. During hard exercise, the entry of CO_2 into venous blood causes the Pv_{CO_2} to increase. The physiological range of approximately 40 mm Hg corresponds to a (v-a)CO_2 of approximately 20 vol % (Figure 5-15).

Buffering of Metabolic Acids by the Bicarbonate Buffer System

The fact that most CO_2 is transported in forms other than as CO_2 means that the dissolved CO_2 in venous blood is less than might be expected. This is a highly desirable situation for several reasons. Cells produce more CO_2 than can be transported in physical solution. As hemoglobin acts for O_2, there must be a carrier for CO_2. Important also is the fact that dissolution of CO_2 in H_2O causes the formation of an acid (H_2CO_3). However, by converting CO_2 in HCO_3^- and H^+ in the erythrocyte, by buffering the H^+ on hemoglobin and shifting

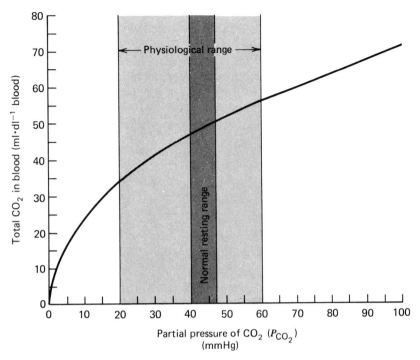

Figure 5-15

The CO_2 carried in the blood depends mainly on the partial pressure of CO_2. The carbon dioxide dissociation curve has a positive, almost linear slope within the physiological range.

the HCO_3^- into plasma, a mechanism to minimize (buffer) the effects of metabolic acids or bases on plasma pH is set up.

In the blood, where the bicarbonate buffer system is the main means to regulate the blood activity (pH), the pH is given by

$$pH = 6.1 + \log\frac{[HCO_3^-]}{CO_2} \qquad (5\text{-}12)$$

This is called the Henderson–Hasselbalch equation; it describes how plasma pH is regulated by the relative, *not* the absolute, quantities of bicarbonate ion and CO_2. In this equation, the constant 6.1 is termed the pK. The pK represents the pH at which buffering capacity is maximal.

Control of Blood pH by Ventilation

Because the pK of the bicarbonate–carbonic acid buffer system (6.1) is quite removed from the normal arterial pH of 7.4, the strength of the buffer system is weak, and small additions of acid or base could markedly affect blood pH.

However, despite this deficiency, the bicarbonate buffer system is an effective physiological buffer system because the concentrations of the system's elements can be regulated.

The main way blood pH is regulated during metabolic transient periods such as during exercise is by ventilation. As noted at the outset of this chapter, ventilation is important for several reasons, one being regulation of blood pH. Ventilation affects pH by changing the CO_2 content of the blood. Arterial CO_2 content is inversely related to the pulmonary minute volume: too little breathing causes CO_2 to build up; too much causes CO_2 to be eliminated from the blood. For example, as a person volitionally hyperventilates at rest, the alveolar partial pressure of CO_2 (P_{ACO_2}) will fall. This change will cause CO_2 to move from blood to alveoli and be expired.

The loss of CO_2 by increasing breathing (hyperventilation) will affect pH in two ways. First, CO_2 forms an acid in H_2O (i.e., H_2CO_3). Eliminating CO_2 in effect eliminates an acid from the blood. Also, according to the Henderson–Hasselbalch equation (E5-12), the pH depends on a constant plus the logarithm of the ratio of HCO_3^- to CO_2. Because CO_2 content is in the denominator of that ratio, eliminating CO_2 from the blood will increase the ratio (and pH). If heavy ventilation during exercise eliminates CO_2 from the blood at the lung, the effect of entry of metabolic acids into the blood can be minimized (buffered). In actuality it must be realized that this description is a bit simplistic because the concentrations of H^+, HCO_3^-, and CO_2 are interrelated. Therefore, if the P_{CO_2} falls as the result of hyperventilation, then HCO_3^- ultimately will also fall.

In the long term, blood pH is determined by those metabolic processes that form or remove metabolic acids, as well as by the kidney, which can regulate blood concentrations of H^+, HCO_3^-, and NH_4^+.

Buffering of Metabolic Acids

During heavy exercise, production of several metabolic acids is increased, lactic acid in particular. Entry of lactic acid into the blood would cause a large drop in pH if not for the bicarbonate buffer system and the ventilatory regulation of that system. The action of the bicarbonate system in buffering lactic acid is illustrated by the following equations:

$$HLA \longrightarrow H^+ \quad + \quad LA^- \tag{5-13}$$

Lactic   Hydrogen   Lactate
acid   ion   ion

$$H^+ \quad + \quad HCO_3^- \longrightarrow \quad H_2CO_3 \tag{5-14}$$

Hydrogen   Bicarbonate   Carbonic
ion   ion   acid

$$H_2CO_3 \longrightarrow H_2O \quad + \quad CO_2 \tag{5-15}$$

Carbonic   Water   Carbon
acid   Dioxide

In summary, lactic acid gives rise to CO_2. This CO_2 is termed *nonmetabolic CO_2*, because it did not arise from the immediate combustion of a substrate. The nonmetabolic CO_2, or its volume equivalent of CO_2, can be eliminated from the blood at the lung. In other words, the effects of adding a strong acid to blood are lessened by forming a weaker acid (H_2CO_3) and then eliminating the weaker acid as CO_2. In this way the R ($R = \dot{V}_{CO_2}/\dot{V}_{O_2}$) can exceed 1.0 during hard exercise when lactic acid enters the blood.

Summary

Life depends on a constant flow of energy to the body's cells and a controlled conversion of that energy into useful forms. The main cellular mechanism of bioenergetics is respiration. (Respiration is the proper term for biological oxidation.) Therefore, life also depends on a continuous flow of O_2 to the body's cells. Entry of O_2 into the body begins with breathing O_2 into the lungs. Ventilating the lungs has the effect of raising the partial pressure of O_2 in the alveoli (i.e., the $P_{A_{O_2}}$). Oxygen then diffuses from the alveoli into the blood where the O_2 combines with hemoglobin in a way determined mostly by the arterial P_{O_2} (i.e., the $P_{a_{O_2}}$).

The gaseous by-products of respiration are H_2O and CO_2. It is important to eliminate most CO_2, because it is toxic even in concentrations that are not really great. During ventilation of the lungs, atmospheric and alveolar air are exchanged. Carbon dioxide elimination occurs during ventilation because CO_2 moves from an area of high partial pressure (mixed venous blood) to an area of low partial pressure (the atmosphere). In the blood, CO_2 is transported in three ways: in simple solution, as bicarbonate ion, and in union with hemoglobin (carbaminohemoglobin).

In addition to CO_2, other by-products of cellular metabolism include strong organic acids such as lactic acid. The effect of metabolic acids on blood pH can be lessened (buffered) by increasing the ventilatory rate to cause diffusion of CO_2 out of the blood. Because CO_2 forms carbonic acid in H_2O, the exit of nonmetabolic CO_2, in effect, makes room for another acid, such as lactic acid.

Breathing, then, has three critically important metabolic functions for exercise: the uptake of O_2, the elimination of CO_2, and the buffering of metabolic acids.

Selected Readings

AMERICAN COLLEGE OF SPORTS MEDICINE. Symposium on ventilatory control during exercise. Med. Sci. Sports 11:190–226, 1979.

ÅSTRAND, P.O., and K. RODAHL. Textbook of Work Physiology. New York: McGraw-Hill, 1970, pp. 185–254.

COMROE, J. Physiology of Respiration. Chicago: Year Book Medical Publishers, 1974.

BROOKS, G.A., and T.D. FAHEY. Exercise Physiology: Human Bioenergetics and Its Applications, Macmillan, New York, 1984, pp. 221–276.

DEJOURS, P. Control of respiration in muscular exercise. In: Fenn, W.O. and H. Rahn (eds.), Handbook of Physiology, Section 3, Respiration, Vol. 1. Washington, D.C.: American Physiological Society, 1964.

DEMPSEY, J.A., and C.E. REED (eds.). Muscular Exercise and the Lung. Madison: University of Wisconsin Press, 1977.

FENN, W.O., and H. RAHN (eds.). Handbook of Physiology, Section 3, Respiration, Vols. I and II. Washington, D.C.: American Physiological Society, 1964.

GUYTON, A.C. Textbook of Medical Physiology. Philadelphia: W.B. Saunders, 1976, pp. 516–529.

MAGEL, J., and K. ANDERSEN. Pulmonary diffusing capacity and cardiac output in young trained Norwegian swimmers and untrained subjects. Med. Sci. Sports. 1:131–139, 1969.

MILLER, W.S. The Lung. Springfield, Ill.: Charles C Thomas, 1947.

PAPPENHEIMER, J.R. Standardization of definitions and symbols in respiratory physiology. Fed. Proc. 9:602–605, 1950.

VANDER, A.J., J.H. SHERMAN, and D.S. LUCIANO. Human Physiology, 3rd ed. New York: McGraw-Hill, 1980, pp. 327–365.

WEST, J.B. Respiratory Physiology—The Essentials. Baltimore: Williams & Wilkins, 1974.

6

Control of Ventilation During Exercise

(AP/Wide World Photos)

Because life depends on energy transduction, and most of the body's cells depend on O_2 for energy transduction, a constant delivery of O_2 is necessary to sustain life. During exercise, energy (ATP) demands are increased and cell respiration must be accelerated. Continuous muscular activity depends on a flux of O_2 from the alveoli of the lungs to the mitochondria in skeletal muscle. Conversely, CO_2 formed in muscle mitochondria must flow to the lungs without disrupting acid–base balance. It is very important, therefore, for O_2 delivery and CO_2 removal to be finely coordinated with cellular respiration, an incredible regulatory task.

Control of Alveolar Ventilation

If a person is forewarned and can anticipate exercise, ventilation will start to increase before the exercise starts (Figure 6-1). When the exercise starts, ventilation will increase very rapidly with a half-response time of 20 to 30 sec. After approximately 2 min, the rate of change in pulmonary minute ventilation ($\dot{V}_E$) will increase less. During submaximal exercise, $\dot{V}_E$ will plateau (stop rising) after 4 to 5 min (Figure 6-1). During maximal exercise, ventilation will continue to increase until either maximum voluntary ventilation (MVV) or the point of fatigue is reached.

The pulmonary minute volume reached during exercise will depend on a number of factors, including the work rate, the state of training, and the muscle group used. Typical ventilatory volumes reached during leg exercise for trained and untrained individuals are illustrated in Figure 6-2. The relationship between $\dot{V}_E$ and $\dot{V}O_2$ (or work rate) has two components. These are a linear rise followed by a curvilinear, accelerated increase in response to exercise work rates eliciting more than 50 to 75% of $\dot{V}O_{2max}$. In general, ventilation is higher in untrained than in trained subjects for given absolute and relative work loads (Figure 6-2A). However, ventilation is higher in trained individuals during maximal exercise (Figure 6-2A and B). This is because the exercise capacity is much greater in the trained. Ventilation is also higher when small muscles (e.g., arms) perform a given amount of work in comparison with the same work rate performed by larger muscles (e.g., legs).

In the following section, the factors that control ventilation during exercise are described. It would be inaccurate to state that our understanding of ventilatory control is complete. In particular, explaining the elevated ventilation (hyperpnea) during exercise has been one of the major challenges in modern physiology. Significant progress has been made, and we look forward to continued research on the regulation of exercise hyperpnea.

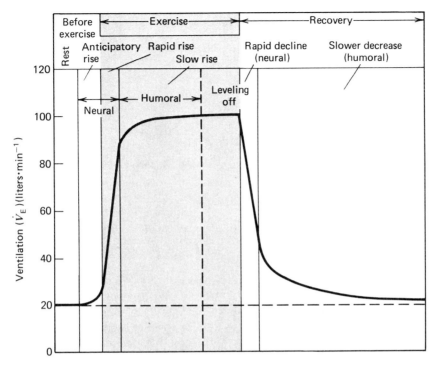

Figure 6-1

The neural–humoral control of ventilation during exercise. The elevated pulmonary ventilation during exercise (exercise hyperpnea) is controlled by at least two sets of mechanisms. One set acts very rapidly when exercise starts and stops. This mechanism has a neural basis and even causes ventilation to increase before exercise. The other set of factors that affect ventilation act slowly and result from the effects of blood-borne factors on the ventilatory (respiratory) center.

Control of Ventilation: An Integrated, Redundant Neural–Humoral Mechanism

The neural center that controls ventilation (i.e., the respiratory center) is located in the lower brain (Figure 6-3 and 6-4). The center is designed to alternate inspiration and expiration rhythmically. The rate and amplitude of those ventilatory movements is under the direct control of the respiratory center. Impinging on the center are a large number of neural and chemical (humoral) inputs. These inputs operate singularly and in concert to set the frequency and amplitude of output from the respiratory center. Not only are

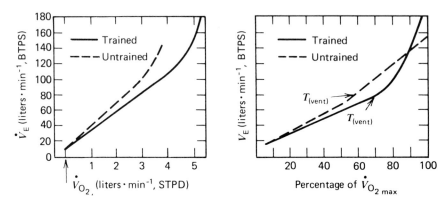

Figure 6-2

Relationship between pulmonary minute ventilation ($\dot{V}_E$) and metabolic rate ($\dot{V}_{O_2}$) during rest and exercise. In both untrained *(broken line)* and trained *(solid line)* subjects, $\dot{V}_E$ increases linearly with $\dot{V}_{O_2}$ up to about 50 to 75% of $\dot{V}_{O_2max}$. Thereafter, $\dot{V}_E$ increases at a rate disproportionately greater than the change in $\dot{V}_{O_2}$. Note that an effect of endurance training is to delay the ventilatory inflection point [T(vent)] in trained individuals.

the various inputs into the respiratory center integrated there to produce a given output, but also the center appears to possess redundant mechanisms (Figure 6-4).

Following nature's example, when human engineers design sophisticated machines for which there is sometimes little opportunity for repair (e.g., airliners and the NASA space shuttle), the engineers build in redundant control systems. In this way, if one system fails, there will be at least one other— and probably several other—systems to take over. Redundancies in the human respiratory center, as well as its anatomical location, have made it very difficult to study. Scientists usually study a system by varying the inputs into the system and seeing what happens to the output. Because the various inputs into the respiratory center alter the relationships among the different inputs, and because the center can compensate for loss of a usual input, the output from the center may be the same even when one or more of the inputs are experimentally perturbed or even ablated (destroyed). This system of operation is most beneficial for us who must breathe continually under a wide range of circumstances. The complexity of the system, however, makes the respiratory physiologist's job a real challenge.

The Respiratory (Ventilatory) Center

The respiratory center is divided into four areas: (1) the medullary expiratory center, (2) the medullary inspiratory center, (3) the apneustic center, and (4)

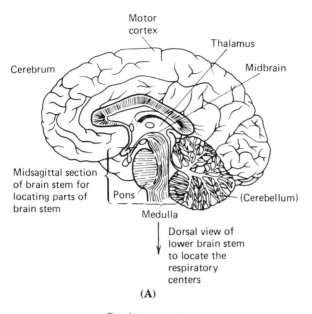

(A)

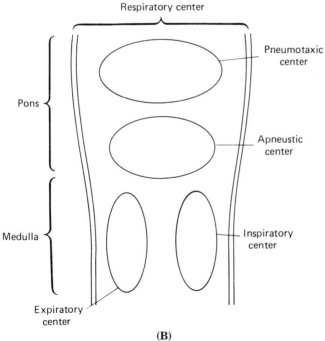

(B)

Figure 6-3

(A) Schematic of a sagittal cross section through the brain showing parts of the ventilatory (respiratory) center in relation to the rest of the brain. **(B)** Expanded view of the respiratory center.

(SOURCE: Modified from J. R. McClintic. Physiology of the Human Body. New York: John Wiley, 1975, p. 209. Used with permission.)

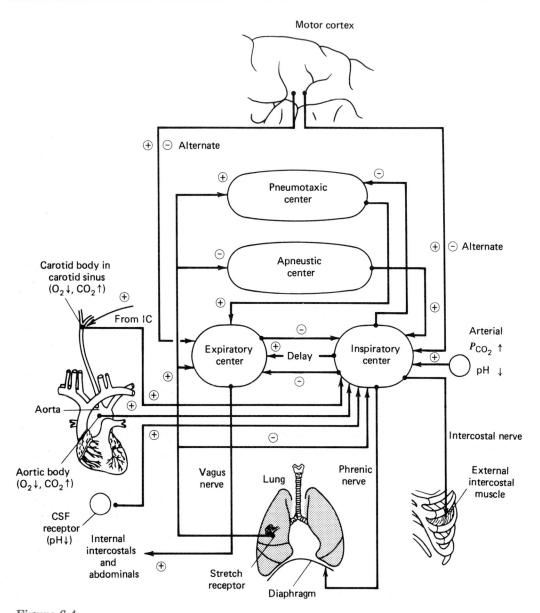

Figure 6-4
Schematic representation of the control of ventilation during rest and exercise in various environmental conditions. See the text for a description.

the pneumotaxic center (Figure 6-3*B*). Both the apneustic and the pneumotaxic centers are located in the pons. Basic rhythmicity of the center is set in the medulla. The apneustic center facilitates (stimulates) the inspiratory center; conversely, the pneumotaxic center facilitates expiration.

There are two populations of neurons in the medullary rhythmicity center—the inspiratory and expiratory neurons—and they tend to be localized in individual areas. The inspiratory and expiratory neurons intermingle, however, as well as interconnect with the apneustic and pneumotaxic centers (Figure 6-4). Rhythmicity of the respiratory center is set in the medullary neurons, which become active spontaneously.

In describing the functioning of any system that acts rhythmically, such as the ventilatory system, it is difficult to select a point at which to begin describing events within that system. Let us begin by describing events leading to an inspiration. Basically, the system works as follows.

Because of facilitatory inputs from other inspiratory neurons, from neurons in the apneustic center, and from central and peripheral sources, increased inspiratory neuronal activity summates to increased phrenic and intercostal nerve activity and contraction of muscles of inspiration (see Figure 6-4). Because the inspiratory and expiratory neurons of the medullary center are reciprocally innervated, inspiratory center activity temporarily inhibits expiratory center activity. However, as inspiratory activity begins to wane, reciprocal inhibition of the expiratory neurons decreases. Because of their own intrinsic rhythmicity, activity of the expiratory neurons increases. This activity is facilitated by synaptic interconnections from other expiratory neurons and from neuronal loops from the inspiratory center. Again, because of the reciprocal inhibitory interconnections between inspiratory and expiratory areas, neuronal discharge in the expiratory area leads to inhibition of inspiratory area activity. During rest, when expiration is passive, inhibition of the inspiratory area is sufficient to result in relaxation of the muscles of inspiration. During exercise when expiration is forced, accessory expiratory muscles are contracted. The ventilatory cycle will begin again as expiratory neuronal activity decreases and inspiratory neuronal activity increases.

Central Inputs to the Inspiratory Center

Neural Input—The Motor Cortex

The motor cortex is primarily responsible for stimulating the respiratory center to achieve the elevated ventilatory rates seen in exercise. The motor cortex is also responsible for the voluntary control of breathing that allows the individual speaking, singing, or playing a wind instrument to be successful. The motor cortex also allows movement and breathing patterns to be integrated during exercise. For instance, a swimmer must take large inspirations when the mouth and nose are out of the water, and expiration occurs under water. A wide range of breathing patterns are learned by swimmers who ventilate at high rates in a variety of stroke events (freestyle, butterfly, backstroke, breaststroke, etc.). During some sports activities, such as sprint running and weight lifting, ventilation must be inhibited.

The rapid increase in pulmonary ventilation with exercise, which is in fact preceded by an anticipatory rise (see Figure 6-1), is the key to the long-standing hypothesis of cortical control over the respiratory center during exercise. The input from the motor cortex into the respiratory center during exercise is an example of a "feed-forward" mechanism in which both ventilation and work rate are proportional to output from the cortical controller.

In addition to the motor cortex, other areas in the brain above the level of the pons (suprapontine) that facilitate the medullary respiratory center include the hypothalamus, the cerebellum, and the reticular formation. The hypothalamus (see Figures 6-3A, and 9-10) is particularly sensitive to increases in body temperature. In humans, effects of the hypothalamic mechanisms are observable during recovery from prolonged hard exercise, which elevates body temperature.

Whereas the cortex exerts feed-forward control over the respiratory center, the cerebellum provides feedback control. Afferents from contracting muscle reach the cerebellum, which then provides facilitatory input to the respiratory center.

The reticular formation is a diffuse subcortical, suprapontine area. The reticular formation is responsible for the general state of central nervous system (CNS) arousal. Exercise is associated with heightened activity in the reticular formation. Facilitatory input to the respiratory center from the reticular formation is thought to amplify the ventilatory response to exercise.

Humoral Input—The Medullary Extracellular Fluid

Any substance that circulates in the blood and has general effects at a site or sites removed from where it is secreted is termed a humor. Blood-borne substances are thought to be responsible for the slow phase of ventilatory adjustment to exercise (see Figure 6-1).

The ventilatory response in resting individuals at sea level altitudes is mediated predominantly by the central chemoreceptors. Specialized cells on the ventral surface of the medulla, which are distinct from inspiratory and expiratory neurons, are sensitive to change in hydrogen ion (H^+) concentration. Some of these chemosensitive cells are influenced by the pH of the medullary interstitial fluid, whereas other cells are sensitive to pH of the cerebrospinal fluid (CSF).

Increases in medullary H^+ concentration (decreases in pH) stimulate ventilation. Increases in arterial H^+ concentration decrease medullary interstitial pH; this pH change, in turn, activates the chemosensitive cells that monitor interstitial pH.

Whereas medullary chemosensitive cells respond to the pH of CSF, the pH perturbations to CSF come not from changes in arterial pH but rather from changes in the Pa_{CO_2}. Hydrogen ions diffuse slowly through the "blood–brain barrier" separating CSF and arterial blood. This barrier is permeable to arterial CO_2. Because the buffer capacity of CSF is rather low, CO_2 penetrating the blood–brain barrier results in carbonic acid formation, which lowers the pH.

It should be emphasized that the central chemoreceptors sensitive to H^+ and CO_2 act to control ventilation during rest when the Pa_{O_2} is around 100 mm Hg. At other times, such as during exercise or acute exposure to high altitude, there is actually an alkalotic response in the medullary extracellular fluid due to high ventilatory rates, which causes decreases in the PA_{CO_2} and Pa_{CO_2}. This increase in pH actually acts to restrain ventilatory response during exercise or acute hypobaric hypoxia.

Peripheral Inputs to the Respiratory System

Neural inputs to the medullary respiratory center that originate outside the brain are said to be peripheral to it. Peripheral inputs to the respiratory center include those from chemoreceptors, mechanical receptors, and baroreceptors.

Peripheral Chemoreceptors

The carotid bodies are located at the bifurcation of the common carotid artery, which becomes the internal and external carotids (see Figure 6-4). Afferent signals from the carotid bodies reach the medullary respiratory center through the carotid sinus and glossopharyngeal nerves. The carotid bodies are stimulated by decreased Pa_{O_2}, and the response is heightened by increased Pa_{CO_2} and decreased pH. The carotid bodies are in an ideal position to detect a decrease in Pa_{O_2} if for some reason the partial pressure of inspired O_2 (PI_{O_2}) decreased or pulmonary ventilation became limited. The PI_{O_2} of sea level residents could fall suddenly if they breathed air in which the O_2 content was lowered by the presence of a contaminating gas or if they ascended to a higher altitude. The mechanical requirements of many sports activities such as swimming frequently impair pulmonary ventilation.

Although a fall in Pa_{O_2} will rapidly stimulate the carotid bodies, the contribution (if any) of the carotid bodies to stimulating ventilation during exercise has remained puzzling. Breathing is so regulated during exercise that mean Pa_{O_2} does not decrease (see Figure 5-9). A range of normal arterial CO_2 responses occurs during exercise, but one frequent response is a decrease in Pa_{CO_2}. Therefore, except during transient situations such as at the start of exercise or during maximal exercise in highly trained persons, the carotid bodies would not see an increase in the Pa_{CO_2} or a decrease in Pa_{O_2}.

During exercise arterial pH does decrease, and the Pa_{O_2} does fluctuate subtly with the arterial pulse wave. These factors have been suggested as stimulants of the carotid bodies during exercise. Hypoxia is known to exaggerate the CO_2 response of the carotid bodies in resting individuals; therefore, it is possible that during exercise pulsatile variations in Pa_{O_2} increase sensitivity of the carotid bodies to CO_2 and H^+. In addition, under the influence of the motor cortex, the medullary respiratory center might be more influenced by input from the carotid bodies during exercise than during rest.

In addition to the carotid bodies, other arterial chemoreceptors exist in the aorta and brachiocephalic arteries. These "aortic bodies" are also sensitive to Pa_{O_2}, Pa_{CO_2}, and pH; the aortic bodies send afferent signals to the medulla through the vagus nerve.

Other Peripheral Chemoreceptors

Along with the arterial chemoreceptors, several other peripheral chemoreceptors have been postulated to exist. Because $\dot{V}_E$ and $\dot{V}_{CO_2}$ are so closely related both at rest and during exercise, increased CO_2 flux to the lungs has long been postulated to be sensed by some receptor in the right heart, pulmonary artery, or lung itself. Concerted efforts, however, have failed to detect such a receptor.

The existence of muscle chemoreceptors has also been postulated. These muscle receptors are believed to be sensitive to the concentrations of local metabolites. As with the postulated pulmonary chemoreceptors, no anatomical or histological evidence of muscle chemoreceptors exists.

Peripheral Mechanoreceptors

When the lungs and chest wall expand rapidly, mechanical receptors there are stimulated; these mechanoreceptors transmit to the respiratory center signals that have the effect of inhibiting inspiration. This action is known as the Hering–Bruer reflex. Because these mechanoreceptors are known to exist and because of the difficulty in identifying a main peripheral receptor that regulates ventilation during exercise, scientists have looked for the presence of mechanical receptors that could be activated during exercise. The muscle spindles, Golgi tendon bodies, and skeletal joint receptors are known to send afferent signals to the sensory cortex, which relays information to the respiratory center. Passive limb movement on awake as well as lightly anesthetized human subjects increases $\dot{V}_E$ without an increase in metabolic rate ($\dot{V}_{O_2}$ or $\dot{V}_{CO_2}$). Unfortunately, whereas peripheral mechanoreceptor stimulation has been observed to increase $\dot{V}_E$ in humans, the increase is small compared to the large and abrupt changes seen during exercise.

Control of Exercise Hyperpnea

The abrupt and very large change in ventilation that occurs as exercise starts and continues (see Figure 6-1) has been and remains a difficult phenomenon for scientists to explain. For the present, the neurohumoral theory is the best explanation. Basic ventilatory rhythmicity is set by the medullary respiratory center. When exercise starts, output of the respiratory center is increased tremendously by neural inputs from motor cortex, muscles, and joints. Once the broad range of ventilatory response is set by these neural components, the ventilatory response is fine-tuned by humoral factors that affect the peripheral and central chemoreceptors. When exercise stops, the exact opposite happens. Cortical and other neural inputs to the respiratory center cease, and ventilation slows dramatically. Then, as humoral disturbances wane, ventilation slowly returns to resting values.

Ventilation as a Limiting Factor in Aerobic Performance

Ventilation is not usually considered to be the factor limiting aerobic performance at altitudes close to sea level. The term *aerobic performance* is sometimes defined as the ability to endure hard and prolonged tasks that are of submaximal intensity. Aerobic performance is sometimes also defined as $\dot{V}O_{2max}$. Whether aerobic performance is defined in terms of submaximal endurance or short-time capacity to achieve $\dot{V}O_{2max}$, the process of ventilation is usually sufficiently robust to continue at high rates for prolonged periods, oxygenating the blood passing through the lungs.

The capacity to increase ventilation during exercise is relatively much greater than the body's capacity to increase cardiac output or oxygen consumption. The alveolar surface area is large in comparison with the pulmonary blood volume; the alveolar partial pressure of O_2 (P_{AO2}) increases during exercise, and the arterial partial pressure of O_2 (P_{aO2}) is maintained close to resting levels even during exercise eliciting $\dot{V}O_{2max}$ at sea level altitudes. A considerable ventilatory reserve exists to oxygenate blood passing through the lungs, and this reserve allows us to perform effectively at altitudes significantly above sea level.

Ventilatory Perfusion Ratio (V̇$_E$/Q̇) during Rest and Exercise

When scientists attempt to understand the limitations in a system such as the the O_2 transport system, they frequently try to identify the factor or step that limits the system (Chapter 1). In the overall scheme of O_2 transport from the atmosphere to tissues, the process of pulmonary ventilation is not generally considered to be limiting at normally inhabited altitudes near sea level.

As the exercise work rate increases from resting levels up through easy to moderate intensities, pulmonary minute ventilation ($\dot{V}_E$) increases linearly (see Figure 6-2). As exercise intensity becomes more severe, however, a

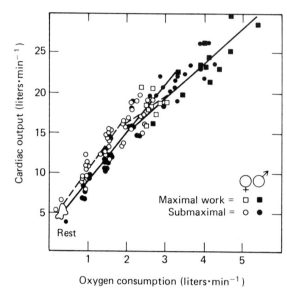

Figure 6-5

Relationship between cardiac output and oxygen consumption during rest and exercise. Given physical limits for arterial O_2 consumption ($\dot{V}_{O_2max}$) is largely a function of the ability to increase cardial output.

(SOURCE: Redrawn from P.-O. Åstrand and K. Rodahl, 1970. Used with permission.)

ventilatory threshold exists beyond which further increments in exercise work rate or $\dot{V}O_2$ result in exaggerated, nonlinear increments in $\dot{V}_E$. Resting values of pulmonary minute ventilatory volume (5 liters·min^{-1}, BTPS) can increase to values of around 200 liters·min^{-1} in a healthy young adult male during exercise. This represents a 35-fold increase. As exercise intensity increases, the volume of blood flowing through (perfusing) the pulmonary vessels also increases. However, this increase in cardiac output is essentially linear from resting levels up through those achieved during maximal exercise (Figure 6-5). In absolute terms, resting cardiac output (5 liters·min^{-1}) can increase five or six times (25 to 30 liters·min^{-1}) during exercise in a young, healthy, and fit adult male.

The ratio of pulmonary minute ventilation to cardiac output (i.e., the ventilation: perfusion ratio, $\dot{V}_E/\dot{Q}$) approximates unity during rest in most individuals. In the robust individual just described, the $\dot{V}_E/\dot{Q}$ seen during exercise is usually presented as one reason pulmonary ventilation is not thought to limit aerobic performances. In individuals less fit than the one just described, the absolute increments in $\dot{V}_E$ and $\dot{Q}$ achieved during exercise will be less, but the $\dot{V}_E/\dot{Q}$ will expand to a similar extent.

The Ventilatory Equivalent of O_2 during Exercise

An argument similar to that on the $\dot{V}_E/\dot{Q}$ is used with the ventilatory equivalent of O_2 (i.e., $\dot{V}_E/\dot{V}O_2$) to exclude pulmonary ventilation as a factor limiting aerobic performance. During rest, $\dot{V}_E$ approximates 5 liters·min^{-1}, whereas $\dot{V}O_2$ can be as low as 0.25 liters·min^{-1} the $\dot{V}_E/\dot{V}O_2$ is 20. During maximal exercise, for the individual we are describing, $\dot{V}_{Emax}$ may expand to 200 liters·min^{-1}, and $\dot{V}O_{2max}$ might be 5 liters·min^{-1}; the $\dot{V}_E/\dot{V}O_2$ increases to 35. The ability to expand ventilation is therefore relatively greater than the ability to expand oxidative metabolism.

$\dot{V}_{Emax}$ Versus MVV during Exercise

Pulmonary minute ventilation can increase tremendously from rest to maximal exercise (see Figure 6-2). The greatest $\dot{V}_E$ observed in an individual during exercise, however, is usually less than the MVV (Chapter 5) capacity of that individual. When an athlete turns into the home stretch in finishing a track race, he or she will be breathing very heavily and will probably feel a degree of breathlessness. If that athlete were to volitionally attempt to increase $\dot{V}_E$ still further, however, he or she could probably do it. The fact that a maximal $\dot{V}_E$ observed during exercise is less than the MVV is another reason ventilation is not thought to limit aerobic performance at sea level altitudes.

Partial Pressures of Alveolar (P_{AO2}) and Arterial Oxygen (P_{aO2}) during Exercise

The real test of adequacy of pulmonary ventilation rests with the partial pressures of O_2 in alveoli (P_{AO2}) and arterial (P_{aO2}) blood during exercise. As described in Chapter 5, O_2 transport around the body is accomplished only because O_2 (like other gases) moves from areas of high concentration (or partial pressure) to areas of lower partial pressure. Respiratory gas exchange is accomplished through ventilation by maintaining the alveolar partial pressure of O_2 relatively high and that of CO_2 low. The adequacy of pulmonary ventilation in maintaining the partial pressure of O_2 in alveoli during exercise up to $\dot{V}O_{2max}$ is illustrated in Figure 11-3. If anything, increased ventilation during exercise raises the P_{AO2}.

The partial pressure of O_2 (P_{aO2}) is systemic arterial blood (i.e., blood that has circulated through the lungs and heart and into the aorta) is also well maintained during exercise (see Figure 5-12). This apparently results from several major factors. First, the P_{AO2} is maintained or increased. Second, the erythrocytes passing through the pulmonary capillaries remain there sufficiently long for equilibration with alveolar O_2 (see Figure 5-9). Third, the sigmoid shape of the O_2 dissociation curve (see Figure 5-11) is such that when the PO_2 is about 100 mm Hg, the saturation of hemoglobin with O_2 does not fall off markedly even if the PO_2 falls off several millimeters of mercury.

Alveolar Surface Area for Exchange

As noted earlier, the alveolar surface area estimated to exist in the average-sized person is 50 m^2, or 35 times the surface area of the person (Chapter 5). This is the area represented by one-half of a singles tennis court. Keeping in mind that the average blood volume is 5 liters, picture the following scene. You are trying to spread the liquid contents of a 5-qt container over one side of the tennis court. How far do you think you could get in spreading the liquid? Could you cover the one side? Now consider that in reality less than 10% of the blood volume is in the pulmonary vessels at any one instant. Therefore, the ratio of alveolar surface area to pulmonary capillary blood volume is enormous. This disproportionality ensures a large capacity for exchange of respiratory gases between blood and alveolar air during ventilation.

Fatigue of Ventilatory Muscles and Limitations in Ventilation

Any muscle, including the diaphragm and accessory ventilatory muscles, can fatigue. When diaphragm muscle preparations isolated from experimental animals are electrically stimulated to contract at high rates, the muscles demonstrate distinct fatigue characteristics. Additionally, during an MVV test, human subjects will usually demonstrate a degree of fatigue and not be able to ventilate at as high a rate at the end of the test as at the beginning of the test. Maximum voluntary ventilation tests repeated in rapid succession will also usually produce decreasing values. The central question regarding ventilatory muscle fatigue during exercise, however, is whether or not ventilatory fatigue precedes or coincides with and results in decrements in body exercise performance. The answer to this question is usually no. As noted previously, $\dot{V}_{Emax}$ during exercise is usually less than MVV, even MVV determined after exercise. Further, most athletes can volitionally increase $\dot{V}_E$ above normally occurring volumes at the end of exercise.

The issue of adequacy of the ventilatory system during maximal exercise in very fit individuals has recently been raised. Decreases in P_{aO2} have been observed when some subjects were stressed to $\dot{V}O_{2max}$. Because the P_{aO2} decreased even though $\dot{V}_E$ approached MVV, the pulmonary system did not adequately oxygenate blood passing through it. Therefore, it was suspected that compliance in the ventilatory system prevented $\dot{V}_E$ from rising sufficiently to maintain arterial O_2 concentration. Compliance is a measure of expansibility of the lungs and thorax. These structures do provide a resistance to ventilatory movements and ventilatory flow. Consequently, a limitation to ventilatory flow is imposed by the internal resistance of the pulmonary tissues. It is therefore possible that in some individuals P_{aO2} could be affected by pulmonary compliance during maximal exercise.

The "Anaerobic Threshold": A Misnomer

As exercise intensity increases, $\dot{V}O_2$ increases linearly, but the blood lactate level changes only slightly until about 60% of $\dot{V}O_{2max}$ has been reached; thereafter, the blood lactate level increases nonlinearly (Figure 6-6). The inflection point in the blood lactate curve has been given several names. These include: The lactate threshold [T(lact)], the anaerobic threshold (AT), and the onset of blood lactate accumulation (OBLA).

Because blood acidity is one of the factors that increases $\dot{V}_E$, it has been hypothesized that an abrupt increase in $\dot{V}_E$ during exercise could be used to indicate that the blood lactate level had increased due to insufficient O_2 delivery to exercising muscle. Finding the point of a nonlinear increase in ventilation [i.e., the ventilatory threshold, or T(vent)] during progressive exercise was considered to represent detection of a muscle anaerobic threshold. The idea of an anaerobic threshold determined from the T(vent) was particularly attractive because it offered the possibility of detecting muscle anaerobiosis by changes in breathing. Unfortunately, it was found that various factors affect determination of the anaerobic threshold, including nutritional status, body mass, mode of exercise, and speed of movement. Perhaps most revealing of the falacy of the anaerobic threshold model were studies on McArdle's syndrome patients. McArdle's syndrome is a genetically linked disease in which victims lack the enzyme phosphorylase (see Figure 3-8), which renders them incapable of catabolizing glycogen and forming lactic acid. Nevertheless, McArdle's syndrome patients demonstrate ventilatory, or "anaerobic," thresholds at the usual place on the lactate–work curve even though there is no change in blood lactate (Figure 6-7).

Because changes in blood lactate concentration cannot be taken as indicative of changes in muscle lactate production, and because exercise ventilatory minute volume does not always track blood lactate levels (e.g., Figure 6-7), determination of the ventilatory (anaerobic) threshold provides no definitive information about the status of muscle metabolism. Therefore, the term *anaerobic threshold* is a misnomer and should not be used.

Even though the AT phenomenon has been widely misunderstood, the

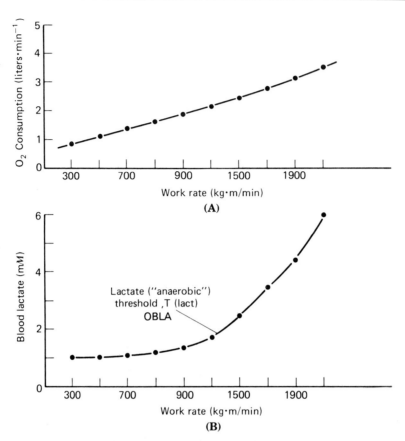

Figure 6-6

O_2 consumption **(A)** and blood lactate **(B)** responses to a continuous, progressive cycle ergometer test in healthy young subjects. $\dot{V}_{O_2}$ responds in almost a linear fashion **(A)**, whereas the lactate level does not change much at first but then begins to rise nonlinearly **(B)**. At the lactate inflection point, lactate entry into the blood exceeds its removal.

(SOURCE: Modified from E. H. Hughes et al., 1982.)

exercise intensity that elicits a blood lactate concentration of 4mM (the OBLA point) has been found to be a good means of predicting performance in various forms of endurance exercise. Use of OBLA determination as well as other techniques to gauge training intensity will be discussed in Chapter 15. However, at this point an explanation of the relationship between the OBLA point and exercise performance is appropriate.

A sudden rise in blood lactate level can indicate a rapid rate of muscle glycogenolysis. Rapid glycogenolysis during exercise can result in glycogen

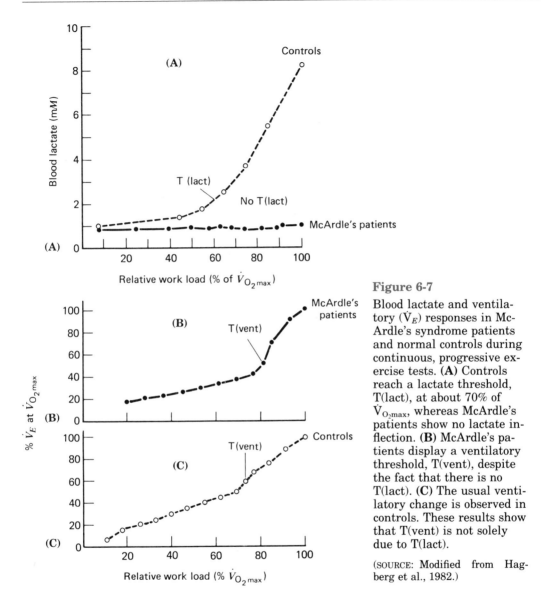

Figure 6-7

Blood lactate and ventilatory ($\dot{V}_E$) responses in McArdle's syndrome patients and normal controls during continuous, progressive exercise tests. **(A)** Controls reach a lactate threshold, T(lact), at about 70% of $\dot{V}_{O_2max}$, whereas McArdle's patients show no lactate inflection. **(B)** McArdle's patients display a ventilatory threshold, T(vent), despite the fact that there is no T(lact). **(C)** The usual ventilatory change is observed in controls. These results show that T(vent) is not solely due to T(lact).

(SOURCE: Modified from Hagberg et al., 1982.)

depletion and muscle fatigue. A rise in blood lactate concentration during exercise also indicates that lactate entry into the blood is higher than can be removed and kept at reasonable levels. The failure to cope with lactate production during exercise results in blood acidosis. Acidosis of the blood also causes a fall in muscle pH because hydrogen ion accumulation in the blood inhibits the efflux of hydrogen ion from muscle. Acidosis is another fatigue factor during exercise.

At this point it is also necessary to recognize that the OBLA point (i.e., the exercise intensity that elicits a 4mM blood lactate concentration) is different from the T(lact) and the ventilatory AT. These latter two thresholds occur at a much lower (approximately 2 mM) blood lactate concentration. As noted earlier, the relationships among the AT, T(lact), and AT are not directly linked, and so it is not always possible to predict one from the other.

Summary

Ventilation of the lungs is under the control of a respiratory center in the medulla of the brain. The respiratory center receives a variety of neural and humoral (chemical) inputs both directly (internally) and indirectly (externally) from receptors in the periphery. These inputs are integrated within the respiratory center to produce an appropriate ventilatory response, but the control circuits within the respiratory center's system of operation contain redundancies. Therefore, the respiratory center can usually produce an appropriate ventilatory response even if one or several inputs are cut off or if the inputs are contradictory.

Physical exercise results in rapid and large ventilatory adjustments noted by both initial (rapid) and secondary (slow) response characteristics. When exercise stops, ventilation first slows abruptly and then declines slowly to resting levels. This fast–slow ventilatory response to the initiation and cessation of exercise is best explained by the neural–humoral theory of ventilatory control. During exercise, neural inputs to the respiratory center come from the motor cortex and from peripheral mechanoreceptors. Of these, the cortical inputs are most important. As exercise continues, humoral (chemical) factors such as fluctuating PO_2 and increased PCO_2 and H^+ are sensed in peripheral chemoreceptors. Of these, the arterial chemoreceptors have been identified as being the most important for controlling ventilatory response to exercise. Chemoreceptors sensitive mainly to CO_2 have been hypothesized to exist in muscles and in the right heart or lung. Serious efforts to identify these receptors have failed to document their existence.

The mechanisms for control of ventilation are redundant in their operation and ensure adequate response under numerous conditions. Similarly, the robust capacity of the pulmonary system usually ensures that O_2 transport from atmosphere to metabolizing tissues is not limited by ventilation. The ventilatory perfusion ratio ($\dot{V}_E/\dot{Q}$) increases several times during exercise, as does the ventilatory equivalent of O_2 ($\dot{V}_E/\dot{V}O_2$). The alveolar partial pressure of O_2 (P_{AO2}) is maintained or increased during exercise, and the partial pressure of O_2 in the systemic arterial blood (P_{aO2}) is maintained at or close to normal resting levels. The rather flat shape of the oxyhemoglobin dissociation curve at partial pressures of 95 to 105 mm Hg ensures that even if P_{aO2}

decreases slightly, the O_2 content of arterial blood (C_{aO2}) will not decrease appreciably.

During exercise tests of increasing intensity, blood lactate levels begin to increase dramatically at about 60% of $\dot{V}O_{2max}$. This inflection point in blood lactic acid level has mistakenly been called the "anaerobic threshold," meaning the point at which muscle becomes O_2 deficient. It was incorrectly believed that O_2 deficiency in muscle during exercise could be detected from measurements of pulmonary ventilation. Unfortunately, it has been discovered that the anaerobic threshold hypothesis is incorrect. Therefore, the term *anaerobic threshold* should not be used.

Selected Readings

ASMUSSEN, E., E.H. CHRISTENSEN, and M. NIELSEN. Humoral or nervous control of respiration during muscular work? Acta Physiol. Scan. 6:160–167, 1943.

ÅSTRAND, P.O., T.E. CUDDY, B. SALTIN, and J. STENBERG. Cardiac output during submaximal and maximal work. J. Appl. Physiol. 19:268–273, 1964.

ÅSTRAND, P.O., and K. RODAHL. Textbook of Work Physiology. New York: McGraw-Hill, 1970, pp. 154–178, 187–254.

BISCOE, T.J. Carotid body: structure and function. Physiol. Rev. 51:427–495, 1971.

BROOKS, G.A., and T.D. FAHEY. Exercise Physiology: Human Bioenergetics and Its Applications, New York: Macmillan, 1984, pp. 221–276.

COMROE, J.H. Physiology of respiration. Chicago: Year Book Medical Publishers, 1974, p. 234.

DEJOURS, P. Control of respiration in muscular exercise. In: Fenn, W.O. and H. Rahn (eds.). Handbook of physiology, Section 3, Respiration, Vol. 1. Washington, D.C.: American Physiological Society, 1964.

DEMPSEY, J.A., P.E. HANSON, and S.M. MASTENBROOK. Arterial hypoxemia during heavy exercise in highly trained runners. Fed. Proc. 40:932, 1981.

DEMPSEY, J.A., D.A. PELLIGRINO, D. AGGARWAL, and E.B. OLSON. The brain's role in exercise hypernea. Med. Sci. Sports. 11:213–220, 1979.

ELDRIDGE, F.L., D.E. MILLHRON, and T.G. WALDROP. Exercise hypernea and locomotion: parallel activation from the hypothalamus. Science 211:844–846, 1981.

GUYTON, A.C. Textbook of Medical Physiology. Philadelphia: W.B. Saunders, 1981, pp. 516–528.

HAGBERG, J.M., E.F. COYLE, J.E. CARROLL, J.M. MILLER, W.H. MARTIN, and M.H. BROOKE. Exercise hyperventilation in patients with McArdle's disease. J. Appl. Physiol.: Respirat. Environ. Exercise Physiol. 52:991–994, 1982.

HILDEBRANDT, J.R., R.K. WINN, and J. HILDEBRANDT. Cardiorespiratory response to sudden releases of circulatory occlusion during exercise, Resp. Physiol. 38:83–92, 1979.

HUGHES, E.F., S.C. TURNER, and G.A. BROOKS. Effects of glycogen depletion and pedaling speed on "anaerobic threshold." J. Appl. Physiol. 52:1598–1607, 1982.

KROGH, A., and J. LINHARD. The regulation of respiration and circulation during the initial stages of muscular work. J. Physiol. London 47:112–136, 1913.

SEGAL, S.S., and G.A. BROOKS. Effects of glycogen depletion and work load on postexercise O_2 consumption and blood lactate. J. Appl. Physiol.: Respirate. Environ. Exercise Physiol. 47:514–521, 1979.

WASSERMAN, K., B.J. WHIPP, S.N. KOYAL, and M.G. CLEARY. Effect of carotid body resection of ventilatory and acid-base control during exercise. J. Appl. Physiol. 39:354–358, 1975.

ZUNTZ, N., and J. GEPPERT. Ueber die Natur der normalen Atomreize un den Ort ihrer Wirkung. Arch. Ges. Physiol. 38:337–338, 1886.

7

Cardiovascular System Responses to Exercise

The body, whether resting or exercising, depends on an adequate supply of oxygen and fuels and must operate within narrow limits of pH and temperature. In addition, many physiological processes are regulated by hormones that are produced at relatively great distances from their active sites. The cardiovascular system helps to satisfy these biological requirements by serving as the body's internal transportation system. Using blood as the transport medium, the heart and circulation help maintain homeostasis by delivering vital substances to various tissues and eliminating metabolic end products (Table 7-1).

The control of the cardiovascular system is geared toward supplying the tissues' metabolic requirements by maintaining blood pressure and perfusion to the tissues. During exercise, when the need for oxygen and fuels in working muscles is greater, changes reflect the increased requirement for blood flow: cardiac output and muscle blood flow increase, while blood flow to less active tissues decreases. However, flow to critical areas such as the brain and heart is either maintained or increased, respectively.

The maintenance of systemic arterial blood pressure and the satisfaction of regional tissue demands require coordination of the pumping action of the heart and the optimal distribution of blood flow. These processes are accomplished by a combination of neural, mechanical, and hormonal regulatory mechanisms that maintain circulatory homeostasis at rest and exercise.

This chapter will examine the control of the heart and circulation during rest and exercise. Chapter 8 will deal with oxygen transport dynamics during exercise.

Structure and Function of the Heart

During exercise, three basic physiological processes occur that increase blood flow to exercising muscles: the rate of blood flow increases because of an increased output from the heart (i.e., an increased cardiac output), blood is di-

---

TABLE 7-1 **Functions of the Cardiovascular System**

Transportation of O_2 to tissues
Transportation of nutrients
Transportation of CO_2 and metabolites to lungs and kidneys
Distribution of hormones and other substances that regulate cell function
Thermoregulation
Urine formation

SOURCE: G. A. Brooks and T. D. Fahey, Exercise Physiology: Human Bioenergetics and Its Applications. New York: Macmillan, 1984, Table 14-1.

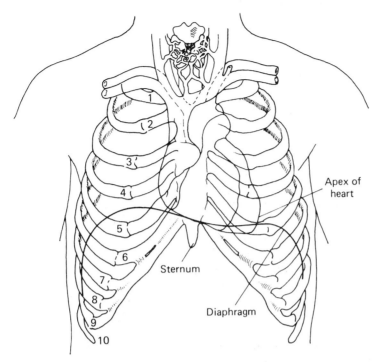

Figure 7-1

Location of the heart in the chest cavity.

(SOURCE: Adapted from C. M. Goss, Grey's Anatomy, 1973. In: G. A. Brooks and T. D. Fahey. Exercise Physiology: Human Bioenergetics and Its Applications. New York: Macmillan, 1984, Figure 14-1.)

rected toward metabolically active tissues (exercising muscles and the heart) by vasodilation (opening) of their blood vessels, and blood is directed away from most relatively inactive tissues by vasoconstriction (closing) of their blood vessels.

The heart is a hollow, four-chambered muscular organ that pumps blood to the lungs and the general circulation. It rests in the chest cavity on the diaphragm between the lower parts of the lungs and below the middle and left of the sternum, with the apex (bottom) descending to about the fifth rib (Figure 7-1). About two-thirds of the heart lies left of the midline of the thorax (chest). The heart is contained in a protective, supportive sac called the pericardium. This structure, composed of fibrous tissue interspersed with adipose, lubricates the heart to reduce friction during cardiac contractions.

The heart is divided into the right and left atria and ventricles. The chambers are distinct, separated by walls called septa. The atria are thin-walled, low-pressure chambers that serve as reservoirs for the ventricles. At rest, the right and left atria play a small role in helping the heart maintain the necessary cardiac output. However, during exercise, the atria are very important in assisting the movement of blood returning from the veins by acting as a ventricular primer pump that greatly facilitates ventricular output. The ventricles bear the major burden of pumping blood to lungs and circulation. Both ventricles pump essentially the same amount of blood. However, the left ventricle walls are thicker than the right walls because of the greater resistance (higher pressure system) provided by the peripheral circulation. Exercise that increases blood pressure, such as heavy weight lifting, tends to increase the thickness of the left ventricular walls.

Four cardiac valves—the tricuspid, mitral, pulmonic, and aortic—maintain the flow of blood in one direction either into or out of the ventricles (Figure 7-2). Exercise training is generally not recommended when these valves are diseased; diseased valves allow blood to regurgitate back into the chambers, resulting in excessive load on the heart during exercise.

The Myocardium

The heart is composed mainly of muscle called myocardium. The outer layer of the myocardium is called epicardium and the inner layer is endocardium. There are two types of cardiac muscle: contractile, which makes up the bulk of the myocardium (Figure 7-3), and electrical, which are specialized exicatory and conductive fibers. The contractile cardiac muscle causes the pumping action of the heart, while the electrical tissue is responsible for the rapid conduction of impulses throughout the heart.

Cardiac and skeletal muscle are similar in many ways (see Chapter 9): both appear striated, both have myofibrils that contain actin and myosin filaments that participate in contraction, and both exhibit an electrical depolarization that precedes shortening. However, cardiac and skeletal muscle differ in several significant ways. Cardiac muscle is largely involuntary (there is some voluntary control of heart rate). Unlike skeletal fibers, cardiac muscle cells are connected by intercalated disks in tight series so that stimulation of one cell results in the stimulation of all the cells. The electrical resistance between cells is minimal so that all the cardiac muscle in the atria or ventricles can contract as a unit (the contractile unit is called a syncytium). In the myocardium, the supply of Ca^{++} is variable. This and the arrangement of the sarcomeres enable the heart to elicit a graded contractile response when stimulated, while a single skeletal muscle motor unit either contracts or does not contract when it is stimulated (the all-or-none principle).

Heart's Blood Supply

The coronary arteries and veins supply blood and remove metabolic wastes from the myocardial tissue (Figure 7-4). The left coronary artery supplies mainly the left ventricle, whereas the right coronary supplies the right and part of the left ventricle. The arteries run on the surface of the heart and

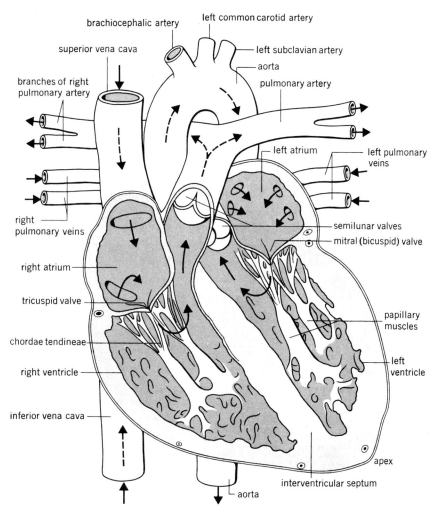

Figure 7-2
The chambers of the heart.

(SOURCE: From J. E. Crouch and J. R. McClintic, 1971. In: G. A. Brooks and T. D. Fahey. Exercise Physiology: Human Bioenergetics and Its Applications. New York: Macmillan, 1984, Figure 14-4.)

penetrate into the heart muscle at right angles, branching off into the various layers of muscle.

The heart depends almost entirely on oxidative metabolism to supply its energy needs. Consequently, the heart muscle is very high in mitochondria, and its demand for blood is high (particularly during exercise). The heart muscle extracts more than 75% of the oxygen delivered to it (highest of any

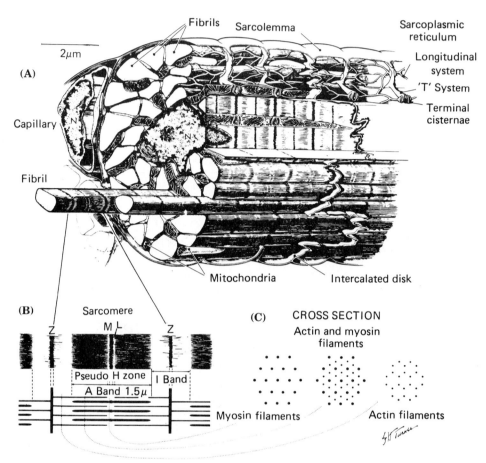

Figure 7-3

Schematic diagram of cardiac muscle as seen under the electron microscope. **(A)** Myocardial cell, showing arrangement of multiple parallel fibrils; **(B)** individual sarcomere from a myofibril. A representation of the arrangement of myofilaments that make up the sarcomere is shown below; **(C)** cross section of the sarcomere, showing specific lattice arrangement of myofilaments. N = nucleus.

(SOURCE: From E. Braunwald, J. Ross, and E. H. Sonnenblick, 1967. In: G. A. Brooks and T. D. Fahey. Exercise Physiology: Human Bioenergetics and Its Applications. New York: Macmillan, 1984, Figure 14-2.)

tissue) during rest as well as during exercise. During exercise, the heart's enhanced oxygen requirement must be met by increased blood flow rather than by increased oxygen extraction from blood. This is not a problem for people with healthy hearts. However, in people with narrowed coronary arteries due to atherosclerosis (see Chapter 16), ischemia (inadequate blood flow) develops, which may result in hypoxemia (low levels of oxygen in the tissues),

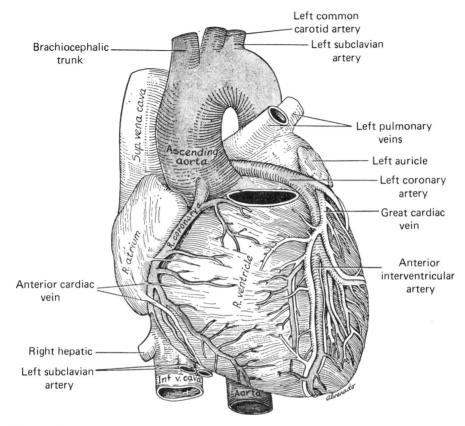

Figure 7-4
The coronary blood vessels of the sternocostal aspect of the heart.

(SOURCE: From C. M. Goss, Grey's Anatomy, Lea & Febiger, Philadelphia, 1973, p. 573. In: G. A. Brooks and T. D. Fahey. Exercise Physiology: Human Bioenergetics and Its Applications. New York: Macmillan, 1984, Figure 15-8.)

angina pectoris (chest pain), electrical conduction abnormalities (arrhythmias), congestive heart failure (diminished pumping capacity of the heart), and myocardial infarction (death of heart tissue, i.e., a heart attack).

The Heart's Electrical Conduction System and the Electrocardiogram

The heart contains special electrical tissue that can spontaneously cause heart muscle to contract. The most important concentration of these autorhythmic cells is found in the sinoatrial node (SA node) located in the right atrium. The SA node acts as the pacemaker for the heart, initiating an electrical impulse over the heart's electrical conduction system that results in a coor-

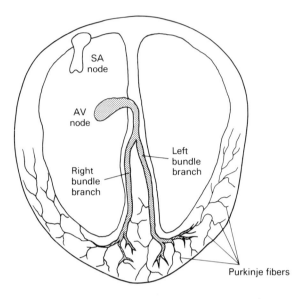

Figure 7-5
The heart's electrical conduction system.

(SOURCE: Redrawn from G. A. Brooks and T. D. Fahey. Exercise Physiology: Human Bioenergetics and Its Applications. New York: Macmillan, 1984, Figure 14-3.)

dinated contraction of heart muscle during the cardiac cycle. A conduction tract connects the SA node with the left atrium. The muscular conduction system of the ventricles consists of the atrioventricular node (AV node), AV bundle, left and right bundle branches, and Purkinje fibers (Figure 7-5). These systems allow impulses to travel much faster and uniformly than they would if they traveled directly across cardiac muscle.

Resting heart muscle is polarized—the cells are negatively charged on the inside and positively charged on the surface. Before heart muscle contracts it must depolarize—the inside becomes positively charged and the outside negatively charged. The electrical wave of depolarization causes a progressive contraction of the cardiac muscle. Because depolarization occurs so rapidly, the ventricles contract as a unit.

The electrical activity of the heart can be measured by the electrocardiograph (ECG). The elements of the electrocardiogram precede the actual mechanical events of the cardiac cycle, as is shown in Figure 7-6.

The SA node (the heart's pacemaker) propagates the electrical impulse that initiates the cardiac cycle. This electrical impulse results in a wave of depolarization (called a P wave) across both atria. The P wave immediately precedes atrial contraction. Neural tracts from the SA node to the left atrium allow simultaneous contraction of the right and left atria.

A slight delay occurs when the atrial depolarization wave reaches the AV node. This delay allows the blood to pass through the AV valves into the ventricles. After the delay, the AV node is stimulated. This results in depolarization of the ventricles, which produces a QRS complex on the electrocardiogram. In this process the electrical impulse proceeds across the heart's

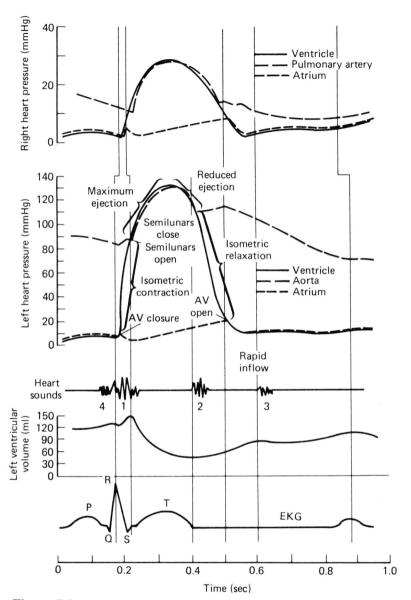

Figure 7-6

The elements of the electrocardiogram and the cardiac cycle.

(SOURCE: From J. E. Crouch and J. R. McClintic, 1971. In: G. A. Brooks and T. D. Fahey. Exercise Physiology: Human Bioenergetics and Its Applications. New York: Macmillan, 1984. Figure 14-5.)

neural conduction system and results in rapid and coordinated stimulation of cardiac muscle. The QRS complex occurs just before the contraction of the ventricles. Repolarization of the atria is usually masked by the QRS complex, so it cannot be seen on the electrocardiogram.

The T wave, caused by repolarization of the ventricles, occurs just after ventricular contraction. There is a pause between the S and T wave called the ST segment. The ST segment, as we will see in Chapter 15, is important in exercise stress testing because it is used to detect deficiencies in coronary blood flow.

Cardiac Cycle

The heart receives blood from the veins and pumps it to the lungs and circulation. This is accomplished by a rhythmic contraction–relaxation process called the cardiac cycle. The cardiac cycle consists of an active phase, called systole, and a relaxation phase, called diastole. During systole the ventricles contract and push blood from their chambers; during diastole, they relax and the chambers fill with blood in preparation for the next systole.

Low-oxygenated blood returns to the heart from the circulation via the inferior and superior vena cavae to the right atrium. It then passes through the tricuspid valve into the right ventricle. Blood is then propelled from the right ventricle through the pulmonary valve into the pulmonary arteries, to the lungs where gas exchange occurs. The blood returns to the left atrium via the pulmonary veins. It then passes through the mitral valve into the left ventricle, where it is finally propelled into the aorta to the systemic circulation (see Figure 7-2).

The amount of blood ejected from the ventricles during systole is called the stroke volume. The stroke volume is determined by the difference between ventricular filling—the end-diastolic volume—and ventricular emptying—the end-systolic volume. The percentage of the end-diastolic volume that is pumped from the ventricles is called the ejection fraction.

The amount of blood pumped by the heart per unit of time is called the cardiac output ($\dot{Q}$). Cardiac output is a product of the heart rate and stroke volume (Eq. 7-1).

$$\dot{Q} = (V_s) \times (f_H) \tag{7-1}$$

where:

$\dot{Q}$ = cardiac output ($1 \cdot min^{-1}$),
V_s = stroke volume, and
f_H = heart rate or frequency of the cardiac cycle.

At rest, the cardiac output is approximately 5 liters·min^{-1}, but during exercise it can exceed 35 liters·min^{-1} in some world-class endurance athletes.

Control of Cardiac Output

Cardiac output is controlled by the regulation of heart rate and stroke volume. Heart rate is paced by the sinoatrial node, influenced by the autonomic nervous system and circulating hormones. Stroke volume is determined by venous return and the extent to which heart muscle fibers contract. Stroke volume and heart rate are regulated through intrinsic (from within the heart) and extrinsic (from outside the heart) control mechanisms. Intrinsic control mechanisms mainly affect stroke volume and make it possible for the heart to automatically pump all the blood returned to it from the circulation. Extrinsic control mechanisms, composed of neural control systems and hormones, work to further increase the rate and strength of cardiac contractions.

Increased cardiac output is affected by metabolic and homeostatic demands. When the body's metabolism increases, such as during exercise, the various control mechanisms (including renal and temperature controllers) increase the output of the heart.

Intrinsic Regulation of the Heart

The normal heart will pump all the blood returned to it from the veins. This is called the Frank–Starling law of the heart (Figure 7-7). The ventricles are stretched when they receive more blood. This causes them to contract more forcefully due to increased tension created by stretching of the elastic components of the cardiac muscle and the placement of the myofilaments (contractile tissue) of the heart muscle in positions more conducive to forceful contraction.

The ability of the Frank–Starling mechanism to increase cardiac output is limited. Any increase in the size of the heart geometrically increases the energy required for contraction. If the linear dimensions of the heart are doubled, then the ventricular muscles must produce a tension four times greater to secure the same systolic pressure. During exercise, most of the increase in cardiac output is due to increased heart rate rather than stroke volume. There is a greater mechanical advantage in contracting the smaller ventricular volume. However, increased stroke volume significantly contributes to cardiac output during lower exercise intensities; under these circumstances, myocardial oxygen consumption ($M\dot{V}o_2$) is less when stroke volume rather than heart rate increases (because of the time–tension factors).

The Frank–Starling principle has many important implications during exercise. Stroke volume depends on the maintenance of central blood volume. In other words, blood must return to the heart for the heart to be able to pump it to the systemic circulation. Factors that facilitate the return of blood to the heart include the pumping action of skeletal muscles and ventilation, blood volume, and vasoconstriction of the blood to inactive areas. Factors that decrease central blood volume include skin blood flow (during exercise in the

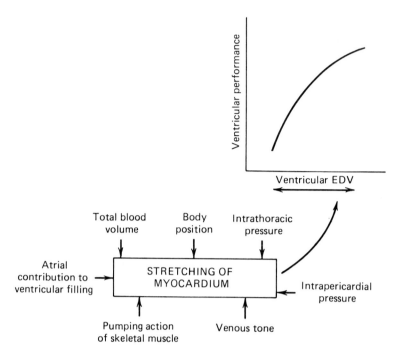

Figure 7-7

The Frank–Starling curve and the factors affecting end-diastolic volume (EDV).

(SOURCE: Braunwald, J. Ross, and E. J. Sonnenblick, 1967. In: G. A. Brooks and T. D. Fahey. Exercise Physiology: Human Bioenergetics and Its Applications. New York: Macmillan, 1984, Figure 14-6.)

heat), dehydration (decreased blood volume), and exercises such as weight lifting that result in increased resistance to blood flow (peripheral resistance).

A number of mechanical reflexes are capable of increasing heart rate during exercise. These include the atrial stretch reflex and pulmonary reflex that cause an increase in heart rate and blood pressure. These reflexes may be particularly important in increasing the output of the heart during the early phases of exercise.

In most people, the Frank–Starling mechanism and mechanical reflexes are capable of increasing cardiac output more than 100% without assistance from the other mechanisms that control the heart. However, the various control mechanisms operate at the same time. Thus, mechanical and neural controls work together to increase heart rate and stroke volume. Exceptions include heart transplant patients who operate with only intrinsic controls.

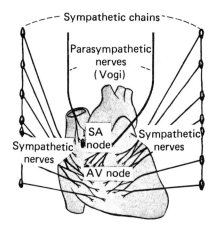

Figure 7-8

The cardiac nerves.

(SOURCE: A. C. Guyton. Textbook of Medical Physiology. Philadelphia; W. B. Saunders, 1976, p. 171. In: G. A. Brooks and T. D. Fahey. Exercise Physiology: Human Bioenergetics and Its Applications. New York: Macmillan, 1984, Figure 14-7.)

Extrinsic Control of the Heart

Extrinsic controls consist of nervous reflexes and hormones. These controls regulate the heart rate and strength of contraction of the heart muscle. Many of these mechanisms are also involved in the control of circulation. In addition, physiological mechanisms that control arterial blood pressure, blood volume, and the intake of fluid and electrolytes ultimately have an effect on the heart.

Circulatory requirements during exercise easily exceed the ability of the mechanical autoregulatory mechanisms to increase cardiac output. Fortunately, the heart is supplied with both sympathetic and parasympathetic nerves from the automatic nervous system (Figure 7-8). The sympathetic nervous system increases both the contractile strength of the heart and the heart rate, while the parasympathetic nervous system decreases the heart rate. A summary of the effects of sympathetic and parasympathetic nerves on cardiovascular function is shown in Table 7-2.

The majority of cardiovascular sympathetic and parasympathetic reflexes are controlled by the vasomotor center of the brain located in the lower third of the pons and the upper two-thirds of the medulla. The center emits constant impulses that maintain the circulation in a sympathetic tone (partially vasoconstricting the circulatory vessels and moderately elevating the heart rate). When the vasomotor center is stimulated, sympathetic fibers, including those to the heart, are stimulated. When the center is inhibited, sympathetic tone is decreased and cardiac function is depressed. The center can be greatly affected by higher brain centers, which explains the effects of emotions on cardiac function. These actions are balanced by a simultaneous supression of cardiac function by the vagus nerve (parasympathetic) that is operational to a heart rate of approximately 150 beats per minute.

TABLE 7-2 Effects of the Autonomic Nervous System on the Cardiovascular Function

Effects of Sympathetic Nerves	Effects of Parasympathetic Nerves
↑ Heart rate	↓ Heart rate
↑ Strength of contraction	↓ Strength of atrial contraction
Vasodilation of coronary arteries	Vasoconstriction of coronary arteries
Mild vasoconstriction of pulmonary vessels	Dilation of skin blood vessels
Vasoconstriction in abdomen, muscle (adrenergic), skin (adrenergic), and kidneys	
Vasodilation of muscle (cholinergic) and skin (cholinergic)	

SOURCE: G. A. Brooks and T. D. Fahey. Exercise Physiology: Human Bioenergetics and Its Applications. New York: Macmillan, 1984, Table 14-2.

Parasympathetic neurons innervate the SA node, the atrial myocardium, and the AV node. Stimulation of the parasympathetic system has a depressant effect on the heart, resulting in cardiac slowing and a delay in atrioventricular conduction. At rest, signals through the vagus nerve elicit a parasympathetic tone on the heart that lowers heart rate. This tone is thought by some to increase with training, which may account for the lower resting heart rates found in endurance athletes (a controversial viewpoint).

Sympathetic neurons innervate the SA node, the atrial myocardium, the AV node, and the ventricular myocardium. Sympathetic stimulation is directed at increasing blood pressure by peripheral vasoconstriction of blood vessels and stimulating heart rate and force of cardiac contraction. At the same time, the sympathetics allow more blood to pass through the coronary arteries.

Baroreceptors

The baroreceptors, which are stimulated by stretch, detect changes in blood pressure. They are located principally in the carotid arteries and aorta but exist in the walls of all the major arteries. When stimulated, they act to inhibit sympathetic centers, which tends to reduce cardiac output. When pressure falls, they produce an opposite reflex: they send fewer impulses to the medulla of the brain, which decreases parasympathetic tone to the heart and increases sympathetic tone to the heart and blood vessels. The result is an increase in cardiac output and vasoconstriction that elevates the blood pressure. The baroreceptors are important for maintaining blood pressure during changes in posture. Their sensitivity is thought to be reduced during exercise.

Hormonal Controls

Large portions of the sympathetic nervous system are stimulated both during exercise and in anticipation of exercise. The sympathetics are turned on as a unit, so that the body is ready for the demands of exercise. These sympathetic effects include an increase in heart rate, cardiac contractility, stroke volume, circulatory vasoconstriction in inactive areas, vasodilation in active muscles, metabolic rate, carbohydrate mobilization, recruitment of motor units, and mental acuity.

The mass action discharge of the system has both specific and general effects on the circulation: individually innervated areas such as the heart and blood vessels are directly stimulated to increase blood pressure, while sympathetic stimulation of the adrenal medulla has general circulatory effects because of the release of the catecholamines—mostly epinephrine and a small amount of norepinephrine. Thus, while the heart is directly innerevated by sympathetic nerves, it is also stimulated by the hormonal action of the adrenal medulla.

Control of Circulation

Circulatory control during exercise is directed toward maintaining blood pressure and central blood volume (facilitating the return of blood to the heart), maintaining blood flow to the brain, and increasing blood flow to the heart, active skeletal muscles, and skin. During exercise, the autonomic nervous system tends to elicit a general circulatory vasoconstriction (restriction of blood flow) that is proportional to the intensity of physical activity. However, this tendency is overridden by local circulatory control mechanisms in the brain, heart, active skeletal muscles, and skin that results in a maintenance or increase in blood flow to these tissues.

At rest, a relatively large portion of the cardiac output is directed to the spleen, liver, kidneys, brain, and heart. Although muscles constitute over 40% of the body's tissue, they receive only about 20% of the total blood flow. During exercise, however, the muscles can receive more than 85% of the cardiac output.

Structure and Function of the Circulation

The blood vessels consist of (1) arteries, which serve to transport blood under pressure to the tissues, (2) arterioles and precapillary sphincters, which act as valves to control blood flow to the various tissues, (3) capillaries, which

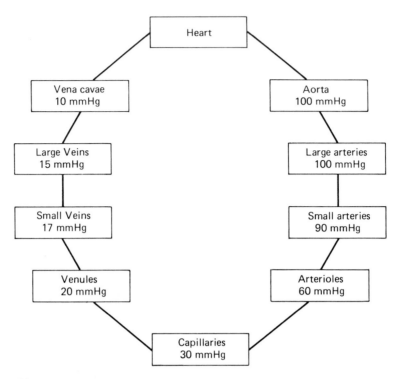

Figure 7-9

Mean internal pressure in the circulation.

(SOURCE: G. A. Brooks and T. D. Fahey. Exercise Physiology: Human Bio-energetics and Its Applications. New York: Macmillan, 1984, Figure 15-2.)

act as an exchange medium between blood and the interstitial spaces, (4) venules, which collect blood from the capillaries, and (5) veins, which return blood to the heart. Another related system, the lymphatics, returns small amounts of plasma and proteins into the veins and is integrally related to circulatory function. The circulation is subdivided into the systemic and pulmonary circulations.

The blood pressure in the arteries is relatively high but diminishes throughout the circulation until it approaches 0 mm Hg. when it reaches the right atrium (Figure 7-9). The greatest resistance to flow occurs in the arterioles, and precapillary sphincters. Blood flow control in these areas is critically important for maintaining blood pressure and ensuring tissue blood supply, particularly during exercise. The regulation of blood flow occurs in these areas as a result of a combination of sympathetic neural control mechanisms and local chemical vasoconstrictors and vasodilators.

At rest, the arterioles in the inactive muscle remain mostly vasocon-stricted, which allows the blood to be directed to other areas. However, dur-

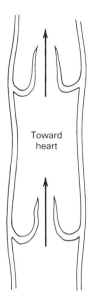

Figure 7-10
Venous valves are structured so that blood can move only toward the heart.

ing exercise, when more blood is needed by the working muscles, the arterioles supplying blood to the muscles vasodilate, thus allowing the transportation of the required oxygen and nutrients.

Blood passes through the arterioles into the capillaries where gases, substrates, fluids, and metabolites are exchanged. Capillary blood flow is controlled by circulatory driving pressure provided by the heart and by resistance provided by the arterioles, precapillary sphincters, and veins. Because the capillaries contain no smooth muscle, they play no role in regulating their own blood flow.

By far the largest portion of the blood volume (approximately 60%) resides in the veins. The veins are sometimes called the "venous capacitance system" because of their storage capacity. The veins can be constricted by sympathetic stimulation and by mechanical compression—both important factors during exercise. Every time muscles are contracted, the veins are compressed, which propels blood toward the heart. Respiration and negative pressure created by the pumping action of the heart can also stimulate blood flow in the veins. Valves in the veins prevent the blood from flowing away from the heart (Figure 7-10).

Determinants of Blood Flow

The rate at which blood flows through the circulation is dictated by the blood pressure. Blood pressure is the product of cardiac output, the amount of blood

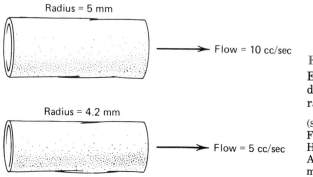

Figure 7-11

Effect of decreasing the radius of a tube 16% on flow rate at a constant pressure.

(SOURCE: G. A. Brooks and T. D. Fahey. Exercise Physiology: Human Bioenergetics and Its Applications. New York: Macmillan, 1984, Figure 15-5.)

pumped from the heart per minute, and peripheral resistance—the resistance to blood flow provided by the circulation (Eq. 7-2).

$$\text{Blood pressure (BP)} = \text{Cardiac output} \cdot \text{Total peripheral resistance} \quad (7\text{-}2)$$

At a constant cardiac output, local tissue blood flow is regulated by increasing or decreasing the size or resistance in the local blood vessels. This is expressed by Poiseuille's law (Eq. 7-3):

$$F = \frac{(P_1 - P_2)\pi R^4}{8LN} \quad (7\text{-}3)$$

where:
F = flow rate,
$(P_1 - P_2)$ = the drop in pressure,
R = the radius of the vessel
L = the length of the vessel, and
N = the viscosity of the fluid.

Pressure is perhaps the most important factor that increases blood flow. Blood flow between two points is directly proportional to the driving force between them. During exercise, blood flow to active muscle can be increased as much as 25 times by increasing the cardiac output and thus the driving force of blood through the circulation.

The distribution of blood is controlled mainly by variations in the size of the arterioles (i.e., flow is proportional to the radius^4). These controls are extremely sensitive. For example, a decrease in the radius by one-half will decrease blood flow to 1/16 of the original value. Thus, a very small increase in a vessel's radius will result in a significant change in its blood flow (Figure 7-11).

Peripheral Vascular Regulation and Control

Vasodilation of blood vessels in active muscle and vasoconstriction in other areas are controlled by intrinsic autoregulation and extrinsic control by the autonomic nervous system. Local regulation of blood flow is directed toward meeting tissue requirements, while extrinsic autonomic neural control is directed toward maintaining blood pressure.

Autoregulation of Blood Flow

Autoregulation or local control of blood flow occurs in response to tissue demands for oxygen and fuels and responses to CO_2, osmolality of the extracellular fluid, adenosine, ATP, K^+, pH, and temperature. Muscle blood flow increases with the intensity of exercise. As oxygen requirements of muscles increase, the arterioles vasodilate to allow more blood flow. At lower levels of metabolism, the precapillary sphincters open and then close. At higher intensities, the vessels tend to stay open.

Changes in arterial pressure, by themselves, have little affect on muscle blood flow because local blood flow control (autoregulation) dictates whether the local circulation vasodilates or vasoconstricts. As discussed, this is very important during exercise because sympathetic stimulation tends to produce a general vasoconstriction. Thus, blood flow can increase in active muscles that need oxygen and nutrients and decrease in inactive muscles and tissues that have lower metabolic requirements.

Muscle blood flow can be blocked during isometric or heavy isotonic contractions, because of the compression of blood vessels. When free flow is restored, blood flow to the area can increase many times above normal, resulting in a phenomenon known as reactive hyperemia. A good example of reactive hyperemia is the increase in muscle size following weight lifting exercise. Many novice weight lifters interpret the increased girth as evidence that the muscle is growing before their eyes; however, it is only the result of increased blood flow, and the muscles will shrink to their normal size in a short time.

Autonomic Nervous System Control of Blood Flow

Although autoregulation is a potent means of ensuring muscle blood flow during exercise, neural and humoral mechanisms are also vital. Exercise requires a rapid redistribution of blood to the active muscles. Hormones and the sympathetic nervous system can cause rapid vasoconstriction in the viscera and inactive muscles so that blood pressure can be maintained or increased and blood can be effectively rechanneled to working muscles.

Sympathetic vasoconstrictor fibers are widely distributed in the circulation but are particularly potent in the spleen, kidneys, skin, and gut. Their distribution in muscle, brain, and heart is much less, which is convenient for the circulatory changes that occur during exercise. Sympathetic stimulation that occurs with exercise stimulates the heart and progressively increases vasoconstriction in the spleen, kidneys, gut, and in many instances, the skin. In addition, sympathetic stimulation of the veins causes them to constrict, resulting in an increased return of blood to the heart.

The sympathetics also have more specific actions that are important during exercise. Blood flow to the skin can be affected independently to cause either vasodilation or vasoconstriction. Thus, while other inactive areas are vasoconstricted during exercise, the skin can be vasodilated to facilitate body cooling. Muscles also contain sympathetic vasodilators that act to increase blood flow during exercise. Although these vasodilators are relatively weak, they definitely contribute to increasing muscle blood flow during physical activity.

During exercise, blood flow to the brain must be maintained at a constant rate, and flow to active muscles and the heart needs to be increased. Because sympathetic stimulation in these areas is less prolific than to organs such as the kidneys and spleen, autoregulatory and other mechanisms facilitate blood flow to the brain, heart, and active muscles.

Hormonal Control Mechanisms

The release of epinephrine and norepinephrine from the adrenal medulla affects the circulation as well as the heart. In the heart both hormones enhance the effect of the specific sympathetic stimulation. However, they have dissimilar effects on circulatory vasoconstriction. Both hormones stimulate the heart by increasing its rate, force and speed of contraction, speed of conduction, and excitability. However, while norepinephrine causes peripheral vasoconstriction epinephrine causes vasodilation.

Long-Term Regulation of Blood Flow

There are also long-term regulatory mechanisms for controlling blood flow to the tissues. The two most important long-term mechanisms having implications in exercise physiology are increased vascularity in response to local metabolism and control of blood and fluid volumes.

Vascularization

Endurance training and long-term exposure to altitude will lead to increased vascularization (increased blood supply) in skeletal muscle. In general, the degree of adaptation reflects the chronic metabolic demands placed on the tissues. The vascularization will also reverse itself if the metabolic demand diminishes.

After myocardial infarction (heart attack), collateral circulation is developed in the heart to improve circulation. Collaterals are accessory vessels that branch from the coronaries to help restore blood flow to an area of the heart. It has been hypothesized that exercise training enhances the development of these collaterals after a myocardial infarction; unfortunately, present evidence suggests that this does not occur in humans. The circulatory benefits of exercise in the myocardial infarction patient are probably due to peripheral changes rather than to changes in the coronary circulation. In addition, presently no evidence indicates that collateral circulation develops in a healthy heart in response to exercise training.

Control of Blood Volume

Total blood volume seems to be related to endurance fitness. Athletes have a higher blood volume, plasma volume (noncellular portion of blood), total hemoglobin content, and erythrocyte (red blood cell) volume. Increased blood volumes facilitates venous return of blood to the heart, which increases cardiac output by the Frank–Starling mechanism (the heart tends to pump the blood returned to it). Increased blood volume also "allows" better perfusion of nonexercising tissues during exercise.

The control of blood volume is an important consideration in cardiovascular performance at rest and during exercise. As we have seen, cardiac output capacity depends on venous return of blood to the heart. If blood volume is too low, then the capacity of the heart is diminished because it has less blood to pump. If blood volume is high, then cardiac output and arterial blood pressure will increase.

Blood volume control is part of an integrated system involving regulation of extracellular fluid, intracellular fluid, and fluid intake. You cannot affect one of these factors without affecting the others.

The kidney regulates the rate of fluid excretion by determining the rate of urine formation and electrolyte reabsorption. The hormone ADH (antidiuretic hormone or vasopressin) controls water output in the kidney. Sodium and potassium are controlled by the hormones aldosterone, ADH, and angiotensin.

Fluid intake is extremely important for the maintenance of blood volume. Usually, the thirst mechanism stays abreast with the body's fluid requirements. (Note: thirst does not always parallel fluid requirement, particularly during exercise in the heat.) Fluid intake is an important consideration in exercise physiology. When fluids are ingested, both blood volume and interstitial fluid volume increase.

Blood volume increases with exercise training. These adaptations occur rapidly: after a few days of endurance training, plasma volume can be increased by almost 400 ml, even in relatively fit individuals. This adaptation is an important consideration in producing the increase in stroke volume that occurs with endurance training.

There appear to be two mechanisms that produce the increase in blood volume with endurance training. The initial increase is due to large increases in plasma renin and ADH levels during exercise. This results in an increased retention of sodium and water by the kidneys. Chronic training leads to an increase in plasma protein, mainly albumin, which increases the osmolality of the blood. This allows the blood to hold more fluid.

Summary

The control of the heart is directed toward satisfying cellular metabolic demands and maintaining blood pressure. A combination of neural, mechanical, and hormonal regulation synchronizes the activity of the heart and circulation to ensure the optimal distribution of blood flow.

The heart is regulated by intrinsic and extrinsic control mechanisms. Intrinsic controls, such as the Frank–Starling mechanism, work largely by adjusting to changes in venous return of blood to the heart. Extrinsic controls consist of nervous regulators and hormones, including sympathetic and parasympathetic nerves, baroreceptors, chemoreceptors, and catecholamines.

During exercise blood must be rapidly directed to working muscles to meet their demands for oxygen and substrates. The mechanisms that control blood flow make it possible to maintain or increase blood pressure, to continue supplying blood to the tissues, and to satisfy the metabolic requirements of working muscles.

Circulation is regulated by autoregulation and neural-hormonal control mechanisms. Autoregulation—self regulation of blood flow according to the local biochemical environment—is the principal mechanism that channels blood to muscles and the heart during exercise. It works by responding to tissue O_2, fuels, CO_2, hydrogen ion, adenosine, K^+, and temperature. Neural-hormonal control mechanisms facilitate distribution of blood to active muscles and away from viscera and inactive muscles. Circulating catecholamines and the renin-angiotensin system are involved in the acute control of blood pressure and flow, whereas changes in vascularization and fluid volumes are more important as long-term controls.

Selected Readings

BADEER, H.S. Cardiovascular Physiology: A synopsis. New York: Karger, 1984.

BERN, R.M. and M.N. LEVY. Cardiovascular Physiology. St. Louis: C.V. Mosby, 1977.

BRODAL, P., F. INGJER, and L. HERMANSEN. Capillary supply of skeletal muscle fibers in untrained and endurance trained men. Am. J. Physiol. 232:H705–712, 1977.

BROOKS, G.A. and T.D. FAHEY. Exercise Physiology: Human Bioenergetics and Its Applications. New York: Macmillan, 1984.

CHRISTENSEN, N.J., and H. GALBO. Sympathetic nervous activity during exercise. Annu. Rev. Physiol. 45:139–153, 1983.

CHUNG, E.K. (ed.). Exercise Electrocardiography: Practical Approach. Baltimore: Williams & Wilkins, 1979.

DUBIN, D. Rapid Interpretation of EKG'S. Tampa Fla.: Cover Publishing, 1980.

ELLESTAD, M.H. Stress Testing. Principles and Practice. Philadelphia: F.A. Davis, 1976.

GUYTON, A. et al. Integration and control of circulatory function. In: Guyton, A. (ed.). Cardiovascular Physiology II. Baltimore: University Park Press, 1976, pp. 341–386.

HONIG, C.R., and T.E.J. GAYESKI. Mechanisms of capillary recruitment: relation to flow, tissue PO_2, and motor unit control of skeletal muscle. In: Advances in Physiological Sciences. Oxford: Pergammon, 1981.

HONIG, C.R., C.L. ODOROFF, and J.L. FRIERSON. Active and passive capillary control in red muscle at rest and in exercise. Am. J. Physiol. 243:H196–H206, 1982.

IKAHEIMO, M.J., I.J. PALASTI, and J.T. TAKKUNEN. Noninvasive evaluation of the athletic heart: sprinters versus endurance runners. Am. J. Cardiol. 44:24–30, 1979.

INGJER, F. Maximal aerobic power related to the capillary supply of the quadriceps femoris muscle in man. Acta Physiol. Scand. 104:238–240, 1978.

MORGANROTH, J., and J. MARON. The athlete's heart syndrome: a new perspective. Ann. New York Acad. Sci. 301:931–941, 1977.

MUMFORD, M. and R. PRAKASH. Electrocardiographic and echocardiographic characteristics of long distance runners. Am. J. Sports Med. 9:23–28, 1981.

PARKER, B.M., B.R. LONDEREE, G.V. CUPP, and J.P. DUBIEL. The noninvasive cardiac evaluation of long distance runners. Chest 73:376–381, 1978.

ROST, R. The athlete's heart. Eur. Heart J. 3(Suppl. A):193–198, 1982.

RUCH, T.C. and H.D. PATTON (eds.). Physiology and Biophysics. Philadelphia: W.B. Saunders, 1974, pp. 120–167.

SOKOLOW, M. and M.B. McILROY. Clinical Cardiology. Los Altos, Calif.: Lange Medical Publications, 1977, pp. 1–29.

STONE, H.L. Control of the coronary circulation during exercise. Annu. Rev. Physiol. 45:213–227, 1983.

STONE, H.L. and I.Y.S. LIANG. Cardiovascular response and control during exercise. Am. Rev. Respir. Dis. 129(Suppl.)S13–S16, 1984.

SUGISHITA, Y., and S. KOSEKI. Dynamic exercise echocardiography. Circulation 60:743–752, 1979.

8

Oxygen Transport Dynamics during Exercise

(AP/Wide World Photos.)

At rest in the healthy person, the cardiovascular system has little difficulty supplying oxygen and fuels to the body's tissues and removing waste products. During exercise, the demands on this system can increase considerably. The amount of oxygen delivered to the working muscles increases with the intensity of exercise. This is accomplished by increasing cardiac output, directing blood to working muscles and vital areas (e.g., the heart and brain), and directing blood away from less active tissues (e.g., the viscera and inactive muscles). In addition, blood is directed to the skin to help dissipate heat produced by the increased metabolism of exercise.

The capacity of the cardiovascular system to transport oxygen to working muscles is critical in determining performance levels in endurance exercise. There is a limit to the body's ability to increase the transport and use of oxygen, called maximal oxygen consumption ($\dot{V}O_{2max}$). $\dot{V}O_{2max}$ largely determines how fast a person can perform endurance exercises and for how long. It is considered the best measure of the capacity of the cardiovascular system and the major determinant of "whole-body" endurance.

This chapter will discuss the responses of the cardiovascular system to exercise, the limits of cardiovascular performance, and the effects of training on the cardiovascular system.

Cardiovascular Responses to Exercise

As discussed in Chapter 7, the heart and blood vessels respond to the metabolic demands of the body by increasing blood flow to active areas and decreasing blood flow to less critical areas. The principal cardiovascular responses to exercise include: (1) activation of the sympathetic nervous system, resulting in local and general circulatory release of catecholamines such as norepinephrine and epinephrine (see Table 7-2 for a summary of the effects of the sympathetic nervous system on the heart and circulation); (2) increased cardiac output, resulting in increased oxygen and substrate (fuel) delivery and increased CO_2 and metabolite removal in active skeletal muscles and the heart; (3) increased skin blood flow to help remove heat; (4) decreased blood flow to the kidneys, resulting in a diminished urinary output; (5) decreased visceral blood flow, resulting in reduced digestion and glandular secretion; and (6) maintenance of blood flow to the brain. Cardiovascular changes with exercise and with training are shown in Table 8-1.

The cardiovascular responses to physical activity depend on the type and intensity of exercise. Dynamic exercise requiring a large muscle mass elicits the greatest response from the cardiovascular system. Large increases occur in cardiac output, heart rate, and systolic blood pressure, with little change in diastolic blood pressure. Strength exercises, which require less muscle mass than whole-body endurance exercises, cause marked increased in systolic,

TABLE 8-1 Changes in Cardiovascular and Pulmonary Function as a Result of Endurance-Type Physical Training[a]

Measurement	Resting Pre		Post	Upright Submaximal "Steady-State" Exercise Pre		Post	Upright Maximal Exercise Pre		Post
Heart rate (beats · min⁻¹)	70	0	63	150	−	130	185	0	182
Stroke volume (ml · beat⁻¹)	72	+	80	90	+	102	90	+	105
Cardiac output (liters · min⁻¹)	5.0	0	5.0	13.5	0	13.2	16.6	+	19.1
(A–V)O₂ Difference (vol %)	5.6	+ 0	5.6	11.0	+	11.3	16.2	0	16.5
O₂ uptake (liters · min)	0.280	0	0.280	1.485	0	1.485	2.685	+	3.150
(ml · kg⁻¹ · min⁻¹)	3.7	0	3.7	19.8	0	19.8	35.8	+	42.0
(METs)[b]	1.0	0	1.0	5.7	0	5.7	10.2	+	12.0
Work load (kg · kg · min⁻¹)	—		—	600	0	600	1050	+	1500
Blood pressure (mm Hg)									
Systemic arterial systolic BP	120	0	114	156	0	140	200	0	200
Systemic arterial diastolic BP	75	0	70	80	0	75	85	0	75
Systemic arterial mean	90	0	88	126	0	118	155	0	152
Total peripheral resistance (dyne sec · cm⁻⁵)	1250	0	1250	750	0	750	450	0	390
Blood flow (ml · min⁻¹)									
Coronary	260	−	250	600	−	560	900	+ 0	940
Brain	750	0	740	740	0	740	740	0	740
Viscera	2400	0	2500	900	+ 0	1000	500	0	500
Inactive muscle	600	±	555	500	0	500	300	0	300
Active muscle	600	−	555	10,360	0	10,000	13,760	+	16,220
Skin	400	0	400	400	0	400	400	0	400
Total	5000		5000	13,500		13,200	16,600		19,100
Blood volume (liters)	5.1	+ 0	5.3						
Plasma volume (liters)	2.8	+ 0	3.0						
Red cell mass (liters)	2.3	0	2.3						
Heart volume (ml)	730	+ 0	785						
Pulmonary ventilation (liters · min⁻¹)	10.2	0	10.3	44.8	0	38.2	129	+	145
Respiratory rate (breaths · min⁻¹)	12	0	12	30	−	24	43	+	52
Tidal volume	850	0	855	1.5	0	1.6	3.0	0	2.8
Lung diffusing capacity (D_L) (ml at STPD)[c]	34.1	0	35.2	40.6	0	42.8	48.2	+	50.6
Pulmonary capillary blood volume (ml)	90.1	+	97.2	129.3	+	141.2	124.5	+	220.0
Vital capacity (liters)	5.1	0	5.2						
Blood lactic acid (mM)	0.7	+ 0	0.7	3.9	−	3.0	11.0	0	12.4
Blood pH	7.43	0	7.43	7.41	0	7.43	7.33	0	7.29
Recovery Rate					+			+	

[a] Estimated for a healthy man, age 45, weighing 75 kg. pre = pretraining; post = posttraining; minus (−) sign means usually decrease in value with training; plus (+) sign means usually increase in value with training; zero (0) sign usually no change in value with training.

[b] A MET is equal to the O₂ cost at rest. One MET is generally equal to 3.5 ml · kg⁻¹ of body weight per minute of O₂ uptake or 1.2 cal · min⁻¹.

[c] STPD is standard temperature (0°C), pressure 760 mm Hg.

SOURCE: G. A. Brooks and T. D. Fahey. Exercise Physiology: Human Bioenergetics and Its Applications. New York: Macmillan, 1984, pp. 332–333; data courtesy of W. Haskell.

diastolic, and mean blood pressure, with more moderate increases in heart rate and cardiac output.

Oxygen Consumption

The rate of oxygen consumption is roughly proportional to the intensity of exercise. Oxygen consumption is determined by the rate at which oxygen is transported to the tissues, the oxygen carrying capacity of blood, and the amount of oxygen extracted from the blood (Eq. 8-1).

$$\dot{V}O_2 = (f_H)(V_S)(a\text{-}\bar{v})O_2 \text{ difference} \tag{8-1}$$

$$\dot{V}O_2 = \dot{Q}(a - \bar{v})O_2 \text{ difference}$$

where:

$f_H = HR =$ heart rate (i.e., the number of heartbeats per minute),
$V_S = SV =$ stroke volume (i.e., the amount of blood ejected from the left ventricle per cardiac contraction expressed in milliliters),
$(a - \bar{v})O_2$ difference = the difference in oxygen content between the arteries and veins, expressed in milliliters per 100 ml of blood or volumes percent (vol %) (This is a measure of oxygen extraction by the tissues.),
$\dot{Q} =$ cardiac output (i.e., the amount of blood pumped by the left ventricle of the heart), expressed in liters · min^{-1}. (Cardiac output is a function of the heart rate and stroke volume.)

During an exercise in which the intensity gradually proceeds from rest to maximal intensity, stroke volume increases during the early phase of exercise (i.e., to 25% of maximum), and heart rate and (a-$\bar{v}$)O$_2$ difference increase almost linearly with intensity (Figures 8-1, 8-2, and 8-3). Cardiac output and (a-$\bar{v}$)O$_2$ difference each account for about 50% of the increase in oxygen consumption during submaximal exercise, but cardiac output (mainly due to increased heart rate) plays an increasing role as the intensity approaches maximum, accounting for approximately 75% of the increased oxygen uptake above rest.

Oxygen carrying capacity of blood is approximately 18 to 20 ml $O_2 \cdot dl^{-1}$ in most healthy people living at sea level (males slightly higher than females because of higher hemoglobin content in males). Oxygen carrying capacity is higher in high altitude natives (as high as 30 vol %) and in people practicing blood doping (i.e., induced erythrocythemia). Blood is withdrawn and stored. After the person's blood volume and red blood cells (RBCs) rise to normal, the RBCs are reinfused, which increases the blood's oxygen carrying capacity (see Chapter 13). In most people, however, oxygen carrying capacity is relatively stable and can be considered a constant in the oxygen consumption equation.

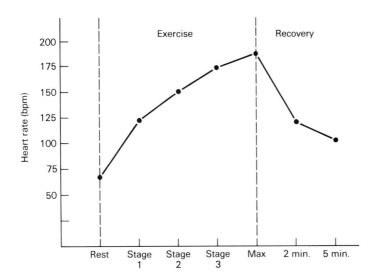

Figure 8-1
Heart rate response of a 30-year-old man during and after a Bruce treadmill test. Maximal heart rate is relatively independent of functional capacity. Resting, submaximal, and recovery heart rates tend to decrease following an extended period of endurance training.

Oxygen consumption increases with exercise intensity until it plateaus near maximal effort (i.e., maximal oxygen consumption, $\dot{V}O_{2max}$). After $\dot{V}O_{2max}$ is reached, further increases in exercise intensity do not lead to a further increase in oxygen consumption. $\dot{V}O_{2max}$ will be discussed in more detail in this chapter and in Chapter 17.

There is very little variability between individuals in oxygen consumption performing at the same power output or exercise intensity. If a world-class cyclist and a sedentary individual ride a bicycle ergometer at the same power output, their oxygen consumptions will be very similar. The power output will represent a lower percentage of maximum for the cyclist but the oxygen cost will be the same. However, the bout of exercise must be con-

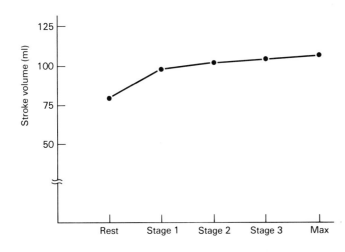

Figure 8-2
Stroke volume of a 30-year-old man during a Bruce treadmill test. Stroke volume increases during the early stages of exercise. Heart rate contributes relatively more to the total cardiac output as the intensity of exercise approaches maximum.

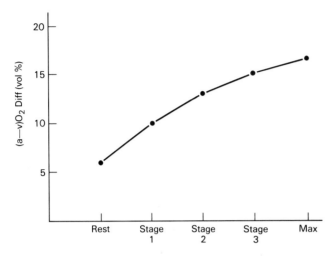

Figure 8-3
$(a-v)_{O_2}$ difference of a 30-year-old man during a Bruce treadmill test. This measure changes very little with training.

ducted under identical conditions (i.e., same environment, pedal revolutions, etc.).

Heart Rate

Heart rate is the most important factor increasing cardiac output during exercise. In dynamic exercise, heart rate rises with exercise intensity and oxygen consumption, leveling off at $\dot{V}_{O_{2}max}$. Typically, heart rate will rise from a resting value of approximately 70 beats/min to a maximum heart rate of as much as 200 beats (or more). The rate and extent of the increase depend on the type of exercise, and the fitness, age, and sex of the individual.

During submaximal exercise, heart rate rises and then levels off when the oxygen transport requirements of the activity have been satisfied. At increasing intensities, this leveling off of heart rate takes longer and is more difficult to achieve. In prolonged exercise the heart rate increases steadily at the same work rate. This phenomenon, called cardiovascular drift, is caused by a diminished capacity of the circulation to return blood to the heart because of a decreased plasma volume (due to filtration and sweating) and, perhaps a decrease in sympathetic tone. Cardiovascular drift results from a decrease in stroke volume, so that the heart rate must increase to maintain cardiac output and blood pressure at the same level.

At rest and during low intensity submaximal exercise, heart rate may be elevated above normal due to factors such as anxiety, dehydration, ambient temperature, altitude, and digestion. "Resting" heart rates of over 100 to 130 beats/min are not unusual before anxiety-producing situations such as treadmill tests and sports competitions.

Heart rates tend to be lower when one is performing strength exercises such as weight lifting than during endurance exercise such as running. During resistive exercise (weight lifting), the heart rate increases in proportion to the muscle mass used and the percentage of maximum voluntary contraction. Thus, a dynamic lift, such as a clean and jerk, using heavy weights, will increase the heart rate more than a one-arm biceps curl using mimimum resistance.

At the same absolute power output, heart rate is higher during upper body exercise (i.e., arm ergometer) than lower body exercise (i.e., bicycle ergometer). In addition, upper body exercise results in a higher level of $\dot{V}O_2$, systolic and mean arterial pressure, and total peripheral resistance. The greater circulatory load probably results from the use of a smaller muscle mass, a greater isometric exercise component, and a less effective muscle pump that results in a decreased venous return of blood to the heart.

Heart rate can be valuable in writing an individual exercise prescription. By measuring the heart rate either during or immediately after exercise, one can estimate the metabolic cost of the activity (see Chapter 17). Exercise heart rate can provide a reasonable estimate of cardiac load (with blood pressure; rate–pressure product (RPP) = heart rate × systolic blood pressure), providing a rough index for such factors as coronary blood flow, myocardial oxygen consumption ($M\dot{V}O_2$), percentage of $\dot{V}O_{2max}$, and respiratory exchange ratio.

Stroke Volume

Stroke volume increases during exercise in the upright posture (see Figure 8-2). Stroke volume increases steadily until about 25% of $\dot{V}O_{2max}$ and then tends to level off. After peak stroke volume has been achieved, additions in cardiac output occur because of increased heart rate. In a sedentary man, stroke volume can increase from about 72 ml to about 90 ml at maximal exercise.

Stroke volume rises with upright exercise but does not change from rest to exercise when the subject is supine (at rest, stroke volume is higher in the supine than in the upright posture). Studies using a technique called radionuclide angiography indicate that left ventricular end-diastolic volume (EDV, the amount of blood in the left ventricle during the resting or diastolic portion of the cardiac cycle) increases slightly during upright exercise but is unchanged during supine exercise. Ejection fraction increases during upright exercise because of an increased cardiac contractility. Consequently, stroke volume is approximately equal in the supine and erect postures during exercise of the same intensity.

Stroke volume is perhaps the most important factor determining individual differences in $\dot{V}O_{2max}$. This is readily apparent when comparing the components of cardiac output of a sedentary man with those of a champion cross-country skier. Both men have maximum heart rates of 185 beats/min, yet the maximum cardiac output of the untrained man is 16.6 liters·min^{-1}, while that of the skier is 32 liters. The maximum stroke volumes of the skier and the sedentary man were 173 and 90 ml, respectively.

Arteriovenous Oxygen Difference

A linear increase in (a-v)O_2 difference occurs with the intensity of exercise (see Figure 8-3). The resting value of about 5.6 vol % (ml O_2/100 ml) is increased to about 16 vol % at maximal exercise. There is always some oxygenated blood returning to the heart even at exhaustive levels of exercise. This is because some blood continues to flow through metabolically less active tissues that do not fully extract the oxygen from the blood. However, oxygen extraction is almost 100% when (a-v)O_2 difference is measured across a maximally exercising muscle.

Blood Pressure

It is very important that blood pressure increases during exercise; blood flow must be maintained to critical areas such as the heart and brain, as well as satisfy the requirements of the working muscles and skin. Blood pressure is a function of cardiac output and peripheral resistance (Eq. 8-2).

$$\text{Blood pressure (mm Hg)} = \dot{Q} \cdot \text{TPR} \tag{8-2}$$

where

$$\dot{Q} = \text{cardiac output (liter} \cdot \text{min}^{-1}), \text{ and}$$
$$\text{TPR} = \text{total peripheral resistance (dyne sec} \cdot \text{cm}^{-5}).$$

Peripheral resistance decreases during exercise, but blood pressure increases. This occurs because of the large increase in cardiac output, and vasoconstriction in nonworking tissues is not quite great enough to compensate for the vasodilation in the working muscles.

Systolic blood pressure rises steadily during exercise from about 120 mm Hg at rest to 180 mm Hg or more during maximal exercise (Figure 8-4). It follows the same general trend as the heart rate. The increase in variable—maximum systolic pressures can vary from as little as 150 to more than 250 mm Hg in a normal individual. Likewise, the mean arterial pressure [MAP = 1/3(systolic blood pressure − diastolic blood pressure) + diastolic blood pressure] rises from about 90 mm Hg at rest to about 155 mm Hg at maximal exercise. Failure to increase systolic and mean arterial blood pressures during exercise (or fall in pressure near the end of an exercise stress test) is an indication of heart failure and an absolute reason for stopping an exercise tolerance test.

There is debate about the maximum safe systolic pressure during exercise. Although some experts do not become overly concerned about pressures above even 250 mm Hg, others suggest terminating stress tests at levels above

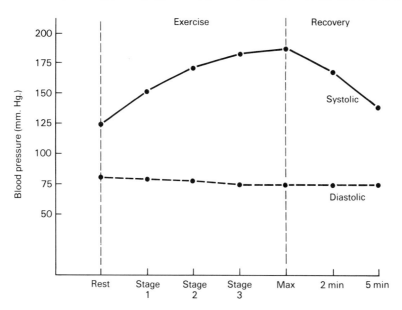

Figure 8-4
Blood pressure response of a 30-year-old man during and after a
Bruce treadmill test. Falling systolic blood pressure or excessive increases in systolic or diastolic blood pressure are absolute indications for stopping an exercise test.

220 mm Hg. It is important to look at the characteristics of the subject. A
high systolic pressure is very significant in a hypertensive patient but is
probably meaningless in a world-class endurance athlete. During exercise,
systolic blood pressure increases with cardiac output. Because endurance athletes have extremely high cardiac output capacities, their systolic blood pressures will naturally be higher. Systolic blood pressure greater than 450 mm
Hg have been reported in weight lifters during exercise with no morbidity.

High systolic pressure during exercise in untrained people is a matter of
concern. The combination of a high heart rate and systolic blood pressure
indicates that the myocardial oxygen consumption (metabolic load on the heart)
is also high. In fact, the rate–pressure–product—(systolic blood pressure)×(heart rate)—is an excellent predictor of myocardial work. If a person
has heart disease, extreme levels of systolic blood pressure could easily result
in myocardial hypoxia (insufficient supply of oxygen for the heart).

Diastolic pressure changes little during exercise in the normal individual. Typically, there is either no change or a slight decrease of less than 10
mm Hg during exercise, and a small decrease during recovery of less than 4
mm Hg. A significant increase in diastolic pressure (greater than 15 mm Hg

or above 110 mm Hg) is associated with a greater prevalence of coronary artery disease.

Blood Flow

During exercise blood is redistributed from inactive to active tissues. Critical areas such as the brain and heart are spared the vasoconstriction that occurs in other areas. There is a progressive increase in the sympathetic vasomotor activity (resulting in vasoconstriction in appropriate tissues) with increasing severity of exercise.

Resting blood flow to the spleen and kidneys is about 2.8 liters·min^{-1}. It is reduced to about 500 ml during maximal exercise. The marked reduction in blood flow to these areas is caused by sympathetic stimulation (sympathetic innervation is particularly potent in these organs) and generally circulating catecholamines. In the kidneys, the reduction in blood flow during exercise is accompanied by postexercise proteinuria (protein in the urine) and, occasionally, by hemoglobinuria and myoglobinuria (hemoglobin and myoglobin in the urine, respectively). These changes are probably due to the decrease in plasma volume (noncellular aspect of blood) that concentrates the blood, increased permeability of the glomeruli, and partial inhibition of reabsorption in the kidney tubules.

Skin blood flow tends to increase during submaximal exercise, but approaches resting values when muscle blood flow is the greatest. The relative skin blood flow (percentage of cardiac output) changes very little during exercise. Peripheral perfusion of cutaneous vessels during exercise, particularly in the heat, contributes to cardiovascular drift and to fatigue during endurance exercise.

Coronary blood flow increases with intensity during exercise from about 260 ml·min^{-1} at rest to 900 ml·min^{-1} at maximal exercise. This large coronary artery reserve is extremely important because it provides adequate blood flow even in the face of significant coronary artery disease. Coronary blood flow is not thought to limit oxygen transport capacity in people without coronary artery disease. However, as discussed in Chapter 6, increases in coronary blood flow occur mainly by autoregulation and mainly during diastole. Therefore, severe coronary artery disease which impedes blood flow will interfere with autoregulatory control of blood flow and may have catastrophic consequences.

Warm-up before endurance exercise is important in facilitating the increase in coronary blood flow during the early stages of exercise. Electrocardiographic changes, which may indicate coronary ischemia (ST segment depression) have been shown to occur in healthy people subjected to sudden strenuous exercise. Although these changes appear to be easily tolerated in healthy individuals, they could be very dangerous in persons with heart disease.

Limits of Cardiovascular Performance: Maximal Oxygen Consumption

Maximal oxygen consumption ($\dot{V}O_{2max}$) is the best measure of the capacity of the cardiovascular system, provided there is no pulmonary disease present. $\dot{V}O_2$ is the product of maximum cardiac output and maximum arteriovenous oxygen difference (Eq. 8-3).

$$\dot{V}O_{2max} = \dot{Q}_{max}\,(a - \bar{v})O_{2\ max} \tag{8-3}$$

where:

$\dot{V}O_{2max}$ = maximal oxygen uptake, expressed in ml · min^{-1},
$\dot{Q}_{max}$ = maximum cardiac output expressed in ml · min^{-1}, and
$(a\text{-}\bar{v})O_{2max}$ = the maximum arterial venous oxygen difference, expressed in ml O_2 · dl^{-1} blood.

Theoretically, $\dot{V}O_{2max}$ is the point at which oxygen consumption fails to rise despite an increased exercise intensity or work load. After $\dot{V}O_{2max}$ has been reached, work can be sustained by nonoxidative metabolism (Figure 8-5). Al-

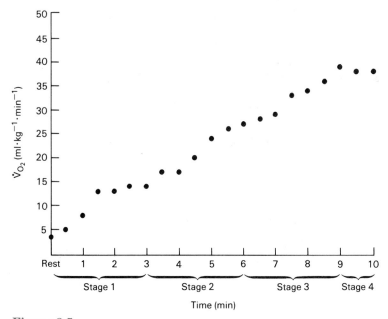

Figure 8-5

$\dot{V}O_2$ (in ml · kg^{-1} · min^{-1}) during a Bruce treadmill test in a 25-year-old woman. Oxygen consumption tends to level off as maximum oxygen transport capacity is reached.

though $\dot{V}O_{2max}$ is the best predictor of cardiovascular capacity, biochemical factors, such as oxidative enzyme activity and the size of the mitochondrial reticulum, are better predictors of endurance (the ability to sustain a particular level of physical effort). In a running race such as the 5000-m run, performance is determined by $\dot{V}O_{2max}$ and biochemical factors that allow the maintenance of a particular level of oxygen consumption.

Cardiac output is the most important factor determining $\dot{V}O_{2max}$. Cardiac output can increase about 20% from endurance training, which accounts for most of the training-induced changes in $\dot{V}O_{2max}$. Maximum arteriovenous oxygen difference, a measure of oxygen extraction, changes very little with training. Also, there is little difference in $(a-\bar{v})O_2$ difference between endurance athletes and the sedentary individual. On the other hand, elite endurance athletes have been known to have maximum cardiac outputs in excess of 35 liters·min^{-1}, almost twice that of the average sedentary person. It is easy to see why the limit of $\dot{V}O_{2max}$ is dictated by the limit of cardiac output.

The measurement of maximal oxygen consumption must satisfy several objective criteria: (1) the exercise must use at least 50% of the total muscle mass continuously and rhythmically for a prolonged period of time; (2) the results must be independent of motivational or skill factors (3) there must be a leveling of oxygen consumption with increasing intensities of exercise; and (4) the measurement must be made under standard experimental conditions—it cannot be made in a stressful environment that exposes the subject to excessive heat, humidity, air pollution, or altitude.

An oxygen consumption measurement made during maximal exercise but not according to the criteria necessary for $\dot{V}O_{2max}$ is called $\dot{V}O_{2peak}$. In many instances, $\dot{V}O_{2peak}$ will equal $\dot{V}O_{2max}$. But it is important to differentiate between the two because of the inferences made regarding the relationship between $\dot{V}O_{2max}$ and oxygen transport capacity.

$\dot{V}O_{2max}$ usually cannot be measured during upper body exercise. An untrained person will fatigue relatively rapidly during this type of work. Typical $\dot{V}O_{2peak}$ on an arm ergometer may be 70% of the $\dot{V}O_{2max}$ measured on a treadmill. However, in a trained rower or canoeist, the difference between the two measurements may be as small as a few percentage points.

$\dot{V}O_{2max}$ is often measured on a bicycle ergometer. However, most studies show that these values are 10 to 15% less than those gathered on a treadmill (see Chapter 17). In addition, cycling skills and body weight affect the results. Thus, even though values gathered on bicycle ergometers are commonly called $\dot{V}O_{2max}$, they are in reality $\dot{V}O_{2peak}$.

An exercise that results in fatigue before the limits of cardiovascular capacity are reached is thus not appropriate for measuring $\dot{V}O_{2max}$ and may not be appropriate for cardiovascular conditioning. An excellent example of this is wheelchair propulsion. Many handicapped individuals use wheelchairs as a means of conditioning their cardiovascular systems (Figure 8-6). However, peak heart rate and $\dot{V}O_{2peak}$ are much less than what could be attained

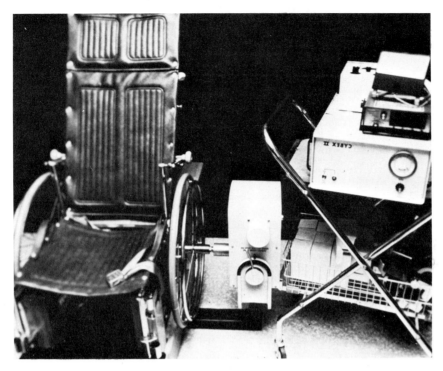

Figure 8-6

An isokinetic wheelchair ergometer. This device is useful for testing subjects who do not have the use of their legs. Local muscle fatigue rather than oxygen transport capacity is limiting in this type of exercise.

(SOURCE: From G. A. Brooks and T. D. Fahey. Exercise Physiology: Human Bioenergetics and Its Applications. New York: Macmillan, 1984, p. 325.)

on other types of exercise. Local muscle fatigue rather than cardiovascular capacity is limiting. Because of this, heavy exercise in a wheelchair may be less useful than other forms of exercise for developing aerobic capacity.

The leveling off criterion of oxygen consumption is sometimes difficult to achieve in untrained subjects. These people are often unable or unwilling to withstand the pain that accompanies work after maximal oxygen consumption has been reached. However, on a treadmill, $\dot{V}O_{2peak}$ usually renders an excellent approximation of $\dot{V}O_{2max}$. A subject typically terminates the test when the limits of cardiovascular capacity have been attained.

There are several practical guidelines for judging whether or not $\dot{V}O_{2peak}$ is equal to $\dot{V}O_{2max}$. Perceived exertion is excellent because there is a high correlation between the perception of exhaustion and $\dot{V}O_{2max}$ (see Chapter 17). There are objective physiological measurements: a respiratory exchange ratio greater than 1.0 ($R = \dot{V}CO_2/\dot{V}O_2$), high blood lactate level (greater than

12 mM), a peak heart rate similar to the age-predicted maximum, or progressively diminishing differences between successive oxygen consumption measurements.

Changes in Cardiovascular Parameters with Training

Endurance training results in adaptive changes in many aspects of cardiovascular function. These changes are summarized in Tables 8-1 and 8-2. In general, the heart improves its ability to pump blood, mainly by increasing its stroke volume. This occurs because of an increase in end-diastolic volume and a small increase in left ventricular muscle mass. These changes are in-

TABLE 8-2   **Cardiovascular Adaptations Resulting from Endurance Training[a]**

Factor	Rest	Submaximal Exercise	Maximal Exercise
Heart rate	↓	↓	0
Stroke volume	↑	↑	↑
$(a-v)$ O_2 difference	0 ↑	↑	↑
Cardiac output	0 ↓	0 ↓	↑
$\dot{V}_{O_2}$	0	0	↑
Work capacity	——	——	↑
Systolic blood pressure	0 ↓	0 ↓	0
Diastolic blood pressure	0 ↓	0 ↓	0
Mean arterial blood pressure	0 ↓	0 ↓	0
Total peripheral resistance	0	0 ↓	0
Coronary blood flow	↓	↓	↑
Brain blood flow	0	0	0
Visceral blood flow	0	↑	0
Inactive muscle blood flow	0	0	0
Active muscle blood flow	↓ 0	↓ 0	↑
Skin blood flow	0	0 ↑	0
Blood volume	↑	——	——
Plasma volume	↑	——	——
Red cell mass	0 ↑	——	——
Heart volume	↑	——	——

[a]Symbols:
   ↑ increase
   ↓ decrease
   0 no change
   —— not applicable

SOURCE: G. A. Brooks and T. D. Fahey. Exercise Physiology: Human Bioenergetics and Its Applications. New York: Macmillan, 1984, p. 326.

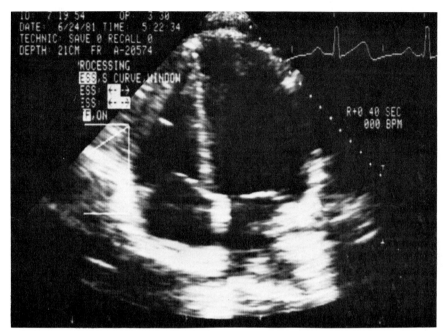

Figure 8-7

Two-dimensional echocardiogram of a world-class discus thrower. Chronic intermittent pressure loads (resistance to outflow of blood from the heart) caused by lifting heavy weights tends to result in increased left ventricular wall size in these types of athletes.

(SOURCE: G. A. Brooks and T. D. Fahey. Exercise Physiology: Human Bioenergetics and Its Applications. New York: Macmillan, 1984, p. 319.)

duced by the increased volume load (increased filling) placed on the heart during endurance exercise. In contrast, strength exercises such as weight lifting subject the heart to a pressure load that results in larger increases in left ventricular muscle mass and little or no change in ventricular volume (Figure 8-7). In addition, endurance exercise decreases the metabolic load on the heart at rest and at any submaximal work rate by increasing stroke volume and decreasing heart rate, thus resulting in a more efficient pressure–time relationship (this has not been consistently demonstrated in cardiac patients).

Endurance, or aerobic, exercise is best for improving the capacity of the cardiovascular system. These exercises require the use of at least 50% of the body's muscle mass in rhythmical exercise, for at least 15 to 20 min, 3 to 5 days a week, and above 50 to 60% of $\dot{V}O_{2max}$ (see Chapter 17). Obviously, considerably more training is required to develop the high levels of fitness required of endurance athletes.

Adaptation to endurance training is somewhat specific. Thus, swimming, for example, will improve cardiovascular performance in that activity but will be much less effective in improving endurance in running. This principle is critically important in multi-endurance events such as triathlons; cycling, running, and swimming must be practiced in order to be a successful triathlete.

Interval training, repeated bouts of short- to moderate-duration exercise, is also used to improve cardiovascular condition. This mode of training manipulates four factors: distance, speed, repetition, and rest. Interval training allows the athlete to train at a higher intensity than is typically employed during competition, and thus acts as an overload. Although this type of training optimizes the development of cardiovascular capacity, it is less effective in eliciting the biochemical changes critical for optimal endurance performance. Therefore, the endurance athlete must practice both interval and over distance training.

Oxygen Consumption

Improvement in maximal oxygen consumption with training will depend on current condition, type of training, and age. Most studies find that $\dot{V}O_{2max}$ can be improved only about 20%. It appears that an athlete must be endowed with a relatively high capacity oxygen transport system to be successful in endurance events. This is not to say that training is not extremely important, but rather that there is only a limited opportunity to improve aerobic capacity ($\dot{V}O_{2max}$).

Heart Rate

Endurance training reduces the resting heart rate. It is not unusual to see resting heart rates of less than 40 beats/min in champion endurance runners. Although some of these extremely low heart rates are probably genetically determined, aerobic training does induce some of it. It is important to note, however, that a low resting heart rate is not necessarily a sign of physical fitness. On the contrary, bradycardia (low heart rate) is sometimes a sign of disease. The reduction in resting heart rate with training is the important sign of fitness, rather than the low heart rate itself.

Training also decreases the heart rate response to a given submaximal level of exercise. Although the metabolic requirement of the work load remains the same (once the movement patterns have been learned), the decline in heart rate does not reduce cardiac output because of a concomitant increase in stroke volume.

Training has only a small effect on maximal heart rate, usually decreasing it by about 3 beats/min. Because maximum heart rate is relatively stable, tending to decrease only with age, it can be used as a reference point for judging the relative intensity of exercise. For example, suppose a person achieved a heart rate of 140 beats/min running a 10-min mile. The person then returned after 6 months of endurance training and ran another 10-min mile, only this time the heart rate was only 130 beats/min. The work load no longer represented the same percentage of maximum heart rate (which remained the same). Because the heart rate decreased at an identical submaximal exercise intensity, the running speed would have to be increased to achieve the same relative intensity of exercise. The use of heart rate for exercise prescription is discussed in Chapter 17.

Stroke Volume

Endurance training increases the stroke volume at rest and during submaximal and maximal exercise. Most studies indicate that training can increase stroke volume by no more than about 20%, the same percentage change as is seen in $\dot{V}O_{2max}$. The tremendous levels seen in world-class runners and cross-country skiers are probably genetically determined.

The training-induced increase in stroke volume seems to be due to a variety of factors: The decreased heart rate results in increased ventricular filling (increased end-diastolic volume), activating the Frank–Starling mechanism (the heart tends to pump the blood that it receives), which enhances ejection. This process is facilitated by an increased ventricular volume, a thickening of the ventricular walls, and an increase in blood volume (principally the plasma volume). The improved myocardial contractility may be due to an increase in Ca^{++}-ATPase activity. Adaptations in heart rate and stroke volume improve the heart's efficiency.

Arteriovenous Oxygen Difference (a-v)O$_2$

(a-v)O$_2$ difference increases slightly with training. Possible mechanisms for the change include a rightward shift of the oxyhemoglobin dissociation curve, mitochondrial adaptations, elevated myoglobin concentration, and increased muscle capillary density. Increased capillary density results in a shorter diffusion distance between the circulation and muscle. The circulatory and biochemical changes appear to be linked. The number of capillaries around each fiber is a good predictor of aerobic power and is related to the mitochondrial content of the fiber. Increased capillarization around muscle fibers is thought to facilitate diffusion during exercise. The adaptation in (a-v)O$_2$ difference does not seem to occur to the same extent in older individuals.

Blood Pressure

Endurance training tends to reduce resting and submaximal exercise systolic, diastolic, and mean arterial blood pressures. Diastolic and mean arterial, but not systolic, blood pressures are reduced at maximal exercise. The mechanism of reduced blood pressure at rest is not known; however, the fact that it occurs is another reason that exercise training is important in reducing the risk of heart disease. However, in some patients with hypertension (high blood pressure), exercise training may increase resting blood pressure.

Blood Flow

With training, coronary blood flow decreases slightly at rest (in some people) and during submaximal exercise. The increased stroke volume and decreased heart rate result in a reduced myocardial oxygen consumption, which decreases the requirements for blood. Coronary blood flow increases at maximal exercise with training, supporting the metabolic requirement of increasing cardiac output. Again, blood flow accommodates to the metabolic load in the normal heart. As discussed, training does not seem to increase myocardial vascularity.

Muscle vascularity (blood vessels in skeletal muscles) increases with endurance training, which facilitates diffusion of oxygen, substrates, and metabolites to the working muscles. In addition, increased vascularity decreased resistance to flow (peripheral resistance), which is a mechanism probably involved in the increased cardiac output observed as a result of endurance training. During submaximal exercise, blood flow to the muscles is lower after training because of increased oxygen extraction (due to improved diffusion capability and muscle respiratory capacity). Decreased muscle blood flow allows more blood to be directed to the viscera. During maximal exercise, muscle blood flow increases by about 10% after training because of a greater cardiac output and muscle vascularity.

The volume of skin blood flow in unaffected by endurance training, but the onset of vasodilation in skin vessels during exercise (along with an earlier onset and increased sweat rate) occurs earlier. This facilitates temperature regulation, which helps the body to cool itself during endurance exercise.

Summary

During the transition from rest to exercise, there is an increase in cardiac output, an increased blood flow to active muscles and the heart, maintenance of blood flow to the brain, and decreased blood flow to the viscera.

Maximal oxygen consumption is the best measure of the capacity of the cardiovascular system and is the product of maximum cardiac output and maximum arteriovenous oxygen difference. The measurement of $\dot{V}O_{2max}$ must satisfy objective criteria of standardization and measurement. $\dot{V}O_{2max}$ is most commonly measured on a treadmill or bicycle ergometer.

Endurance exercise is best for improving the capacity of the cardiovascular system. Training results in increased maximum cardiac output, stroke volume, and blood volume and in decreased resting and submaximal exercise heart rate.

Selected Readings

BHAN, A., and J. SCHEUR. Effects of physical training on cardiac myosin ATPase activity. Am. J. Physiol. 228:1178–1182, 1975.

BROOKS, G.A., and T.D. FAHEY. Exercise Physiology: Human Bioenergetics and Its Applications. New York: Macmillan, 1984.

CLAUSEN, J.P. Effect of physical training on cardiovascular adjustments to exercise in man. Physiol. Rev. 57:779–815, 1977.

COOPER, K., J.G. PURDY, S.R. WHITE, M.J. POLLOCK, and A.C. LINNERUD. Age-fitness adjusted maximal heart rates. BAG Medicine and Sport. 6:1–10, 1976.

FORTNEY, S.M., E.R. NADEL, C.B. WENGER, and J.R. BOVE. Effect of acute alterations of blood volume on circulatory performance in humans. J. Appl. Physiol. 50:292–298, 1981.

FOSTER, C., J.D. ANHOLM, C.K. HELLMAN, J. CARPENTER, M.L. POLLOCK, and D.H. SCHMIDT. Left ventricular function during sudden strenuous exercise. Circulation 63:592–596, 1981.

FRANKLIN, B.A., D. WRISLEY, S. JOHNSON, M. MITCHELL, and M. RUBENFIRE. Chronic adaptations to physical conditioning in cardiac patients. Clin. Sports Med. 3:471–511, 1984.

GISOLFI, C.V., and C.B. WENGER. Temperature regulation during exercise: old concepts, new ideas. Exercise Sports Sci. Rev. 12:339–372, 1984.

KEUL, J., H.H. DICKHUTH, G. SIMON, and M. LEHMANN. Effect of static and dynamic exercise on heart volume, contractility, and left ventricular dimensions. Cir. Res. (Supp. I)48:162–170, 1981.

MAHLER, D.A., and J. LOKE. The physiology of endurance exercise: the marathon. Clin. Chest Med. 5:63–76, 1984.

MELLEROWICZ, H., and V.N. SMODLAKA (ed.). Ergometry: Basics of Medical Exercise Testing. Baltimore: Urban & Schwarzenberg, 1981.

PATE, R.R., and A. KRISKA. Physiological basis of the sex differences in cardiorespiratory endurance. Sports Med. 1:87–98, 1984.

ROWELL, L. Human cardiovascular adjustments to exercise and thermal stress. Physiol. Rev. 54:75–159, 1974.

SANDERS, M., F.C. WHITE, T.M. PETERSON, and C.M. BLOOR. Effects of endurance exercise on coronary collateral blood flow in miniature swine. Am. J. Physiol. 234:H614–H619, 1978.

SCHAIBLE, T.F., and J. SCHEUER. Response of the heart to exercise training. In: Zak, R. (ed.). Growth of the Heart in Health and Disease. New York: Raven Press, 1984, pp. 381–417.

SCHEUER, J., and C.M. TIPTON. Cardiovascular adaptations to physical training. Annu. Rev. Physiol. 39:221–251, 1977.

SLUTSKY, R. Response of the left ventricle to stress: effects of exercise, atrial pacing, afterload stress, and drugs. Am. J. Cardiol. 47:357–364, 1981.

SNELL, P.G., and J.H. MITCHELL. The role of maximal oxygen uptake in exercise performance. Clin. Chest Med. 5:51–62, 1984.

SNOECKX, L., H. ABELING, J. LAMBREGTS, J. SCHMITZ, F. VERSTAPPEN, and R.S. RENE-MAN. Echocardiographic dimensions in athletes in relation to their training programs. Med. Sci. Sports Exercise 14:428–434, 1982.

STROMME, S.B. and F. INGJER. The effect of regular physical training on the cardiovascular system. Scand. J. Soc. Med. (Suppl. 29):37–45, 1982.

SUGA, H., R. HISANO, S. HIRATA, T. HAYASHI, and I. NINOMIYA. Mechanism of higher oxygen consumption rate: pressure-loaded vs. volume-loaded heart. Am. J. Physiol. 242:H942–H948, 1982.

SUTTON, J.R. Control of heart rate in healthy young men. Lancet 2:1398–1400, 1967.

TONER, M.M., M.N. SAWKA, L. LEVINE, and K.B. PANDOLF. Cardiorespiratory responses to exercise distributed between the upper and lower body. J. Appl. Physiol.: Respirat. Environ. Exercise Physiol. 54:1403–1407, 1983.

9

Neuromuscular Structures and Functions

Many of the events of daily living, including those involving physical work performed on the job, magnificent physical performances in athletics and the performing arts, as well as migrations, predatory chases, and flights of survival in the animal kingdom, are but a few of the behaviors supported by muscle contraction. These sometimes fantastic feats of strength and endurance are possible because of the conversion of chemical energy to mechanical energy in muscle. In previous chapters (Chapters 2 through 4), we have described the conversion of the potential chemical energy in foodstuffs into chemical energy forms (glycogen, ATP, CP) used in muscle and other cells. In Chapters 5 through 8, we described the uptake of O_2 from the air by the lungs, oxygenation of the blood, and circulation of blood around the body. Those processes support energy transduction in cells of the body. In this chapter we explain the process by which this stored cellular energy is used to swim, run, jump, and lift and throw things.

Skeletal, cardiac, and smooth muscles are chemomechanical transducers; they convert chemical energy to mechanical and heat energy. By nature, this process is at best 30% efficient, and so 70% of the energy released appears as heat (Chapter 2). At present, the chemical events of muscle contraction are fairly well understood. Progress has also been made toward understanding how those chemical events lead to muscle shortening.

Skeletal Muscle Structure

Skeletal muscle tissue is composed of individual muscle cells (fibers). These fibers are arranged in bundles (fasciculi) and subdivided into myofibrils and myofilaments (Figure 2-A). Integrally arranged in the structure of muscle is connective tissue made up largely of the substance collagen. Connective tissue runs from end to end of muscle (i.e., from the tendon of origin to the tendon of insertion) and exists within muscle tissue surrounding the fibers and giving rise to muscle bundles. In some muscles, the cells run from end to

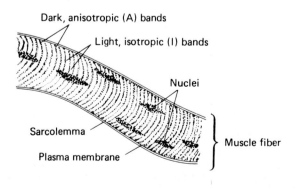

Figure 9-1
Skeketal muscle fibers have a striated (striped) appearance because of the banding of actin and myosin myofilaments.

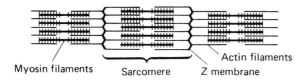

Myosin filaments   Sarcomere   Z membrane   Actin filaments

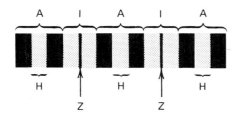

Figure 9-2

Dark (anisotropic, A) bands in striated muscle are due to the overlap of thick (myosin) and thin (actin) myofilaments. Light (isotropic, I) bands obtain their appearance from a lesser density and greater penetration of light.

end, whereas in other muscles the fibers attach to connective tissue within the muscle. Consequently, in some muscles (e.g., gastrocnemius) the fibers do not run exactly in the direction of the muscle tissue.

Under a magnifying glass or a light microscope, skeletal muscle fibers have a striped (striated) appearance (Figure 9-1). These striations are due to the presence of actin and myosin, the two main proteins of contraction. The lighter I (isotropic) band allows more polarized light to pass because of the presence of the thin actin filaments and mitochondria. The darker A (anisotropic) bands block more light because of the presence of both the thick myosin and the thin actin filaments. Under higher magnification, a thin H band appears in the center of the A band; the H band results from to the structure of the myosin filament, which is less dense at the center (Figure 9-2).

How the fine (ultra) structure of skeletal muscle gives rise to the striated appearance under the light microscope is illustrated in Figure 9-2. This figure also shows how the thin actin filaments are attached to the Z line. The Z line is actually a latticelike structure that forms the foundation for the molecular mechanism of shortening in muscle. The distance between one Z line and the next makes up the *sarcomere*, which represents the basic functional unit of the muscle.

The Motor Unit

A motor unit consists of an alpha (α)-motor neuron and its associated muscle cells (fibers). The motor unit (Figure 9-3) is the functional unit of the neural control of muscular activity. All muscle fibers are innervated by at least one motor neuron, and an action potential in the neuron will result in action

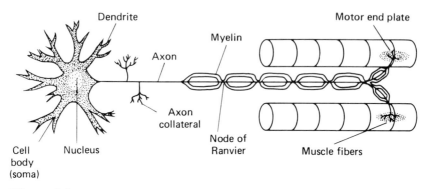

Figure 9-3

A motor unit, consisting of an α-motor neuron and the muscle fibers
(cells) it innervates. All the muscle cells in a motor unit are of the same
fiber type.

potentials in all the muscle cells. The number of fibers in a motor unit can
vary considerably (from perhaps 10 fibers in an eye muscle to approximately
1000 fibers in a gastrocnemius muscle). Normally, all the fibers within a motor unit will have identical biochemical and physiological properties.

Figure 9-4 illustrates that motor units can be classified in two ways on
the basis of speed of contraction, and three ways on the basis of metabolic
characteristics. Muscle fiber types within motor units are usually identified
by histochemical techniques on muscle samples taken during biopsy. In histochemistry, various biochemical characteristics allow reactions with specific
stains. The characteristics are then identified in a light microscope.

Histochemically, speed of contraction of a fiber is suggested by the myofibrillar–ATPase (M–ATPase) stain. Myofibrils are the contractile proteins in
muscle (see Figure 3-9). Fast-contracting (fast-twitch) fibers stain dark with
alkaline (high pH) M–ATPase, and light with acid M–ATPase (Ac–ATPase).
Usually there is a good correlation between M–ATPase histochemistry and
physiological contraction characteristics of individual muscle fibers. In histochemistry, the metabolic characteristics of a muscle fiber are usually identified with stain that reacts with an oxidative enzyme or enzyme complex in
the fiber. A stain for succinic dehydrogenase (SDHase) is frequently used. If
a fiber stains dark for SDHase, it is assumed to be an oxidative fiber. Usually,
if a fiber stains weakly with SDHase, it is assumed to have a nonoxidative,
glycolytic metabolism. Sometimes the glycolytic characteristics of a fiber are
determined by staining specifically for a glycolytic enzyme such as alpha (α)-
glycerol phosphate dehydrogenase (α-GPDase). Because M–ATPase activity
correlates with glycolytic capacity, in practice high M–ATPase activity, as
indicated by histochemical appearance, is also taken as evidence for a high
glycolytic capacity.

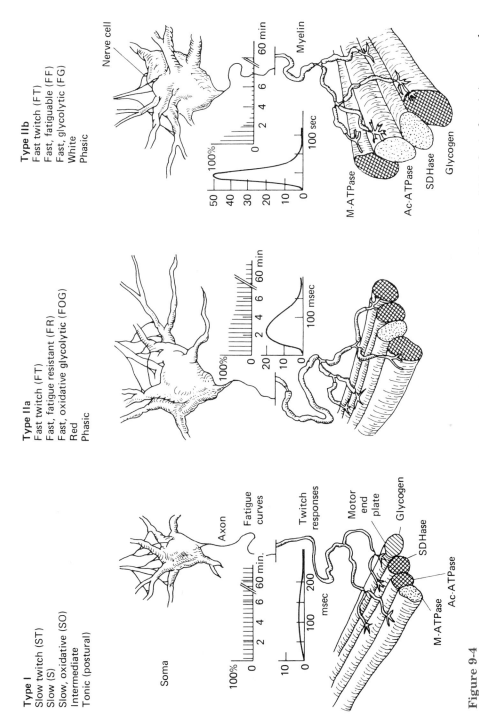

Type I
Slow twitch (ST)
Slow (S)
Slow, oxidative (SO)
Intermediate
Tonic (postural)

Type IIa
Fast twitch (FT)
Fast, fatigue resistant (FR)
Fast, oxidative glycolytic (FOG)
Red
Phasic

Type IIb
Fast twitch (FT)
Fast, fatiguable (FF)
Fast, glycolytic (FG)
White
Phasic

Nerve cell

Myelin

M-ATPase

Ac-ATPase

SDHase

Glycogen

Soma

Axon

Fatigue curves

Twitch responses

Motor end plate

Glycogen

SDHase

M-ATPase

Ac-ATPase

Figure 9-4

In adult mammalian muscles, microscopic examination after transverse cross sectioning and histological staining reveals three fiber types (see Figure 3-9). Fibers are classified as either Type I (slow) or Type II (fast), depending on the intensity of staining with alkaline myofibrillar ATPase). With the oxidative marker succinic dehydrogenase (SDH), Type I and Type IIa fibers stain dark, whereas Type IIb fibers stain light. Glycogen content is revealed by the Periodic Acid Schiff (PAS) stain. The three fiber types differ in ease of recruitment, metabolism, twitch characteristics, and rate of fatigue. The alternative terminologies used to classify skeletal muscle fiber types are indicated at the top.

(SOURCE: Modified from D. W. Edington and V. R. Edgerton, 1976, p. 53. Used with the permission of the authors.)

183

On the basis of these twitch and metabolic characteristics, three main skeletal muscle fiber types have been identified: (1) fast glycolytic (FG), the classic phasic or white fiber; (2) fast oxidative glycolytic (FOG), the classic red fiber; and (3) slow oxidative (SO), or the classic tonic, intermediate fiber. To the eye, FG fibers are pale or white, whereas both FOG and SO fibers are red.

Muscle fibers may also be classified by their resistance to fatigue. The FG fiber is alternatively termed fast fatigable (FF). The FOG fiber is also termed fast fatigue-resistant (FR), and the SO fiber is also termed slow (S) fiber. In this classification, the metabolic profile of fibers is implied.

The Size Principle in Fiber Type Recruitment

According to the size principle, the frequency of motor unit utilization (recruitment) is directly related to the size and ease of triggering an action potential in the soma. In general, the smaller the soma (neuron cell body), the easier it is to recruit. According to the size principle, those motor units with the smaller cell bodies (S motor units) will be used first and, overall, most frequently. Those motor units with larger cell bodies (FF and FR) will be used last during a recruitment and, overall, least frequently. Whatever terminology is used, fiber recruitment is usually determined not by the speed of a movement but rather by the force necessary to perform a movement. For instance, S motor units may be exclusively recruited while lifting a very light weight fairly rapidly. However, in lifting a very heavy weight, necessarily very slowly, all motor units will be recruited. It is known that fast fibers are used to support low-frequency, high-resistance bicycle ergometer exercises. More rapid cycling at higher speeds but against less resistance was supported by slow muscle fibers.

Evidence exists that fast motor units can be recruited alone when rapid, unloaded movements are made. For instance, when a cat steps on a piece of adhesive tape, the cat will attempt to flick the tape off its paw by recruiting fast motor units before slow units.

Muscle Fiber Types in Athletes

Outstanding performers at far ends of the athletic spectrum have been shown to possess specialized muscle fiber type characteristics. For instance, sprint runners have been found to possess fast-twitch glycolytic fiber types, whereas slow-twitch, high-oxidative fiber types have been found to predominate in distance runners. Figure 9-5 illustrates differences between athletes. In that

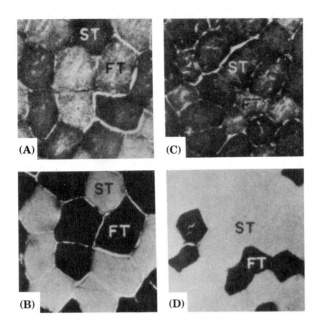

Figure 9-5
Serial sections of quadriceps muscle from two athletes, stained with two different stains: **A** and **B** from an outstanding sprinter, **C** and **D** from an outstanding distance runner. **A** and **C** are stained for succinic dehydrogenase (SDHase); **B** and **D** are stained for alkaline M–ATPase stain. Note that fast fibers, which stain dark with M–ATPase, are usually pale and stain weakly with SDHase. FT, fast-twitch fibers; ST, slow-twitch fibers. Usually, most ST fibers are SO, and FT fibers are FG. Note the two dark FT fibers in **D**, which also stain dark for SDHase in **C**. These are FOG fibers (see Figure 9-4).

(SOURCE: Courtesy of P. D. Gollnick.)

figure, A and B are from one subject, a sprinter; C and D are from a distance runner. A and C are stained for SDHase, whereas B and D are stained for M–ATPase. Note the pale appearance in A, the oxidative marker of the sprinter. In the sprinter, however, note the dark appearance of fibers when fixed for the contractibility marker, M–ATPase (B). The results obtained on the distance runner are the inverse: high-oxidative capacity is indicated in C, but low-contractile activity is indicated in D.

It should again be pointed out that results such as those in Figure 9-5 typify histological characteristics in athletes at the far ends of the athletic spectrum. These results are consistent with other observations made in the biosphere, where species noted for speed (e.g., cats) possess fast-twitch fiber characteristics whereas species noted for endurance (e.g., dogs) possess slow-twitch fiber type characteristics. In humans, a significant range of fiber type characteristics exists in athletes who are successful in middle-distance competition requiring both speed and endurance. Clearly muscle fiber type is but one factor that affects human motor performance.

The characteristics of all tissues are largely genetically determined. However, compared with other types of tissues, skeletal muscle displays a great deal of plasticity. This means that a muscle fiber can change dramatically in response to certain types of (appropriate) stimuli. The histological appearance and biochemical characteristics of muscle have been observed to change in response to cross-innervation, transplantation, continuous electrical stimulation, and endurance training.

In response to training, some muscle cell characteristics appear to be more adaptable than others. In particular, endurance training can significantly raise muscle mitochondrial content. It appears, however, that neither sprint nor endurance training can greatly affect muscle contractile characteristics. It probably is not possible, therefore, for the muscle cells of the sprint athlete displayed in Figure 9-5A and B to assume, by training, the histological appearance of the endurance athlete displayed in Figure 9-5C and D. Similarly, the endurance athlete cannot by training become like the sprint athlete. Properly used, training can enhance the histochemical and underlying biochemical properties of muscle, but it cannot reverse a muscle's intrinsic, genetically determined qualities.

Gross Anatomy of the Nervous System

The central nervous system (CNS) consists of the brain and spinal cord (Figure 9-6). The peripheral nervous system (PNS) consists of all the nerves extending from the brain or spinal cord. Nerves consist of bundles of myelinated neuronal axons that may carry either sensory information to (afferents) or motor information from (efferents) the CNS. In connection with the nervous system, the terms *afferent* (toward) and *efferent* (away from) are used to describe the direction of information flow. In the nervous system, information is transmitted in the form of action potentials. During an action potential the chemical–electrical equilibrium of the nerve (or muscle) cell membrane is briefly perturbed. This perturbation propagates over the surface of the cell so that all points on its receive the signal. Under appropriate conditions, an action potential in one nerve cell can cause the release of the chemical messenger substance (e.g., acetylcholine) from the terminal (end) branches of the cell. In sufficient quantity, the chemical messenger can cause an action potential in the postsynaptic nerve or muscle cell.

Spinal Cord

Seen in a cross section, the spinal cord (SC) is divided into white and gray areas (Figure 9-7). The central gray matter consists of neuronal cell bodies with associated dendrites, short interneurons that do not leave the spinal cord, and terminal axon processes from other neurons whose cell bodies are located elsewhere. It is in the gray area that synapses occur and integration can take place. Some areas in the gray matter can appear especially dark because of the high concentration of cell bodies. Such an area, where cell bodies having related function cluster together, is called a **nucleus.**

The gray matter of the spinal cord is surrounded by white matter consisting of bundles of myelinated neuronal axons running in parallel. These neuronal bundles are called tracts or pathways and are analogous to nerves

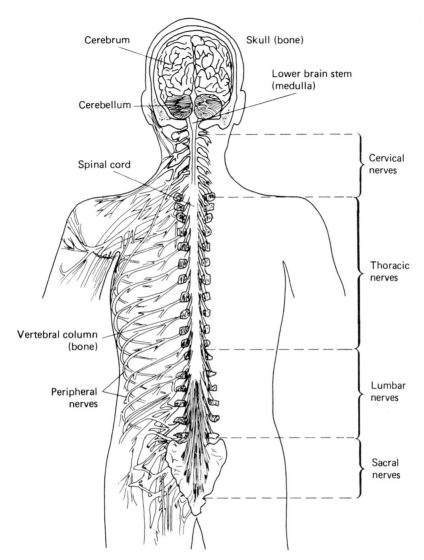

Cerebrum

Skull (bone)

Lower brain stem
(medulla)

Cerebellum

Spinal cord

Cervical
nerves

Thoracic
nerves

Vertebral column
(bone)

Peripheral
nerves

Lumbar
nerves

Sacral
nerves

Figure 9-6
Dorsal (back) view of the nervous system. The CNS consists of the
brain and spinal cord. PNS consists of nerves (bundles of nerve cell
axons) extending from the brain and spinal cord.

(SOURCE: Adapted from J. A. Vander, J. H. Sherman, and D. S. Luciano, 1980,
p. 180, and R. T. Woodburne, Essentials of Human Anatomy, 5th ed. New York:
Oxford University Press, 1973.)

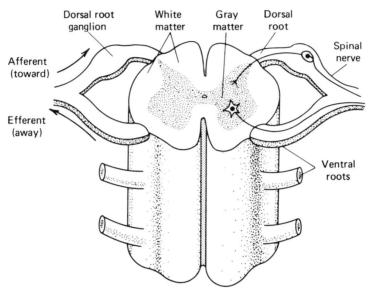

Figure 9-7
Cross-sectional view through the spinal cord and joining nerves.
Gray matter contains cell bodies for motor nerves, which send
axon processes out of the ventral root, as well as cell bodies of
interneurons. Cell bodies for sensory nerves exist in the dorsal
root ganglion. Sensory neurons also synapse in the gray matter.
The SC white matter contains tracts for ascending (sensory) and
descending (motor) signals.

in the PNS. Nerve tracts run both up (ascending) and down (descending) the
spinal cord and carry sensory and motor signals. No synapses are possible in
white matter, but axons may enter the gray matter to receive or transmit
information (action potentials).

Groups of afferent fibers carrying sensory information enter the spinal
cord on the dorsal (back) side of the body. Cell bodies of these sensory nerves
are located immediately outside the spinal cord, in the dorsal root ganglion
(Figure 9-7). Groups of efferent fibers carrying motor signals leave the spinal
cord on the ventral (belly) side of the body.

Brain

The brain consists of six major areas: the cerebrum, cerebellum, diencephalon, midbrain, pons, and medulla (Figure 9-8).

The **cerebral cortex** (derived from the Greek word meaning "tree bark")
covers most of the brain's surface (Figure 9-8A). The cortex is responsible for
those functions of intellect and motor control that set human beings apart.
Four different sections (lobes) of the cortex are associated with specific func-

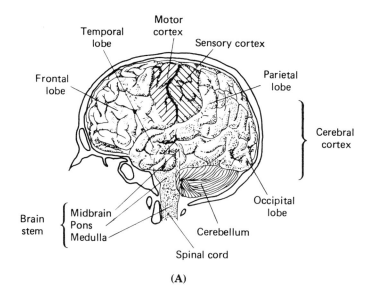

(A)

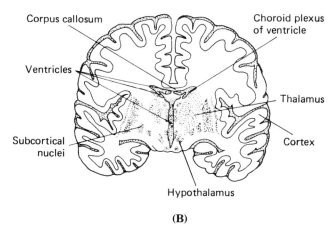

(B)

Figure 9-8
The human brain. The side view (**A**) shows major divisions of the brain, and the cross-sectional view (**B**) reveals the interior structures.

(SOURCE: From J. A. Vander, J. H. Sherman, and D. S. Luciano. New York: McGraw-Hill, 1980, pp. 181–183. Used with permission.)

tions. The **frontal** lobe is responsible for fine intellect and motor control. The motor cortex is at the rear of the frontal lobe. The **parietal** lobe is associated with sensation and interpretation of sensory information. The sensory cortex is at the front of the parietal lobe. The **temporal** lobe is associated with auditory sensation and interpretation, and the **occipital** lobe is associated with visual sensation and interpretation.

The large core of the brain, the **diencephalon,** is made up of two areas: the thalamus and hypothalamus. The **thalamus** is an important integration center through which most sensory inputs pass. From the thalamus, neuronal signals arise for input to the cortex and cerebellum. In addition, descending signals from the cortex can be integrated with incoming sensory information by synapses in the thalamus.

The **hypothalamus** is an important area where neural and hormonal functions effect a constancy of the internal body environment. The hypothalamus governs appetite and regulates body temperature.

The **cerebellum** is an area especially important for motor control. Motor coordination, balance, and smooth movements are accomplished through the action of the cerebellum. Damage to the cerebellum results in impaired motor control.

All afferent and efferent signals pass through the brain stem, which consists of the midbrain, pons, and medulla. The **brain stem** is an area that sets the rhythmicity of breathing and controls the rate and force of breathing movements and heartbeat. Also within the brain stem is an area called the reticular formation that allows us to focus on specific sensory inputs and influences arousal and wakefulness. For instance, in baseball the reticular formation allows a batter to focus on the pitch rather than the taunts of opposing players and spectators.

Neural Control of Reflexes

Reflexes are the simplest type of movement of which we are capable. The knee jerk reflex (Figure 9-9) involves at least four components: (1) the receptor (in this case a muscle stretch receptor, the **spindle**), (2) the gamma (γ)-afferent neurons, which synapse in the gray matter of the spinal cord (e.g., at A in the Figure 9-9), (3) the α-motor neurons with a cell body in the spinal cord, and (4) the muscle fibers within the motor unit. Contrary to immediate appearance, the knee jerk reflex and other reflexes are not all-or-none responses.

Although the knee jerk response is involuntary, control is experienced at several levels. Although stretching does depolarize the spindle receptor, an action potential in the γ-afferent does not always result. There must be a summation of receptor potentials to generate an afferent action potential or a train (series) of potentials. At the level of synapse with the α-motor neuron, γ-afferent activity results in excitatory postsynaptic potentials (EPSPs). These must summate to result in an action potential in the α-motor neuron. Because the α-motor neuron resting membrane potential is also subject to inhibitory postsynaptic potentials (IPSPs), a degree of voluntary inhibition is possible.

The simplest reflexes are monosynaptic. As illustrated in Figure 9-9, synapses with other neurons such as interneurons are also possible. At B, the interneuron stimulated will result in release of an inhibitory neurotransmitter on the soma of an antagonistic motor neuron—in this case, one that in-

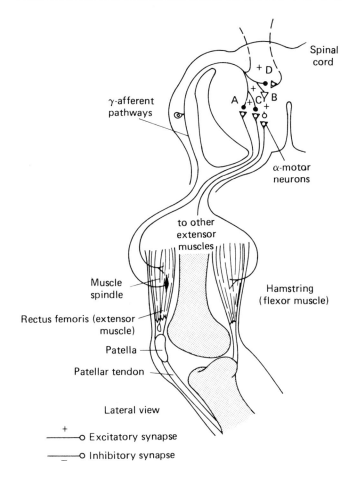

Figure 9-9

The knee jerk reflex involves a minimum of four components: the muscle spindle stretch receptor, the γ-afferent neuron, the α-motor neuron for the rectus femoris extensor muscle, and the rectus femoris. Sufficient rapid stretching of the spindle results in reflex contraction of the rectus femoris (A) and other extensors in the quadriceps (B), inhibition of the soma of motor neurons innervating the antagonist hamstring flexors (C), and ascending signals (D), perhaps to motor units in the arms and back.

(SOURCE: From J. A. Vander, J. H. Sherman, and D. S. Luciano. New York: McGraw-Hill, 1980, p. 594. Used with permission.)

nervates a motor unit in the hamstring muscle. Thus, the antagonist hamstring will stay relaxed while the quadriceps agonist contracts to perform the actual knee jerk. In this terminology, the **agonist** is the muscle primarily responsible for movement, and an **antagonist** is a muscle that retards movement.

Other synapses possible during a knee jerk reflex are those that activate synergists to the knee jerk (at *C* in Figure 9-9) or that send ascending signals to the brain or to motor units innervating a contralateral limb (at *D*).

Gamma-Loop and Muscle Spindle

Muscle spindles (Figure 9-10) respond to the amount and rapidity of stretch. The rapid stretching (lengthening) of spindles in the quadriceps that results when the patellar tendon is struck is a rather extreme example of the spindle's range of responses. In real life, we use the full jerk response in emer-

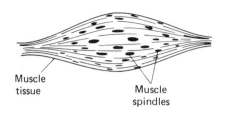

Muscle
tissue

Muscle
spindles

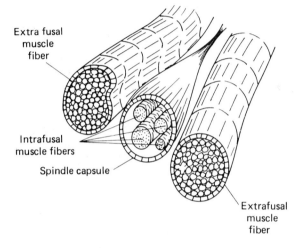

Extra fusal
muscle
fiber

Intrafusal
muscle fibers

Spindle capsule

Extrafusal
muscle
fiber

Figure 9-10
Muscle spindles exist in parallel with extrafusal muscle fibers. Stretch of the muscle results in stretch of the spindle capsule and its contents.

(SOURCE: Modified from D. W. Edington and V. R. Edgerton, 1976, p. 98.)

gency situations only, such as when a foot slips and it is necessary to maintain posture and keep from falling. The spindle, however, works continuously to monitor muscular movement. Muscle spindles exist in parallel with normal extrafusal muscle fibers (Figure 9-10). When a volitional muscular activity is initiated by activation of α-motor neurons, activation (coactivation) of smaller γ-motor neurons also occurs. These efferent γ neurons cause contraction of muscle fibers within the muscle spindle (Figure 9-10). Contraction of the fibers within muscle spindle capsules (intrafusal fibers) in effect takes up the slack within the spindle capsule during contraction of the larger extrafusal fibers. In this way, the central receptor portion of the spindle stays at relatively the same length. The receptor can then respond to sudden changes in length throughout almost the full range of limb movement. The system through which muscle spindles participate in monitoring muscular activity is the γ-loop (Figure 9-11).

Tension Monitoring and Golgi Organs

Golgi tendon organs (GTOs) are receptors that respond to tension (rather than to length as the muscle spindles do). Golgi tendon organs are high-threshold receptors that exert inhibitory effects on agonists and facilitatory affects on

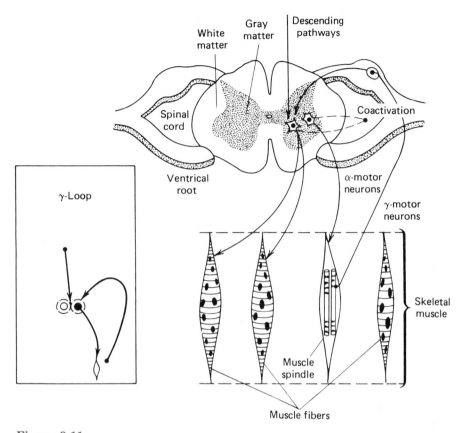

Figure 9-11
The γ-loop (in heavy lines) allows for fine control of muscle position in complex movement patterns. Descending signals result in activation of both α- and γ-motor neurons (coactivation). Stretch on the spindle receptors provides feedback on muscle position through the γ-afferents. Input of the γ-loop back to the α-motor neuron cell body affects its activity.

antagonists. When forces of muscle contraction, together with forces resulting from external factors, sum to the point at which injury to the muscle tendon or bone becomes possible, then the GTOs cause IPSPs on the cell body of the agonistic motor units. Similarly, when shortening during muscle contraction progresses to the point that continued shortening could damage the joint because of hyperextension or hyperflexion, then GTOs act to shut off the agonist and stimulate the antagonist. In this way, GTOs bring about smooth retardation of muscular contractions.

The GTO mechanism is not, however, a failsafe mechanism. Although GTOs influence motor neuron cell bodies with inhibitory signals (IPSPs), their effects can be counterbalanced by additional excitatory signals from higher

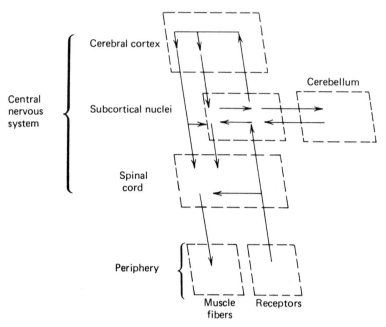

Figure 9-12

General scheme of motor control. The cerebral motor cortex initiates movement by sending descending signals to muscle fibers and
to subcortical areas, which relay signals to the cerebellum. Various
receptors provide sensory feedback, and the cerebellum allows a
comparison (integration) of actual and intended movements. Subsequent activity initiated by the motor cortex is varied depending on
the initial results.

(SOURCE: From J. A. Vander, J. H. Sherman, and D. S. Luciano. New York:
McGraw-Hill, 1980, p. 590. Used with permission.)

centers. The process of minimizing the influence of GTOs is referred to as
disinhibition. Indeed, practicing disinhibition appears to be part of athletic
training, the purpose of which is to push performance to the limits of tissue
capacity. In the sport of wrist wrestling, ruptured muscles or tendons and
broken bones occasionally occur. In highly motivated and disinhibited individuals, the combination of active muscle contraction plus tension exerted by
the opponent can exceed the strength of tissues.

Volitional and Learned Movements

The general scheme by which the brain controls motor activities is illustrated
in Figure 9-12. According to this scheme, movement is initiated in the motor
cortex, which sends commands (action potentials) directly over a spinal axon
to α-motor neurons whose cell bodies are located in the spinal cord. Simulta-

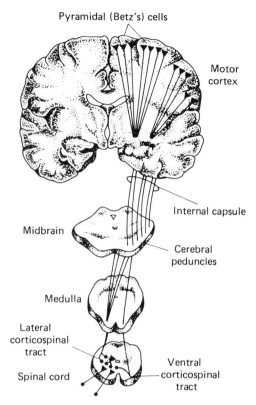

Pyramidal (Betz's) cells

Motor cortex

Internal capsule

Midbrain

Cerebral peduncles

Medulla

Lateral corticospinal tract

Spinal cord

Ventral corticospinal tract

Figure 9-13

The pyramidal (corticospinal) tract originates from the pyramid-shaped Betz's cells in the cerebral corex. Axons from the motor cortex cross over in the medulla and run down in the ventral and lateral white matter of the spinal cord. Bundles of descending axons make up a tract. Synapses occur with motor neurons in the gray area of the spinal cord at appropriate levels.

(SOURCE: Adapted from J. A. Vander. J. H. Sherman, and D. S. Luciano. New York: McGraw-Hill, 1980, p. 598. Used with permission.)

neously, or perhaps with a slight delay, the cortex signals subcortical nuclei which receive input from sensory receptors. Meanwhile, the cerebellum constantly compares the intended with actual movements and integrates each sequential movement component into a coordinated effort.

Corticospinal (Pyramidal) Tract

The corticospinal tract (Figure 9-13) consists of bundles of neurons whose cell bodies exist in the motor cortex, whose axons extend through the spinal cord, and whose terminal processes communicate with α-motor neurons in the gray matter of the spinal cord. Because portions of the corticospinal tract run from the top of the head to the lower back, the tract can be quite long. The cell bodies from which the corticospinal tract originates are pyramidal in shape, therefore, the tract is alternatively referred to as the pyramidal tract, pathway, or system.

The corticospinal pathway is the major effector of complicated and rapid volitional movements. Functioning of the motor cortex has been compared to the running of a computer program. According to this theory, intricate movements that depend on the precise contraction of motor units in different muscles ordered specifically in terms of space, time, intensity, and duration are "programmed" by an incredibly precise order of depolarization of pyramidal cells in the motor cortex. At present, the precise mechanism by which memory is accomplished is not understood. Learning may well involve the synthesis of proteins or neurotransmitters in specific neurons or areas of neurons. The precise imprinting mechanism involved in learning rapid, precise performance of an intricate motor task depends on a computer-programlike sequencing of events in the motor cortex.

Multineuronal, Extrapyramidal Pathways

As indicated in Figure 9-12, descending motor pathways exist in addition to the pyramidal pathway. These extrapyramidal pathways are multineuronal in structure. Extrasynaptic connections slow the conduction velocity, but they allow integration of motor programs with sensory inputs including progress on the result of programs originating in pyramidal cells. Additionally, the extrapyramidal system allows the cerebellum to become involved in coordinating motor activities.

Sensory Inputs during Motor Activities

During motor activities, an individual will, at various times, use most of the sensory information available. The contributions of various forms of sensory information in leading to successful completion of an activity will vary depending on the activity, but afferent inputs from the eyes, inner ear, muscle spindles, joints, and skin are very important. Various individuals may, in fact, perform identical motor tasks while relying on the different sensory inputs to various degrees. Depending on the activity and sense involved, some individuals can adapt and successfully complete motor tasks even though deprived of a usually important form of sensory input. Sometimes, also in the performance of motor tasks, receiving too much information confuses individuals, distracting them from relevant inputs. Concentration and focusing are tasks governed by the frontal cortex and the reticular formation.

Summary

Muscle tissue is made up of individual cells, or fibers. The type of cell found in a muscle tissue ranges from slow-twitch-oxidative (SO), to fast-twitch-glycolytic (FG). A fast-twitch-oxidative and glycolytic (FOG) fiber also exists. By heredity and training endurance athletes possess more SO fibers, whereas sprinters possess more FG fibers.

The biological control of muscular movement depends on the CNS. Even the simplest form of movement involves at least two neurons and a synapse in the CNS. As motor activities become more complex, the center of neuromuscular control tends to move up the CNS and include the cerebral cortex of the brain. The learning of intricate motor tasks involves programming of the area of the brain's frontal lobe called the motor cortex. Once the motor cortex is imprinted with a program, the program can be played back very rapidly and accurately. Thus, the performance of learned, highly skilled motor activities involves pyramidal cells of the motor cortex, the pyramidal tract in the spinal cord, and α-motor neurons and their respective motor units. Also, feedback to the CNS from muscle spindles, joint receptors, skin, eyes, and ears allows for modification of motor programs depending on the situation.

Selected Readings

BROOKS, G.A., and T.D. FAHEY. Exercise Physilogy: Human Bioenergetics and its applications. New York: Macmillan, 1984, pp. 343–376.

CAREW, T.J. Descending control or spinal circuits. In: Kandel, E.R., and J.H. Schwarts (eds.). Principles of Neural Science. New York: Elsevier/North-Holland, 1981, pp. 312–322.

CAREW, T.J. Spinal cord I: Muscles and muscle receptors. In: Kandel, E.R., and J.H. Schwarts (eds.). Principles of Nueral Science. New York: Elsevier/North-Holland, 1981; pp. 284–292.

EVARTS, E.V. Relation of pyramidal tract activity to force exerted during voluntary movement. J. Neurophysiol. 31:14–27, 1968.

GHEZ, C. Introduction to the motor systems. In: Kandel, E.R., and J.H. Schwartz (eds.). Principles of Neural Science. New York: Elsevier/North-Holland, 1981, pp. 272–283.

GUYTON, A.C. Textbook of Medical Physiology. Philadelphia: W.B. Saunders, 1981, pp. 560–697.

HENRY, F.M. The evolution of the memory drum theory of neuromotor reaction. In: Brooks, G.A. (ed.). Perspectives on the Academic Discipline of Physical Education. Champaign, Ill.: Human Kinetics, 1981, pp. 301–322.

KANDEL, E.R., and J.H. SCHWARTZ (eds.). Principles of Neural Science. New York: Elsevier/North-Holland, 1981.

KATZ, B. Nerve, Muscle and Synapse. New York: McGraw-Hill, 1966.

MERTON, P.A. How we control the contraction of our muscles. Sci. Amer. 226:30–37, 1972.

VANDER, A.J., J.H. SHERMAN, and D.S. LUCIANO. Human Physiology, 3rd ed. New York: McGraw-Hill, 1980, pp. 144–190.

10

Muscle Function during Exercise

The performance of muscle during exercise is determined at several levels of organization. Ultimately, the CNS (Chapter 9) is responsible for controlling muscle movements, whether they be simple reflexes or learned skills. Within the cell, interactions of the contractile proteins (actin and myosin) are precisely regulated by the interaction of calcium ion (Ca^{++}) with the troponin–tropomyosin protein complex. These factors regulate the extent of actin–myosin interaction and the contraction process.

Muscular performance is determined by not only the characteristics of the contractile apparatus (i.e., the intracellular proteins and Ca^{++}) but also the elastic characteristics of muscles and tendons. Additionally, the anatomical arrangement of muscle cells within muscle tissue, as well as the attachment of muscles to the skeleton, affect the quality of movement.

The Sliding Filament Mechanism of Muscle Contraction

When muscle shortens, the I band shortens, but the A band does not change in length (see Figure 9-2). The mechanism of how this occurs and how the thick and thin filaments operate to cause muscle shortening (contraction) was developed largely by H. E. Huxley. According to this mechanism, the protruding heads of myosin filaments interact with actin filaments, and movement occurs as a result of a ratchet or oarlike interaction between the two contractile proteins (see Figure 2-2B). At present, the chemistry of muscle contraction is fairly well understood, but the precise mechanism by which chemical energy is converted to shortening is a subject under active investigation.

The structures of myosin (Figure 10-1) and actin (Figure 10-2) reveal that the filamentous structures are made up of individual subunits. Whereas filamentous actin (F-actin) is a helical structure composed of globular subunits (G-actin), the structure of filamentous myosin is like a double-ended bottle brush (Figure 10-1B). Like actin filaments, myosin filaments are also made up of individual myosin subunits, or molecules. In addition to supporting the basic structure of muscle, both actin and myosin subunits contain enzymatic activities. Each has a complementary binding site for the other, and each can bind ADP or ATP. Furthermore, F-actin binds two regulatory proteins, troponin and tropomyosin, which are involved in triggering muscle contraction.

The Molecular Mechanism of Muscle Movement

All the essential elements for muscle contraction (ATP, actin, myosin, troponin, tropomyosin, Mg^{++}, Ca^{++}) are normally present in muscle. Yet con-

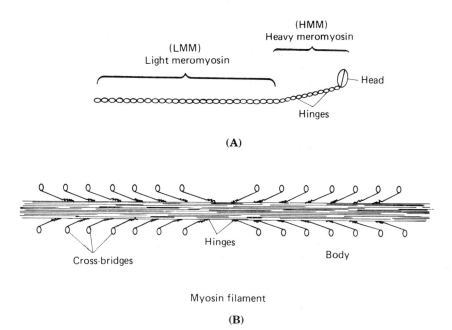

Figure 10-1
Myosin molecules have structural (light) and enzymatic (heavy) ends (**A**).
The light meromyosin provides a connecting link to similar units in the
myosin filament, which appears as a double-ended bottle brush (**B**). The
head of heavy meromyosin contains binding sites for actin and ATP.
Myosin in fast-contracting muscle has a higher ATPase activity than does
myosin in slow muscle.

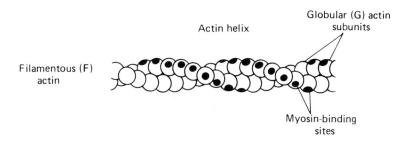

Figure 10-2
Filamentous (F) actin is a helix made up of individual globular (G)
actin subunits. Each G-actin subunit contains a myosin-binding
site. Tropomyosin (not shown) provides structural support to the
helical structure and allows for enzymatic control.

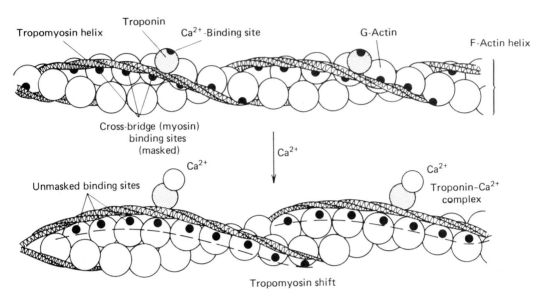

Figure 10-3

The binding of Ca^{++} to troponin causes a conformational (shape) change in that protein and a movement of the tropomyosin helix. The tropomyosin shift causes the myosin-binding sites on actin to become unmasked. Thus, Ca^{++} binding to troponin indirectly allows for actin and myosin to interact.

tractions result only in particular circumstances. Normally (Figure 10-3), tropomyosin blocks or screens out the possible interaction between actin and myosin. The release of Ca^{++} from the sarcoplasmic reticulum provides the stimulus for actin–myosin interaction and muscle contraction because it causes the movement of the troponin–tropomyosin complex and exposure of the myosin-binding sites.

Huxley's ratchet mechanism of muscle filament sliding is diagrammed in Figure 10-4. Although at present there is fair agreement on the fact of actin–myosin interaction, as suggested earlier, the precise mechanism by which the energy of ATP is utilized to effect filament sliding is somewhat uncertain. As

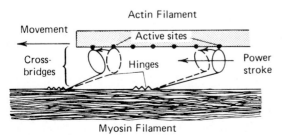

Figure 10-4

Muscle contraction (shortening) is thought to occur when cross-bridges extend from myosin to actin and a conformational change occurs in the cross-bridge. The specifics of this schematic model are yet to be worked out.

(SOURCE: Modified from H. E. Huxley, 1958.)

originally proposed by Huxley, a rotation of the myosin head toward the direction of movement could result in filament sliding. Alternatively, movement in the "hinge" area could produce shortening. Other possibilities also exist. Solution of this problem is probably worthy of a Nobel prize, and some of the best minds in biology, chemistry, and physics are currently working on it.

The cyclic events of muscle contraction are summarized in Figure 10-5. Description of this model starts with the resting state (Figure 10-5A). In the presence of magnesium ion (Mg^{++}), ATP unites with myosin to energize it. Thus, in Figure 10-5A, myosin is like a loaded and cocked revolver ready to discharge. The energized myosin can then combine with actin if Ca^{++} affects the troponin–tropomyosin complex to reveal (unmask) the actin-binding sites. The binding of actin to myosin triggers the release of potential energy stored in the myosin head. Mechanical work (movement) and heat release are consequences of this energy release. For the myosin cross-bridge to be used again (i.e., to recycle), it must be dislodged from the actin-binding site and be re-energized. This is done by ATP in several ways. Ca^{++} must be pumped back into the lateral sacs of the sarcoplasmic reticulum. This process is endergonic and requires ATP (see Figure 10-7). Additionally, ATP must be present to break up (dissociate) the actin–myosin (Figure 10-5C) complex and to react with the myosin to reenergize it (Figure 10-5D).

Excitation–Contraction Coupling

The process by which nerve signals result in muscular movement is referred to as excitation–contraction coupling. This process (Figures 10-6 and 10-7) involves a series of events by which action potentials in α-motor neurons cause actin and myosin to interact. The release of acetylcholine at the neuromuscular junction causes an action potential in the postsynaptic muscle cell (Figure 10-6). The muscle action potential spreads over the cell surface and likely also down the transverse (T) tubules (Figure 10-6). As a result, calcium ion (Ca^{++}) is released from the lateral sacs of the sarcoplasmic reticulum, and Ca^{++} is released into the sarcoplasm. Calcium ion then binds to troponin and causes tyopomyosin to shift its orientation along the F-actin helix. As indicated in Figure 10-7, the myosin cross-bridge binding sites on actin are exposed, thereby allowing actin and myosin to interact.

The postsynaptic muscle cell membrane (Figure 10-6) possesses two important features in the control of muscle contraction. Acetylcholine (ACH) released into the synaptic cleft from the terminal branches of the motor neuron finds binding sites on the muscle cell membrane. The binding of ACH has the effect of increasing the permeability of sodium ion (Na^+), which depolarizes the postsynaptic muscle cell membrane, giving rise first to an end-plate

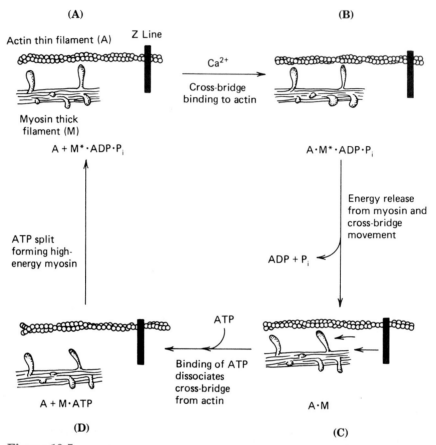

Figure 10-5

The cyclic process of muscle contraction and relaxation. In the resting state (**A**), actin (A) and energized myosin (M*.ADP.Pi) cannot interact because of the effect of tropomyosin. Upon the release of Ca^{++} from the sarcoplasmic reticulum, actin binds to M*.ADP.Pi (**B**). Tension is developed and movement occurs with the release of ADP and Pi (**C**). Dissociation of actin and myosin requires the presence of ATP to bind to myosin and to pump Ca^{++} into the SR(**D**). Myosin is energized upon return to the resting state (**A**).

(SOURCE: From J. A. Vander, J. H. Sherman, and D. S. Luciano. Human Physiology, 1980, p. 218. Used with permission.)

potential (EPP) and then to an action potential (AP), which spreads across the muscle cell surface and down the T tubules. The effect of ACH is short lived, as it is degraded by the presence of the enzyme acetylcholinesterase. Thus, the release of ACH constitutes the first muscle signal to "switch on" contraction, and the activity of acetylcholinesterase is the signal to "switch off" the contraction.

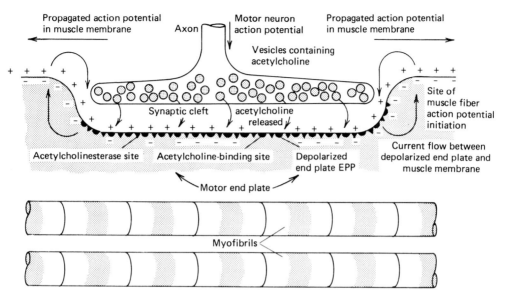

Figure 10-6

The motor end plate is the site where α-motor neurons communicate with muscle cells. At the motor and plate (myoneural junction), terminal axon branches contain acetylcholine, which can be released into the synaptic cleft and bind to receptor sites on the muscle cell surface. Enzymatic degradation of ACH by acetylcholinesterase means that continual α-motor neuron activity is required for continued muscle cell contraction.

(SOURCE: From J. A. Vander, J. H. Sherman, and D. S. Luciano. Human Physiology, 1980, p. 224. Used with permission.)

Whereas muscle contraction depends on the release of Ca^{++} from the lateral sacs of the sarcoplasmic reticulum (Figure 10-6, upper right), muscle relaxation depends on sequestering Ca^{++} back into the lateral sacs. The pumping of Ca^{++} into the lateral sacs is an endergonic process and requires ATP. Fast contracting muscle fiber types, such as Type IIb (see Figures 9-4 and 9-5), have high contents of sarcoplasmic reticulum and high sarcoplasmic reticulum ATPase activity levels. These characteristics facilitate rapid contraction and relaxation.

Characteristics of Muscle Contraction

Classically, the contractile characteristics of muscle have been studied at several levels. These have been in the intact living, moving organism (*in vivo*), with the muscle in place in an anesthetized animal preparation (*in situ*), and

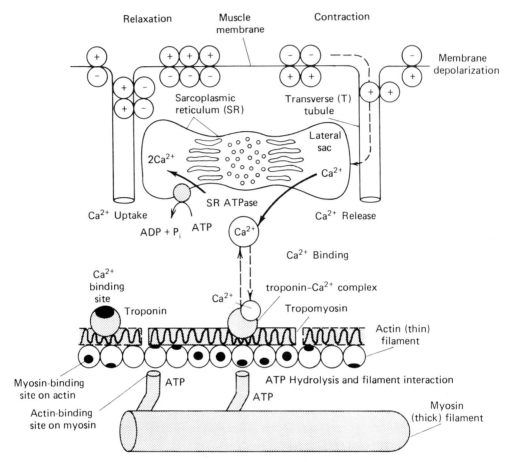

Figure 10-7

Excitation–contraction coupling is regulated in several steps. Muscle cell membrane depolarization (Figure 10-1) causes the release of Ca^{++} from the lateral sacs of the sarcoplasmic reticulum. Calcium ion released into sarcoplasm finds binding sites on troponin, forming a troponin–Ca^{++} complex. Binding of Ca^{++} to troponin causes a direct conformational change in troponin and an indirect shift of tropomyosin. The shift in tropomyosin relieves its inhibition between actin and myosin, so that cross-bridges can be formed and contraction can occur. Relaxation depends on pumping Ca^{++} back into the lateral sacs.

(SOURCE: Modified from J. A. Vander, J. H. Sherman, and D. S. Luciano. Human Physiology, 1980, p. 222. Used with permission.)

with the muscle in a physiological fluid bath isolated from the individual (*in vitro*). Small muscles from frogs and small mammals have particularly lent themselves to study *in vitro*, but detailed studies on muscles of larger mammals have also provided useful information.

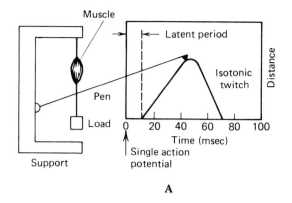

Figure 10-8

Schematics of apparatus to study the contractile properties of isolated muscles. When a loaded muscle shortens against a load, the shortening record produces a linear, isotonic response (**A**). When a muscle's length is fixed, isometric twitch characteristics can be recorded (**B**).

(SOURCE: Adapted from J. A. Vander, J. H. Sherman, and D. S. Luciano. Human Physiology, 1980, p. 226. Used with permission.)

Isometric and Isotonic Contractions

Isolated muscles can be arranged in an apparatus (Figure 10-8) so that the muscle can shorten (A) or be prevented from shortening following stimulations (B). When the muscle's length is fixed, an isometric (same length) condition exists. A recording of the isometric tension developed can be made following a single electrical stimulus (Figure 10-8B). When the load on the muscle is light enough to be lifted, the rate of shortening is constant (Figures 10-8A and 10-9A). Because the lifting of a constant weight by an isolated muscle produces a linear response, the maximal tension produced is constant. The contraction is therefore said to be isotonic (i.e., same tension). The terms isometric and isotonic are also used, or rather misused, in athletic training (Chapter 15). These terms were developed by muscle physiologists and correctly apply to contractile properties of isolated muscles. In the intact individual, it is difficult to establish an isometric condition and almost impossible to establish an isotonic condition. In the isotonic situation, increasing the weight lifted decreases both the distance shortened and the velocity of shortening following a single stimulus (Figure 10-9A). Additionally, the response of the muscle to shorten is delayed as a result of the extra time required to develop sufficient tension to move the heavier weight. Also in Figure 10-9, note that although strengthening a muscle does not affect its maximum rate of unloaded contraction, because of the hyperbolic nature of the relationship, heavy loads can be lifted at significantly faster rates (Figure 10-9B).

Another special characteristic of muscle contraction also bears mention. The initial length at which a muscle begins to contract affects the maximal tension that it develops (Figure 10-10). At the muscle's full resting length (L_0), the overlap between actin and myosin is greatest. Consequently, the probability of maximum cross-bridge development exists and the greatest tension is developed. For the biceps, L_0 would exist at full elbow extension. As the muscle's length changes from L_0, the probability of actin–myosin interaction decreases, and the maximal tension developed during an isometric tetanus also decreases.

Properties of Muscle Contraction in the Body

Although studies on isolated muscles provide a great deal of useful information, the properties of isolated muscles do not always predict the properties *in vivo*. For instance, the body muscles act across a system of bone levers. Whereas maximal isometric tension of the biceps muscle is developed at L_0, or at full elbow extension, maximal tension during elbow flexion is developed at an elbow angle of approximately 90 degrees. Additionally, the forces developed through muscular contraction will not be the same as those developed in the muscle (Figure 10-11). In the body, factors such as lever length, location of origin and insertion of the tendon, and angle of pull affect the speed and force of contraction. In real life, also, external forces placed on a muscle by the circumstances of movement (e.g., through an opponent's efforts or a fall) are additive to the tension developed by the contractile apparatus. These forces can sometimes exceed the tensile strength of a muscle's supporting contractile apparatus and connective tissue. In such cases, injury results.

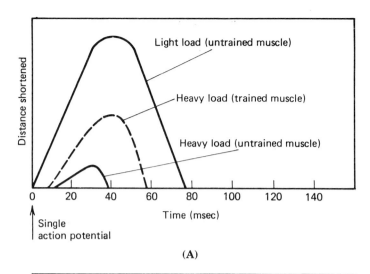

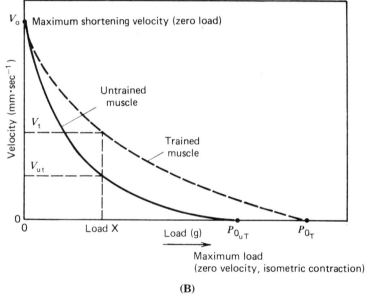

Figure 10-9

Characteristics of isotonic contractions. Compared with those
when lifting light loads, isotonic responses to given stimuli when
lifting heavy loads result in a greater latent period, slower
movement, and less movement (**A**). The effect of strength training is one that appears to make the load lighter. The force–
velocity relationship (**B**) is hyperbolic in nature. Greater loads
produce slower speeds but greater tension. The effect of strength
training is to increase P_0 (maximum isometric tension) but not
V_0 (maximum unloaded velocity). However, a stronger trained
muscle can move a given isotonic load (x) at a greater velocity
($V_t > V_{ut}$).

209

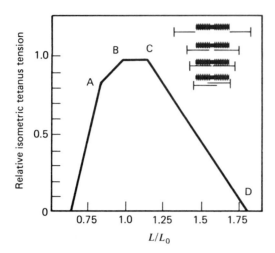

Figure 10-10

The length–tension relationship for skeletal muscle. At full resting muscle length (L_0), the probability of actin–myosin interaction (*B* and *C*) is maximal, and the greatest isometric tension is recorded. At muscle lengths significantly less than L_0 (*A*), or greater than L_0 (*D*), isometric tension declines.

(SOURCE: Adapted from Gordon, Huxley, and Julian, 1966.)

Muscle Length and Cross Section

The characteristics of muscle contraction *in vivo* will also depend on several other factors. In general, the longer a muscle is, the faster it will contract. In general, also, the thicker a muscle is, the greater its maximal tension will be.

Given that in most individuals sarcomere length does not vary much, longer muscles mean more sarcomeres arranged end to end. If these all shorten at the same rate, the individual having the longer muscle will achieve the greatest shortening per unit time (Figure 10-12A). The maximal tension developed by a muscle is directly related to its thickness, or cross-sectional area. Greater area means more cross-bridges pulling in parallel (Figure 10-12B). The tension developed by human skeletal muscle has been estimated to be 1 to 2 kg/cm^2.

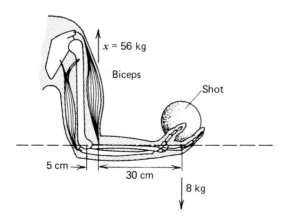

Figure 10-11

In the body, muscles act across bone levers so that the force exerted will usually be different from the force of muscular contraction.

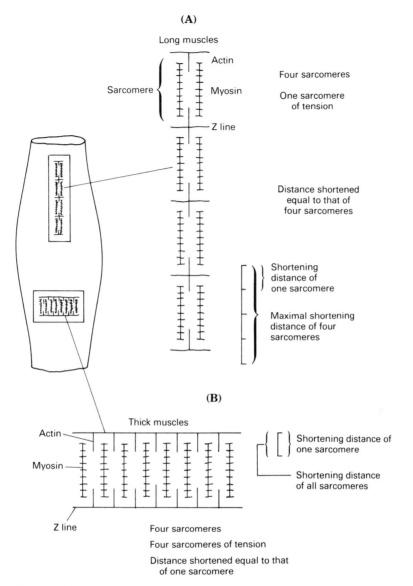

Figure 10-12

Illustration of how the anatomical arrangement of sarcomeres results in greater speed of shortening (**A**) and tension development in thicker muscles (**B**). In anatomically long muscles (**A**), the series (end-to-end) arrangement of sarcomeres produces a rapid contraction in the unloaded state because the distance shortened per unit of time will be great. In anatomically thick muscles (**B**), the parallel (side-by-side) arrangement of sarcomeres produces a forceful contraction.

The maximal tension and speed of muscle contraction will also vary depending on the muscle fiber type and the recruitment pattern (Chapter 9). Because few movements in sports require tetanic contractions, maximal force achieved during movement likely depends on the coordination and skill of the competitor. For instance, the velocity of Jimmy Connors' backhand shot in tennis is likely greater than that of Arnold Schwartzeneger, the body builder. Even in sports such as wrist wrestling, where the individual with the thickest muscle is potentially the strongest, muscular recruitment depends on pyramidal tract activity mediated by the inhibitory influences of Golgi tendon organs (Chapter 9). Here again, muscular performance does not necessarily depend completely on the muscle.

The neural control of muscle recruitment affects speed of movement in another important way. Many movement patterns (e.g., running and swimming) are cyclic in nature. Although muscle strength certainly affects the rate at which a limb can be moved, continued movement depends on both contraction and relaxation of agonists as well as antagonists. The individual with the strongest legs is therefore not necessarily the fastest runner or swimmer.

Summary

Physical activities are the result of chemical to mechanical energy transduction in skeletal muscle. In muscle and other cells two main components to energy transduction exist. Through the processes of intermediary metabolism, potential energy contained in the by-products of foodstuffs is captured in the form of high-energy phosphate compounds (ATP and CP). The second major component of energy transduction in muscle is the conversion of potential chemical energy in ATP into mechanical work by the two contractile proteins, actin and myosin.

Together, actin and myosin make up a majority of the muscle mass, which in turn can represent a majority of the body's mass. In a lean, muscular individual, therefore, much of the body is composed of these two contractile proteins. Thus, not only do actin and myosin determine the body's structure, their enzymatic properties also largely determine the body's capacity for movement.

The contractile characteristics of isolated muscle, in terms of speed of movement and during tension development, are mediated by a number of factors in the body during muscular exercise. These include the bone lever system, motor unit recruitment pattern, muscle fiber type, and the neural mechanisms of muscular control.

Selected Readings

BRISKEY, E.J., R.G. CASSENS, and B.B. MARSH (eds.). The Physiology and Biochemistry of Muscle as a Food, II. Madison: University of Wisconsin Press, 1970.

BRISKEY, E.J., R.G. CASSENS, and J.C. THAUTMAN (eds.). The Physiology and Biochemistry of Muscle as a Food, I. Madison: University of Wisconsin Press, 1966.

BROOKS, G.A., and T.D. FAHEY. Exercise Physiology: Human Bioenergetics and Its Applications. New York: Macmillan, 1984, pp. 377–394.

COHEN, C. The protein switch of muscle contraction. Sci. Amer. 233:36–45, 1975.

DONOVAN, C.M., and G.A. BROOKS. Muscular efficiency during steady-rate exercise II. Effects of walking speed and work rate. J. Appl. Physiol.: Respirat. Environ. Exercise Physiol. 43:431–439, 1977.

GORDON, A.M., A.F. HUXLEY, and F.J. JULIAN. The variation in isometric tension with sarcomere length in vertebrate muscle fibers. J. Physiol. London 184:170–192, 1966.

GUYTON, A.C. Textbook of Medical Physiology. Philadelphia: W.B. Saunders, 1981, pp. 122–136.

HILL, A.V. Chemical change and the mechanical response in stimulated muscle. Proc. Roy. Soc. London B. 141:314–321, 1953.

HUXLEY, H.E. The contraction of muscle. Sci. Amer. 199:66–82, 1958.

SZENG-GYORGI, A. Chemistry of Muscular Contraction. New York: Academic Press, 1951.

VANDER, A.J., J.H. SHERMAN, and D.S. LUCIANO. Human Physiology. New York: McGraw-Hill, 1980, pp. 211–252.

WILKIE, D.R. The efficiency of muscular contraction. L. Mechanochem. Cell Motility 2:257–267, 1974.

11

Exercise, Body Composition, and Nutrition

Exercise, nutrition, and body composition are integrally involved in health, aesthetics, and physical performance. To a large extent, body composition (the relative proportion of fat and fat-free weight) is a product of caloric intake from the diet and the caloric expenditure from physical activity. Excessive fat (obesity) is usually caused by eating too much and not getting enough exercise.

Body composition is an important component in physical performance. In sports such as distance running, body composition is a critical component determining success or failure. Excessive fat is also of significance to the physical capacity of the average person. Obesity seriously affects physical performance because increased energy is required to move a larger mass, which forces the overweight person to work harder at most tasks. Unfortunately, overweight people are usually less fit, which compounds their handicap; chronic inactivity deprives them of a potent means of weight loss.

Athletes are also concerned about the role of nutrition on physical performance. Nutrition has achieved almost mystical status among athletes and people interested in exercise. There are constant efforts to manipulate the diet to increase the ability to perform at high metabolic rates for extended periods in athletic training and competition. Although a proper diet is necessary for performing at an optimal level, metabolism is directly controlled by biochemical processes that are influenced only indirectly by the previous diet. Extreme dietary manipulation is more likely to hinder than help performance.

This chapter will discuss the interaction of body composition, diet, and exercise. Emphasis will be placed on the role of exercise in reducing body fat and on the relationship between body composition, nutrition, and physical performance. Basic principles of nutrition for athletics will also be discussed.

Obesity and Health

Obesity refers to excess body fat and is the direct result of consuming more energy than is expended. It affects nearly 30% of the adults in Western countries and constitutes a serious health problem. High levels of body fat are associated with an increased risk of coronary heart disease, stroke, hypertension, hyperlipidemia, diabetes, osteoarthritis, gallstones, gallbladder disease, renal disease, hepatic cirrhosis, accident proneness, surgical complications, and back pain.

The association between obesity and increased mortality is controversial. Although the higher incidence of many diseases among the obese is well established, obesity as a cause of premature death has been questioned. In the absence of serious risk factors, such as hypertension and diabetes, obesity seems to pose a much less serious risk to overall mortality. However, the

216

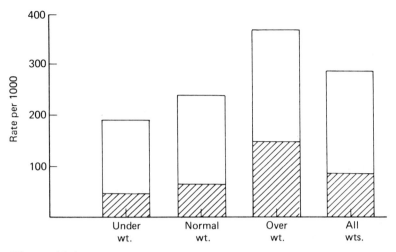

Figure 11-1

The frequency of hypertension in various weight categories (men and women). The darker bars represent the 20- to 39-year age group, and the lighter bars represent 40 to 64 years.

(SOURCE: Data from P. Berchtold, V. Jorgens, C. Finke, and M. Berger, 1981. In G. A. Brooks and T. D. Fahey. Exercise Physiology: Human Bioenergetics and Its Applications. New York: Macmillan, 1984, Figure 25-1.)

possibility exists that obesity may be a cause of diabetes and hypertension and thus be vitally linked with coronary heart disease, the number-one killer (see Chapter 16).

Hypertension (both systolic and diastolic pressure) is twice as common in overweight persons as it is in those with normal weight, and three times as common than those who are underweight (Figure 11-1). This relationship is most striking in white women and blacks of both sexes, but the problem exists throughout the general population in all age groups, even in children as young as 5 years of age.

Obese individuals have a greater risk of developing diabetes, with the risk increasing with the severity and duration of the problem. Obesity often fosters resistance to insulin by decreasing the number of active insulin receptors (see Chapter 16). In addition, chronically elevated oral glucose loads are associated with a positive energy balance (higher energy intake than expenditure). The pancreas is sometimes unable to handle the increased insulin requirement, resulting in glucose intolerance. Obesity-related pancreatic islet failure may take as long as 15 to 20 years to develop.

Hyperlipidemia (high blood fats) is common in obesity, with more than 31% of obese persons exhibiting this disorder. In obese persons with hyperlipidemia, three-quarters have high triglycerides, one-quarter have high cholesterol, and half have a combination of both. Additionally, there is a strong negative correlation between plasma high-density lipoproteins (HDL) and relative weight (proximity to ideal weight). HDL and triglyceride levels increase during weight reduction in the obese. Exercise reduces triglycerides and increases HDL, which reinforces the importance of physical activity in weight reduction.

Obesity greatly increases the risk of a variety of musculoskeletal disorders, particularly osteoarthritis and backache. The increased mass places chronic stress on joints, eventually leading to arthritic changes. A sagging abdomen, especially prominent in obese men, results in an increased lumbar lordosis that has been implicated as a frequent cause of back pain. This problem is compounded by generally weak and inflexible abdominal, spinal, and leg muscles.

Energy Balance: The Role of Exercise and Diet

The body's energy balance determines whether the amount of fat increases, decreases, or remains the same. The metabolism is in energy balance when energy intake equals energy expenditure (Eq. 2-1, Figure 11-2). Obesity occurs when this balance becomes positive (more energy is consumed than expended). Once gained, the body fat will remain unless there is also a period of negative energy balance. Superficially, obesity appears to be simply a mat-

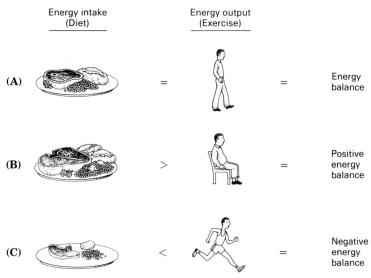

Figure 11-2
Energy balance is dependent on caloric intake and expenditure.

ter of putting a reign on gluttony and burning up more calories through physical activity. However, the problem is considerably more complex than this. For example, there are individual differences in the desire for energy consumption and the rate of energy expenditure. Although the cause of the positive energy balance in obese people is not totally understood, the answer probably lies in the complex physiological and psychological factors that control food intake and energy expenditure.

Control of Food Intake

The control center for food intake, consisting of separate regulators of hunger and satiety, is found in the hypothalamus. A number of agents have been suggested as factors triggering the hypothalamic hunger center. These include glucose, stored triglycerides, plasma amino acid levels, and hypothalamic temperature. The glucostatic theory of hunger regulation proposes that glucose controls hunger and satiety with glucose sensors located in the hypothalamus. These sensors are thought to be sensitive to the effects of insulin and elicit satiety signals as glucose utilization increases within the sensor cells.

The lipostatic theory proposes that appetite is controlled over the long term by the amount of stored triglycerides. A faulty lipostatic thermostat may be involved in obesity. This theory is only conjecture at present, and considerable research is required to substantiate it. Other researchers have proposed an aminostat—control of hunger by plasma amino acids—as a regulator. More experimental support is likewise required for this theory.

Hypothalamic temperature may be involved in the control of appetite. This theory, called the thermostatic theory, proposes that the specific dynamic activity of food, the heat given off during digestion, stimulates the satiety center. This is consistent with the often observed phenomenon of increased appetite in the cold and decreased appetite in the heat.

A number of other factors have been implicated in the hunger–satiety mechanism. These include gastrointestinal (GI) stretch receptors, nutrients, osmotic changes, GI hormones, such as cholecystokinin, hepatic nutrient receptors, hormones sensitive to nutrient status such as insulin, glucagon, growth hormone, and plasma levels of nutrients.

Psychological factors can affect food intake. This is extremely important as a cause of obesity and perhaps the most difficult to alter. Psychosocial factors such as food-centered social gatherings, structured mealtime, and anxiety-stimulated eating binges are often independent of physiological hunger stimulatory mechanisms. A summary of hunger–satiety mechanisms appears in Figure 11-3.

Energy Expenditure

The components of energy expenditure include basal metabolic rate (BMR), thermal effect of food, facultative thermogenesis, and physical activity. Indi-

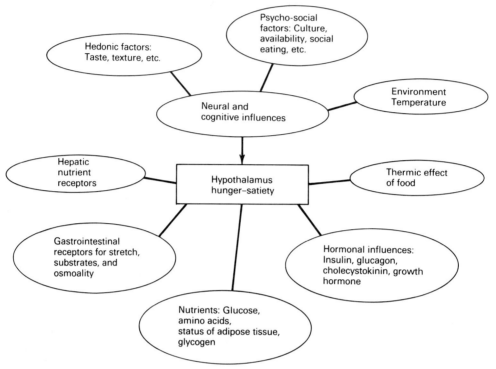

Figure 11-3
Hunger and satiety, regulated by the hypothalamus, are influenced by number of physiological and psychological cues.

vidual differences can exist in each of these factors, which accounts for the considerable variation in body fat between individuals on diets with similar caloric content.

Basal metabolic rate is the energy requirement of an awake person during absolute rest. It is measured under stringent laboratory conditions and requires that the subject had not eaten in 12 hr, had a restful night's sleep, performed no strenuous exercise after sleeping, and was reclined in a comfortable, nonstressful environment (68 to 80 degrees) for 30 min before the measurement.

Although BMR tends to decrease with age, and is higher in men than in women, it varies less than 10%. While BMR tends to be higher in lean people than in obese people of the same weight (muscle has a higher metabolic rate than fat), the difference is not enough to account for the sometimes large differences in fat weight between the two groups. The increased body fat in older individuals may be partially caused by gradual decrease in BMR with

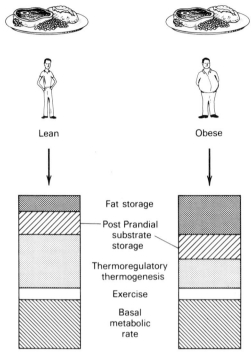

Fate of Energy from Food

Figure 11-4
Thermoregulatory thermogenesis from tissues such as brown fat may be lower in the obese and may contribute to their overweight problem.

(SOURCE: Adapted from W. P. T. James and P. Trayburn, 1981. In: G. A. Brooks, and T. D. Fahey. Exercise Physiology: Human Bioenergetics and Its Applications. New York: Macmillan, 1984, Figure 25-4.)

age. A small deficit in caloric expenditure may become quite substantial when accumulated over a period of many years.

Metabolic rate increases during digestion and absorption of food (thermic effect). The energy cost of digestion is highest for protein, lower for carbohydrates, and lowest for fats. Some fad diets advocate the consumption of high amounts of protein because of its higher energy loss during digestion. Close examination of these diets, however, demonstrates that their ability to help people lose weight stems from a low caloric content rather than the paltry number of calories dissipated during digestion.

Facultative thermogenesis is heat production in addition to basal metabolic rate, the thermic effect of food, and physical activity. When food is ingested, the portion of energy not required for metabolism is either stored as fat or dissipated as heat. It appears that humans vary in their efficiency in utilizing food energy. Some are very efficient and store most of the unneeded energy in adipose tissue, whereas others lose a portion as heat. This phenomenon may account for individual differences in fat deposition among people with seemingly identical caloric intake (Figure 11-4).

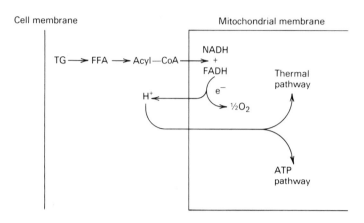

Figure 11-5
Thermogenesis in brown adipose tissue. Lean people may have a more active thermal pathway in their brown adipose tissue.

Brown adipose tissue (BAT) may be an important center for facultative thermogenesis in man (Figure 11-5). Small amounts of this tissue exist in the interscapular, axillary, and perirenal regions and around the great vessels in the thorax. The thermogenic property of BAT stems from the ability of its mitochondria to perform controlled uncoupling of oxidative phosphorylation (see Chapter 4). Thermally active BAT allows a portion of the consumed calories dissipate as heat rather than be stored as fat. The significance of BAT in humans is controversial and is currently under study.

Exercise and Energy Balance   The amount of physical activity is probably the most significant and variable factor of energy expenditure. Basal metabolic rate is less than 1000 kcal $\cdot$ day^{-1} (depending on body size), but the additional caloric cost of physical activity can vary tremendously. While a sedentary person typically expends approximately 1800 kcal $\cdot$ day^{-1}, the endurance athlete may use as much as 6000 kcal (during an endurance event such as an ultramarathon or triathlon).

Many health experts place little emphasis on the importance of exercise in caloric expenditure. However, observing the threefold difference in caloric expenditure between the sedentary and extremely active should dispel this notion. Even small differences in caloric expenditure can become quite substantial over many months.

During exercise, approximately 5 kcal are utilized for the consumption of every 1 liter of oxygen. However, an increase in metabolic rate after exercise, due to the Q_{10} effect (heat increases metabolic rate) and anabolic process elicited by the exercise stimulus, is almost equal to the caloric cost of the exercise itself. These postexercise effects add to the potent effect of physical activity in caloric expenditure.

Many studies have demonstrated that the amount of physical activity is the most important difference between the lean and obese. Obese individuals typically lead a sedentary life-style and, when involved in sports, pursue them

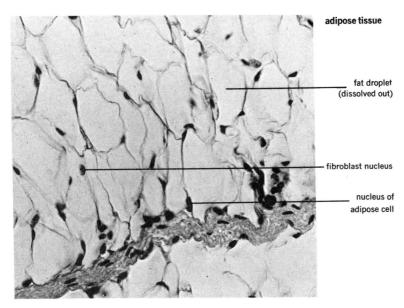

adipose tissue

fat droplet
(dissolved out)

fibroblast nucleus

nucleus of
adipose cell

Figure 11-6
Micrograph of adipose tissue.

(SOURCE: J. E. McClintic, 1971, p. 112. In: G. A. Brooks and T. D. Fahey. Exercise Physiology: Human Bioenergetics and Its Applications. New York: Macmillan, 1984, Figure 25-6.)

less vigorously than lean people. These patterns were evident in studies of children as well as adults. However, critics of these studies point out that physical activity in the obese has a higher metabolic cost.

Hypercellularity of Adipose

Obesity can occur because of an increase in adipose cell size, number, or both (Figure 11-6). Severely obese individuals have been shown to have three times as many fat cells that can be 40% larger than those in lean people. Fat cells increase in both size and number during childhood and, to a certain extent, during adolescence. In the adult, the number of cells becomes fixed and they increase only in size (except in extreme obesity). Weight loss results in a decrease in the size of the fat cells but not in the number. Animal studies show that the development of fat cells can be reduced by endurance exercise and diet *during growth*. Efforts should be directed toward preventing the initial development of fat cells during the growth period.

Diet, Exercise, and Weight Control

The most successful weight loss programs seem to be those that use a combination of diet and exercise. The success or failure of any diet depends on its effect on energy balance. While caloric restriction is an essential component of any weight control program, it is probably doomed to failure in the long run if the person is physically inactive. Dietary restriction without exercise has been shown to result in a decrease in metabolic rate, probably due to a substantial loss of lean body weight. (Approximately 40 percent of weight lost in this type of program is lean body mass.) Fat is lost at a slower rate than expected and it is difficult to remain on the dietary regimen. When exercise is added to the weight control program, metabolic rate is increased above normal and lean body mass tends to be maintained, which accelerates the weight loss. In addition, exercise complements dietary restriction because it depresses appetite, making a program of caloric reduction more bearable. The calories burned during exercise also often allow the dieter to consume more calories and still lose weight, which presents a more acceptable approach to long-term weight control.

Exercise is a vital part of a lifelong weight control program because it allows the consumption of enough calories to supply the body with adequate nutrients as well as energy. Caloric restriction alone often leads to malnourishment because the diet may not contain enough food to provide the necessary vitamins and minerals. Chronic caloric and fluid restriction (fad diets often restrict fluids in an effort to reduce weight) may eventually have serious health consequences. Although a single session of exercise results in little fat loss, regular training can make a substantial difference in the weight control program. The expenditure of 300 cal during exercise, three or four times a week, can result in the loss of 13 to 23 lb of fat in a year, provided the caloric intake remains the same. While that may not seem like much to a crash dieter, the weight loss consists of fat and not a combination of water, lean tissue, and fat, which is commonly lost on most fad diets.

As fitness improves, exercise has a more potent effect on caloric utilization. A change in maximal oxygen consumption from 3 liters $\cdot$ min^{-1} to 3.5 liters $\cdot$ min^{-1} increases the ability to burn calories by about 16%. Exercise for weight control should center on long-term endurance activity for a minimum of 20 min (see Chapter 17). The amount of fat loss from exercise is directly proportional to the duration and intensity of the activity. At the same intensity of exercise, in activities which are greatly affected by gravity, the obese lose more fat than the lean because they do more work.

Harmful Weight-Loss Techniques   Chronic dieters usually overemphasize excessive weight rather than excessive fat. They often see the loss of water or lean mass as desirable and concentrate on the rate of weight loss rather than its permanence. They fail to realize that food provides nutrients as well as energy and that an adequate caloric intake is necessary for good health. The long-term solution lies in achieving a balance between energy intake and expenditure.

The loss of 1 lb of fat requires a caloric deficit of approximately 3500 cal. A sedentary person of average size does not even expend that many calories in a day, so it is impossible to lose more than a few pounds of fat in a week. Diets that promise large decreases in fat in a short time are fraudulent.

Exercising with impermeable clothing (rubber suits and belts) is a popular technique of losing weight and inches. The weight loss is caused by fluid depletion, however, and does not represent loss of fat. The resulting dehydration of the cells under the clothes does cause a temporary loss of circumference; however, the change is short-lived as normal fluid balance is quickly restored. Chronic dehydration can also result in kidney disorders.

Starvation diets can result in a considerable weight loss, but unfortunately much of it consists of lean body mass. These diets can have serious side effects such as arrhythmias (ECG), gout, anemia, hypotension, and various metabolic disturbances. In addition, starvation does little to modify eating habits that will help the person maintain his lost weight.

Just as misleading are calisthenic exercise programs that promise to decrease fat in specific locations. Exercise does not result in the spot-reduction of fat. Although the improved muscle tone that results from training will usually make a particular area of the body look better, the subcutaneous adipose layer that lies over the muscles is unaffected (except as it is affected by any negative caloric balance). However, increasing muscle girth results in a thinner layer of fat (although total subcutaneous fat remains the same), which improves appearance.

Body Composition

Body composition can be divided into two components: lean body mass, or fat-free weight, and body fat. The lean body mass encompasses all of the body's nonfat tissues including the skeleton, water, muscle, connective tissue, organ tissues, and teeth. The body fat component includes both the essential and nonessential lipid stores. Essential fat includes lipid incorporated into organs and tissues such as nerves, brain, heart, lungs, liver, and mammary glands. The storage fat exists primarily within adipose tissue.

Ideal Body Composition

Perhaps the three most important considerations determining the ideal body composition are health, aesthetics, and performance. The average person tends to be most concerned with the two latter factors, whereas the athlete is concerned with all three.

Although the absolute range of the ideally "healthy fat percentage" has not been clearly established, it is generally agreed to be between 16 and 25% for women and less than 20% for men. Figure 11-7A and *B,* present the 90th, 50th, and 10th percentiles of percentage fat for men and women in different age groups. Notice that the average man and woman fall above the recommended fat percentage in almost all age categories.

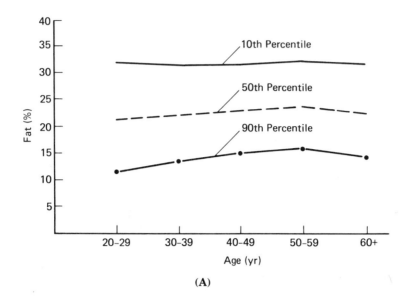

(A)

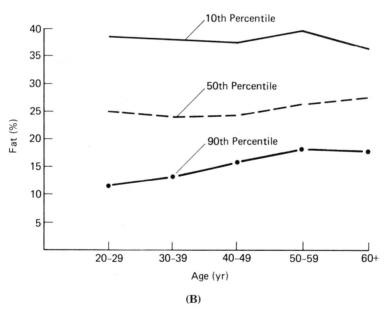

(B)

Figure 11-7

Fat percentage in (**A**) males and (**B**) females as a function of age.

(SOURCE: From data presented in M. Pollock, J. H. Wilmore, and S, M. Fox. Health and Fitness Through Physical Activity. New York: Macmillan, 1978.)

The ideal aesthetic body composition is even more difficult to establish. These days, the lean, athletic look is prized, while the more corpulent look of the turn of the century is disdained. Unfortunately, the quest for the "lean look" often leads to unhealthy dietary habits. This is especially disturbing among athletes, who usually have very high caloric requirements because of heavy training. Teenage female athletes seem to be especially prone to over-zealous caloric restriction that can be dangerous.

Body composition is an extremely important consideration in many sports. In sports with weight categories, such as wrestling, boxing, and weight lift-ing, serious abuses have taken place in an attempt to lose weight, which have sometimes compromised the health of the athletes. Successful athletes in various sports usually possess a characteristic body composition (Table 11-1). The variability in body fat seems to depend on the metabolic requirement of the activity and the relative disadvantage of carrying an extra load. For example, successful male distance runners are almost always less than 9% fat. For these athletes, excess fat is a decided disadvantage, and the tremendous caloric cost of running long distances makes the deposition of large amounts of fat extremely difficult.

TABLE 11-1   **Body Composition Values in Athletes**

Athletic Group or Sport	Sex	Age (year)	Height (cm)	Weight (kg)	Relative Fat (%)
Baseball	Male	20.8	182.7	83.3	14.2
	Male	——	——	——	11.8
	Male	27.4	183.1	88.0	12.6
Basketball	Male	26.8	193.6	91.2	9.7
	Female	19.1	169.1	62.6	20.8
	Female	19.4	167.0	63.9	26.9
Football	Male	20.3	184.9	96.4	13.8
	Male	——	——	——	13.9
Defensive backs	Male	17–23	178.3	77.3	11.5
Offensive backs	Male	17–23	179.7	79.8	12.4
Linebackers	Male	17–23	180.1	87.2	13.4
Offensive linemen	Male	17–23	186.0	99.2	19.1
Defensive linemen	Male	17–23	186.6	97.8	18.5
Defensive backs	Male	24.5	182.5	84.8	9.6
Offensive backs	Male	24.7	183.8	90.7	9.4
Linebackers	Male	24.2	188.6	102.2	14.0
Offensive line	Male	24.7	193.0	112.6	15.6
Defensive line	Male	25.7	192.4	117.1	18.2
Quarterbacks, kickers	Male	24.1	185.0	90.1	14.4

TABLE 11-1 Body Composition Values in Athletes (*Continued*)

Athletic Group or Sport	Sex	Age (year)	Height (cm)	Weight (kg)	Relative Fat (%)
Gymnastics	Male	20.3	178.5	69.2	4.6
	Female	19.4	163.0	57.9	23.8
	Female	20.0	158.5	51.1	15.5
	Female	14.0	——	——	17.0
	Female	23.0	——	——	11.0
	Female	23.0	——	——	9.6
Ice hockey	Male	26.3	180.3	86.7	15.1
Jockeys	Male	30.9	158.2	50.3	14.1
Skiing	Male	25.9	176.6	74.8	7.4
Swimming	Male	21.8	182.3	79.1	8.5
	Male	20.6	182.9	78.9	5.0
	Female	19.4	168.0	63.8	26.3
Track and field	Male	21.3	180.6	71.6	3.7
	Male	——	——	——	8.8
Runners	Male	22.5	177.4	64.5	6.3
Distance	Male	26.1	175.7	64.2	7.5
	Male	40–49	180.7	71.6	11.2
	Male	50–59	174.7	67.2	10.9
	Male	60–69	175.7	67.1	11.3
	Male	70–75	175.6	66.8	13.6
	Male	47.2	176.5	70.7	13.2
	Female	19.9	161.3	52.9	19.2
	Female	32.4	169.4	57.2	15.2
Sprint	Female	20.1	164.9	56.7	19.3
Discus	Male	28.3	186.1	104.7	16.4
	Male	26.4	190.8	110.5	16.3
	Female	21.1	168.1	71.0	25.0
Jumpers and hurdlers	Female	20.3	165.9	59.0	20.7
Shot put	Male	27.0	188.2	112.5	16.5
	Male	22.0	191.6	126.2	19.6
	Female	21.5	167.6	78.1	28.0
Tennis	Male	——	——	——	15.2
Volleyball	Female	19.4	166.0	59.8	25.3
Weight lifting	Male	24.9	166.4	77.2	9.8
Power	Male	26.3	176.1	92.0	15.6
Olympic	Male	25.3	177.1	88.2	12.2
Body builders	Male	29.0	172.4	83.1	8.4
Wrestling	Male	26.0	177.8	81.8	9.8
	Male	27.0	176.0	75.7	10.7
	Male	22.0	——	——	5.0
	Male	19.6	174.6	74.8	8.8
	Male	15–18	172.3	66.3	6.9

SOURCE: From J. H. Wilmore and J. A. Bergfeld. A comparison of sports: physiological and medical aspects. In: Strauss, R. J. (ed.). Sports Medicine and Physiology. Philadelphia: W. B. Saunders, 1979.

Football linemen, on the other hand, are almost always greater than 15% fat. This may be advantageous because of the added mass and padding provided by the subcutaneous fat and the increase in lean mass that accompanies excess weight (muscle mass accompanies gains in fat to support the extra weight). Unfortunately, many younger athletes gain too much fat in an attempt to attain the high body weights of the professional football player.

Body Composition Measurement

The morning weighing ritual on the bathroom scale is really an attempt to estimate body composition. Using this method, it is impossible to accurately determine whether a fluctuation in weight is due to a change in muscle, body water, or fat. The method cannot differentiate between overweight and overfat. A 260-lb muscular football player may be overweight according to population height–weight standards, yet actually have much less body fat than average. Likewise, a 40-year-old woman may weigh exactly the same as when she was in high school, yet have a considerably different body composition.

Several methods have been developed that can provide a more precise estimation of body composition. Laboratory methods include densitometry (underwater weighing), potassium-40 (^{40}K), nuclear magnetic resonance (NMR), radiography and neutron activation analysis. Field test methods include ultrasound, anthropometry, and electrical impedance. The field tests are usually validated with standard laboratory techniques.

Hydrostatic Weighing   Hydrostatic or underwater weighing is considered the most accurate indirect means of measuring body composition and serves as a standard for other indirect techniques such as skinfolds (Figure 11-8). This procedure was popularized by researchers such as Behnke and Pace in the early 1940s and has become an important tool in exercise physiology and medicine. The equations used in this method stem from the direct chemical analysis of human cadavers.

Chemical analyses of human cadavers have demonstrated several universal characteristics of body composition that have made possible the indirect measurement of body fat. These studies have shown that the density of fat (density is a measure of compactness) and muscle and the ratios of skeletal weight and body water to lean body weight are relatively constant. Further, numerous animal studies showed an inverse relationship between the density of the animal and its percentage of fat.

Density is equal to mass divided by volume. Unfortunately, the irregular shape of the human body makes a simple geometric estimation of its volume impossible. The volume of the body can be measured by using Archimedes' principle of water displacement. This principle states that "A body immersed in water is buoyed up with a force equal to the weight of the water displaced." The volume of the body can be measured by determining the weight loss by complete immersion in water. The density of the body, and thus its percent-

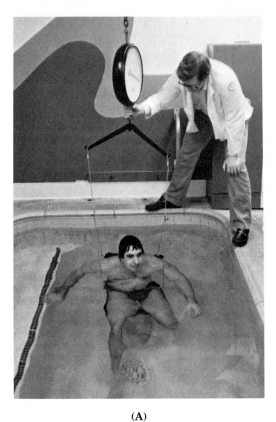

(A)

Figure 11-8
The underwater weighing technique (**A, B, C**). (**A**) Subject maximally expires from lungs. (**B**) Subject submerges and is weighed. (**C**) Data is corrected for residual lung volume (O_2 washout method is shown).

(SOURCE: G. A. Brooks and T. D. Fahey, pp. 540–541).

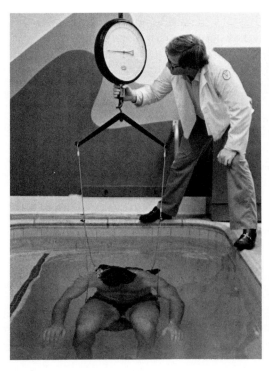

(B)

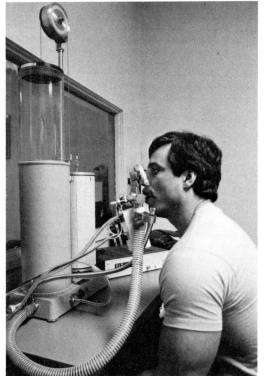

(C)

age fat, can be calculated by dividing the body weight (scale weight) by the body volume (calculated by underwater weighing).

In this procedure, the subject is submerged and weighed underwater. Muscle has a higher density and fat a lower density than water (approximately 1.1 g/cm^3 for muscle, 0.91 g/cm^3 for fat, and 1 g/cm^3 for water). Therefore, fat people tend to float and weigh less underwater, whereas lean people tend to sink and weigh more underwater. At a given body weight, a fat person has a larger volume than a thin one and thus a smaller density.

A number of errors are possible even in this relatively precise laboratory procedure (the error of underwater weighing is estimated as 2.5% fat). Failure to consider factors such as residual lung volume, intestinal gas, and water density will decrease the underwater weight and result in an overestimation of volume. During the measurement, the subject is weighed completely submerged in water while attempting to expel as much air as possible from the lungs. A small but variable amount of air called the residual lung volume remains, which must be taken into account in the equation. Although residual lung volume can be estimated, accurate assessment of body composition requires that it be measured directly. Further, intestinal gas will also increase buoyancy and confound the results. Finally, water has a density of 1 g/cm^3 only at a temperature of 39.2° F. The calculation of volume must be corrected for a difference in water density if the water temperature is other than 39.2° F. Another problem with this technique is that tissue densities may vary in different populations (thus a basic assumption of the procedure is violated).

The two most widely used equations for the calculation of lean body mass and percentage fat were derived by Brozek et al. and Siri. Their slight variance stems from different estimations of the density of fat and muscle. These equations, together with sample calculations of density, percentage fat, and lean mass appear in Table 11-2.

Biochemical Techniques A number of biochemical techniques have been employed in the measurement of body composition and are based on biological constants observed during the direct chemical analysis of the body. These methods include potassium-40 (^{40}K), total body water, inert gas absorption, neutron activation analysis, and nuclear magnetic resonance.

The lean body mass contains a relatively constant proportion of potassium. Part of this potassium is in the form of ^{40}K, a naturally occurring isotope. The gamma-rays emitted by the ^{40}K can be measured with a whole body scintillation counter, which allows the prediction of total body potassium and lean body mass. The results of this method are very similar to those of hydrostatic weighing. Because of the expense of the scintillation counter, this method is almost completely restricted to research.

Various diffusion techniques rely on the property of various substances to diffuse into specific tissues or compartments. Tracers such as deuterium

TABLE 11-2   Equations for the Calculation of Body Density, Percentage Fat, Body Fat, and Lean Body Mass

1. Body density $= \dfrac{BW}{\dfrac{BW - UWW}{D_{H_2O}} - RLV}$

   where BW = body weight (kg), UWW = underwater weight, D_{H_2O} = density of water (at submersion temperature), and RLV = residual lung volume.

2. Percentage fat $= \left(\dfrac{4.950}{D_b} - 4.50\right) \times 100$
   (Siri equation)
   where D_b = body density

3. Percentage fat $= \left(\dfrac{4.570}{D_b} - 4.142\right) \times 100$
   (Brozek equation)

4. Total body fat (kg) = Body weight (kg) $\times \% \dfrac{Fat}{100}$

5. Lean body weight = Body weight – Fat weight

SOURCE: Brooks and Fahey, Exercise Physiology: Human Bioenergetics and Its Applications, New York: Macmillan, 1984, p. 543.

oxide, tritium oxide, antipyrine, and ethanol have been used to estimate total body water. Lean body mass can thus be estimated because body water represents an almost constant 73.2% of body weight and the water is contained almost entirely within the lean body mass. Fat-soluble, inert gases such as krypton and cyclopropane have been used to estimate the percentage fat by measuring their rate of absorption into the body.

Measurements of creatinine excretion, 3-methylhistidine excretion, and nitrogen balance are useful in estimating muscle mass and assessing changes in lean body mass. Urinary creatinine concentration is roughly proportional to muscle mass. Unfortunately, levels are affected by heavy exercise, emotional stress, disease, and diet. However, used with other techniques, its measurement may help to make estimates of body composition more accurate. 3-methylhistidine excretion is an excellent marker of myofibrillar breakdown (the myofibril is the basic contractile component of the muscle cell) and muscle mass. However, it is unlikely that it will be widely used outside of the research laboratory because its measurement places excessive demands on subject (i.e., repeated 24 hr urine samples and 3 days on a meat-free diet).

Nitrogen balance is considered the best method of measuring small, short-term changes in body protein. The method assumes a ratio of 6.25 g of protein per g of nitrogen. Nitrogen balance (and thus the net gain or loss of body protein) is calculated by measuring the difference between nitrogen intake in the diet and nitrogen excretion in urine, feces, sweat, etc. A positive nitrogen balance indicates a net gain in body protein, while a negative nitrogen balance indicates a net loss. While accurate, this is an extremely difficult procedure for both subject and researcher.

Two new and promising techniques for measuring body composition are nuclear magnetic resonance (NMR) and neutron activation analysis (NAA). In NMR the body is surrounded by a strong and uniform magnetic field which causes certain naturally occurring atomic nuclei (i.e., hydrogen-1, carbon-13, fluoride-19, sodium-23, and phosphorous-31) to line up in relation to the field. When an occilating magnetic field is applied at right angles to a static one, the nuclei will resonate at a particular frequency. The resonance will cause the nuclei to emit low level radio frequency energy. The characteristics of this energy reveals precise information about the makeup of the body's tissues. NAA works by scanning the body with two neutron fields and measuring the gamma radiation emitted as a consequence of this procedure. This technique accurately measures body nitrogen which, as discussed, exists in a fixed proportion to body protein.

Ultrasound, Computerized Tomography (CT), and Electrical Impedance Ultrasound is widely used in cardiology to noninvasively examine heart walls and valves and in obstetrics to observe the developing fetus. Several investigators have used ultrasound to estimate thicknesses of layers of fat and muscle. The instrument emits sound waves that are directed at specific parts of the body. A characteristic echo occurs as it strikes tissues of differing thickness and density. This echo is quantified by the instrument. This technique may provide an alternative to anthropometric techniques of quickly and accurately estimating body composition.

CT is an x-ray technique that provides a three-dimensional view of the body. CT scans allow accurate assessment of the volumes and thicknesses of various organs and tissue spaces and should add considerably to our knowledge of body composition. It is unlikely that this technique will become widely used to measure body composition outside of research applications because the procedure is expensive and involves radiation exposure.

Measurement of total body electrical conductivity (TOBEC) and bioelectric impedance (BIA) are new and popular methods of measuring body composition. TOBEC works by surrounding the body with an electromagnetic field and measuring the rate that the body conducts electrical energy. The operating principle is that lean tissue and body water conduct electricity more rapidly than fat. While the TOBEC technique is an excellent predictor of body composition measured by underwater weighing, the required instrument currently costs between $50,000–100,000. In BIA, an electric current is applied to an extremity (i.e., arm) and the impedance to the electrical flow measured at an opposite extremity (i.e., leg). Impedance is greater in people with more fat and less in people with more lean tissue. Most studies have shown that BIA is less accurate than the skinfold in estimating body composition. Investigators have estimated an average measurement error of approximately 6% fat. So, based on current technology, BIA must be considered an inaccurate, expensive gimmick.

Anthropometric Techniques Anthropometric assessment of body composition utilizes various superficial measurements such as height, weight, skinfolds, and anatomical circumferences. Of these, height–weight is by far the most popular. Height–weight tables, periodically produced by insurance companies, are inadequate because they are subject to individual interpretation by requiring people to decide if they are of small, medium, or large frame and do not take into consideration individual differences in lean body mass and relative fat.

Sheldon devised a rating system for assessment of body composition based on three components, rated on a seven-point scale. The three components were endomorphy, relative predominance of corpulence and roundness; mesomorphy, relative predominance of muscularity; and ectomorphy, relative predominance of linearity and fragility of body build. This method is very subjective and requires a test administrator who is well trained in the photographic protocol and rating system.

Behnke presented an anthropometric technique for estimating body composition that compares various circumferences of a subject with those of a reference man or woman. Like other field test methods, however, it requires experience to obtain the precise measurements necessary for accurate results.

Skinfold measurements are probably the most popular "scientific" means of assessing body composition (Figure 11-9). This method is inexpensive, rapid, and takes little time to learn. Skinfold equations are derived using a statistical technique called multiple regression, which predicts the results of the hydrostatic weighing procedure from the measurement of skinfolds taken at various sites. It is absolutely essential that a subject be measured using an equation derived from a similar population. For example, it would be inappropriate to use a skinfold equation to estimate the body fat of a 40-year-old man that was derived from 18-year-old college females.

Several models of skinfold calipers are available. The ideal caliper should have parallel jaw surfaces and a constant spring tension, regardless of the degree of opening. Many inexpensive, plastic calipers have become available recently, but these should be avoided because of the potential for error.

The skinfold method is subject to severe limitations and should be used only in field studies or in circumstances when only gross estimations of body composition are required. This technique has been shown to render considerable measurement error, even among experienced observers. Dehydration will decrease a skinfold thickness by as much as 15%, so would likely cause variability between measurements taken in the morning and evening. In addition, skinfold measurements have been shown to be of no value in predicting changes in body composition following weight loss. The accuracy of this

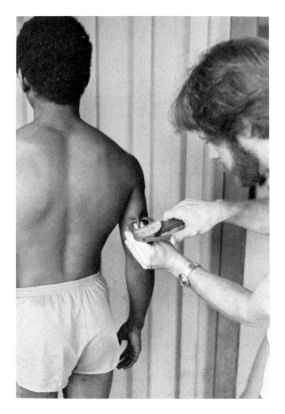

Figure 11-9
The skinfold technique.
(SOURCE: G. A. Brooks and T. D. Fahey, p. 545.)

method can be improved through the use of multiple measurements by a single, experienced observer.

Nutritional Practice in Athletics

Perhaps no greater mythology exists in sports than in the area of athletic nutrition. To gain an immediate competitive edge, athletes have engaged in all sorts of odd dietary habits that are perpetuated if the athlete is successful because of genetic endowment. Sound nutritional practices of what to eat, how much to eat, and when to eat it will allow an athlete to perform up to his or her potential in practice and competition. Sound nutrition combined with habitual overload training can enable athletes to achieve incredible feats. At present, however, no known foodstuff will allow a mediocre, moderately conditioned athlete to become an Olympic champion. It is more likely that the miracle diet consumed before a competition will result in problems than in outstanding performance. To perform to its maximum, the body requires specific nutritional elements. However, those elements are available in a wide variety of foods. The body even has some flexibility in terms of interconversions of materials. Regarding nutrition and sports, it is *not* true that you are what you eat, and it is *not* true that you metabolize what you consume. A balanced diet consists of at least three square meals a day, wherein the daily protein content is 15 to 20%, carbohydrate content is 45 to 55%, and fat consumption is 35% or less of total calories. These calories should be consumed in the form of (1) milk and milk products, (2) protein foods including lean meats, fish, poultry, eggs, cheese, and beans, (3) vitamin C fruits such as citrus and tomatoes, (4) dark green and yellow fresh vegetables, (5) potatoes and other starchy vegetables, (6) whole grain products, and (7) fats. The consumption of fats and refined sugar products should be held to a minimum. If necessary, the reader should review Chapters 2 to 4 before proceeding to the following sections on diet and sports nutrition.

The Normal Balanced Diet

To assist the general population in selecting from available foods to form a daily nutritional adequate and balanced diet, the U.S. Department of Agriculture (USDA) in 1957 classified foods into four basic groups and made recommendations about how many items from the four groups should be consumed daily. These four food groups became known as "the basic four." They include the following:

1. milk and calcium equivalent foods,
2. meat and protein equivalent foods,
3. fruits and vegetables, and
4. grains.

Today, to assist in educating people on the composition of foods and how to select foods for a nutritious diet, various nutrition advisory boards, such as the U.S. National Dairy Council, publish tables (e.g., Table 11-3), which are very helpful in identifying the nutrients present in various foods and the physiological functions served by those foods.

It must be realized that it is very difficult to make specific dietary recommendations for the general population because individual dietary needs can be quite unique. Periods of growth and physical activity will require extra calorie and protein intake, whereas in older individuals the dietary essentials should be present among fewer calories. During unique physiological situations such as pregnancy, proper nutrition becomes especially important. Another reason dietary recommendations are difficult to make is that our knowledge of essential dietary constituents as well as their proportions is inadequate. Therefore, in making dietary recommendations today, it is be-

TABLE 11-3 Food Sources and Physiological Functions of Nutrients

Nutrient	Important Sources of Nutrient	Some Major Physiological Functions		
		Provide Energy	Build and Maintain Body Cells	Regulate Body Processes
Protein	Meat, poultry, fish Dried beans and peas Egg Cheese Milk	Supplies 4 kcal/g.	Constitutes part of the structure of every cell, such as muscles, blood, and bone; supports growth and maintains healthy body cells.	Constitutes part of enzymes, some hormones and body fluids, and antibodies that increase resistance to infection.
Carbohydrate	Cereal Potatoes Dried beans Corn Bread Sugar	Supplies 4 kcal/g. Major source of energy for central nervous system.	Supplies energy so protein can be used for growth and maintenance of body cells.	Unrefined products supply fiber—complex carbohydrates in fruits, vegetables, and whole grains—for regular elimination. Assists in fat utilization.
Fat	Shortening, oil Butter, margarine Salad dressing Sausages	Supplies 9 kcal/g.	Constitutes part of the structure of every cell. Supplies essential fatty acids.	Provides and carries fat-soluble vitamins (A, D, E, and K).
Vitamin A (retinol)	Liver Carrots Sweet potatoes Greens Butter, margarine		Assists formation and maintenance of skin and mucous membranes that line body cavities and tracts, such as nasal passages and intestinal tract, thus increasing resistance to infection.	Functions in visual processes and forms visual purple, thus promoting healthy eye tissues and eye adaptation in dim light.
Vitamin C (ascorbic acid)	Broccoli Orange Grapefruit Papaya Mango Strawberries		Forms cementing substances, such as collagen, that hold body cells together, thus strengthening blood vessels, hastening healing of wounds and bones, and increasing resistance to infection.	Aids utilization of iron.
Thiamin (B$_1$)	Lean pork Nuts Fortified cereal products	Aids in utilization of energy.		Functions as part of a coenzyme to promote the utilization of carbohydrate.

TABLE 11-3 Food Sources and Physiological Functions of Nutrients (*Continued*)

Nutrient	Important Sources of Nutrient	Some Major Physiological Functions		
		Provide Energy	Build and Maintain Body Cells	Regulate Body Processes
				Promotes normal appetite. Contributes to normal functioning of nervous system.
Riboflavin (B$_2$)	Liver Milk Yogurt Cottage cheese	Aids in utilization of energy.		Functions as part of a coenzyme in the production of energy within body cells. Promotes healthy skin, eyes, and clear vision.
Niacin	Liver Meat, poultry, fish Peanuts Fortified cereal products	Aids in utilization of energy.		Functions as part of a coenzyme in fat synthesis, tissue respiration, and utilization of carbohydrate. Promotes healthy skin, nerves, and digestive tract. Aids digestion and fosters normal appetite.
Calcium	Milk, yogurt Cheese Sardines and salmon with bones Collard, kale, mustard, and turnip greens		Combines with other minerals within a protein framework to give structure and strength to bones and teeth.	Assists in blood clotting. Functions in normal muscle contraction and relaxation, and normal nerve transmission.
Iron	Enriched farina Prune juice Liver Dried beans and peas Red meat	Aids in utilization of energy.	Combines with protein to form hemoglobin, the red substance in blood that carries oxygen to and carbon dioxide from the cells. Prevents nutritional anemia and its accompanying fatigue. Increases resistance to infection.	Functions as part of enzymes involved in tissue respiration.

SOURCE: National Dairy Council. Used with permission.

lieved that individuals should eat a wide variety of foods to increase the probability that all the essentials will be included.

In recognition of the need to include more fruits, vegetables, and whole grain cereals in the diet, it has been recommended that

the "basic four" of 30 years ago be broadened to the "basic seven."

These include the following:

1. milk and milk products (including yogurt, cottage cheese, and ice cream),
2. protein foods (including lean meat, fish, poultry, cheese, eggs, and beans),
3. vitamin C fruits and vegetables (including citrus and tomatoes),
4. dark green and yellow vegetables,
5. potatoes and other starchy vegetables,
6. whole grain products (including breads and cereals), and
7. fats (margarine and vegetable oils).

The effect of these recommendations (Table 11-4) is to "lighten up" our diet by diluting the input from meats and milk and meat products containing cholesterol and saturated fats and to include more fruits, vegetables, and cereals. Fats are included as a separate group to ensure assimilation of fat-soluble vitamins.

Muscle Glycogen

Figure 4-10A illustrated the relationship between the respiratory gas exchange ratio ($R = \dot{V}CO_2/\dot{V}O_2$) and relative work load. From the R, a crude estimate can be made of the relative contribution to energy yield of carbohydrates (glycogen and hexoses) and fats. Once exercise starts, the metabolism of carbohydrates contribute most of the energy released to support the exercise, and the relative contribution provided by carbohydrates increases as the relative work load increases. Endurance training has the effect of shifting the curve (Figure 4-10A) slightly down and to the right, indicating a greater reliance on fats as fuels. As indicated in Figure 4-10B, fat oxidation increases in importance as the duration of exercise increases. Endurance training has the effect of shifting the relationship (Figure 4-10B) up and to the left.

Introduction of the muscle biopsy technique in the late 1960s by Scandinavian scientists, has contributed significantly to our understanding of exercise metabolism. Information contained in the now-famous one-legged experiments (Figure 11-10) summarizes much of what was learned by the biopsy technique. In these experiments, two subjects pedaled the same bicycle ergometer; each subject used one leg to pedal, and exercise continued until exhaustion. During the days following the exercise, subjects rested and ate a high-carbohydrate diet. These one-legged and subsequent studies indicated the following:

TABLE 11-4 The Basic Seven Food Groups and Daily Recommended Servings of Each[a]

Food Groups	Servings to Have Each Day	Serving Sizes
1. Milk and milk products	2	1 cup $1\frac{1}{2}$ cups cottage cheese 1 cup plain yogurt 2 oz. cheese
2. Protein foods (meat, fish, poultry, legumes, nuts)	2	3 oz meat, fish or poultry 2 eggs $\frac{1}{4}$ cup peanut butter 1 cup dried peas, or beans, cooked
3. Vitamin C fruits and vegetables (citrus fruits, tomatoes, green peppers, melons, raw cabbage, dark greens, strawberries)	1	$\frac{3}{4}$ cup
4. Dark green or yellow vegetables	2	$\frac{1}{2}$ cup
5. Potatoes and other fruits and vegetables	1	$\frac{1}{2}$ cup 1 medium potato
6. Whole grain products (breads and cereals)	4	1 slice bread $\frac{1}{2}$–$\frac{3}{4}$ cup cooked cereal 1 cup dry cereal
7. Fat (margarine, vegetable oils)	1	1 tablespoon

[a] Additional calories for active individuals should be selected from all groups with a *minimum* emphasis on Group 7.

SOURCE: M. A. Burkman. Department of Nutritional Sciences, University of California, Berkeley.

1. Prolonged exercise of submaximal intensity can result in glycogen depletion of the active muscle.
2. Glycogen level is little affected in inactive muscle.
3. Following exhausting exercise and a high-carbohydrate diet, glycogen level in the exercised muscle is restored to a higher level than before exercise.
4. Glycogen level in the inactive muscle is little affected by the exercise and diet procedure.

The relationship between muscle glycogen content and endurance during hard but submaximal exercise (at about 75% $\dot{V}O_{2max}$) is illustrated in Figure 11-11. In these experiments, muscle glycogen content was manipulated by diet and previous exercise. Subjects then attempted to maintain a given work load on a bicycle ergometer for as long as possible. From these studies, it is apparent that for exercises such as cycling, the amount of glycogen present when exercise begins can determine the endurance time.

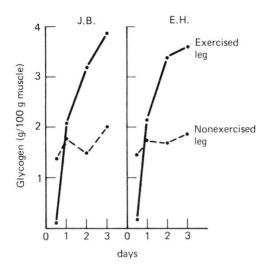

Figure 11-10

Effects of exhausting exercise and diet on quadriceps muscle glycogen content. Exhausting exercise depletes glycogen content in active muscle. Rest and a high carbohydrate diet results in a glycogen overshoot (supercompensation) in the exercised muscle only.

(SOURCE: Based on the data of Bergstrom and Hultman, 1967.)

Carbohydrate Loading and Glycogen Supercompensation

The process by which glycogen concentration is raised to levels two or three times greater than normal is called glycogen supercompensation. Glycogen supercompensation results from a program of exercise (submaximal exercise

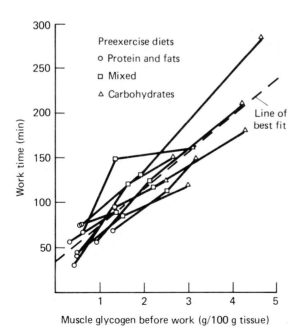

Figure 11-11

Exercise duration on a bicycle ergometer at a net power output for subjects on three different diets. Endurance (exercise duration) depends on the muscle glycogen content before exercise. The diet several days before exercise affects the muscles' glycogen content and, therefore, exercise endurance.

(SOURCE: Based on the data of Bergstrom et al., 1967.)

to exhaustion) and a high-carbohydrate diet. This procedure, sometimes called carbohydrate (carbo) loading, is performed as follows. Three or 4 days prior to competition, the athlete exercises continuously to exhaustion. For some sports it may also be advisable to include some very hard intervals of exercise during and after a brief recovery from the prolonged exercise. These sprints deplete FG and FOG fibers of glycogen. The athlete then rests or trains mildly during the intervening days until competition, and eats a normal, balanced diet that contains substantial carbohydrate. The athlete will then be well prepared to compete in activities requiring hard continuous exercise (e.g., cycling, marathon running) or activities in which activity is not continuous but includes intervals of very hard exercise (e.g., soccer, American football).

Problems with Carbohydrate Loading

From the more than 10 years of experience with carbohydrate loading, it appears that the practice is not universally successful. Some individuals apparently do not respond to the procedure. Further, the precise biochemical mechanism by which the practice works is not understood. Obviously glycogens synthase activity in the affected muscles is increased, but the practice in effect fools the biochemical regulation of this enzyme to produce an abnormal effect. Apparently after repeated attempts to glycogen-supercompensate, the biochemistry "smartens up," and the supercompensation effect is diminished.

Another problem encountered with carbohydrate loading is that, with inexperienced individuals, malnutrition can result. A carbohydrate loading diet should be one rich in whole grain cereals and potatoes. Care should also be taken to include fresh vegetables (for vitamins and minerals) as well as meats or meat substitutes (for protein). Refined sugar products (cakes, pies, candies) and alcohol should be avoided. An example of such a diet is given in Table 11-5. In manipulating an athlete's diet immediately before competition, care should be taken to include necessary nutrients as well as calories. Too little protein or calorie input will result in lean tissue wasting, and too much carbohydrate will result in fat gain. Moreover, a preliminary trial is necessary to ensure that the diet is agreeable and palatable to the athlete.

Another potential problem or asset in glycogen supercompensation, depending on the activity, is that glycogen storage is associated with H_2O retention. Because each gram of glycogen requires almost 3 g of H_2O for storage, each gram in effect adds 4 g of body weight. In some sports (e.g., gymnastics or wrestling), added weight would be a liability. For endurance exercise, the added H_2O would be useful for preventing dehydration.

It has sometimes been advocated that during the interim between exercise to exhaustion and carbohydrate loading, a 2-day period of carbohydrate starvation be imposed. Supposedly, this period when protein and fats are allowed, but no sugars or starches, results in a heightened glycogen supercompensation effect—a super-supercompensation. However, it has never been

TABLE 11-5 Sample High-Energy, High-Carbohydrate Diet for a 75-kg Male during Hard Training or Glycogen Loading[a]

Breakfast
 1 cup orange juice or $\frac{1}{2}$ grapefruit
 1 cup hot cereal
 2 eggs
 Bacon, ham, or sausage (3 oz)
 2–4 slices of whole grain toast or hot cakes with margarine
 Hot chocolate (1–2 cups)

Lunch
 Bowl of clam chowder
 Broiled fish (3–6 oz)
 Cooked rice ($\frac{1}{2}$ cup)
 Green salad with dressing
 Bread (2 slices)
 Milk (1–2 cups)

Dinner
 Cream of potato soup
 Broiled chicken (2 pieces)
 Baked potato(s) (1–2)
 Cooked broccoli (1–2 pieces)
 Strawberries ($\frac{3}{4}$ cup)
 Milk (1–2 cups)

[a] Note the minimal use of refined sugars.
SOURCE: Modified from Åstrand, "Diet and Athletic Performance" *J Appl Physiol* 26:1772–1780, 1967.

convincingly demonstrated that such a carbohydrate-free period is beneficial; on the contrary, carbohydrate starvation after exhausting exercise has often been reported to produce serious side effects. Inducing a period of depression and lethargy immediately before a competition is perhaps not the best way to prepare an athlete psychologically. Furthermore, there is a natural tendency to restore glycogen reserves after exhausting exercise. If adequate carbohydrate is not consumed to accomplish this, lean tissues will be catabolized in the attempt to supply gluconeogenic precursors. The dietary input of proteins may be inadequate to prevent this.

Fat Utilization during Exercise

Although the ability to store glycogen in the body is limited, for practical purposes during athletics the stores of lipid in adipose tissue are essentially inexhaustible. In addition to that stored in adipose tissue, significant amounts

243

of lipid are also deposited in muscle and liver. On the basis of dry weight, more than twice as many calories are stored in fatty acids (9 kcal · g^{-1}) than in glycogen (4 kcal · g^{-1}). Because the storage of lipid entails far less additional water weight than glycogen storage does, the kilocalories stored per gram of lipid plus associated water may exceed that in glycogen by six to eight times. Consequently, storing calories in adipose tissue rather than in glycogen is far more efficient in terms of weight and space. Adipose tissue should be considered as a great fuel reserve. As described in Chapter 4, the mobilization of calories from adipose tissue, their delivery to muscle, as well as their uptake and utilization in muscle, constitute a complicated and lengthy process. Furthermore, untrained subjects seldom have the circulatory capacity or the muscle enzyme activity to utilize fats as the predominant fuels during endurance exercise. Consequently, glycogen becomes the preferred fuel (see Figure 4-10). Through training, however, both circulatory capacity (Chapter 7) and muscle oxidative capacity (Chapter 4) improve, so that the CHO curve in Figure 4-10A shifts down and to the right, while the fat curve in Figure 4-10B shifts up and to the left.

Given the fact that even the leanest endurance athlete has stored away more lipids than he or she will ever use in a competition, athletes do not need to eat extra fat during the days prior to a competition. However, because the uptake of fatty acids by muscle depends to a great extent on circulating levels, anything that raises those levels could potentially benefit endurance. As we will see, some lipid content in the precompetition meal might even be desirable. Also, caffeine present in coffee, tea, and other beverages may slightly enhance lipid mobilization and hence its oxidation.

Dietary Protein Requirements for Athletes (Bulking Up)

For most individuals, including those who are moderately active, a dietary protein content of from 0.8 to 1.0 g of protein · kg^{-1} body weight · day^{-1} is recommended to ensure nitrogen balance. On a normal, balanced North American or European diet, this figure is easily met, especially in active individuals who tend to eat more.

Unfortunately, few studies have evaluated nitrogen balance in athletes during training. As discussed, determination of nitrogen loss involves collection and analysis of all nitrogen-containing materials from the body (including feces, urine, whiskers, semen, menses, and phlegm). This is a difficult task, to say the least. Studies by Gontzea et al. indicate that individuals on a normal recommended diet for protein content (1 g · kg^{-1} · day^{-1}) go into negative nitrogen balance (net loss of body protein) when initiating a program of exercise training (Figure 11-12). Within several days to a week, however, nitrogen balance is restored on the normal diet. It has also been found

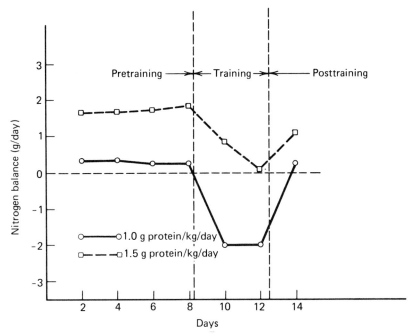

Figure 11-12

The initiation of endurance training causes individuals on a diet containing "normal" amounts of dietary protein (i.e., 1.0 g protein per kilogram body weight per day) to go into negative nitrogen balance (net loss of protein). The negative nitrogen balance condition, which occurs when training intensity increases, may be prevented by increasing dietary protein content.

(SOURCE: Based on the data of Gontzea et al., 1975.)

that the period of negative nitrogen balance can be eliminated if the protein intake is raised to 1.5 to 2 g · kg^{-1} · day^{-1} when training starts. When initiating training or when increasing training intensity, it is therefore advisable to increase protein intake.

On the basis of experimentally determined protein requirements for normal-sized individuals engaged in endurance activity, 1 g · kg^{-1} · day^{-1} is also usually recommended adequate for heavy-weight athletes and those attempting to maintain or increase lean body mass ("bulk up"). Unfortunately, there is inadequate information on the dietary protein content required to bulk up. Increasing lean body mass is often a requirement for success in some track and field events, American football, wrestling, and weight lifting. In one study on Polish Olympic weight lifters preparing for competition, some athletes were unable to maintain nitrogen balance despite extremely high meat and vegetable protein consumptions. As was discussed in Chapter 12, dietary protein supplementation by means of consuming concentrated protein materials may result in superior strength and weight gains in those undergoing very heavy weight training and taking anabolic steroids. The testimonials by athletes who believe their success depends on consuming large amounts of protein and calories, and the examples of such athletes as Polish weight lifters and Japanese sumo wrestlers suggest there is a need for further laboratory investigation. The possibility exists that high-protein, high-calorie diets coupled with extremely high resistance training can positively affect lean body mass. In Chapter 12, the negative side effects of such practices are described.

The Precompetition Meal

The timing, size, and composition of the pregame meal are all important considerations in performing optimally. Ideally, the athlete will enter competition with neither feelings of hunger or weakness (from having eaten too little or not at all) nor fullness from having eaten too much or too recently. Depending on the event, an athlete may want to be glycogen loaded. Ideally, also the blood glucose level will be in the high-normal range ($100 \text{ mg} \cdot \text{dl}^{-1}$ or 5.5 mM) and will not be falling. Blood insulin levels should be constant or falling slightly, but not rising.

It is important for athletes to eat a moderate-sized meal 2½ to 3 hr before competition. The nervous athlete who cannot eat or the athlete with an unfavorable competition schedule could be severely disadvantaged in terms of maintaining blood glucose homeostasis. Even in well-nourished glycogen-loaded athletes during the morning after 8 hr of sleep, the liver will essentially be empty of glycogen, and the blood glucose level will be falling. The hepatic glucose output will be the result of protein catabolism and gluconeogenesis. Therefore, a nutritious breakfast is necessary to stop the fall in blood glucose and begin replenishing liver glycogen content.

The practice of carbohydrate loading has, unfortunately, encouraged the habit, among some athletes, of consuming large amounts of simple starches, syrups, and sugars immediately before competition. The fact is that a glycogen-supercompensated athlete has no real place, except in adipose tissue, to store much of the glucose in a high-sugar, high-carbohydrate diet. Even worse, simple sugars and refined carbohydrates are rather rapidly digested. The rush of glucose into the bloodstream results in a tremendous release of insulin; the insulin clears the glucose from the circulation, but the hormone lingers, causing a continuous fall in blood glucose and increased utilization of muscle glycogen. Soon after a glucose jolt to the circulation, glucose falls lower than if no glucose had been consumed. This is no way to be entering competition.

Prior to the advent of carbohydrate loading, athletes were frequently advised to consume a moderate-sized meal of steak or eggs and toast or pota-toes. This precompetition meal remains an excellent choice and is perhaps the best way to top off a carbohydrate-loading regimen. A lean steak and eggs present minimal problems with digestibility. Furthermore, their digestion re-sults in the release of some fat and amino acids into the circulation. Amino acids do serve as substrates for exercise, and more important, they in effect represent "glucose timed-release capsules." A significant portion of the amino acids will be deaminated in the liver and converted into glucose. A protein meal is actually a means of supplying glucose and avoiding an exaggerated insulin response. It has long been recommended that people who suffer from hypoglycemia (low blood sugar) consume protein-rich meals and avoid sugars and simple, highly refined carbohydrates. Hypoglycemics are those with ex-aggerated insulin responses to elevations in blood sugar (glucose); they re-semble the athlete who packs away sugar at the last minute.

The complex carbohydrates in whole grain bread, cereals, and potatoes are digested more slowly than are sugars or simple carbohydrates. Conse-quently, glucose is released more slowly from the GI tract. Blood glucose rises more slowly and does not peak as high, but it remains elevated longer as a result of the slower release and lower insulin response. Circulating free fatty acid levels after a meal high in complex carbohydrates are more likely to be higher than after a meal containing sugars and simple carbohydrates of the same calorie value. Free fatty acid uptake by muscle is concentration depen-dent.

The old standard pregame meal of steak, eggs, toast, and potatoes, con-sumed 2½ to 3 hr before competition, raises blood glucose and fatty acids and keeps them elevated longer than either no meal or one rich in sugars and simple carbohydrates.

Glucose Ingestion during Exercise

Rather than consuming glucose or simple carbohydrates shortly before com-petition—a practice that may actually hamper performance—consuming di-lute glucose solutions during exercise may enhance performance (Figure 11-13). When dilute, aqueous solutions are taken during exercise, the fuel can enter the circulation without eliciting a large insulin response. Thus, the glucose fuel becomes available to working muscle, and "normal" blood glu-cose levels are maintained to benefit other glucose-requiring tissues such as the brain. As discussed in Chapters 12 and 13, glucose should be taken in dilute aqueous solution to maximize the rate of entry into the blood.

Fructose Versus Glucose   Fructose is an intensely sweet sugar found in honey and fruits. Fructose has the same chemical composition as glucose $(C_6H_{12}O_6)$, but the arrangement of atoms in the molecule differs. Because fructose does no provoke the same high insulin response on entry into the blood as glucose, researchers have attempted to substitute fructose for glu-

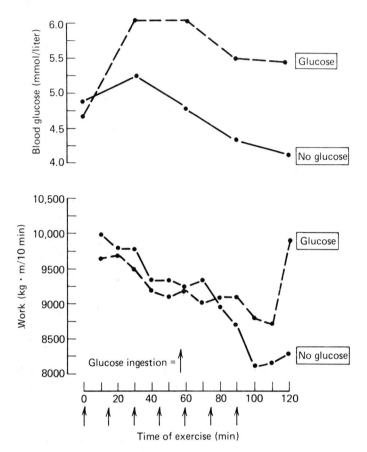

Figure 11-13

Injection of aqueous glucose solutions during prolonged exercise can result in greater work output and endurance. This procedure avoids an insulin response and the result is much different from that obtained when glucose is taken shortly before exercise.

(SOURCE: Based on data from Ivy et al., 1979)

cose in foods and beverages taken before, during, and after exercise. As is often the case, fructose administration has disadvantages as well as benefits.

Although fructose in the blood will not elicit an insulin response as glucose does, in practical terms fructose consumption before or after exercise has little advantage over glucose consumption. There are several reasons for this, many of which are related to how dietary sugars enter the blood. Cells in the intestinal wall possess an enzyme that converts fructose to glucose. Consequently, much of the sugar entering the blood will be glucose although fructose was ingested.

Fructose that does enter the portal circulation (see Figure 3-2) is taken up preferentially by the liver. In the liver, fructose compared with glucose, promotes glycogen and fat (triglyceride) synthesis. Consequently, fructose goes into storage and is less effective in relieving hypoglycemia (low blood glucose) after exercise or in replenishing muscle glycogen levels. In contrast with fructose, glucose is a more potent stimulator of glycogen synthesis in muscle. Additionally, many other types of cells prefer glucose to fructose as a fuel.

Moreover, high-fructose diets consumed over a long time can result in a fatty liver.

As is the case with other forms of dietary manipulation, dietary substitution of fructose for glucose and sucrose (table sugar) should be used judiciously.

Summary

Body composition and nutrition are important considerations for people interested in health and physical performance. Obesity is associated with a variety of diseases, such as coronary heart disease, hypertension, and diabetes, and places an increased load on the body that hampers exercise capacity.

The tendancy to gain or lose body fat is dictated by the body's energy balance. The body is in positive energy balance (and tends to gain fat) if more calories are consumed than burned and is in negative energy balance (and tends to lose fat) when more calories are burned than consumed. Appetite and satiety are controlled by the hypothalamus, which is influenced by a variety of factors such as substrates (fuels) in the blood, temperature, gastrointestinal stretch receptors, liver nutrient receptors, and social programming.

While dietary restrictions is central to any weight (fat) control program, exercise training is probably essential to the program's success. Exercise helps to maintain lean body mass, which is the most important factor determining metabolic rate. Moderate exercise has a depressing effect on appetite and raises metabolic rate for some time during and after the training session (thus, the person continues to burn calories at a higher level than before).

The three principle considerations in determining the ideal body composition are health, aesthetics, and performance. For good health it is recommended that women be less than 25% fat and men less than 20%. Because beauty is in the eye of the beholder, it is difficult to make recommendations about the ideal aesthetic fat percentage. However, excessive preoccupation with leanness is recognized as a psychological disorder (anorexia nervosa). The ideal body composition for physical performance varies with the sport: distance runners must be extremely lean, while summo wrestlers and NFL linemen can be considerably fatter.

A number of methods are used to estimate body composition that range in complexity from CT scans, nuclear magnetic resonance, and underwater weighing to skinfolds and body weight. Underwater weighing is currently considered to be the most accurate method of assessing body composition. However, even this method is sometimes subject to considerable error. New methods may help us to become more accurate and enable us to develop more precise equations for traditional measurement techniques.

The normal balanced diet has not been surpassed for supporting daily life or athletic training and competition. Eating a wide variety of foods ensures the input of necessary calories, proteins, carbohydrates, fats, vitamins, minerals, and trace elements. Further, consumption of such a diet develops sound nutritional habits necessary to sustain the individual throughout his or her life.

Extreme manipulation of the diet immediately before competition can more likely upset or handicap the athlete than trigger outstanding performance. Two exceptions to this rule bear mentioning, however. Carbohydrate loading can potentially benefit athletes engaged in sports requiring endurance and activities causing problems of dehydration. In heavyweight athletes concerned with increasing body mass and lean body mass, the dietary protein content may have to be emphasized to improve deposition of lean tissue. The precompetition meal following carbohydrate loading should be either a balanced meal or one high in protein.

Selected Readings

American Association for Health, Physical Education, and Recreation. Nutrition for the Athlete. Washington, D.C.: AAHPER, 1971.

Angel, A. Pathophysiologic changes in obesity. CMA J. 119:1401, 1406, 1978.

Bailey, C.J. On the physiology and biochemistry of obesity. Sci. Prog., Oxf. 65:365–393, 1978.

Behnke, A.R., and J.H. Wilmore. Evaluation and Regulation of Body Build and Composition. Englewood Cliffs, N.J.: Prentice-Hall, 1974.

Berchtold, P., V. Jorgens, C. Finke, and M. Berger. Epidemiology of obesity and hypertension. Int. J. Obesity 5:1–7, 1981.

Bergstrom, J., L. Hermansen, E. Hultman, and B. Saltin. Diet muscle glycogen, and performance. Acta Physiol. Scand. 7:140–150, 1967.

Bergstrom, J., and E. Hultman. Muscle glycogen synthesis after exercise: an enhancing factor localized to the muscle cells in man. Nature 210:309–310, 1966.

Bray, G.A., J.A. Glennon, L.B. Salans, E.S. Horton, E. Danforth, and E.A. Sims. Spontaneous and experimental human obesity: effects of diet and adipose cell size on lipolysis and lipogenesis. Metabolism 26:739–747, 1977.

Brooks, G.A. and T.D. Fahey. Exercise Physiology: Human Bioenergetics and its applications. New York: Macmillan, 1984.

Brown, C.H., and J.H. Wilmore. The effects of maximal resistance training on the strength and body composition of women athletes. Med. Sci. Sport 6:174–177, 1974.

Buskirk, E.R. Obesity: a brief overview with emphasis on exercise. Fed. Proc. 33:1948–1951, 1974.

Butterfield, G., and D. Calloway. Physical activity improves protein utilization in young men. Brit. J. Nutr. 51:171–184, 1984.

Celejowa, I., and M. Homa. Food intake, nitrogen balance, and energy balance in Polish weight lifters during a training camp. Nutr. Metabol. 12:259–274, 1970.

Clarke, H.H. Exercise and fat reduction. Phys. Fit. Res. Digest. 5:1–27, 1975.

Costill, D.L., E. Coyle, G. Dalsky, W. Evans, W. Fink, and D. Hopes. Effects of elevated plasma FFA and insulin on muscle glycogen usage during exercise. J. Appl. Physiol. 37:679–683, 1974.

CURREY, H., R. MALCOLM, E. RIDDLE, and M. SCHACHTE. Behavioral treatment of obesity. JAMA 237:2829–2831, 1977.

EPSTEIN, L.H. and R.R. WING. Aerobic exercise and weight. Addictive Behav. 5:371–388, 1980.

FAHEY, T.D. Athletic Training: Principles and Practice. Palo Alto: Mayfield Publishing Co., 1986.

FAHEY, T.D., L. AKKA, and R. ROLPH. Body composition and $\dot{V}O_{2max}$ of exceptional weight-trained athletes. J. Appl. Physiol. 39:559–561, 1975.

FRANKLIN, B.A., and M. RUBENFIRE. Losing weight through exercise. JAMA 244:377–379, 1980.

GONTZEA, I., R. SUTZESCU, and S. DUMATRACHE. The influence of adaptation to physical effort on nitrogen balance in man. Nutr. Rep. Int. 11:231–236, 1975.

HENDERSON, S.A., A.L. BLACK, and G.A. BROOKS. Leucine turnover and oxidation in trained and untrained rats during rest and exercise. Med. Sci. Sports Exercise 15:98, 1983.

HICKSON, R.C., M.J. RENNIE, W.W. WINDER, and J.O. HOLLOSZY. Effects of increased plasma fatty acids on glycogen utilization and endurance. J. Appl. Physiol. 43:828–833, 1977.

HIMMS-HAGEN, J. Obesity may be due to a malfunctioning of brown fat. CMA J. 121:1361–1364, 1979.

IVY, J.L., D.L. COSTILL, W.J. FINK, and R.W. LOWER. Influence of caffeine and carbohydrate feedings on endurance performance. Med. Sci. Sports 11:6–11, 1979.

JAMES, W.P.T., and P. TRAYHURN. Thermogenesis and obesity. Br. Med. Bull. 37:43–48, 1981.

KATCH, F., and W.D. MCARDLE. Nutrition, Weight Control, and Exercise. Boston: Houghton Mifflin, 1977, pp. 101–134.

KLEIBER, M. The Fire of Life. New York: John Wiley, 1961, pp. 41–59.

LEMON, R.W.R., and J.P. MULLIN. Effect of initial muscle glycogen levels on protein catabolism during exercise. J. Appl. Physiol.: Respirat. Environ. Exercise Physiol. 48:624–629, 1980.

LEWIS, S., W.L. HASKELL, H. KLEIN, J. HALPERN, and P.D. WOOD. Prediction of body composition in habitually active middle-aged men. J. Appl. Physiol. 39:221–225, 1975.

MALCOLM, R., P.M. O'NEIL, A.A. HIRSCH, H.S. CURREY, and G. MOSKOWITZ. Taste hedonics and thresholds in obesity. Int. J. Obesity 4:203–212, 1980.

MOTT, T., and J. ROBERTS. Obesity and hypnosis: a review of the literature. Am. J. Clin. Hypnosis 22:3–7, 1979.

NATIONAL DAIRY COUNCIL. Nutrition and human performance. Dairy Council Dig. 51:13–17. 1980.

OSCAI, L.B., S.P. BABIRAK, J.A. MCGARR, and C.N. SPIRAKIS. Effect of exercise on adipose tissue cellularity. Fed. Proc. 33:1956–1958, 1974.

POLLOCK, M.L., E.E. LAUGHRIDGE, B. COLEMAN, A.C. LINNERUD, AND A. JACKSON. Prediction of body density in young and middle-aged women. J. Appl. Physiol. 38:745–749, 1975.

ROCHE, A.F. Body Composition assessments in youth and adults. Columbus, Oh: Ross Laboratories, 1985.

SHARP, J.T., M. BARROCAS, and S. CHOKROVERTY. The cardiorespiratory effects of obesity. Clin. Chest Med. 1:103–117, 1980.

STERN, J.S. and M.R.C. GREENWOOD. A review of development of adipose cellularity in man and animals. Fed.Proc. 33:1952–1955, 1974.

WHITE, T.P. and G.A. BROOKS. [U-^{14}C]glucose, -alanine, and -leucine oxidation in rats at rest and two intensities of running. Am. J. Physiol. (Endocrinol. Metab.) 3:E155–165, 1981.

WILMORE, J.H. Body composition in sport and exercise: directions for future research. Med. Sci. Sports Exercise 15:21–31, 1983.

WILMORE, J.H., C.H. BROWN, and J.A. DAVIS. Body physique and composition of the female distance runner. Ann. NY Acad. Sci. 301:764–776, 1977.

WILMORE, J.H., R.N. GIRANDOLA, and D.L. MOODY. Validity of skinfold and girth assessment for prediction alterations in body composition. J. Appl. Physiol. 29:313–317, 1970.

WILMORE, J.H. and W.L. HASKELL. Body composition and endurance capacity of professional football players. J. Appl. Physiol. 33:564–567, 1972.

12

Environmental Stress and Exercise: Altitude, Cold, Heat, Polluted Air, and Travel

(UPI/Bettmann Newsphotos)

The stress of exercise is often exacerbated by the environment. The low oxygen pressure at high altitude can stress the oxygen transport systems of even the most fit athletes. Cold temperatures can numb the flesh and sometimes suppress cellular metabolism to dangerous levels. Hot temperatures can result in a competition for blood between the skin and muscles that can severely limit physical performance and subject the body to thermal injury. Smoggy air an leave the athlete gasping for air during exercises, while traveling across time zones can make athletes fatigued and less able to compete.

Thousands ski and hike every year at altitudes over 3000 m (9840 ft), subjecting sportspersons to both cold and altitude stresses. With the influx of adventure travel companies, even novice mountaineers can climb some of the peaks in the rarefied air of the Andes, Himalayas, Alps, and Rockies. Low-pressure environments place extraordinary stresses on the human body. Exposure to moderate altitudes above 1524 m (5000 ft) result in decreased maximal oxygen consumption. Prolonged exposure to extremely high altitudes over 6000 m (19,685 ft) leads to progressive deterioration that can eventually cause death unless the person is moved to a lower altitude. The combined effects of cold and altitude create a hostile environment for physical activity.

High environmental temperatures are perhaps the most widespread environmental adversary facing the active person. Health and well-being can be maximized in the heat by understanding the physiology of temperature regulation and heat stress, dehydration, clothing, fluids and electrolytes, and physical conditioning.

Smoggy air can have negative effects on physical performance, health, and well-being. The active person should have an understanding of the nature of polluted air and its effect on exercise.

Traveling across time zones can sometimes have devastating effects on athletic performance. Jet lag, cramped muscles resulting from prolonged sitting, and dehydration caused by the dry air of pressurized aircraft can sometimes override the effects of even the most carefully planned physical conditioning program.

This chapter will examine the physiology of exercise in commonly encountered environments. Particular attention will be paid to the effects of these conditions on acute and long-term exercise responses and to acclimatization.

Altitude

The study of altitude physiology began during the early part of the century by physically active physiologists, such as Douglas and Barcroft, who made investigations in conjunction with their alpine recreational pursuits. Further research was stimulated by aviation problems encountered during the World

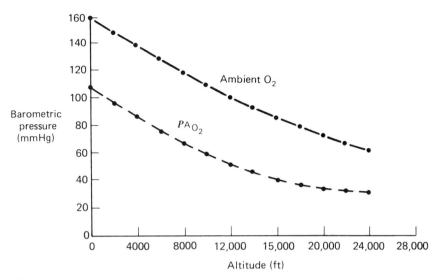

Figure 12-1
Ambient and alveolar (P_{AO_2}) partial pressure at altitude.

(SOURCE: Brooks and Fahey, Exercise Physiology: Human Bioenergetics and Its Applications, New York: Macmillan, 1984, p. 474.)

War II, mountain climbing expeditions, and the 1968 Olympics that were held at Mexico City. An understanding of altitude physiology has become important because of the many athletic contests held at moderate altitude and the tremendous popularity of mountain sports.

Exercising at high altitude is stressful because there is less oxygen available (P_{O_2}) than at sea level. Barometric pressure decreases with increasing altitudes, resulting in less oxygen per volume of air (Figure 12-1). However, the percentage of oxygen in the air (F_IO_2) at altitude is the same as at sea level. Although there are several mechanisms for adjusting to hypoxia (i.e., increased heart rate and ventilation), the ability to maintain maximal sea level oxygen transport capacity becomes increasingly limited at higher and higher altitudes. Maximal oxygen consumption ($\dot{V}O_{2max}$) begins to decrease at about 1524 m (5000 ft). Initially, $\dot{V}O_{2max}$ decreases about 3% for each increase of 300 m (1000 ft) of elevation. However, the rate of decrease is more severe at higher altitudes (Figure 12-2).

Diffusion from the alveoli to the pulmonary capillary blood largely depends on the movement of gases from a high to a lower concentration. The partial pressure of oxygen (independent pressure of oxygen exerted in the total gas mixture) determines the driving force of the gas moving from one place to another. At high altitude, this driving force is diminished. Gases are composed of individual molecules that can be either compressed or expanded. The low pressure of altitude allows the gases to expand, resulting in fewer

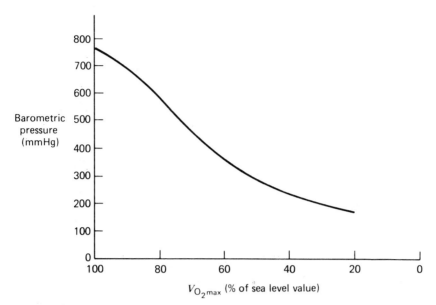

Figure 12-2

Maximal O_2 consumption at decreasing barometric pressures. $\dot{V}_{O_2\text{max}}$ remains largely unchanged until 5000 to 6000-ft altitudes because of the shape of the oxyhemoglobin dissociation curve.

(SOURCE: Brooks and Fahey, p. 475.)

molecules per unit volume. As discussed in Chapters 6 and 7 (ventilation), the ability to move oxygen from the ambient environment to the bloodstream depends on the extent and coordination of ventilation (movement of air into the lungs), diffusion (movement of oxygen from the alveoli to the pulmonary capillaries), and pulmonary perfusion (blood flow). Of these, diffusion is most affected at high altitude. When the pressure is low, as at high altitude, the system is stressed because there is less oxygen available, which results in a slower rate of diffusion between the alveoli and the pulmonary circulation.

At sea level, blood entering the pulmonary capillaries has a P_{O_2} of about 40 mm Hg. At rest, blood takes approximately 0.75 sec to travel the length of the capillary. Oxygen in the capillaries equilibrates with the air in the alveoli within 0.25 sec to a P_aO_2 of approximately 98 to 100 mm Hg, illustrating the tremendous diffusion reserve of the lungs (Figure 12-3). During heavy exercise, blood travels through the capillaries more rapidly (0.25 sec) but still reaches equilibrium with the alveoli. Diffusion is therefore not a limiting factor of endurance performance in the normal lung at sea level (except, perhaps, in elite endurance runners).

Diffusion is severely affected during exercises at high altitudes. While

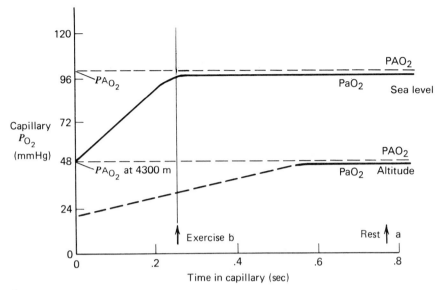

Figure 12-3

Resting (a) and exercise (b) pulmonary PaO_2 at sea level and high altitude. At rest at sea level and at 4300 m, blood is in the capillary long enough to achieve approximate equilibrium with alveolar O_2. However, during exercise at high altitude the transit time of blood through the capillaries is too rapid to allow equilibrium, resulting in a diminished PaO_2. Thus, pulmonary diffusion is a major factor limiting oxygen transport during endurance exercise at high altitude.

(SOURCE: Brooks and Fahey, Exercise Physiology: Human Bioenergetics and Its Applications, Macmillan: New York, 1984, p. 476, Figure 23-4.)

the transit time in the pulmonary capillaries remains at 0.25 sec, the driving force for diffusion is much less than at sea level. The diffusion driving force is equal to the difference between the alveolar (PO_2) and venous PO_2. As shown in Figure 12-3, the diffusion driving force is 66 mm Hg at sea level [calculated by subtracting the PO_2 of mixed venous blood (44 mm Hg) from the P_{AO2} (106 mm Hg) from the equilibrated pulmonary capillary blood] and only 30 mm Hg at 5486 m (18,000 ft). This results in a drastic reduction in hemoglobin saturation, which produces a decrease in maximal oxygen consumption.

In the resting subject at high altitude, relatively large decreases in oxygen partial pressure can be tolerated because of the shape of oxyhemoglobin dissociation curve (see Chapter 6). Notice in Figure 12-4 that at a PO_2 of 50 mm Hg. (a value found at an altitude of 4300 m) the hemoglobin is about 85% saturated. This explains why some acclimatized men are quite comfortable at rest for short periods of time without external oxygen supplies at

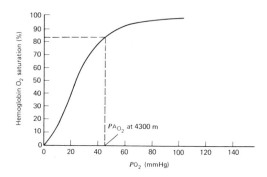

Figure 12-4

The oxyhemoglobin dissociation curve. At an altitude of 4300 m the hemoglobin of a resting subject is approximately 85% saturated with normal bicarbonate and $P_{c}O_{2}$.

(SOURCE: Brooks, G. A. and Fahey, T. D., Exercise Physiology: Human Bioenergetics and Its Applications. New York: Macmillan, 1984, p. 476, Figure 23-5.)

altitudes as high as 8000 m (26,246 ft). Of course, the physiological changes of acclimatization such as increased hemoglobin and 2,3-DPG levels contribute to this "comfort."

Acute Exposure to Altitude

Slow ascent to about 5486 m (18,000 ft) can be accomplished with few adverse symptons other than diminished exercise capacity, shortness of breath, and Cheyne-Stokes breathing at night (Cheyne-Stokes is an irregular breathing pattern). If the ascent is rapid, as when going to high altitude in a car or plane, acute mountain sickness (AMS) will often appear within 2 hrs (Table 12-1). Symptoms include headache, insomnia, irritability, weakness, vomiting, tachycradia, and disturbance of breathing. The individual differences in

TABLE 12-1 Effects of Acute Exposure to Altitude

Change	Effect
Increased resting and submaximal heart rate	Increased O_2 transport to tissue
Increased resting and submaximal ventilation	Increased alveolar P_{O_2}
	Decreased CO_2 and H^+ in CSF and blood
	Predominance of hypoxic ventilatory drive
	Left shift of oxyhemoglobin dissociation curve
	Acute mountain sickness
Decreased $\dot{V}_{O_2max}$	Decreased exercise capacity
Few acute changes in blood, muscle, or liver	

SOURCE: G. A. Brooks and T. D. Fahey. Exercise Physiology: Human Bioenergetics and Its Applications. New York: Macmillan, 1984, p. 477.

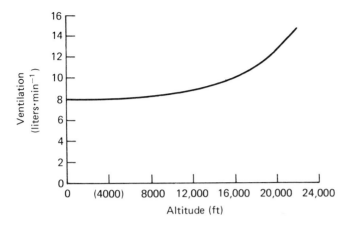

Figure 12-5
The effects of acute exposure to high altitude on resting ventilation.

(SOURCE: Brooks, G. M. and Fahey, T. D., Exercise Physiology: Human Bioenergetics and Its Applications. New York: Macmillan, 1984, p. 478.)

the onset of and susceptibility to AMS seem to lie in the susceptibility to fluid retention and in the ventilatory response to high altitude. AMS can be prevented to a certain extent by a slow rate of ascent and the use of acetazolamide (a diuretic that promotes the loss of bicarbonate and sodium).

Resting respiratory minute volume increases exponentially beginning at an altitude of about 2438 m (8000 ft) (Figure 12-5). Hypoxia, by its effect on the aortic and carotid bodies, is the driving force for this increase in ventilation. At sea level, the most important factors in the regulation of ventilation are P_{CO_2} and H^+ through their effect on the central chemoreceptors located in the medulla. These controls are diminished at high altitude because hyperventilation results in a decrease of CO_2. Some of the adaptive changes that occur with exposure to high altitude are aimed at restoring normal respiratory responsiveness to changes in P_{CO_2}.

Resting and submaximal exercise heart rate increase at high altitude. The increase in heart rate makes up for the decreased oxygen carrying capacity of the blood by increasing the blood flow to the tissues. Heart rate increases as a function of the relative percentage of maximal oxygen consumption. Although the oxygen cost of a given intensity of exercise is identical at sea level and at altitude, the exercise is more difficult at high altitude because it represents a higher percentage of maximum capacity. Stated simply, maximal exercise capacity is less at high altitude, so a given work load is more difficult.

Acclimatization to Altitude

The body begins to acclimatize to altitude within the first few days of exposure. The initial adaptation includes changes in acid–base balance that improve the regulation of ventilation and hemoglobin–oxygen binding and increased levels of 2,3-DPG that also affects oxygen binding to hemoglobin. More long-term adaptations include increases in oxygen carrying capacity, cellular metabolic efficiency, pulmonary and muscular vascularity and decreased plasma volume (Table 12-2).

During the first few days of exposure to altitude changes take place in the control of ventilation that enable both the hypoxic and CO_2 drives to control ventilation. The first effect is to decrease the amount of bicarbonate in the cerebrospinal fluid and blood. Bicarbonate levels are reduced in the CSF by active transport and reduced in blood through excretion in the kidneys. The second effect is an increased ventilatory sensitivity to CO_2. These changes normalize the pH of the blood and CSF, allowing almost normal respiratory responsiveness to changes in Po_2. In addition, a higher resting ventilation is possible in the face of the hypoxia of altitude.

The reestablishment of near-normal blood pH also affects the binding of hemoglobin and oxygen. The hyperventilation that accompanies the early stages of altitude exposure has two conflicting effects: a relative increase in blood Po_2 and a shift in the oxyhemoglobin dissociation curve to the left (Figure 12-6). The left shift of the curve causes hemoglobin to bind more tightly to oxygen so that a lower Po_2 is necessary to release oxygen to the tissues.

TABLE 12-2 Acclimatization to Altitude

Change	Effect
Decreased bicarbonate in CSF and excretion of bicarbonate by kidneys	Increases $CO_2 - H^+$ control of ventilation
	Shifts oxyhemoglobin dissociation curve to the right
Increased RBC 2,3-DPG	Shifts HbO_2 curve to right
Decreased plasma volume; increased hemoglobin, RBC, and hematocrit	Improves O_2-carrying capacity of blood
Reduction in resting and submaximal heart rate (below increases of early altitude exposure)	Restores more normal circulatory homeostasis
Increased pulmonary BP	Improves pulmonary perfusion
Increased pulmonary vascularity	Improves pulmonary perfusion
Increased size and number of mitochondria and in quantity of oxidative enzyme	Improves muscle biochemistry
Increased skeletal muscle vascularity	Improves O_2 transport
Increased tissue myoglobin	Improves cellular O_2 transport
$\downarrow [HCO_3]$ plasma	Reduces LA tolerance at altitude and SL

SOURCE: G. A. Brooks and T. D. Fahey. Exercise Physiology: Human Bioenergetics and Its Applications. New York: Macmillan, 1984, p. 480.

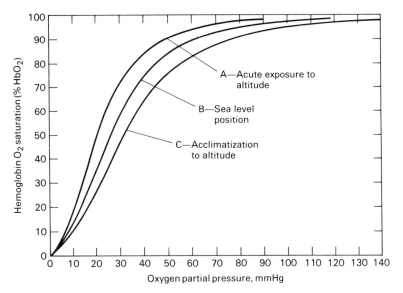

Figure 12-6
Changes in the oxyhemoglobin dissociation curve with acute exposure to high altitude and acclimatization. (A) On initial exposure, hyperventilation results in a decrease in blood P_{CO_2}, which causes the curve to shift to the left. (B) Decreases in blood and cerebrospinal fluid pH cause the curve to shift to the right. (C) Increases 2,3-DPG production by the red blood cells causes the curve to shift further to the right. The rightward shift of the oxyhemoglobin dissociation curve is beneficial at high altitude because it increases the P_{O_2} at which O_2 is released from the erythrocytes.

An added disadvantage is that the lower Po_2 decreases the capillary-tissue diffusion gradient, which slows the movement of oxygen. The bicarbonate excretion that occurs with acclimatization shifts the curve to the right, restoring the normal binding relationship between oxygen and hemoglobin and increasing the diffusion gradient. This improves oxygenation because more oxygen can be delivered at the same or higher oxygen tension.

Also occurring during these first few days is a gradual increase in the concentration of 2,3-diphosphoglycerate (2,3-DPG) in the erythrocytes. This compound decreases the affinity of hemoglobin for oxygen and further shifts the oxyhemoglobin dissociation curve to the right without affecting blood pH.

A more long-term mechanism of increasing oxygen supply is to improve the oxygen-carrying capacity of blood. A gradual increase in hemoglobin is induced by stimulation of the bone marrow by erythropoietin (which is produced in the kidneys) in response to hypoxia. Hemoglobin can increase from a sea level average of 14 to 16 g · dl^{-1} to as much as 35 g · dl^{-1} at high altitude. Each gram of hemoglobin is capable of combining with approximately 1.34 ml of oxygen. Thus, although hemoglobin saturation is impaired at high altitude, acclimatization improves the actual oxygen-carrying capacity above the initial exposure values. Permanent residents at 4267 to 4572 m (14,000 to 15,000 ft) sometimes have an oxygen-carrying capacity of more than 30 ml $O_2 \cdot$ 100 ml^{-1} of blood.

Hematocrit increases with the increase in red blood cells and the decrease in plasma volume. Although this improved oxygen-carrying capacity, it has a mixed effect on exercise capacity, particularly prolonged activity. Prolonged exercise is accompanied by a gradual increase in cardiovascular load (increased heart rate and decreased venous return of blood to the heart), a phenomenon called cardiovascular drift. This is caused at least in part by a decrease in central blood volume, which impairs venous return of blood to the heart. The combination of an initial decrease in central blood volume and increased viscosity of the blood introduces an added load during prolonged exercise at altitude.

As oxygen-carrying capacity and oxygen affinity improve, heart rate and cardiac output decrease at rest and during submaximal exercise. The initial increase in cardiac output seems to be a stopgap method of improving oxygen transport until the development of slower-acting mechanisms of increased oxygen-carrying capacity. There is a gradual increase in pulmonary diffusing capacity. This is accomplished by increases in pulmonary blood pressure (which makes pulmonary perfusion more uniform), pulmonary vascularity, and pulmonary blood volume and by hypertrophy of the right side of the heart. Pulmonary adaptation is a very slow process and is of negligible benefit to the temporary visitor.

Chronic exposure to high altitude also induces cellular changes similar to those experienced in endurance training. Increases in mitochondrial mass, the amount of oxidative enzymes, and active tissue vascularity occur. As would be expected, fit individuals acclimatize more readily then the unfit; however, the best sea level performers are not always the best performers at high altitude.

Competitive Athletics at Altitude

Most of the information on the effects of altitude on competitive athletics comes from research stemming from the 1968 Olympics held at Mexico City. These studies have provided valuable information about altitude exercise physiology and useful techniques for maximizing performance and comfort. Altitude causes marked improvements in events of short duration and high intensity (sprints and throwing events) and deterioration in events of long duration and lower intensity (endurance events). Table 12-3 compares the Olympic performances of the top three athletes in selected sprint events at the Mexico City Olympics with their previous personal bests. High-altitude performances were much better in almost every instance. In the long jump and triple jump (not shown on the table), for example, the world records were surpassed by margins of 21¾ and 14¼ in., respectively. In these types of events,

TABLE 12-3 Comparison of Personal Best and Mexico City Olympic Performances of Selected Sprint Athletes

Event, Placement, and Athlete's Name	Mexico City Olympics Time (sec)	Previous Personal Best Time (sec)
100m—Men		
1st J. Hines (U.S.A.)	9.9	9.9
2nd L. Miller (Jamaica)	10.0	10.0
3rd C. Green (U.S.A.)	10.0	9.9
100 m—Women		
1st W. Tyus (U.S.A.)	11.0	11.1
2nd B. Farrell (U.S.A.)	11.1	11.2
3rd I. Szewinska (Poland)	11.1	11.1
200 m—Men		
1st T. Smith (U.S.A.)	19.8	19.9
2nd P. Norman (Australia)	20.0	20.5
3rd J. Carlos (U.S.A.)	20.0	19.7[a]
200 m—Women		
1st I. Szewinska (Poland)	22.5	22.7
2nd R. Boyle (Australia)	22.7	23.4
3rd J. Lamy (Australia)	22.8	23.1
400 m—Men		
1st L. Evans (U.S.A.)	43.8	44.0
2nd L. James (U.S.A.)	43.9	44.1
3rd R. Freeman (U.S.A.)	44.4	44.6
400 m—Women		
1st G. Besson (France)	52.0	53.8
2nd L. Board (Great Britain)	52.1	52.8
3rd N. Burda (U.S.S.R.)	52.2	53.1
400 m Hurdles—Men		
1st D. Hemery (Great Britain)	48.1	49.6
2nd G. Hennige (Federal Republic of Germany)	49.0	50.0
3rd J. Sherwood (Great Britain)	49.0	50.2
110 m Hurdles—Men		
1st W. Davenport (U.S.A.)	13.3	13.3[a]
2nd E. Hall (U.S.A.)	13.4	13.4[a]
3rd E. Ottoz (Italy)	13.4	13.5

[a] Previous personal best set at high altitude.

SOURCE: G. A. Brooks and T. D. Fahey. Exercise Physiology: Human Bioenergetics and Its Applications. New York: Macmillan, 1984, p. 484.

some of the energy cost stems from overcoming air resistance, which is less at altitude.

In throwing events, performances can be helped or hindered by altitude. In events such as the discus or javelin, air mass provides lift to the implements, so performance tends to be hampered. In the shotput and hammer throw, where the implements have minimal aerodynamic characteristics, performances will be improved marginally because of the decreased air resistance.

At high altitude, performance in running events greater than 800 m declines. At the Mexico City games, many athletes who dominated distance running at sea level were soundly defeated by athletes native to high altitude. High-altitude natives placed first or second in the 5000-m run, 3000-m steeplechase, 10,000-m run, and the marathon.

Athletes who must compete at high altitude will benefit from a period of acclimatization of from 1 to 8 weeks. Athletes involved in activities of short duration such as sprints, jumps, and throws need acclimatize only long enough to get over the effects of mountain sickness. Although the adjustments in acid–base balance takes less than a week, the changes in oxygen-carrying capacity can take many months. Athletes in championship form may risk losing their peak conditioning by too much acclimatization because they will be unable to train as hard at high altitude as at sea level.

Controversy exists over the effects of high-altitude training on subsequent performance at sea level. Most studies show no improvement in maximal oxygen consumption or maximal work capacity when returning from high altitude. In the studies that show an improvement, the subjects may not have been in good condition to start with. At high altitude, they improved their exercise capacity, but the improvement was no greater than they would have achieved by training at sea level.

The physiological adapatations to altitude are not necessarily beneficial at sea level. Although the increase in hemoglobin is probably helpful, the decreases in plasma volume and alkaline reserve (bicarbonate, HCO_3^-) are decided disadvantages. During high-intensity exercise, the decrease in HCO_3^- may result in a decreased lactate efflux from muscle to blood, resulting in a decreased pH in muscle and, perhaps, earlier onset of fatigue. Also, the decreased blood volume and increased hematocrit will increase blood viscosity, which may have negative effects on oxygen transport capacity. Finally, the increased ventilation at high altitude is worthless at sea level where the oxygen tension is much higher.

Training intensity and duration are the most important factors in improving exercise performace. Athletes cannot train as hard at high altitude. Even though they can reach the same relative percentage of maximum, their maximum is less.

Temperature and Exercise

Animal body temperatures either remain constant (homeotherms) or vary with the environment (poikilotherms). Advanced animals such as humans, mon-

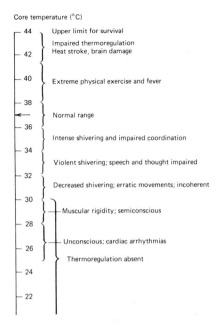

Core temperature (°C)

44 — Upper limit for survival
Impaired thermoregulation
42 — Heat stroke, brain damage

40 — Extreme physical exercise and fever

38 —

← Normal range
36 —

Intense shivering and impaired coordination
34 —

Violent shivering; speech and thought impaired
32 —

Decreased shivering; erratic movements; incoherent
30 —

Muscular rigidity; semiconscious
28 —

Unconscious; cardiac arrhythmias
26 —

Thermoregulation absent
24 —

22 —

Figure 12-7

The effects of alterations in core temperature on physiological function. The human temperature regulation system attempts to maintain core temperature within a narrow range.

(SOURCE: Brooks and Fahey, p. 445.)

keys, dogs, cats, and birds are homeotherms. They are able to function relatively independent of the environment because of their ability to maintain constant temperatures. Processes such as oxygen transport, cellular metabolism, and muscle contraction remain unimpaired in hot and cold environments as long as the internal temperature is maintained. Various physiological mechanisms, such as neural function, depend on a normal body temperature to function properly. Abnormal increases and decreases in body temperature are catastrophic to the organism. Important cell structures begin to deteriorate at temperatures above 41°C. Heat stroke and permanent brain damage can ensue if the body temperature is not quickly brought under control. At temperatures below 34°C, cellular metabolism slows greatly, leading to unconsciousness and cardiac arrhythmias (Figure 12-7).

Principles of Temperature Regulation

Man experiences normal resting body temperatures that typically lie between 36.5 and 37.5°C. There is considerable temperature variation throughout the body. The internal temperature of the core remains relatively constant, whereas the skin temperature is closer to that of the environment. Core temperature tends to reflect metabolic rate and the balance between heat production and heat loss while skin temperature reflects environmental temperature, metabolic rate, clothing, and state of hydration. Body temperature is typically expressed in terms of the core temperature.

Core temperature is usually defined as the temperature of the hypothal-

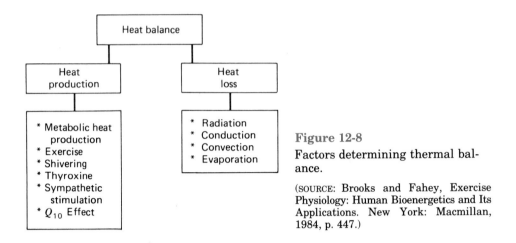

Figure 12-8

Factors determining thermal balance.

(SOURCE: Brooks and Fahey, Exercise Physiology: Human Bioenergetics and Its Applications. New York: Macmillan, 1984, p. 447.)

amus, the temperature regulatory center of the body. The most common method of measuring core temperature is orally. This method has severe limitations, however, particularly during or immediately after exercise, as increased ventilation will result in evaporative cooling of the mouth. In research, core temperature is most often measured rectally. Rectal temperature is typically 0.6°C. higher than oral temperature. Although rectal temperature is more accurate, it also has its limitations. Vigorous exercise of leg muscles will produce a higher regional temperature by means of the warmed venous blood, which will render spurious results. Additionally, there are temperature variations in the rectum itself. Researchers also estimate core temperatures by taking measurements in the auditory canal (tympanic temperature) and in the stomach.

Body temperature is regulated by controlling the rate of heat production and heat loss. When the rate of heat production is exactly equal to the rate of heat loss, the body is said to be in heat balance. When out of balance, the body either gains or loses heat. Heat balance is controlled centrally by the hypothalamus, with feedback from peripheral heat and cold receptors in the skin. The hypothalamus works like a thermostat by initiating an increase in heat production when body temperature falls and an increase in the rate of heat dissipation when it rises.

The mechanism for temperature regulation can be divided into physical and chemical processes. Physical temperature regulation works principally by changing the resistance to heat flow, while chemical mechanisms work by increasing the body's metabolic rate. The factors determining heat balance (the balance between heat production and heat loss) are shown in Figure 12-8.

Heat Production   Metabolism is the body's source of internal heat production. Even when the body is in deep sleep, a certain amount of heat is produced. During exercise, the heat production is considerable. The principle mechanisms of heat production include voluntary (exercise) and involuntary (shivering) muscle contraction and biochemical heat production (caused by the secretion of thyroxin and catecholamines).

Shivering is the primary mechanism of increasing heat production in response to cold. Maximal shivering can increase the body's heat production by up to five times. Compared with muscular exercise, it is a very efficient way of increasing body temperature because no work is done by the shivering muscles. Thus, most of the expended energy appears as heat. However, shivering adds to heat loss by increasing the thermal gradient (the difference in temperature between the person and the environment).

Increased thyroxin secretion from the thyroid and catecholamine secretion from the adrenals also increase metabolic rate. Thyroxin increases the metabolic rate of all the cells in the body. The catecholamines, principally norepinephrine, cause the release of fatty acids, which also increase metabolic heat production because fats are a less efficient fuel to metabolize.

Increased temperature can be self-perpetuating and dangerous. This is because the metabolic rate increases with rising temperature due to the Q_{10} effect (the rate of chemical reactions doubles with each 10°C increase in temperature). At high temperatures, the hypothalamus begins to lose its ability to cool the body. Unfortunately, the rate of temperature increase is faster at these higher temperatures. At core temperatures above 41.5°C, the only recourse is external cooling because the hypothalamus may no longer be functional.

Heat Loss   The body loses heat by radiation, conduction, convection, and evaporation. At room temperature, when skin temperature is greater than air temperature, most heat is lost by outward heat flow caused by the negative thermal gradient. In the heat, or during heavy exercise, evaporation becomes the dominant mechanism of heat dissipation.

Radiation is the loss of heat in the form of infrared rays. At room temperature and at rest it accounts for 60% of the total heat loss. Radiant heat loss will vary with body position and clothing. Any substance not at absolute zero will radiate such waves. However, the body is both radiating and receiving them at the same time. If the body temperature (nude body) is greater than that of the surrounding environment, then more heat is radiated from the body than to it. If the temperature of the radiating bodies around it is greater, then the net flow of radiation is inward. Of course, the insulation provided by clothing will affect gain and loss of heat by radiation.

Conduction is the transfer of heat from the body to an object. About 3% of the total heat loss at room temperature occurs by means of this mechanism. A good example of conduction is the transfer of heat to a chair while a person is sitting on it. Heat loss in the urine and feces is another example of conduction.

The conduction of heat to a fluid (air or water) is called convection. This accounts for about 12% of the heat loss at room temperature. In convection, heat conducted to air or water moves so that other particles can also be heated. As heat is transmitted to the surrounding air, it rises, allowing additional heat transfer to the surrounding air. Heat loss by convection occurs much more rapidly in water than in air.

Heat loss by convection is greater in the wind because warmed air is quickly replaced by colder air lowering the effective temperature. For example, the heat loss at 10°C in a 2.2-mph wind is the same as that at −10°C in still air (Figure 12-9). The effect of wind on temperature is called the wind-chill factor and is expressed in kilocalaries per hour per square meter (kcal · hr^{-1} · m^2) exposed skin surface. Wind speeds above 40 mph have no additional effect on heat loss because the heat transfer to the skin does not occur rapidly enough.

At rest in a comfortable environment, about 25% of heat loss is due to evaporation. However, it is the only means of cooling at high environmental temperature and is critically important during exercise. When the environmental temperature is greater than that of the skin, the body gains heat by radiation, conduction, and convection. If the body cannot lose heat by evaporation under these circumstances then body temperature rises. This occurs in a steam bath, athletic whirlpool, or hottub.

The body loses 0.58 kcal of heat for each gram of water that evaporates. Sweating is effective for cooling only if it evaporates. If the humidity is high, the rate of evaporation may be greatly reduced or totally prevented, so that the sweat remains in the fluid state. Effective evaporation is hampered by lack of air movement because the air surrounding the body becomes saturated with water vapor, just as it does inside a "sweatsuit" or football uniform. This explains why fans are desirable on a hot day.

Evaporation occurs because fluid (sweat or insensible water loss) is changed to a gaseous state by increasing the temperature of the fluid. Water evaporates insensibly from the skin and lungs at a rate of about 600 ml · day^{-1}. This amounts to a continual heat loss of about 12 to 18 kcal · hr^{-1}. Insensible water loss cannot be controlled and it occurs regardless of body temperature. However, evaporative sweat loss can be controlled by regulating the rate of sweating.

Except for insensible water loss, sweat rates are essentially zero when the skin temperature is low. In hot weather, an unacclimatized individual (person not used to the heat) has a maximum sweat rate of about 1.5 liters · hr^{-1}, while an acclimatized person can sweat up to 4 liters · hr^{-1}. During maximum sweating a person can lose 3.6 kg · hr^{-1}.

Temperature Regulatory Control by the Hypothalamus   The temperature regulatory center is located in the hypothalamus (Figure 12-10). The responses to heat are primarily controlled by heat-sensitive neurons in

WINDCHILL FACTOR

$$K_0 = (\sqrt{100v + 10.45 - v})(33 - T_a)$$

K_0 = Windchill as $kcal \cdot hr^{-1}/m^2$ exposed skin surface in shade, ignoring evaporation

v = Wind velocity in $m \cdot sec^{-1}$ = 2.2369 mph)

T_a = Ambient air temperature in °C

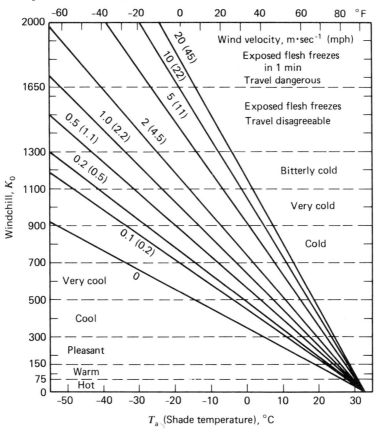

Figure 12-9

Nomogram for the calculation of windchill.

(SOURCE: N. Pace, p. 39. In Brooks and Fahey, *Exercise Physiology, Human Bioenergetics and Its Applications*. New York: Macmillan, 1984, p. 450.)

the preoptic area of the anterior hypothalamus, whereas responses to cold are controlled by the posterior hypothalamus. Although some temperature control is attributed to peripheral receptors, the hypothalamus is by far the most important. Hot and cold skin temperature receptors transmit nerve impulses to the spinal cord and then to the hypothalamus, which then initiates the appropriate response.

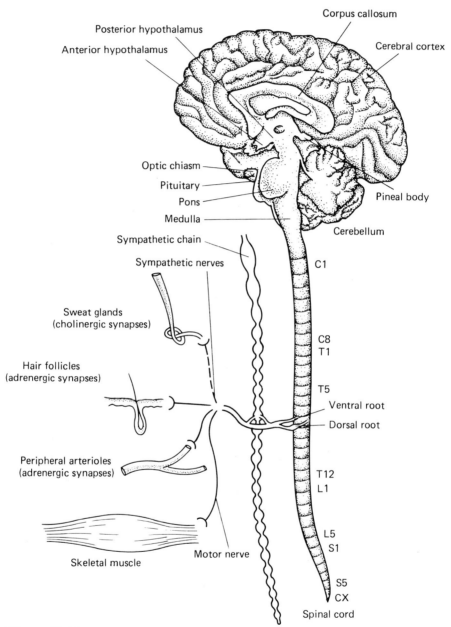

Figure 12-10

Temperature regulation schema for humans. The hypothalamus is the body's temperature regulation. It is influenced by peripheral sensors and uses a variety of structures (i.e., sweat glands, blood vessels, etc.) to control body temperature.

(SOURCE: N. Pace, 1972, p. 31. In Brooks and Fahey, p. 454.)

Overheating the preoptic area of the hypothalamus results in the stimulation of heat loss mechanisms. The anterior hypothalamus stimulates the sweat glands, resulting in evaporative heat loss from the body. Additionally, the vasomotor center in the posterior hypothalamus is inhibited. This removes the normal vasoconstrictor tone to the skin vessels allowing increased loss of heat through the skin. The anterior hypothalamus may also increase the local release of bradykinin, which causes further vasodilation.

When cold receptors in the skin and other places are stimulated, various processes increase heat production and insulation, which effectively increases the insulation of the core. The vasomotor center is stimulated, which results in vasoconstriction of blood vessels in the skin. However, intermittent vasodilation occurs, particularly in the hands and feet, to maintain the health of the skin. Stimulation of the shivering center causes shivering. The pilomotor center is stimulated, causing piloerection (goose bumps), which is probably a reflex used by our "hairy evolutionary ancestors" to increase the insulation air space over the skin. The posterior hypothalamus also initiates the release of norepinephrine, which results in the mobilization of fatty acids and an increase in metabolic heat production. It indirectly increases thyroxin production by secreting thyrotropin-releasing factor, which in turn stimulates the secretion of thyrotropin by the pituitary gland.

The hypothalamus functions as the body's thermostat by keeping the core temperature within a normal range. When the core temperature goes above or below its "setpoint" the hypothalamus initiates processes to increase heat production or heat loss. Normally, sweating begins at almost precisely 37°C and heat production begin below this point (Figure 12-11).

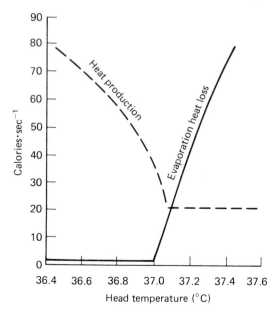

Figure 12-11

The effect of hypothalamic temperature on heat production and heat loss. The body's temperature-regulatory system works very much like a thermostastat in a house: When the temperature increases, cooling mechanisms such as sweating and peripheral vasodilation, are stimulated. When the hypothalamus is cooled, heat production mechanisms, such as shivering and incresed thyroxine and catecholamine secretion, are activated.

(SOURCE: A. C. Guyton. Textbook of Medical Physiology, 1976, p. 962.

Human behavior is an important component in temperature regulation. A person who has the sensation of being hot or cold will do something about it. When hot, he may drink a cold glass of water, removed some clothing, or turn on the air conditioning, and when cold he may put on some clothes, turn up the heat, move around, or go inside.

Exercise in the Cold

Until quite recently, hypothermia was a factor in sports and exercise only when survival was at stake following mishaps in skiing, climbing, or camping. People rarely experienced cold stress during exercise because the resulting increased metabolism largely prevented negative heat balance, and they could put on more clothing when they did get cold. However, beginning about 10 years ago, large numbers of marginally conditioned people began participating in endurance contests, such as triathlons (competitions involving long-distance swimming, bicycling, and running) and marathons, that sometimes exposed them to cold temperatures for many hours. People became hypothermic because the heat production of exercise could not keep pace with heat loss, and they did not have the opportunity to protect themselves with adequate clothing.

The cold does present problems for athletes, as is readily apparent during athletic contests played in extremely adverse wintertime weather. Athletes, such as football players, are handicapped by the numbing of exposed flesh and the awkwardness and extra weight of protective clothing. Manipulative motor skills requiring finger dexterity such as catching and throwing are tremendously impaired in the cold because the cold effectively anesthetizes sensory receptors in the hands. Exposed flesh, particularly on the face, is susceptible to frostbite, which can become a serious medical problem.

Clothing is an important consideration during physical activity in the cold. The insulation value of the clothing must be balanced with the increased metabolic heat production of exercise. If too much clothing is worn, the individual risks becoming a tropical man in a cold environment. There have been instances of heat stroke in overclothed persons exercising in extremely cold climates.

Clothes are valuable in the cold because they increase the body's insulation. Clothing entraps warm air next to the skin and decreases heat loss by conduction. The best clothing for exercise in the cold allows for the evaporation of sweat while providing added protection from the cold. Clothing should be worn in layers so that it may be removed as the metabolic heat production increases during exercise. Tremendous progress has been made by clothing manufacturers in recent years in developing lightweight clothing that pro-

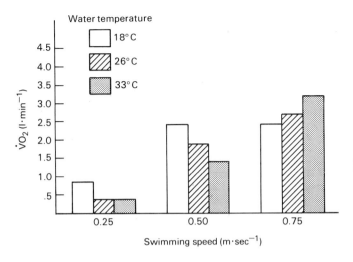

Water temperature

□ 18°C

▨ 26°C

▨ 33°C

Figure 12-12

The effects of swimming speed and water temperature (T_w) on O_2 consumption in swimmers.

(SOURCE: Adapted from the data of E. Nadel, 1980.)

vides sufficient insulation and freedom of movement during exercise and still allows the loss of water vapor (e.g., Gortex).

Exercise can partially or totally replace the heat production of shivering during exposure to a cold environment. The peripheral blood vessels vasodilate during physical activity, which effectively decreases the body's insulation to the cold. Heat production from exercise and shivering must be adequate to maintain heat balance, or hypothermia will result.

Maximal oxygen uptake and the oxygen cost of submaximal exercise are unaffected in the cold. However, the metabolic cost of submaximal exercise by subjects in wet clothing exercising in the wind is about 15 to 20% higher than the same exercise practiced in a comfortable environment. The increased oxygen cost is due to shivering.

It is theoretically possible for cold to impair exercise capacity, particularly in short-term, high-intensity exercise. Muscle functions best at a temperature slightly over 40°C. In a start-and-stop sport such as downhill skiing, it is very possible for muscle temperature to drop substantically during the long, windy chairlift rides between ski runs. In addition to impaired function, increased risk of injury may be caused by enhanced muscle tone or shivering.

Swimming in cold water can cause marked deterioration in exercise capacity and $\dot{V}O_{2peak}$ (in this case, $\dot{V}O_{2peak}$ is the maximal oxygen consumption measured during swimming) (Figure 12-12) since heat conductance is about 25 times greater in water than in air. Body fat percentage is an important factor in determining heat loss in cold water. Greater amounts of body fat increases insulation, which slows the transfer of heat to the water. Long-distance channel swimmers typically have high fat percentages, which slow the rate of heat loss during their prolonged swims. It is unclear if this characteristic represents an adaptation to the cold or simply a conscious effort on the part of the swimmer to increase insulation. Loss of flexibility contributes to the performance decrement probably because the cold water increases the viscosity of muscle and connective tissue.

Acclimatization and Habituation to Cold

People exposed to environmental stresses, such as heat, cold, and altitude, usually make adjustments to improve their comfort. Adjustments to these environments include acclimatization and habituation. Acclimatization is defined as physiological compensation to environmental stress occurring over a period of time. Habituation is the lessening of the sensation associated with a particular environmental stressor. Simply stated, in acclimatization definite physical alterations occur that improve physiological function. In habituation, the person learns to live with the stressor.

It is difficult to demonstrate acclimatization in persons not chronically exposed to cold. Except for primitive societies, humans do not commonly have the opportunity for chronic exposure to cold. There are three basic tests of acclimatization to cold in humans. The first is the threshold skin temperature that results in shivering. Several studies indicate that shivering occurs later in subject exposed to several weeks of cold temperatures. Cold-acclimatized individuals maintain heat production with less shivering by increasing nonshivering thermogenesis. They increase the secretion of norepinephrine, which results in uncoupled oxidative phosphorylation—heat is released without the production of ATP.

The second test of acclimatization involves measuring the temperatures of the hands and feet. In the unacclimatized person, hand and foot temperatures drop progressively with time during cold exposure. However, the acclimatized person is able to maintain almost normal temperature. Acclimatization results in improved intermittent peripheral vasodilation to make the hands and feet more comfortable. Habituation also seems to play a part. Some individuals seem to lose the pain or learn to tolerate the pain sensations associated with cold feet and hands, even though there is little improvement in circulation or temperature.

The third test is the ability to sleep in the cold. Unacclimatized people will shiver so much that it is impossible to sleep. Some studies show that it is possible to acclimatize enough to sleep, but these findings have not been consistently replicated. The ability to sleep in the cold seems to depend on the extent of nonshivering thermogenesis induced by increased secretion of norepinephrine. Some primitive peoples, such as the aborigines of Australia, are capable of sleeping in the cold with little or no clothing without an increase in metabolism. These individuals almost resemble poikilotherms in this regard.

Physical conditioning seems to be beneficial in acclimatization to the cold, just as it is in the heat and at high altitude. Physical conditioning results in a higher body temperature in sleep tests in the cold. Consequently, the individual can sleep and is more comfortable.

Cold Injury

Hypothermia As noted in Figure 12-7, the hypothalamus ceases to control body temperature at extremely low core temperatures. Hypothermia depresses the central nervous system, which results in an inability to shiver, sleepiness, and eventually coma. The lower temperature also results in a lower cellular metabolic rate, creating a vicious circle: decreases metabolism leads to less heat production, which further depresses metabolism. As discussed, hypothermia can be a problem if the rate of heat production during exercise does not keep pace with the rate of heat loss induced by the cold environment. This is a serious problem in endurance competitions held in cold climates. Deaths have been reported from hypothermia in road races held in mountainous areas. Athletes at risk include those who are not properly conditioned, slow runners (who are exposed longer and cannot generate sufficient heat through exercise, particularly during the later stages of endurance races), those who become wet, and those who become hypoglycemic (low blood sugar). When a risk of hypothermia exists in an athletic competition, race personnel should made sure that supplies such as "space blankets," blankets, and warm drinks are available as a preventive measure.

Frostbite Frostbite is frozen tissue and typically occurs to exposed body parts such as the earlobes, fingers, and toes. The injury is relatively common in extremely low air temperatures [-20 to $-30°C$ (-4 to $-22°F$)] or when air movement results in high windchill factors (see Figure 12-9). It can cause permanent circulatory damage, and sometimes the frostbitten part is lost because of gangrene.

Frostbite is treated by placing the frostbitten area in water heated to 37.8 to 42.2°F (100 to 108°F) until the tissue is thawed. The water temperature should be monitored to keep it from becoming too hot. Tissue damage may occur if the water temperature rises above 42.8°C (109°F). After the body part is thawed, it should be kept cool to lessen metabolism and minimize inflammation. The part should not be thawed if there is danger of refreezing. The affected part should also be covered. The person should be kept warm with blankets to facilitate peripheral circulation.

Exercise in the Heat

A nude human in still dry air can maintain a constant body temperature at an ambient temperature of 54 to 60°C (129 to 140°F). However, exercise in the heat sets the stage for a positive thermal balance. The rate of exercise is

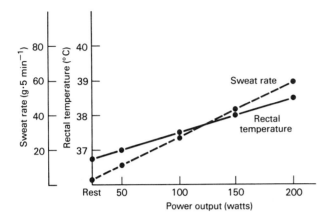

Figure 12-13

The effects of work load during prolonged exercise on sweat rate and rectal temperature. Exercise intensity is the most important factor increasing rectal temperature and sweat rate during physical activity, even in the heat.

(SOURCE: Adapted from the data of B. Neilson, 1938.)

the most important factor precipitating this increase. Core temperature increases proportionally with increasing intensities of exercise. While there is considerable variability in core temperature at any absolute work load, very little variation occurs when the load is expressed as a percentage of maximum capacity (Figure 12-13).

The extent of the effect of environmental temperature on exercise capacity depends on the body's ability to dissipate heat and maintain blood flow to the active muscles. During exercise in the heat, the combined circulatory demands of muscle and skin can effectively impair oxygen transport capacity. An added problem is that the general vasodilation caused by the inhibition of the vasomotor center results in an increase of blood in the venous system (capacitance vessels). Additionally, there is a decrease in plasma volume during exercise that becomes increasingly acute as the intensity of the effort increases. The decrease in plasma volume can be augmented by the loss of body fluids through sweating. This can become a particularly acute problem during dehydration. During exercise in the heat, there may not be enough blood to go around. A decrease in central blood volume can occur with a resulting decrease in return of blood to the heart.

Unacclimatized humans have several physiological mechanisms for dealing with heat stress during exercise. Sweating is the primary means of heat dissipation under these circumstances. During submaximal exercise, heart rate increases. This mechanism becomes less effective at higher intensities of exercise, however, because the maximum heart rate is approached. At maximal levels of exercise, peripheral vasoconstriction overrides the vasodilation originally elicited in response to heat stress. This helps maintain blood pressure and cardiac output. Unfortunately, this response has a negative effect on heat transfer. In this instance, circulatory regulation takes precedence over temperature regulation. These circumstances help to emphasize the danger of heat injury during exercise in hot climates.

Maximal oxygen consumption, as measured during a laboratory treadmill test, is not impaired in the heat unless the subject is suffering heat stress when the test begins. Athletes rarely have the luxury of going from the comforts of air conditioned normal room temperature into the heat of an environmental chamber for athletic contests; they usually have to sleep, eat, and train in the adverse environment before they perform. Dehydration, lack of sleep, and anxiety can combine to cause a degree of physiological and psychological stress. Most studies show that $\dot{V}O_{2max}$ is decreased by 6 to 8% in preheated subjects.

Acclimatization to Heat

During the first week of heat exposure, the body makes several adjustments resulting in lower heart rate, core temperature, and skin temperature at rest and during submaximal exercise. Additionally, stability in blood pressure increases during prolonged exercise. The primary physiological adjustments of acclimatization to heat include increased peripheral conductance, increased plasma volume, increased sweating capacity, a fall in the threshold of skin temperature for the onset of sweating, and a better distribution of sweat over the skin (Table 12-4). Acclimatization to heat is not complete unless the exposure is accompanied by exercise training.

Blood flow to the skin decreases with acclimatization. This adjustment helps to restore central blood volume, which is vitally important for maintaining stroke volume and muscle blood flow during exercise. However, core temperature is lower during exercise in acclimatized humans. The decrease in skin blood flow is accompanied by a large increase in sweating and evaporative cooling capacity, resulting in greater peripheral conductance of heat.

Acclimatization to heat induces an approximately 12% increase in plasma volume, provided that heat exposure is accompanied by exercise training. This increase is percipitated mainly by an increase in plasma protein. For every increase of 1 g of plasma protein 15 g of water are added to the plasma. The

TABLE 12-4 **Acclimatization to Heat**

Change	Effect
Increased sweat rate	Increases evaporative cooling and peripheral heat conductance
Improved sweat distribution	Decreased skin temperature
Earlier onset of sweating	Prevents early rise in core temperature
Increased plasma volume due to increased plasma proteins	Decreases heart rate, increases stroke volume, and facilitates maintenance of central blood volume during exercise in the heat

increased plasma volume helps to ensure the maintenance of stroke volume, central blood volume, and sweating capacity. It also enables the body to hold more heat.

Along with the increase in plasma volume is an almost threefold increase in sweating capacity from about 1.5 liters $\cdot$ hr^{-1} to 4 liters $\cdot$ hr^{-1}. This is accompanied by a more complete and even distribution of sweating, which is an advantage in heat accompanied by high humidity. Sweat losses of sodium chloride decrease because of increased secretion of aldosterone.

The fall in sweating threshold is important for keeping core temperature under control during the early stages of exercise. As discussed, increased temperature tends to cause further increases in temperature because of the Q_{10} effect. The early onset of sweating serves to partially negate this. This phenomenon probably reflects a lower setting of the hypothalamic setpoint.

Exercise training is essential for acclimatization to the heat. Training, by itself, however, will not provide a full measure of heat adaptation. An individual from a temperate environment who must compete in the heat can become acclimatized for the effort by exercising (endurance training) in a hot room.

Thermal Distress

Thermal distress and heat injury are becoming increasingly common with the popularity of distance running and competitive sports for the weekend athlete. Fortunately, many of the severe effects of heat stress in athletics can be avoided if the necessary precautions are taken. Thermal distress includes dehydration (loss of body fluid), heat cramps (involuntary cramping of skeletal muscle), heat exhaustion (hypotension and weakness caused by an inability of the circulation to compensate for vasodilation of skin blood vessels), and heat stroke (failure of the temperature regulatory function of the hypothalamus).

Dehydration

Dehydration is the loss of fluid from the body. Dehydration can decrease sweat rate, plasma volume, cardiac output, maximal oxygen uptake, work capacity, muscle strength, and liver glycogen. Although this is a common condition during exercise in the heat, it can occur even in thermally neutral environments.

A water deficit of 700 ml (approximately 1% of body weight) will cause thirst. At a fluid deficit of 5% of body weight, the person feels discomfort and alternating states of lethargy and nervousness. Irritability, fatigue, and loss of appetite are also characteristic of this level of dehydration. Five percent dehydration is extremely common in athletics such as football, tennis, and

distance running. Dehydration level greater than 7% are extremely dangerous. At these levels, salivating and swallowing food become difficult. At fluid
losses above 10%, the ability to walk is impaired and is accompanied by un-
coordination and spacticity. As 15% dehydration approaches, delirium and
shriveled skin are experienced along with decreased urine volume, loss of the
ability to swallow food, and difficulty swallowing water. Above 20% weight
loss, the skin bleeds and cracks. This is the upper limits of tolerance of dehydration before death ensues.

Osmoreceptors in the hypothalamus stimulate the drive to drink fluids.
Unfortunately, thirst does not keep up with the fluid requirements, so it is
very easy to experience fluid deficits of 2 to 4% of body weight. It is very
important for dehydrating athletes to have regular fluid breaks rather than
rely only on their thirst for fluid replacement and to get weighed before each
practice, especially during early season and in hot weather.

The inadequacy of the thirst mechanism can be compounded by the type
of fluid replacement. Fluids with a high carbohydrate content (glucose or sucrose greater than $2.5 \text{ g} \cdot \text{dl}^{-1}$) have been shown to delay the rate of gastric
emptying. Some commercially available fluid replacements are counterprod-
uctive in that their high sugar content delays the replenishment of water
while satiating thirst. Cold water is the best fluid replacement, although some
commercial fluids have almost equal rates of gastric emptying. Some athletes
prefer the commercial fluids because they are more palatable. As long as a
suitable fluid is selected, the wishes of the athletes should be honored. The
important thing is to get them to drink enough fluid. A common practice
among distance runners and other athletes is to dilute (by about half) high-
glucose, commercial preparations, which satisfies the requirement for good
taste and replenishes fluids.

Heat Cramps

Heat cramps are characterized by involuntary cramping and spasm in muscle
groups used during exercise. They stem from an alteration in the relationship
of sodium and potassium at the muscle membrane and result from dehydra-
monary disease (see Chapter 16). The effects of polluted air are often additive
and sweated heavily. Often the individuals are conditioned and heat acclimatized.

The treatment of heat cramps is somewhat controversial. The classic
treatment includes oral or intravenous salt replacement and rehydration.
Unfortunately, most of the emphasis has been placed on the salt replacement,
which can actually compound the problems. Disproportionate salt and water
intake will lead to intracellular dehydration. The kidneys and sweat glands
have a remarkable ability to conserve salt, particularly in the acclimatized
individual. Present evidence suggests that in most instances providing copi-
ous quantities of fluid during and after exercise is sufficient for treating and
preventing this condition. Most people consume more than enough salt in

their diets to prevent electrolyte depletion and heat cramps, even in extremely hot, humid climates.

Heat Exhaustion

Heat exhaustion and heat stroke are not really distinct entities but rather represent two degrees of thermal injury. Heat exhaustion is characterized by a rapid, weak pulse, hypotension, faintness, profuse sweating, and psychological disorientation. It results from an acute volume loss and the inability of the circulation to compensate for the concurrent vasodilation in the skin and active skeletal muscles. Although core temperature may be evaluated somewhat [usually less than 39.5°C (103.1°F)], it does not reach the extremely high level seen in heat stroke [greater than 41°C (105.8°F)]. The degree of thermal distress can be estimated by measuring rectal temperature.

The treatment for heat exhaustion includes supine rest in a cool area and fluids. Intravenous fluid administration may be appropriate in some instances. The athlete should not participate in any further activity for the rest of the day and should be encouraged to drink plenty of fluids for the next 24 hr.

Heat Stroke (Hyperpyrexia or Sunstroke)

Heat stroke is the failure of the hypothalamic temperature regulatory center and represents a major medical emergency. It is principally caused by a failure of the sudomotor (sweating) center, which results in an explosive rise in body temperature due to the lack of evaporative cooling. It is characterized by a high core temperature (greater than 41°C), hot, dry skin, and extreme confusion or unconsciousness. In exercise-related heat stroke, the individual may still be sweating. The cardiovascular effects are variable, with some experiencing hypotension and others experiencing a full bounding pulse and high blood pressure.

A heat stroke victim should be packed in ice and transported to a hospital as soon as possible. In the hospital treatment includes submersion in an ice bath accompanied by massage to counteract peripheral cutaneous vasoconstriction. Rectal temperature is monitored to guard against rebound hypothermia. Fluids are administered to counteract hypotension. More drastic measures are sometimes required in the event of continued shock or renal failure.

Preventing Thermal Distress

The problems of thermal distress can be minimized by following a few simple principles:

- Ensure that athletes are in good physical condition. There should be a gradual increase in intensity and duration of training until the athletes are fully acclimatized.

- Schedule practice sessions and games during the cooler times of the day.
- Modify or cancel exercise sessions when the wet bulb globe temperature is 25.5°C or greater. Wet bulb temperature is used to determine humidity and globe temperature is an indication of radiant heat.
- Plan for regular water breaks.
- Supply a drink that is cold (8–13°C), low in sugar (less than 2.5 g%), with little or no electrolytes.
- Encourage athletes to "tankup" before practice or games by drinking 400 to 600 ml of water 30 min before activity.
- Encourage fluid replacement particularly during the early stages of practice and competition. As exercise progresses, splanic blood flow tends to decrease, which diminishes water absorption from the gut.
- Weigh athletes every day before practice. Any athlete showing a decrease in weight of 3% or more should not be allowed to participate until he or she is rehydrated. People who tend to lose a lot of weight in the heat should be identified and closely monitored.
- Prohibit salt tablets; however, encourage athletes to consume ample amounts of salt at mealtime.
- Discourage athletes wearing rubberized "sauna suits" in an effort to lose weight. Rather, emphasize attaining the optimal body composition for the sport.

Exercise and Air Pollution

Air pollution is common in urban centers throughout the world. Smog can have a serious effect on the physical performance, particularly in people suffering from pulmonary disorders such as asthma and chronic obstructive pulmonary disease (see Chapter 16). The effects of polluted air are often additive to other environmental stressors, such as heat (Los Angeles or New York), and altitude (Denver or Mexico City).

Air pollutants directly emitted from automobiles, energy plants, and so on are classified as primary, whereas pollutants derived from the interaction of primary pollutants and ultraviolet rays or other agents found in the environmental are called secondary. Examples of primary pollutants include carbon monoxide, nitrogen oxide, sulfur dioxide, and particulate matter. Secondary pollutants include ozone, peroxyacetyl nitrate, aldehydes, and nitrogen dioxide.

Studies of smog and exercise have tended to examine the effects of one substance at a time. The principal substances studied include ozone, peroxyacetyl nitrate, nitrogen dioxide, sulfur dioxide, particulates, and carbon monoxide. Few studies have examined the effects of combinations of these substances. In addition, little data are available on elite athletes. It may be possible to make generalizations for athletes by examining the studies that have been done on young people.

Smog may negatively affect exercise performance because it causes tightening in the chest, difficulty in deep breathing, eye irritation, pharyngitis, headache, lassitude, malaise, nausea, and dryness of the throat. The effects of air pollution are exaggerated during physical activity (ventilation is greater, so more smog enters the pulmonary system) and become increasingly severe as the level of air pollution increases. Although most of these factors will have little effect on measurable physiological factors, such as $\dot{V}O_{2max}$, they will certainly have a negative psychological impact. Studies of athletes in competition show marked decrements in performance when the air is significantly polluted. It has been suggested that the increased airway resistance in the lungs leads to discomfort, which limits the athletes' motivation to perform.

Smoking compounds the negative effects of smog. Carbon monoxide (CO), which is found in smoke and polluted air, competes with oxygen for hemoglobin in the blood, resulting in a decrease in oxygen transport capacity. CO increases resting and submaximal exercise heart rates and reduces functional capacity (see Chapter 17).

Particulate air pollutants, such as dust and pollen, can have serious effects on the exercise performance of allergy-prone athletes. Great athletes, such as the miler Jim Ryan, have suffered from the effects of airborne particulate matter to such an extent that it seriously compromises their athletic careers. Antihistamines, drugs that combat allergic reactions, can cause marked drowsiness that can hurt performance. Some people benefit from desensitization procedures available from allergy specialists.

Practices and competitions should be limited during periods of peak concentrations of air pollution. Air pollution levels tend to be higher during the commuting hours (6–9 A.M. and 4–7 P.M. in most places) and during the middle of the day when the temperature is highest. Air pollution is a fact of life in many areas, and there is no evidence that the human body can acclimatize to it. Attempts should be made to limit exposure, particularly in people with respiratory problems.

Biological Rhythms and Travel Across Time Zones

A variety of physiological functions follow a rhythm that varies approximately every 24 hr (circadian), weekly (circaspetian), monthly (circalunar), and yearly (circa-annual). Factors that exhibit a regular rhythm include sleep, body temperature, heart rate, blood pressure, metabolic rate, gonadotropin hormone secretion (menstrual cycle), and performance characteristics such as strength, power, reaction time, perceived exertion, and pattern recognition.

Most studies indicate that physical performance is maximized in the afternoon. This time is characterized by the highest values in body temperature, strength, reaction time, pattern recognition, and heart rate, and a reduced level of perceived exertion and respiratory response to exercise. Unfortunately, studies of biological rhythms are invariably conducted in the laboratory; the increased stimulation of competition may supersede any arousing effect of a biological rhythm.

Athletic contests are often scheduled great distances from the home area, requiring the athlete to endure long airplane, bus, or automobile rides. These long trips may hamper performance by disturbing normal living habits and altering biological rhythms.

Jet lag is characterized by fatigue, malaise, sluggishness, decreased reaction time, and disorientation. This condition is caused by factors such as loss of sleep due to the excitement of travel, irregular and unfamiliar meals, dehydration, and disturbance of the biological clock. Some athletes may experience muscle stiffness and constipation caused by sitting for prolonged periods.

East bound travel seems to cause the most problems because it has the greatest effect of sleep. Proper travel scheduling can help alleviate the symptoms. If possible, the journey should be timed for arrival in the evening so that the athlete can get a full night's sleep. Several days before the trip is scheduled, the athlete should attempt to gradually shift the hours of eating and sleeping toward the time schedule of the destination. The athlete should be well rested before the beginning of the journey.

Traveling in an airplane can lead to dehydration. The cabins of pressurized airplanes have a relative humidity of approximately 20%, resulting in an increased loss of body water through evaporation. Athletes should be encouraged to consume more water than normal both before and during the trip to prevent this problem. In addition, constipation, which occurs following prolonged sitting in some people, can often be prevented by ensuring adequate fluid intake.

A summary of guidelines to prevent jet lag include the following: (Source: Fahey, T. D. Athletic Training: Principles and Practice, p. 467)

- Make eastbound flights during daylight hours, leaving as early as possible—earlier as the distance increases.
- Make westbound flights late in the day, arriving as close to the retiring hour as possible.
- Drink plenty of water during the trip.
- Eat light meals and keep the intake of fatty foods low.
- At regular intervals, get up from the seat and stretch or walk.

The negative effect of travel on performance can be minimized if the trip is well planned and the athlete's normal schedule is minimally disrupted by the time change.

Summary

Increasing numbers of people are exercising at moderate and high altitudes, which places increased stress on physiological systems. Maximal oxygen consumption begins to deteriorate at an altitude of approximately 5000 ft, with pulmonary diffusion being the major limiting factor. As the partial pressure of oxygen decreases with altitude, the driving force of oxygen from the environment to the pulmonary circulation is impaired.

Acclimatization to high altitude begins within the first few days of exposure. Early exposure diminishes the role of CO_2 in controlling ventilation. The early effects of acclimatization are to restore the CO_2 ventilatory control mechanisms by reducing bicarbonate levels in the blood and cerebrospinal fluid and by increasing the ventilatory sensitivity to CO_2. Bicarbonate excretion and an increased concentration of 2,3-diphosphoglycerate shift the oxyhemoglobin dissociation curve to the right, which decreases the affinity of hemoglobin for oxygen. Long-term changes include increased hemoglobin, hematocrit, pulmonary diffusion capacity, and skeletal muscle vascularity.

Humans can tolerate extremely hot and cold climates because of a well-developed ability to control body temperature. Body temperature is regulated by controlling the rate of heat production and heat loss. Mechanisms of heat production include basal metabolic rate, shivering, exercise, thermogenic hormone secretion, and the Q_{10} effect. The body loses heat by radiation, conduction, convection, evaporation, and excretion. The hypothalamus is the main center for temperature regulation.

Clothing is the most important limiting factor when exercising in the cold. However, swimming in the cold or exercising with wet clothing can result in greatly diminished performance because of an accelerated heat loss. Acclimatization to cold is difficult to demonstrate but is known to occur.

The ability to exercise in high ambient temperatures depends on the ability to dissipate heat and maintain blood flow to active muscles. Sweating is the primary means of cooling in the heat. An increased sweat rate is the most important adaptation that occurs with heat acclimatization. Exercise training is necessary to maximize this process.

Thermal injuries are a serious problem in both competitive and recreational sports. Thermal injuries include heat cramps, heat exhaustion, and heat stroke. These injuries are typically preceded by dehydration. Preventive measures include adequate physical conditioning, exercising during cooler periods of the day, planning regular water breaks, and limiting workout sessions until adequate acclimatization is achieved.

Air pollution can have both psychological and physiological effects that limit performance. Smog can produce tightening in the chest, difficulty taking deep breaths, eye irritation, pharyngitis, headache, lassitude, malaise, nausea, and dryness in the throat. Practice and competitions should be restricted during periods of extremely poor air quality, particularly for athletes with pulmonary diseases such as asthma.

A number of physiological factors exhibit rhythms that may span a day, week, month, or year. Available evidence suggests that several aspects of exercise performance are maximized in the late afternoon. Jet lag, which can cause fatigue and sluggishness, is caused by the effects of crossing time zones and the disrupting effects of travel. Problems can be minimized by scheduling eastbound flights in the daylight hours and westbound flights late in the day.

Selected Readings

ADAMS, W.C., W.M. SAVIN, and A.E. CHRISTO. Detection of ozone toxicity during continuous exercise via effective dose concept. J. Appl. Physiol. 51:415–422, 1981.

BALKE, B. Variations in altitude and its effects on exercise performance. In: Falls, H. (ed.) Exercise Physiology. New York: Academic Press, 1968, pp. 240–265.

CERRETELLI, P. Gas exchange at high altitude. In: West, J.B. (ed). Pulmonary Gas Exchange, Vol. II, Organism and Environment. New York: Academic Press, 1980.

CONVERTINO, V., J. GREENLEAF, and E. BERNAUER. Role of thermal and exercise factors in the mechanism of hypervolemia. J. Appl. Physiol. 48:657–664, 1980.

COYLE, E., D. COSTILL, W. FINK, and D. HOOPES. Gastric emptying rates for selected athletic drinks. Res. Quart. 49:119–124, 1978.

DEMPSEY, J.A., and H.V. FORSTER. Mediation of ventilatory adaptations. Physiol. Rev. 62:262–346, 1982.

DRINKWATER, B., L.J. FOLINSBEE, J.F. BEDI, S.A. PLOWMAN, A.B. LOUCKS, and S.M. HORVATH. Response of women mountaineers to maximal exercise during hypoxia. Aviat. Space Environ. Med. 50:657–662, 1979.

ELLIOTT, P.R., and H.A. ATTERBOM. Comparison of exercise responses of males and females during acute exposure to hypobaria. Aviat. Space Environ. Med. 49:415–418, 1978.

FAHEY, T.D. Athletic Training: Principles and Practice, Palo Alto: Mayfield Publishing Co., 1986.

FOLK, G. Textbook of Environmental Physiology. Philadelphia: Lea & Febiger, 1974, Chapters 3, 4, 5.

GISOLFI, C.V., and C.B. WENGER. Temperature regulation during exercise: old concepts, new ideas. Exercise Sport Sci. Rev. 12:339–372, 1984.

GREENLEAF, J., and F. SARGENT II. Voluntary dehydration in man. J. Appl. Physiol. 20:719–724, 1965.

HANSON, P. Heat injuries in runners. Physician Sports Med. 7:91–96, 1979.

HORVATH, S.M. Exercise in a cold environment. Exercise Sport Sci. Rev. 9:221–263, 1981.

HULTGREN, H. Circulatory adaptation to high altitude. Annu. Rev. Med. 19:119–130, 1968.

KOLLIAS, J., and E.R. BUSKIRK. Exercise and altitude. In: Johnson, W.R. and E.R. Buskirk (eds.). Structural and Physiological Aspects of Exercise and Sport. Princeton, N.J.: Princeton Book Co., 1980. pp. 211–227.

LAHARI, S. Physiological responses and adaptations to high altitude. In: Robertshaw, D. (ed.). Environmental Physiology II. Baltimore: University Park Press, 1977, pp. 217–251.

LENFANT, C., and K. SULLIVAN. Adaptation to high altitude. N. Eng. J. Med. 284:1298–1309, 1971.

LENFANT, C., J.D. TORRANCE, R. WOODSON, and C.A. FINCH. Adaptation to hypoxia.

In: Brewer, G.J. (ed.). Red Cell Metabolism. New York: Plenum Press, 1972, pp. 203–212.

LUCE, J. Respiratory adaptation and maladaptation to altitude. Physician Sport. Med. 7:55–69, 1979.

NADEL, E. Circulatory and thermal regulations during exercise. Fed. Proc. 39:1491–1497, 1980.

NADEL, E., I. HOLMER, U. BERGH, P.O. ASTRAND, and J. STOLWIJK. Energy exchanges of swimming man. J. Appl. Physiol. 36:465–471, 1974.

NUNNELEY, S. Physiological responses of women to thermal stress: review. Med. Sci. Sport. 10:250–255, 1978.

O'DONNELL, T.F. Management of heat stress injuries in the athlete. Ortho. Clin. N. Am. 11:841–855, 1980.

PATAJAN, J.H. The effects of high altitude on the nervous system and athletic performance. Semin. Neurol. 1:253–261, 1981.

PIRNAY, F., R. DEROANNE, and J. PETIT. Maximal oxygen consumption in a hot environment. J. Appl. Physiol. 28:642–645, 1970.

RENNIE, D., B. COVINO, B. HOWELL, S. SONG, B. HANG, and S. HANG. Physical insulation of Korean diving women. J. Appl. Physiol. 17:961–966, 1962.

ROBERTS, M., and C.B. WENGER. Control of skin circulation during exercise and heat stress. Med. Sci. Sport 11:36–41, 1979.

ROWELL, L. Human cardiovascular adjustments to exercise and thermal stress. Physiol. Rev. 54:75–159, 1974.

SHEPHARD, R.J. Sleep, biorhythms, and human performance. Sports Med. 1:11–37, 1984.

SUTTON, J., A.C. BRYAN, G.W. GRAY, E.S. HORTON, A.S. REBUCK, W. WOODLEY, I.D. RENNIE, and C.S. HOUSTON. Pulmonary gas exchange in acute mountain sickness. Aviat. Space Environ. Med. 47:1032–1037, 1976.

WEST, J.B., and S. LAHIRI (eds). High Altitude and Man. Bethesda, Md.: American Physiological Society, 1984.

13

Athletic Training of Men and Women

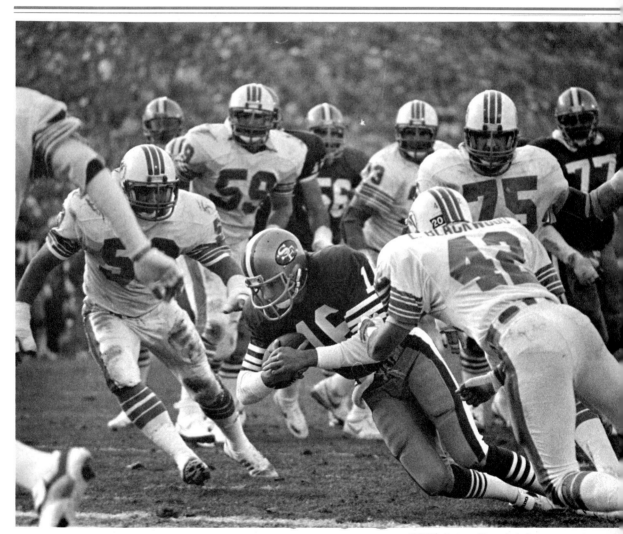

(UPI/Bettmann Newsphotos)

It would seem that studying the physiology of various training methods to identify those methods that produce the greatest improvements in endurance or strength would be a simple matter compared to, for instance, studying the biochemistry of fat metabolism in muscle. However, such is not the case. It has proved extremely difficult to manipulate scientifically, the training regimens of quality athletes. It is very understandable that athletes do not want their training regimens "tampered" with. Therefore, studies of various training regimens frequently use only a few trained athletes or more untrained volunteers who train intensively for from 8 to 15 weeks. Such results are not directly applicable to the training of talented individuals engaged in intense training for many years. Moreover, the very large number of training regimens and the possible combinations of these make it very difficult to include in a single study sufficient subjects to analyze benefits of the many different training protocols.

Conditioning for Endurance and Speed Athletic Events

The sports of running and swimming epitomize those rhythmical activities in which speed and endurance depend on physiological power. In general, running is the most universal sport, not only because of the worldwide interest in it, but also because skill in running is essential to success in many other sports. Conditioning for running is of interest because internationally recognized (Olympic) competition events span the range of pure sprint to pure endurance. In general, many of the same training principles that apply to running also apply to swimming. As we will see, however, swimming differs in that Olympic swimming competition does not include pure sprint events. Furthermore, in swimming, stroke technique is exceedingly important, perhaps more important than physiological power.

This chapter is based on three sources of information: (1) the limited studies on training methods, (2) the application of basic physiological principles to athletic training, and (3) the practical experiences of athletes and coaches.

Training for Athletic Competition

It should be made clear that the following discussion refers to training for athletic competition and not training of middle-aged, older, or even recreational younger asymptomatic individuals. The training stimulus necessary to maintain or improve cardiovascular function in the population at large, as described by the American College of Sports Medicine (ACSM), is less in terms

288

of both intensity and volume than the training of competitive athletes described here. The training stimulus recommended to maintain cardiovascular fitness (Chapters 11 and 17) will not develop the exceptional performance levels required for success in competitive athletes. However, the ACSM training guidelines are probably as effective for developing fitness for daily living and for promoting longevity as training for competitive athletics.

Overload, Stimulus, and Response

The principle of overload is a rephrasing of the well-known general adaptation syndrome (Chapter 1), wherein physiological adaptations occur in response to appropriate stimuli. The amount of overload to a system can be varied by manipulating four basic factors:

1. training intensity,
2. training volume,
3. training duration, and
4. rest interval between training repetitions or sessions.

In general, the greater the overload, the greater the resulting adaptation and increase in functional capacity. Because it takes *time* for physiological responses to occur following application of a training stimulus, the progressive application of a training stimulus must be accomplished within particular constraints. The application of the stimulus (i.e., the increase in training intensity, volume, and duration) must be gradual and progressive. Rather than a rapid and continuous increase in training to achieve an increase in athletic performance (Figure 13-1*A*), the training progression should be gradual and discontinuous. Periods (cycles) of heightened training should be interspersed with recovery periods or cycles involving decreased training intensity and volume. Adequate rest on each day of training is also important. Additionally, hard-training days should be interspersed with easy days. The training schedule of a serious athlete should therefore look more like the broken sawtooth in Figure 13-1*B* than the smooth blade in Figure 13-1*A*. Recuperation periods at the beginning of a training cycle are to be considered an essential part of the training regimen and should be followed scrupulously, for it is during recuperation periods that adaptation occurs.

Specificity, Skill Acquisition, and Developing Metabolic Machinery

Increasing performance as the result of training requires that the training be appropriate for the event. Two factors are involved in the specificity of train-

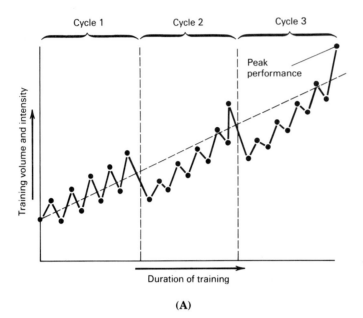

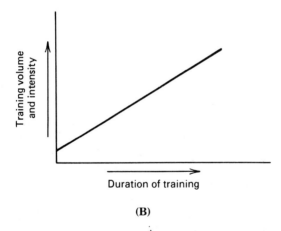

Figure 13-1
(A). Over the course of a training season, training volume and intensity should increase in a cyclic, discontinuous manner. Days and weeks of heightened training should be followed by recovery days and weeks of lesser intensity. Similarly, each training cycle begins at an intensity less than that of the previous cycle. In this system, the stimulus of progressive training is accompanied by periods of recovery and adaption. *(B)* The linear increase in training illustrated here is probably *not* the best protocol for increasing training intensity.

ing response: learning the event of interest and developing the metabolic machinery to support the event. In sports such as running, and especially in swimming, in which the skill level can tremendously affect the performance outcome, long hours of training develop the neuromuscular control mechanisms to optimize results by minimizing the effort necessary to achieve a given result or by maximizing the work output for a given metabolic power output.

The principle of specificity requires that the training regimen overload the metabolic system that supports the activity. In evaluating the relative contributions of immediate, glycolytic, and oxidative energy sources in supporting an activity, the duration of the activity is of primary importance in determining which energy system is most important (see Figures 2-1 and 2-4). Activities lasting a few seconds (e.g., the shot put) depend mainly on immediate energy sources (ATP and CP) muscle strength. Activities lasting from a few seconds to a minute (e.g., 100- to 400-m track running) depend mostly on glycogenolysis, the glycolytic formation of lactic acid, muscle power, and speed. Events lasting longer than a minute become increasingly dependent on oxidative metabolism and cardiovascular and muscular endurance. Because most athletic events last longer than a minute, training of the cardiovascular mechanism of O_2 transport and of the muscular mechanism of O_2 utilization is of primary importance. For endurance-type activities, training the systems of O_2 delivery and utilization is so important that its emphasis can allow athletes to be very successful, even if they overlook and neglect training of the other energy systems. At the conclusion of endurance events, the athletes with the strongest finishing kicks are not necessarily the best sprinters; they are the freshest individuals with the best capabilities of prolonged oxidative metabolism.

Many types of training regimens to develop oxidative capacity exist, but they can be divided into two basic types: over-distance training and high-intensity interval training. Both types of training appear to be important, and clever coaches will work athletes through a range of combinations and variations of these two to optimize adaptation and avoid boredom.

Over-Distance Training

The usually stated objectives of over-distance training [sometimes called long, slow distance training (LSD)] are twofold: (1) to increase $\dot{V}_{O_2max}$ and (2) to increase tissue respiratory (mitochondrial) capacity. Of these two, increasing respiratory capacity appears to be the more important. Although it is true that endurance athletes, such as marathon runners, display very high values of $\dot{V}_{O_2max}$, $\dot{V}_{O_2max}$ actually correlates poorly with performance in events such as the marathon. Middle-distance runners sometimes record higher values of $\dot{V}_{O_2max}$ than do long-distance runners. Obviously, however, top marathon runners are faster in their event than are top mile runners. Some marathon runners can apparently sustain a pace eliciting over 90% of $\dot{V}_{O_2max}$ for several hours. The basis for this phenomenal endurance ability lies in the muscles and other tissues rather than in the O_2 transport apparatus.

Over-distance training, consisting of running or swimming mile after mile at a speed less than the competitive pace, causes a proliferation of mitochondrial protein in muscle (Chapter 4). In detailed animal studies, muscle mitochondrial density has correlated better with endurance capacity than has $\dot{V}_{O_2max}$. The ability to utilize fats as fuels and the ability to protect mitochondria against damage during prolonged work are qualities developed through over-distance training.

Each training regimen has its advantages and disadvantages. The advantage of over-distance training is that it develops tissue respiratory capacity; the disadvantages come from the fact that the training regimen overlooks the basic principle of specificity. All athletic activities, even the most basic such as running, require practice in technique. Therefore, an endurance athlete must prepare for competition by training at or near the race pace. A mile runner practicing to break 4 min by running at an 8-min-mile pace makes about as much sense as a gymnast attempting to practice a double somersault in slow motion. Athletes must learn to pace and improve skill by performing at high rates in practice. Over-distance training can build tissue respiratory capacity but does not develop the sense of pace, skill, or the capacity to achieve a high $\dot{V}_{O_2max}$. Athletes who attempt to practice at or near race pace, however, cannot possibly sustain much of a training volume. An approach to providing specific skill and pace training with volume training is the interval training regimen.

Interval Training

The interval training regimen is one in which periods of intense training intensity during a workout are interspersed with relief or rest periods. For instance, an interval workout for the runner practicing to dip under 4 min might consist of 10 repeated 60-sec quarter-mile runs with a 2-min relief or rest interval each run.

The advantage of interval training is that the athlete learns pace; he or she practices the specific competitive skill, and the cardiovascular training stimulus intensity will be greater than in over-distance training. The interval training stimulus will possibly maximize the improvement in $\dot{V}_{O_2max}$ as well as result in significant improvements in mitochondrial density.

In addition to these aerobic training benefits, high-intensity interval training will stress the glycolytic system in muscle and will result in significant lactate accumulation. Because the accumulation of lactate is distressing to a competitor, he or she must practice tolerating its presence by repeated exposure to it. More important, radiotracer studies of lactate metabolism in animals indicate that training can improve the pathways of lactate removal (Chapter 4). The sites of lactate removal are heart and red skeletal muscle (which oxidize lactate), and gluconeogenic tissues (liver and kidney), which participate in the Cori cycle. Because the rate of lactate removal is directly dependent on its concentration (i.e., the greater the concentration, the greater the removal), interval training that increases blood lactate levels will stimulate improvement in the capacity to remove lactate.

Training Variation and Peaking

With just two basic aerobic training regimens (over-distance and interval), the permutations and combinations of varying distance, speed, duration of rest interval, and so forth, result in an almost infinite combination of training possibilities. The existence of such a large number of choices can be used to benefit by coaches who must often work to sustain interest and desire in athletes over months if not years of training. Varying the training regimen is one way to maintain the interest in athletes.

As the training year progresses and the competitive season approaches, the training regimen should be adjusted to achieve peak performance. Let us illustrate by continuing to describe the training of a miler trying to break 4 min. Early in the training year (i.e., fall and winter), the athlete should concentrate on over-distance training, with interval training sessions only once or twice a week. The athlete should alternate hard and easy days, with an interval-training day substituted for the hard over-distance day. The hard over-distance day might consist of a 10-mile cross-country run at a pace of 6 min to 6 min, 30 sec· mile^{-1}. An easy over-distance day would consist of a 5-mile run at the same pace. Interval training on the track might focus on developing the 4-min mile rhythm. Therefore, an interval day might consist of either 10 quarter-mile runs at a 60-sec pace, each with a 5-min rest interval between; 20 30-sec, 220-yd runs, each with 2 min between; or 5 880-yd ($\frac{1}{2}$ mile) runs in 2 min with 5-min rest intervals. During rest intervals, the athlete should walk or jog to stimulate oxidative recovery. By following such a training regimen, the athlete will be accumulating a large volume of training, which will lay a solid base for the competitive season.

As the competitive season approaches, the athlete should gradually convert from a basic over-distance program to an interval program more specifically designed around the competitive event of interest. Instead of one or two interval sessions and five or six over-distance sessions a week, these training protocols should be reversed. Again, hard days should be alternated with easy days. If minor competitions begin to appear on the schedule, such as on every other Saturday, then the heavy volume of training should be countered early in the week (Sunday, Monday, Tuesday), and the training intensity and volume should taper at the end of the week. On hard interval training days, the 4-min-mile race pace should be the cornerstone of the interval training. For variety, the rest interval between runs may be shortened, distances lengthened, pace quickened, or number of interval repeats increased. If the distances and numbers of repeats are increased, care should be taken to not let the pace fall much below the intended race pace. In practice, if an athlete can manage 10 quarter-mile runs with only 2-min intervals between, then he or she might expect to break 4 min.

Sprint Training

True sprints are events that last from a few seconds to approximately 30 sec. Sprinting requires an extreme degree of skill, coordination, and metabolic power. This power comes from immediate and nonoxidative energy sources present in muscle before the activity starts. Although proficiency in sprinting certainly can be improved through training, the nature of the activity is such that genetic endowment determines in a major way the success that can be achieved by an individual in sprinting.

Whereas endurance athletes require daily training to develop the cardio-vascular and muscle respiratory capacities necessary to be competitive, sprint training requires more intense but less frequent training.

An adequate training frequency for sprinters might be 3 to 5 days a week. The highly specialized nature of sprinting requires that the training must develop the specific skills used in sprinting. Some of these skills might include starting, accelerating, relaxing while sprinting, and finishing. Running and sprinting drills should be all out, but the distances should be kept less than the competitive distances so that repeated bouts at maximal intensity can be practiced.

In addition to high-intensity intervals at maximal speed, analysis of a particular sprinter's performance may reveal a need for exercises to improve other specific aspects of his or her performance. For instance, exercises to develop hip flexion (knee lift) can be particularly important. Weight lifting and isokinetic exercises can be used to develop both quadriceps and hamstring strength. High-speed filming may reveal inefficiencies in form that can be corrected in practice.

Although over-distance training is not strictly necessary for sprinting, under particular circumstances the training volume required by sprinters should be increased. Over-distance training early in the training session may be used to effect a weight loss in overfat athletes. Long sprints (e.g., 400-m track running) require a significant aerobic component, therefore, interval training should be employed. Over-distance training can also be successful if the particular competition involves trials, quarter-, and semifinals, as well as final heats, or a competition may involve participation in several events plus a relay. Even in American football and soccer, repeated sprinting is required. Therefore, the ability to recover rapidly is essential. Recovery is an aerobic process that can be improved through over-distance, interval training. Over-distance conditioning of sprinters may also reduce the incidence of injury.

Volume Versus Intensity of Training

A perpetual question in athletic training is whether or not increasing the volume (frequency and duration) of training is more beneficial than increasing the intensity. There appears to be no simple answer to this question, but consideration should be given to the type of event involved and the phase of training in relation to the competitive season. In general, the more intense (sprint) types of activities require higher intensities of training. This is because of the principle of specificity, which dictates that attention be given to developing the metabolic apparatus and skill levels necessary to compete in the event. Of necessity, more intense training requires reduced training volume.

In general, during the early training season, athletes should focus on increasing the training volume. As the competitive season approaches, training intensity should be emphasized and the volume diminished. In preparing for a major competition, both training volume and intensity should be reduced.

The Taper for Competition

The period before major competition, when athletes rest by decreasing training volume and intensity to very low levels so that peak performances can be achieved, is termed the taper period. The taper can be understood generally in terms of the adaptive response syndrome. It is during the taper that athletes recover from the hard training and adaptive responses peak. The taper period used varies from sport to sport. In track, the most frequently used taper period ranges from 1 to 2 weeks; in swimming, the taper is frequently twice that used in track. Unfortunately, at present we have an insufficient research basis from which to calculate duration of the optimal taper period.

Two to three days after training should be sufficient to result in maximum glycogen supercompensation. Within a week following intense training, minor injuries should have healed, soreness disappeared, and nitrogen balance returned to zero form positive levels. In other words, the response to training overload should have peaked. On physiological bases, then, a taper period of around a week to 10 days would seem to be ideal.

The best information available at present on the half-life of muscle respiratory proteins (mitochondria) indicates that the adaptation period has a half-life of 2 weeks. Therefore, a layoff longer than 1 to 2 weeks should result in physiological decrements. Despite the research data available, however, most athletes and coaches who use a taper regimen believe a taper period longer than a week is superior. At present, therefore, the physiology of the taper is not completely understood.

Three Components of a Training Session: Warm-Up, Training, and Cool-Down

Each training session should consist of three components: warm-up, training, and cool-down. Preliminary exercise (warm-up) has several objectives. The athlete attempts to increase temperatures of the tissues to take advantage of the fact that muscle enzyme activity doubles for each 10-degree-celsius increase in temperature (Q_{10} effect.) Therefore, the Q_{10} effect raises muscle metabolic rate and the speed of contraction. Preliminary exercise also raises the cardiac output and dilates capillary beds in muscle. In this way circulation of blood and O_2 is raised before hard exercise starts. Additionally, during a warm-up, an athlete attempts to stretch out the active tissues by stretching exercises and warming of the tissues. Prior stretching and warming up through exercise and wearing heavy clothing is thought to minimize the possibility of injury. Preliminary exercise also provides a "last-minute" practice session. Motor skills are fine-tuned and adjusted for the prevailing conditions. The warm-up precedure also provides a time for the athlete to make psychological preparation for the practice or competition. This neural aspect of preparing for exercise may be more important than the other benefits of preliminary exercise.

The nature of the preliminary exercise (warm-up bout) depends on the specific activity to be performed. In general, however, several considerations apply. The exercise performed should utilize the major muscles to be involved in training or competition. The activity performed should be the same or very similar to that to be engaged in, and it should progress from mild to hard intensity. Because about 10 min of exercise at a particular work intensity is required to reach a steady muscle temperature, a warm-up should be at least 10 min long. Because the athlete should avoid fatiguing exercise prior to practice or competition, and because tissues cool down more slowly than they heat up, frequent rest periods will allow warming up without imparting fatigue. Once an athlete has warmed up, a brief recovery period should intervene before training or competition. Ideally, this period may be 5 to 10 min, although a well-clothed athlete may remain "warmed up" for 20 to 30 min.

Whereas most athletes, by habit or tradition, include time in a training session to warm up, the cool-down period following training is usually overlooked. A cool-down period is very much like the reverse of a warm-up. The exercise intensity is gradually decreased, followed by a period of passive stretching, wherein heavily used muscles are held in elongated positions for two 1-min intervals. For instance, in runners the hamstrings and gastrocnemius muscles are those usually stretched after training. Particularly in older or less fit individuals, a cool-down period may effectively minimize soreness and stiffness during the days following hard training or competition.

Methods of Evaluating Training Intensity

Is a workout schedule too hard, too easy, or just right? At various times, both coaches and athletes desire some objective evaluation of an athlete's training regimen. To answer these questions several approaches can be taken, all of which involve evaluation of both performance and physiological criteria.

Of primary importance is an evaluation of the athlete's performance. If the athlete is meeting or exceeding performance criteria during workouts, time trials, and competitions, then the training regimen is obviously having good results. If the athlete feels tired immediately after but good an hour or so after training, and if the athlete feels good the day after training, then the training regimen is probably appropriate. If an athlete is sleepy or loses appetite as the result of training, he or she probably is training too hard.

Heart Rate as a Training Guide

Application of the preceding subjective criteria may answer the question whether the training schedule is too easy or too hard, but it cannot identify an optimal training regimen or provide an objective assessment of training intensity. For this evaluation, determination of exercise heart rate can be useful. During interval training, the exercise intensity should be sufficient to stimulate heart rate to near maximum. Maximal heart rate can be determined during an exercise stress test (Chapter 17) or immediately after a time trial by ECG or palpation (counting the pulse). The recovery interval should end and the next training interval should begin when heart rate falls to two-thirds of maximum (i.e., about 120 beats·min^{-1}). Such a regimen would constitute a very hard interval training program. Heart rate during submaximal, over-distance training (e.g., continuous runs or swims lasting 20 min or longer) should stabilize at three-quarters of maximum and progress to maximum as the training session is completed.

Blood Lactate (OBLA) as a Training Guide

Determination of blood lactic acid level has been purported to be another "objective" means of evaluating intensity of the training stimulus. Lactate level can easily be measured in a tiny drop of blood taken by means of a pinprick to the earlobe or fingertip. The East German swim team has reportedly identified the work intensity that elicits a 4-mM blood lactic acid level as the optimal aerobic (over-distance) training intensity. Unfortunately, no data have been put forward to justify a 4-mM blood lactic acid level as the ideal, and no theoretical basis exists to justify use of the 4-mM value. Certainly, for interval exercise, a 4-mM blood lactate level would lack sufficient intensity. Probably also for over-distance training, a 4-mM blood lactate level might be too easy. For instance, many individuals have been able to maintain for an hour exercise loads that elicit blood lactic acid levels from 6 to 8 mM. Because the ability to remove lactic acid is related to its concentration, an athlete should occasionally experience high circulating lactate levels (10 mM) to develop the mechanisms of lactate removal (Chapter 4).

The OBLA point (Chapter 6) has been identified as a means to predict the maximal exercise intensity that can be maintained over extended periods such as in the marathon run. Predicting race pace in long-distance competi-

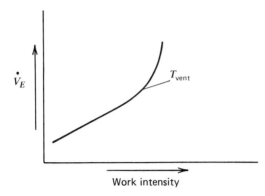

Figure 13-2
Pulmonary minute ventilation ($\dot{V}_E$) is a function of work intensity. As work rate increases, $\dot{V}_E$ increases linearly up to a particular work load, after which $\dot{V}_E$ increases disproportionately. This break in the ventilation versus work rate curve is termed the ventilatory threshold [$T_{(vent)}$]. Blood lactate level (see Figure 6-6*B*) and other factors affect the $T_{(vent)}$; please refer to Chapter 6.

tions is, however, very different from gauging training intensity, particularly with intense interval training.

Ventilatory ("Anaerobic") Threshold as a Training Guide

The ventilatory threshold [$T_{(vent)}$] (Figure 13-2) is that point at which ventilation begins to increase nonlinearly in response to increments in work rate. The $T_{(vent)}$ is sometimes called the "anaerobic threshold" and is usually associated with an increase in the blood lactic acid level (see Figure 6-6*B*). However, other stress factors can elevate ventilation during exercise, and as such, determination of the ventilatory inflection point [$T_{(vent)}$] is probably a less appropriate training criterion than the determination of a blood lactate inflection point [$T_{(lact)}$] or a blood lactate level of 4 mM (OBLA). The problem, however, with using either the $T_{(lact)}$ or $T_{(vent)}$ as a training guide is that their measurement requires special apparatus not ordinarily available to the athlete and coach. If a laboratory is available to a runner, the treadmill pace that elicits and $T_{(lact)}$ or $T_{(vent)}$ can be determined with precision and then utilized in the field. Repeated laboratory tests will be required, however, as the athlete improves. As previously noted, the $T_{(lact)}$ point would provide insufficient training intensity for anything but the longest of endurance competitions.

Common Mistakes in Training

In preparing for competition, many athletes expend a great deal of effort but are unsuccessful for some simple reasons. Athletic training is in some cases, at some times, a very important endeavor. Therefore, a system or training strategy should be constructed and written out. A particular training schedule should be prescribed, and a log of training adherence and performance should be kept. Perhaps the most common failing of some training regimens is that insufficient overload is applied. Either training volume or intensity is too little to result in training adaptations that will distinguish a particular competitor.

Some training regimens are often too shortsighted in their approach. Many athletes expect rapid improvements and become discouraged even as the basis of real adaptation is being achieved. The progression of an athlete in training and competition should realistically be planned to extend over several seasons. Particularly in American track and field competition, where rapid progress is frequently desired, hard interval training has been used to optimize performance in the short run, but athletes become discouraged when they fail to improve consistently from season to season, because no real basis has been laid to support the improvement. The temptation to develop racers rather than physiologically superior athletes must be suppressed.

Sometimes athletes fail to reach their level of competitive aspiration because they lack an individualized training program. In a group of 10 cross-country runners running interval quarter miles together, perhaps 5 will be running very hard to keep up. Several others will not be training very hard, and at least 1 or 2 will be receiving a minimal training stimulus. Such a predicament happens when there are more athletes to train than can interact with the coach.

Sex Differences in Performance

Today, even though we know that women can develop an extremely high level of fitness, the legacy of past beliefs persists. For example, until recently, the longest women's race in Olympic track and field was the 3000-m run, yet thousands of women compete very successfully in marathons every year with no more ill effects than male runners. (The marathon was included in the 1984 Olympics.)

There are sex differences in physical performance. Males tend to be larger with more muscle mass and larger hearts, which gives them more strength, power, and endurance. Sex differences in performance are much less than once thought. Today's top female marathoners equal the performance of their male counterparts of only 3 decades ago, while female swimmers are equaling or surpassing the times of the top male athletes who competed in the 1960s. However, regardless of differences in performance and work capacity, sports and physical activity affect and benefit both sexes.

Sex chromosomes are responsible for the anatomical differences that give males an advantage in physical performance. The genetic material contained in the chromosomes acts as a blueprint for respective sexual characteristics in muscle mass, heart size, body fat, and probably even psychological traits such as aggression.

Growth and Maturation

Girls tend to mature faster than boys. It is not unusual for some girls to be bigger and more physically skilled than some boys during childhood. The pubertal growth spurt begins between 10 and 13 years in girls and 12 and 15 in boys. Young adolescent girls are usually taller than boys of the same age. However, boys catch up and eventually surpass girls.

The hormonal changes of puberty affect the body composition of both sexes, with girls showing a greater growth of fat and boys a greater growth of lean tissue. The body composition during puberty seems to be caused by increased secretion of gonadotropin hormones from the pituitary (controlled by their releasing factors in the hypothalamus). These hormones act to increase estrogen levels in girls and androgen levels in boys. Estrogens tend to increase adipose tissue and have a slight retardant effect on lean body mass, while androgens tend to increase lean tissue and inhibit the development of body fat. These hormone-controlled changes of puberty ultimately cause the evident sex differences in work capacity and physical performance.

Boys tend to have slightly more muscle mass than girls throughout growth. At puberty, boys experience pronounced muscle growth while girls experience much less. The difference in muscle mass between the sexes is due largely to the male hormones. Anthropometric characteristics change considerably during puberty. Boys develop larger shoulders while girls develop larger hips. The smaller shoulder girdle makes it much more difficult for women to develop upper body strength. The wider hips makes the angle of the femur much more pronounced than in males, making it more difficult for women to develop the same running speed as males. However, the larger hips give women a slightly lower center of gravity that gives them an advantage in activities requiring balance.

Body Composition

Adult males tend to have less fat and more muscle mass than adult females. These sex differences remain in athletes who participate in high-energy sports that tend to reduce body fat, such as distance running. Sex differences in fat distribution are caused by a combination of natural and social factors. Active women tend to have lower fat percentages than average (Table 13-1), generally falling below 22% in recreational runners. Women in higher social classes also tend to be leaner. Ideal fat percentages are dictated as much by individual interpretation of fashion as by natural fat deposition patterns.

Differences in body composition affect the work capacity and performance capability of women. Women are at a distinct disadvantage in sports in which they must lift or move their mass against gravity. In activities such as running, climbing, and jumping, they must propel more body fat with less muscle mass than men. The greater body fat also gives women a disadvantage in releasing body heat during exercise.

TABLE 13-1 **Sex Differences in Fat
Percentage (50th percentile)**

Age (year)	Males	Females
20–29	21.6	25.0
30–39	22.4	24.8
40–49	23.4	26.1
50–59	24.1	29.3
Over 60	23.1	28.3

SOURCE: Data from Pollock, J. H. Wilmore, and
S. M. Fox. Health and Fitness Through Physical
Activity. New York: John Wiley, 1978.

Women's higher body fat is an advantage in swimming. The higher body fat allows women to swim higher in the water with less body drag. In swimming, sex differences in performance are smaller than in most other sports. For example, in the 400-m freestyle, the winning time for women in the 1976 Olympics was faster than for men in the 1964 games.

Body fat can be reduced to extremely low levels in endurance-trained women. Body fat levels of less than 12% have been reported for top marathon runners, whereas levels of less than 16% are typical for women involved in metabolically taxing activities. Strenuous endurance programs resulting in substantial reduction of fat may affect the estrous cycle by causing an absence or irregularity of the menses.

Amenorrhea: Amenorrhea (absence of menstruation) and oligomenorrhea (reduced or irregular menstruation) with concomitant anovulation (failure to ovulate) are common in endurance athletes. This phenomenon may be related to low levels of body fat, weight loss, or chronically high energy expenditure. In a study of track and cross-country runners, for example, 45% of women who ran more than 80 miles a week experienced irregular menstrual cycles. This condition is also common in women experiencing body fat losses from other causes such as dieting and anorexia nervosa. Menstrual irregularities associated with rigorous physical training appear to be benign and reversible.

More likely, endurance training probably acts to reduce estrogen levels, which directly affect menstruation. There is a decrease in hypothalamic gonadotropin releasing factors, pituitary gonadotropins and ovarian steroids in amenorrheic distance runners compared with nonrunners with normal menstrual cycles. In addition to secretion from the ovaries, estrogens are produced by peripheral aromatization of androgens catalyzed by the enzyme aromatase found in fat cells. A reduction in fat may decrease the peripheral production of estrogens, which are thought to be important in stimulating the hypothalamic-pituitary axis during the early follicular phase of the normal menstrual cycle.

301

TABLE 13-2 Sex Differences in Maximal Oxygen Consumption (ml $O_2 \cdot kg^{-1} \cdot min^{-1}$) (50th percentile)

Age (year)	Males	Females
20–29	40.0	31.1
30–39	37.5	30.3
40–49	36.0	28.0
50–59	33.6	25.7
Over 60	30.0	22.9

SOURCE: Data from Pollock, J. H. Wilmore, and S. M. Fox. Health and Fitness Through Physical Activity. New York: John Wiley, 1978.

Oxygen Transport System

Men exceed women by about 20% in maximal oxygen consumption. However, training can either equalize or reverse these differences, so that some women will exceed the endurance capacity of some men. Differences in $\dot{V}_{O_2max}$ can be attributed to greater cardiac output, blood volume, and oxygen-carrying capacity. Sex differences in maximal oxygen consumption with age are shown in Table 13-2.

Males have a larger heart size and heart volume. The larger heart size enables greater myocardial contractility while the larger heart volume allows a greater end-diastolic volume. These advantages give males larger maximal stroke volume and maximal cardiac output.

Resting, submaximal exercise, and maximal exercise heart rates tend to be higher in women (Table 13-3). Oxygen requirements for a given work load are similar in men and women, so the female heart must beat faster to make up for its lower pumping capacity. In similarly trained individuals, there is

TABLE 13-3 Sex Differences in Resting and Maximal Heart Rate (50th percentile)

	Heart Rate (beats·min^{-1})			
	Resting		*Maximal*	
Age (year)	Males	Females	Males	Females
20–29	64	67	192	188
30–39	63	68	188	183
40–49	64	68	181	175
50–59	63	68	171	169
Over 60	63	65	159	151

SOURCE: Data from Pollock, J. H. Wilmore, and S. M. Fox. Health and Fitness Through Physical Activity. New York: John Wiley, 1978.

little difference in maximal heart rate between the sexes. Because of their larger maximal cardiac output, males tend to have a higher systolic blood pressure during maximal exercise. Heart rate recovery is slower in women because their hearts must beat faster to produce a particular cardiac output.

Pulmonary ventilation is higher in men, mainly because of differences in body size. Until puberty, maximal ventilation is similar but becomes disproportionate during adolescence. There are no sex differences in pulmonary diffusion capacity and hemoglobin saturation either at rest or during exercise.

Both the amount and the concentration of hemoglobin is higher in males, thus giving their blood a greater oxygen-carrying capacity. Women average about 13.7 g Hb·dl^{-1} blood while men average 15.8 g Hb·dl^{-1} blood. The difference is attributed to the potent effect of the androgens on hemoglobin production and the effects of menstrual blood loss.

Some women are prone to iron difficiency and iron difficiency anemia because of the combined effects of low dietary iron intake, limited rates of iron absorption, and iron loss during menstruation. Such women can benefit from dietary iron supplementation. However, universal administration of iron supplements does not appear to be warranted as studies have shown that iron supplements administered to nonanemic women athletes had no effect on hemoglobin or iron status.

Physical Performance

Males have about a 20% greater capacity for both endurance and short-duration, high-intensity exercise. This is largely due to factors already mentioned: body size and oxygen transport capacity. Sex differences in exercise capacity tend to be somewhat greater in activities that benefit from strength and body mass, such as weight lifting and sprinting. Sex differences in performance are reduced to 7 to 13% in swimming because of the greater buoyancy of women.

Boys tend to be slightly superior to girls in sprint running, long jump, and high jump and considerably superior in throwing skills. At puberty, males accelerate their development of motor skills while females change very little. Sex differences in sports participation probably account for much of this phenomenon.

Males and females seem to experience similar effects from most types of physical training. However, the literature often provides conflicting results. When evaluating these studies, it is important to consider the relative fitness of the male and female subjects. Although some studies show that females improve more than males, this is usually due to a relatively higher initial fitness in males (i.e., males in these studies are usually closer to their maximum physical potential). Recent, well-controlled studies show that both sexes respond similarly to interval and continuous-endurance training.

Sex differences in temperature regulation are somewhat controversial. Numerous early studies found that males were better able to tolerate exercise in the heat. However, these early investigations usually employed fit male subjects and sedentary female subjects. Sweat rates during exercise in the heat are generally less in women, but the abilities to acclimatize and control body temperature were similar. Women may rely on circulatory mechanisms, such as altering vascular tone, to achieve the same degree of thermoregulatory control as men. Relative fitness seem to be more important than sex differences in determining heat tolerance and the ability to acclimatize to heat.

Muscle Metabolism

In equally trained male and female subjects, muscle glycogen, blood lactate levels (at the same relative percentage of $\dot{V}_{O_2max}$), fat metabolism capacity, and muscle fiber composition are similar. There is some evidence that certain aspects of female muscle biochemistry (e.g., the ability to synthesize muscle glycogen and to oxidize fats) do not respond to training as readily as they do in males.

Strength

Males are stronger than females throughout childhood, with the gap widening during adolescence. Body weight accounts for much but not all of the sex differences in strength. Even during childhood, when body weight and muscle mass are similar in boys and girls, male muscle can develop more tension per unit volume. In the adult, males are 50% stronger than females in most muscle groups.

Muscle fibers in female athletes and nonathletes are similar to those in males, both histochemically and in their distribution. However, all fiber types in females have a smaller cross-sectional area than those in males.

Higher androgen levels in males account for the large strength differences between the sexes. Androgens are potent anabolic hormones that are responsible for much of the muscle hypertrophy seen in males during the adolescent growth spurt as well as from strength training. Because women have only low levels of androgens, they experience little muscle hypertrophy from strength training. They can greatly improve their strength, but they just do not get big muscles. Women apparently gain strength by improving their ability to recruit motor units rather than significantly altering the contractile structures of the muscles. Old men, who have low levels of testosterone, also rely principally on enhanced motor unit recruitment to increase strength.

Strength Training

The history of strength training goes back many years, beginning with the great Olympic champion Milo of Crotono, who lived in Greece in the 6th century B.C. Milo is said to have hoisted a baby bull on his shoulders to improve his strength. He repeated this every day, and as the bull grew heavier with age, Milo improved his strength. Since then, progressive strength training has become an important part of the training program of many types of athletes, ranging from football and track and field to swimmers and figure skaters.

Classification of Strength Exercises

Strength exercises can be classified into three categories: isometric (static), isotonic (dynamic), and isokinetic. Isometric exercise involves the application of force without movement, isotonic exercise involves force with movement, and isokinetic exercise involves the exertion of force at a constant speed.

Isometric Exercise Hettinger and Meuller caused a stir in 1953 when they reported that 6 sec of isometric exercise at 75% effort increased strength in hospital patients. However, subsequent research has shown that isometrics have limited applications in the training programs of athletes. Although this type of training received considerable attention in the 1950s and 1960s, it is seldom practiced unless it is included with other techniques in the training program.

Isometric exercise does not increase strength throughout the range of motion of a joint but rather is specific to the joint angle at which the training is being applied. Likewise, isometric training does not improve (and may hamper) the ability to rapidly exert force. And isometric exercise produces less muscular endurance and muscle hypertrophy than dynamic resistive exercise. Athletes will sometimes use isometrics to help them overcome "sticking points" in the range of motion of an exercise. For example, if an athlete has difficulty pushing a weight from his chest in the bench press, he may perform the exercise isometrically at the point where he is experiencing difficulty (Figure 13-3). Isometrics are often used in injury rehabilitation. Exercises, such as "quad sets" (isometrically contracting the quadriceps), are useful when normal joint mobility is impaired.

Most of the benefits of isometrics seem to occur during the early stages of training. Maximal contraction is essential for the optimal effect, and the duration of contraction should be long enough to recruit as many fibers in a muscle group as possible. The greatest gains in strength occur when isometrics are practiced several times a day. As with other strength training techniques, however, excessive training will eventually lead to deterioration in performance (overtraining).

Isotonic Exercise Isotonic exercise is the most familiar strength training technique to most athletes and coaches. Isotonic loading methods include constant, variable, eccentric, speed, and plyometric resistance.

In constant resistance exercise, the load remains constant, but the difficulty in overcoming the resistance varies with the angle of the joint. For

Figure 13-3

Isometric squat on the power rack.

(SOURCE: G. A. Brooks and T. D. Fahey. Exercise Physiology: Human Bioenergetics and Its Applications. New York: Macmillan, 1984, Figure 20-1.)

example, in the "free weight" bench press, it is easier to move the weight at the end of the range of motion than when the weight is on the chest. Barbells and dumbbells are the best example of constant resistance exercise devices and continue to be the most popular with the majority of athletes who depend on strength and power for maximal performance (Figure 13-4).

Variable resistance exercise is done on specially designed weight ma-

Figure 13-4

Constant resistance exercise: the power snatch.

(SOURCE: G. A. Brooks and T. D. Fahey. Exercise Physiology: Human Bioenergetics and Its Applications. New York: Macmillan, 1984, Figure 20-2.)

Figure 13-5
Variable resistance exercise: Nautilus pullover machine.

(SOURCE: G. A. Brooks and T. D. Fahey. Exercise Physiology: Human Bioenergetics and Its Applications. New York: Macmillan, 1984, Figure 20-3.)

chines, which impose an increasing load throughout the range of motion so that a more constant stress is placed on the muscles (Figure 13-5). This is accomplished by changing the relationship of the fulcrum and lever arm in the weight machine as the exercise progresses. Although the concept of placing a muscle group under a relatively uniform near-maximal stress throughout the range of motion is intellectually appealing, the experimental evidence for the superiority of variable resistance over constant resistance exercise remains equivocal.

Eccentric loading is tension exerted during the lengthening of a muscle. In a bench press, for example, the muscles work eccentrically by resisting the movement of the bar as it approaches the chest. Several studies have shown that this is an effective means of gaining strength, although it is not superior to other isotonic techniques. One drawback of eccentric training is that it seems to create more muscle soreness than other methods. Eccentrics, by themselves, are not widely practiced by strength athletes except as an adjunct to other training methods. This type of exercise is often used in athletic rehabilitation for the treatment of tendinitis. Of course, there is almost always an eccentric component any time an athlete trains with free weights.

Plyometric loading involves sudden eccentric loading and stretching of muscles' elastic components (composed of connective tissue and the elastic property of myosin) followed by forceful concentric contraction. The sudden stretch causes an elastic recoil and a stretch reflex by the muscle spindles that results in a more forceful concentration. This type of exercise is sometimes called implosion training or plyometrics. An example of plyometrics is jumping from a box to the ground, then rebounding into the air or to another box (Figure 13-6). Although plyometrics have been shown to increase strength and jumping ability, they carry with them an increased risk of injury. Plyometrics have become very popular with track and field athletes, but more research is needed to assess their effectiveness and safety.

Speed loading involves moving the resistance as rapidly as possible. Most studies have found that constant resistance isotonic exercise is superior to speed loading for gaining strength. Speed loading may not allow sufficient tension to elicit a training effect. This was demonstrated in the 1920s when Hill established that tension diminishes as the speed of contraction increases. Nevertheless, this technique is often practiced by strength athletes at various times in their training schedule, particularly during the competitive period when maximum power is desired.

Proprioceptive neuromuscular facilitation (PNF), is manual resistive exercise that utilizes a combination of isotonic and isometric loading and stretching (Figure 13-7). This technique is widely used by physical therapists and athletic trainers to reeducate motor pathways and improve strength and flexibility following athletic injuries. Unfortunately, there is little comparative data on traditional loading techniques. It appears, however, to be a promising method of resistance training (particularly in injury rehabilitation).

Isokinetic Exercise Isokinetic exercise controls the rate of muscle shortening. It is sometimes called accommodating resistance because the exerted force is resisted by an equal force from the isokinetic dynamometer (Figure 13-8). As with variable resistance isotonic exercise, isokinetics require a specially designed machine to produce the isokinetic loading. Isokinetics have become extremely popular with athletic trainers and physical therapists because they allow the training of injured joints with a lower risk of injury. Isokinetic dynamometers also provide a speed-specific indication of the absolute strength (torque) of a muscle group.

(A)   (B)

(C)   (D)

Figure 13-6

Plyometric loading. The subject jumps from the bench *(A)* to the floor *(B)*, absorbs the shock, and then jumps to the bench *(C* and *D)*.

(SOURCE: G. A. Brooks and T. D. Fahey. Exercise Physiology: Human Bioenergetics and Its Applications. New York: Macmillan, 1984, Figure 20-4.)

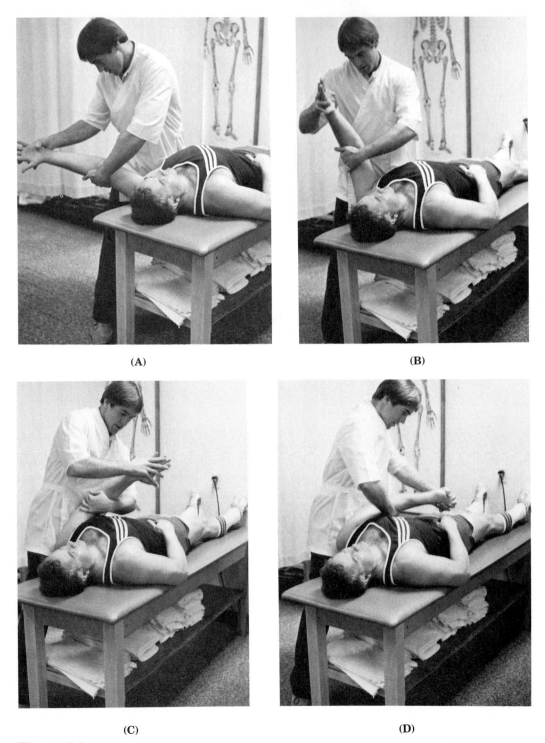

(A)

(B)

(C)

(D)

Figure 13-7
Proprioceptive neuromuscular facilitation.

(SOURCE: G. A. Brooks and T. D. Fahey. Exercise Physiology: Human Bioenergetics and Its Applications. New York: Macmillan, 1984, Figure 20-5.)

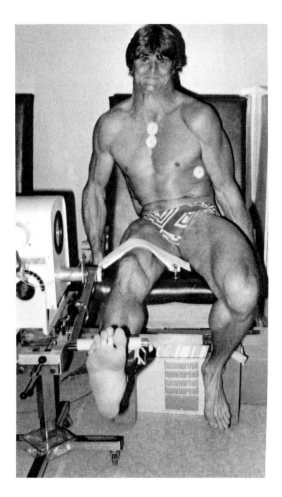

Figure 13-8
The Cybex isokinetic dynamometer.

(SOURCE: G. A. Brooks and T. D. Fahey. Exercise Physiology: Human Bioenergetics and Its Applications. New York: Macmillan, 1984, Figure 20-6.)

The most effective strength gains have come from slower training speed (60 degrees per second or less). Training at fast speeds of motion has been found to increase the ability to exert force rapidly, but no more than traditional isotonic techniques. Although this appears to be a promising method of loading, more research is needed to establish its role in strength training and to determine the ideal isokinetic training protocol.

Factors Involved in Muscular Adaptation to Resistance Exercise

Muscles are strengthened by increasing their size, and by enhancing the recruitment and firing rates of their motor units. It appears that both of these processes are involved in the adaptive response to resistive exercise. There seem to be age and sex differences in the mechanism involved in effecting strength gains. For example, old men and women of all ages seem to increase strength mainly by neural adaptation (with some hypertrophy), while young men rely more on increases in muscle size. There is a limit to the neural contribution to muscular strength increases. The development of superior strength levels (required by top-level football players, weight lifters, discus throwers, etc.) depends on the ability to increase the mass of muscle. However, in these athletes, factors such as improving the ability to recruit motor units and inhibiting Golgi tendon organs (receptors within muscle that inhibit the generation of muscle tension) are probably also important.

Countless exercise devices and training programs are available that are hailed as the best way to gain strength. In most instances, as long as a threshold tension is developed, increases in strength will occur. However, the type of strength developed is the important consideration in exercise and sports. Long-distance running up steep hills, for example, will develop a certain amount of muscular strength, but the muscular adaptations that result will differ from those produced from high-resistance, low-repetition squats (knee bends). The distance runner tends to develop sarcoplasmic protein (factors that improve endurance rather than strength, such as increasing oxidative enzymes, mitochondrial mass, etc.), while the weight lifter tends to develop contractile protein. The nature of the adaptive response must always be considered when designing the training program. Overload and specificity are two important factors that determine the rate and type of strength that result from a resistance training program (see Chapter 1).

Overload and Strength

Muscles increase their strength and size when they are forced to contract at tensions close to their maximum. If muscles are not overloaded, they do not improve in strength and they do not hypertrophy. A number of experimental and empirical observations have allowed some generalizations concerning the amount of overload necessary for strength gains.

Weight training studies and empirical observations of athletes have reinforced the importance of generating muscular tension, at an adequate intensity and duration, for the optimal development of strength. The majority of studies have found that the ideal number of repetitions are between four and eight repetitions maximum (RM), practiced in multiple sets (three or more). Strength gains are less when either fewer or greater numbers of repetitions are used. These findings are consistent with the strength training practices of athletes.

Proper rest intervals are important for maximizing tension, between both exercises and training sessions. Insufficient rest results in inadequate recovery and a diminished capacity of the muscle to exert full force. Unfortunately, the ideal rest interval between exercises has not been determined. Most athletes strength train 3 to 4 days a week, with large muscle exercises such as the bench press and squat seldom practiced more than twice a week. This practice has been empirically derived, as it appears to allow adequate recovery between training sessions.

Athletes involved in speed-strength sports, such as discus throwing and shot putting, practice low-repetition, high-intensity exercise during or immediately preceding the competitive season. Such training seems to improve explosive strength (power), while allowing sufficient energy reserves for practicing motor skills. However, the effectiveness of this practice has not been established experimentally.

The overload must be progressively increased for consistent gains in strength to occur. Because of the great dangers of overtraining in strength building exercises, however, constantly increasing the resistance is sometimes counterproductive. A relatively new practice among strength-trained athletes is periodization of training. This practice varies the volume and intensity of exercises so that the nature of the exercise stress changes frequently. Many athletes believe that this practice produces a faster rate of adaptation.

Muscles will atrophy as a result of disease, immobilization, and starvation. Just as muscles adapt to increasing levels of stress by increasing their function, disuse leads to decreasing strength and muscle mass. Atrophy results in a decrease in both contractile and sarcoplasmic protein.

Specificity of Strength

Muscles tend to specifically adapt to the nature of the exercise stress. The strength training program should stress the muscles in a manner similar to how they are to perform. The most obvious characteristic of specificity is that the muscle exercised is the muscle that adapts to training; in other words, if you exercise the leg muscles, they hypertrophy and not the muscles of the shoulders.

There is specific recruitment of motor units within a muscle depending on the requirements of the contraction. As discussed in Chapters 9 and 10, the different muscle fiber types have characteristic contractile properties. The slow-twitch fibers are relatively fatigue resistant but have a lower tension capacity than the fast-twitch fibers. The fast-twitch fibers have the capacity to contract more rapidly and forcefully, but they also fatigue rapidly.

The use of a motor unit is dependent on the threshold levels of its α-motor neuron. The low-threshold, slow-twitch fibers are recruited for low-intensity activities such as jogging (and, for that matter, for most tasks of human motion). For high-speed or high-intensity activities such as weight lifting, however, the fast-twitch motor units are recruited. The amount of training that occurs in a muscle fiber is determined by the extent to which it is recruited. As discussed, high-repetition, low-intensity exercise, such as distance running, relies on the recruitment of slow-twitch fibers and results in improvements in the fibers' oxidative capacity. Low-repetition, high-intensity activity, such as weight training, causes hypertrophy of fast-twitch fibers, with some hypertrophy to the lower-threshold slow-twitch fibers. The training program should be structured to produce the desired training effect.

Muscle fiber type appears to play an important role in determining success in some sports. Successful distance runners have a high proportion of slow-twitch muscles (the percentage of slow-twitch fibers is highly related to $\dot{V}O_{2max}$), while sprinters have a predominance of fast-twitch muscles. Several studies have shown that a high content of fast-twitch fibers is a prerequisite for success in strength training. This is understandable, as the fast-twitch fibers experience selective hypertrophy as a result of high-resistance, low-repetition exercise.

However, all sports do not require prerequisite fiber characteristics and the fiber types of some athletes may be due to self selection. Coyle et al., for example, found a surprisingly diverse muscle fiber composition in the gastrocnemius of eight world-class shot putters. In those athletes, selective adaptation, rather than the percentage, of the fast-twitch fibers accounted for their performance. Although there is tremendous variability in the relative percentage of fast-twitch fibers in explosive-strength athletes, they exhibit a higher fast-to-slow-twitch fiber area ratio than sedentary subjects and endurance athletes. It appears that individual differences in training intensity and technique can make up for deficiencies in the relative percentage of fast-twitch fibers in these athletes.

Noakes has suggested that selection factors may have forced athletes with higher percentages of slow-twitch fibers into long endurance events such as the marathon. He hypothesized that athletes who currently excel in the longer races (and who exhibit a high percentage of slow-twitch fibers) may have chosen the endurance events because they lack the speed required in the middle distances (800-1500 m) because their muscles have too few fast-twitch fibers. He speculated that as the longer races become more financially lucrative, faster athletes will compete in and dominate them. As examples he cited the domination of the women's marathon by top middle distance runners and the success of Geoff Smith, a world class middle distance runner (3:55 mile), in the marathon (2:09:10 marathon).

Recent research on muscle fiber types has shown that much of the previous work may have been overly simplistic. Fiber type often varies within a specific muscle, so that the predominant fiber in one part of the muscle is not the same as that in another. In addition, the contractile characteristics of a specific muscle fiber type in one muscle may be different from its characteristics in another muscle. More research is needed to determine the practical significance of these findings.

Hypertrophy and Hyperplasia

An ongoing controversy in muscle physiology concerns whether or not resistance training induces the muscle to increase the number of muscle cells

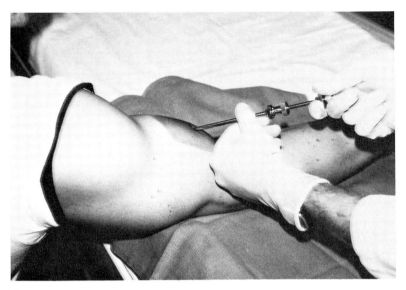

Figure 13-9
Needle biopsy being taken from biceps brachius of an elite body builder.

(SOURCE: G. A. Brooks and T. D. Fahey. Exercise Physiology: Human Bioenergetics and Its Applications. New York: Macmillan, 1984, Figure 20-9a.)

(hyperplasia) as well as increase their size (hypertrophy). For many years it was believed that muscles increased in size only, and that hyperplasia was possible only until the neonatal period. However, recent research has raised questions about this. Histological comparison of muscle cells of elite weight-trained athletes and sedentary controls by MacDougall et al. revealed no apparent differences in fiber areas or muscle fiber type, despite large differences in strength between the two groups (Figure 13-9). The authors hypothesized that the elite group possessed a greater total number of muscle fibers than the controls did (these athletes probably inherited more muscle fibers).

Some researchers have reported fiber splitting (longitudinal division of muscle fibers resulting in a new muscle cell), as well as hypertrophy, in response to resistive exercise. Fiber splitting seems to require a sufficient tension to result in the hypertrophy of Type IIb fibers (fast twitch, glycolytic). Below that intensity, no fiber splitting occurred. Fiber splitting is very controversial, as some researchers have criticized the methodology used in these studies. The bulk of the most recent evidence indicates that fiber splitting probably does not occur in response to muscular overload. *Hypertrophy is the major mechanism involved in enlarging muscle in response to overload stress.* Muscle fibers increase in size by increasing the number and size of their myofibrils.

Muscle Soreness

Delayed muscle soreness (muscle soreness that appears 24 to 48 hr after strenuous exercise) is an overuse injury that is a common experience (and a definite factor to contend with) in persons attempting to develop muscular strength. A number of explanations have been proposed for the cause of muscle soreness including metabolite accumulation, torn tissue, muscle spasm, and connective tissue damage.

Available evidence suggests that delayed muscle soreness probably results from tissue injury caused by excessive mechanical forces exerted on muscle and connective tissue. Direct examination by electron microscopy of sore muscles that were previously eccentrically loaded (subjects who exercised by running downstairs) showed extensive tissue damage, principally in the area of the Z-disk. Similar findings have been observed in well-trained body builders.

Armstrong has developed a model of the physiological consequences of tissue injury that results in delayed onset muscle soreness: (1) high mechanical forces disrupt structural proteins in muscle fibers, connective tissue, sarcolemma, and alter the permeability of cell membranes; (2) abnormal amounts of Ca^{++} accumulate in the mitochondria, which inhibits cellular respiration; (3) the build-up of Ca^{++} results in the activation of a proteolytic enzyme (an enzyme that breaks down protein) that degrades the Z-disks, troponin, and tropomyosin (all three are components of the sarcomere, the basic contractile structural unit of the muscle fiber); (4) this cell destruction causes an inflammatory response characterized by the increased activity of macrophages, mast cells, histocytes, and lysozomal proteases; and (5) the accumulation of histamines, kinins, and potassium in the interstitial spaces along with the accompanying edema and increased temperature stimulates sensory nerve endings, resulting in pain (delayed muscle soreness).

Strength Training Programs of Athletes

Athletes are faced with an incredible array of strength training devices and programs to help them develop strength and power. No doubt, all of them will increase their ability to exert force to a certain extent. It is beyond the scope of this text to provide in-depth analysis of the many programs available. Although there are undoubtedly exceptions, the vast majority of truly strong athletes train with free weights. While this does not necessarily mean this is the best way to gain strength, it does imply a *de facto* recognition of the superiority of this type of training. Athletes are extremely pragmatic and will generally gravitate to the techniques that produce the best results.

The strength training programs of athletes involved in speed–strength sports employ three major types of exercises: presses, pulls, and squats. Examples of presses include the bench press, incline press, jerk, seated press, and behind-the-neck press. These lifts are important for developing the muscles of the shoulders, chest, and arms. Pulling exercises include the clean, snatch, high pull, and dead lift. These lifts develop the muscles of the legs, hips, back, and arms. Squats include the squat and leg press. These exercises develop the legs and back (the leg press develops very little back strength). These three types of lifts represent the most important part of the program and are usually supplemented by auxiliary exercises such as biceps curls, situps, pullovers, and bar dips (exercises designed to develop specific strength for the sport).

Successful strength athletes usually train 3 or 4 days a week during strength-building periods and 1 to 3 days a week during competitive periods. However, the major lifts (press, pulls, and squats) are seldom practiced more than 2 days a week. If these lifts are practiced too frequently, and too intensely, overtraining invariably results. As discussed, heavy training probably causes muscle damage that must be allowed to repair or performance may deteriorate.

Overtraining results in an increased risk of injury and a decrease in performance, probably due to the inability to train heavily during training sessions. Constant, severe training schedules do not provide adequate recovery, and thus the training stimulus cannot be maximal. The intensity and duration of tension are the most important factors eliciting strength increases. The strength requirements of each sport must be assessed in order to develop an appropriate, specific program. In general, sports requiring muscular endurance employ strength-training schedules involving a greater number of repetitions, while those requiring strength use fewer repetitions. Strength-training exercises should be chosen to develop the muscles used in the sport.

Flexibility Training

The ability to move joints through their full range of motion is an important asset in many sports. Unfortunately, little research is available on the physiology of flexibility or the proper way of developing this important fitness characteristic. Most coaches and sports medicine specialists, however, recommend stretching exercises as a way of preventing injury and improving performance.

Static stretching, continuously holding a stretch, is thought to be superior to "bounce" or ballistic stretching. Bounce stretching stimulates the muscle spindles, causing a reflex muscle contraction (stretch reflex). The knee-jerk reflex is an example of a stretch reflex. Tapping the patellar ligament with a rubber hammer stimulates the muscle spindles in the thigh to initiate a reflex contraction of the quadriceps. Ballistic stretching counteracts the desired increase in flexibility induced by stretching and may produce an injury by placing a sudden load on a muscle that is experiencing a reflex contraction. Ballistic stretching is more specific to athletic events, however, so it may have applications under certain circumstances.

Preceding a static stretch with an isometric contraction (a PNF technique) is a particularly effective technique for improving flexibility. The isometric contraction is thought to stimulate Golgi tendon organs (muscle receptors sensitive to tension) within the muscle, resulting in muscular relaxation and the possibility of a greater stretch.

Flexibility training is probably important for preventing injury because it allows the musculotendon unit to move through its range of motion with less strain. Static stretches should be held for 10 to 30 sec and should ideally be practiced after active exercise because the muscles are warmer and are capable of being stretched further. The stretch should be mild and should not involve pain. Maximum flexibility development, as with other types of fitness, occurs when the stretching program is systematically applied over a long period of time.

Summary

As with strength training, training for rhythmical events involves application of the basic training principles of overload, specificity, individuality, and reversibility. According to the principle of overload, application of an appropriate stimulus will result in adaptation; the greater the stimulus, the greater the adaptation. According to the principle of specificity, the adaptations will be specific to the type of stimulus provided and will occur only in the tissues and organs stressed. In other words, preparation for particular events involves very specific training regimens. Whereas according to the principles of overload and specificity two individuals of equal initial ability will respond in the same direction as a result of a particular training regimen, the degree of response will likely be different. This is because of each person's uniqueness and the principle of individuality. Because the improvement of functional capacity (performance) resulting from training is really an example of biological adaptation, we must be mindful that training adaptation requires time and rest. Too little time for recovery and adaptation following hard training often results in decreased performance and injury.

Strength building exercises have become an important component of the training programs of many athletes. Strength exercises include isometrics, isotonic-variable resistance, isotonic-constant resistance, plyometrics, eccentrics, speed loading, and isokinetics. The ideal strength-building technique and protocol has yet to be determined.

A variety of factors must be considered when designing a program to build strength, including overload, specificity, reversibility, individual differences, and injury. The programs of proficient strength-trained athletes increasingly emphasize maximum loads but provide enough rest to prevent overtraining.

Flexibility training may be important for preventing injury and enhancing performance. Flexibility exercises should be practiced statically, with the stretch held for 10 to 30 sec. Stretching is most effective after exercise because the muscles are warmer and can be stretched further.

Selected Readings

ABRAHAM, W.M. Factors in delayed muscle soreness. Med. Sci. Sports 9:11–20, 1977.

American College of Sports Medicine. The recommended quality and quantity of exercise for developing and maintaining fitness in healthy adults. Med. Sci. Sports 10:vii–x, 1978.

ARMSTRONG, R.B. Mechanisms of exercise-induced delayed onset muscular soreness: a brief review. Med. Sci. Sports Exercise 16:529–538, 1984.

ATHA, J. Strengthening Muscle. Exercise Sport Sci. Rev. 9:1–73, 1981.

BAKER, E.R. Menstrual dysfunction and hormonal status in athletic women: a review. Fertil. Steril. 36:691–696, 1981.

BERGER, R. Optimum repetitions for the development of strength. Res. Quart. 33:334–338, 1962.

COSTILL, D.L., E.F. COYLE, W.F. FINK, G.R. LESMES, and F.A. WITZMANN. Adaptations in skeletal muscle following strength training. J. Appl. Physiol. 46:96–99, 1979.

COSTILL, D., J. DANIELS, W. EVANS, W. FINK, G. KRAHENBUHL, and B. SALTIN. Skeletal muscle enzymes and fiber composition in male and female track athletes. J. Appl. Physiol. 40:149–154, 1976.

COSTILL, D.L., W.J. FINK, L.H. GETCHELL, J.L. IVY, and F.A. WITZMANN. Lipid metabolism in skeletal muscle of endurance-trained males and females. J. Appl. Physiol. 47:787–791, 1979.

COYLE, E.F., S. BELL, D.L. COSTILL, and W.J. FINK. Skeletal muscle fiber characteristics of world class shot-putters. Quart. 49:278–284, 1978.

DONS, B., K. BOLLERUP, F. BONDE-PETERSEN, and S. HANCKE. The effect of weightlifting exercise related to muscle fiber composition and muscle cross-sectional area in humans. Eur. J. Appl. Physiol. 40:95–106, 1979.

DRINKWATER, B.L. Physiological responses of women to exercise. Exercise Sport Sci. Rev. 1:125–153, 1973.

EDDY, D.O., K.L. SPARKS, and D.A. ADELIZI. The effects of continuous and interval training in women and men. Eur. J. Appl. Physiol. 37:83–92, 1977.

EDGERTON, V.R. Mammalian muscle fiber types and their adaptability. Am. Zool. 18:113–125, 1978.

EDGERTON, V.R. Neuromuscular adaptation to power and endurance work. Can. J. Appl. Sport Sci. 1:49–58, 1976.

EKBLOM, B. Effect of physical training on the oxygen transport system in man. Acta Physiol. Scand. 328(Suppl.):11–45, 1969.

EKBLOM, B., and L. HERMANSEN. Cardiac output in athletes. J. Appl. Physiol. 24:619–625, 1968.

FAHEY, T. *Athletic Training: Principles and Practice.* Palo Alto: Mayfield Publishing Co., 1986.

Fox, E.L. Difference in metabolic alteration with sprint versus endurance interval training programs. In: Howald, H., and J. Poortmans (eds.). Metabolic Adaptation to Prolonged Physical Education. Basel: Birkhauser Verlag, 1975. pp. 119–126.

Goldberg, A.L. Mechanisms of growth and atrophy of skeletal muscle. In: Cassens, R.G. (ed.). Muscle Biology New York: Marcel Dekker, 1972.

Gollnick, P., R. Armstrong, B. Saltin, C. Saubert, W. Sembrowich, and R. Shepherd. Effect of training on enzyme activity and fiber composition of human skeletal muscle. J. Appl. Physiol. 34:107–111, 1973.

Gollnick, P.D., R.B. Armstrong, C.W. Saubertt, K. Piehl, and B. Saltin. Enzyme activity and fiber composition in skeletal muscle of trained and untrained men. J. Appl. Physiol. 33:312–319, 1972.

Gonyea, W.J. Role of exercise in inducing increases in skeletal muscle fiber number. J. Appl. Physiol. 48:421–426, 1980.

Gonyea, W.J., and D. Sale. Physiology of weight lifting. Arch. Phys. Med. Rehabil. 63:235–237, 1982.

Hickson, R.C. Interference of strength development by simultaneously training for strength and endurance. Eur. J. Appl. Physiol. 45:255–263, 1980.

Ho, K.W., R.R. Roy, C.D. Tweedle, W.W. Heusner, W.D. Van Huss, and R.E. Carrow. Skeletal muscle fiber splitting with weight-lifting exercise in rats. Am. J. Anat. 157:433–440, 1980.

Hoppeler, H., P. Luthi, H. Claussen, E.R. Weibel, and H. Howard. The ultrastructure of the normal human skeletal muscle. A morphometric analysis of untrained men, women, and well-trained orienteers. Pflugers Arch. 344:217–232, 1973.

Klissouras, V. Heritability of adaptive variation. J. Appl. Physiol. 31:338–344, 1981.

Komi, P.V., J.H.T. Viitasalo, M. Havy, A. Thorstensson, B. Sjodin, and T. Karlsson. Skeletal muscle fibers and muscle enzyme activities in monozygous and dizygous twins of both sexes. Acta Physiol. Scand. 100:385–392, 1977.

Lesmes, G.R., D. Costill, E.F. Coyle, and W.J. Fink. Muscle strength and power changes during maximal isokinetic training. Med. Sci. Sports 10:266–269, 1978.

MacDougall, J.D., G.R. Ward, D.G. Sale, and J.R. Sutton. Biochemical adaptation of human skeletal muscle to heavy resistance training and immobilization. J. Appl. Physiol. 43:700–703, 1977.

Moritani, T., and H.A. deVries. Potential for gross muscle hypertrophy in older men. J. Gerontol. 35:672–682, 1980.

Noakes, T. *Lore of Running*. Cape Town, SA: Oxford University Press, 1985.

O'Shea, P. Effects of selected weight training programs on the development of strength and muscle hypertrophy. Quart. 37:95–102, 1964.

Pate, R.R., M. Maguire, and J. Van Wyk. Dietary iron supplementation in women athletes. Physician Sportsmed. 7:81–101, 1979.

Saltin, B., K. Nazar, D.L. Costill, E. Stein, E. Jansson, B. Essen, and P.D. Gollnick. The nature of the training responses; peripheral and central adaptations to one-legged exercise. Acta Physiol. Scand. 96:289–305, 1976.

Sjostrom, M., and J. Friden. Muscle soreness and muscle structure. Med. Sport Sci. 17:169–186, 1984.

Staron, R.S., F.C. Hagerman, and R.S. Hikida. The effects of detraining on an elite power lifter. J. Neurol. Sci. 51:247–257, 1981.

Surburg, P.R. Neuromuscular facilitation techniques in sportsmedicine. Physician Sportsmed. 9:115–127, 1981.

Thomas, C.L. Factors important to women participants in vigorous athletics. In: Strauss, R.H. (ed.). Sports Medicine and Physiology. Philadelphia: W.B. Saunders, 1979, pp. 304–319.

Thorstensson, A. Muscle strength, fibre types and enzyme activities in man. Acta Physiol. Scand. (Suppl.) 443:1–45, 1976.

VERKHOSHANSKY, U. How to set up a training program in speed-strength events (part 1). Legkaya Atletika 8:8–10, 1979. Translated in: Sov. Sports Rev. 16:53–57, 1981.

VERKHOSHANSKY, U. How to set up a training program in speed-strength events (part 2). Legkaya Atletika 8:8–10, 1979. Translated in: Sov. Sports Rev. 16:123–126, 1981.

WEINMAN, K.P., Z. SLABOCHOVA, E.M. BERNAUER, T. MORIMOTO, and F. SARGENT. Reactions of men and women to repeated exposure to humid heat. J. Appl. Physiol. 22:533–538, 1967.

WELLS, C.L. Sexual differences in heat stress response. Physician Sports Med. 5:79–90, 1977.

WILT, F. Training for competitive running. In: Falls, H. (ed.). Exercise Physiology. New York: Academic Press, 1968.

14

Ergogenic Aids and Human Performance

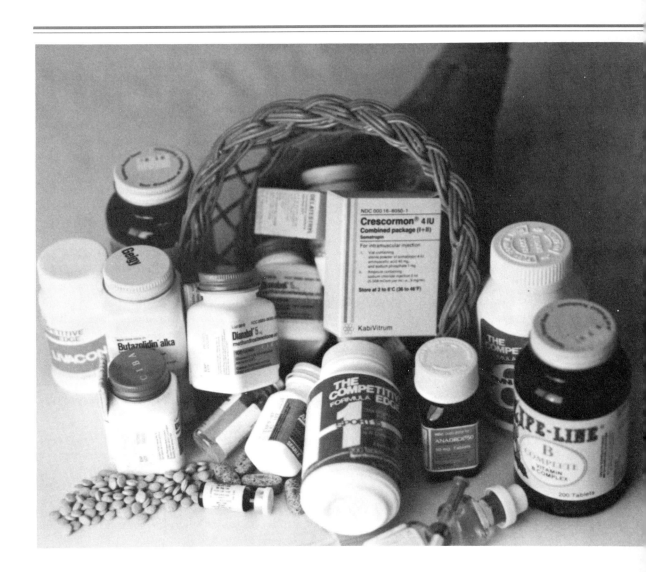

Ergogenic aids are substances or techniques (other than training) that are used to improve athletic performance. They are employed to enhance physiological capacity, depress psychological inhibition to maximum performance, or provide a mechanical advantage in the performance of sports skills. The use of ergogenic aids is extremely widespread in athletics. For example, in sports such as weight lifting and the throwing events (discus, hammer, shotput, and javelin), the use of anabolic steroids is thought to be almost universal. This should not be surprising because the extreme competitiveness within the sports world has forced athletes to grasp at any substance or technique that might provide an edge over the competition.

The vast majority of ergogenic aids provides no benefit other than the placebo effect. A *placebo* causes an improvement through the power of suggestion (if a person wants it to work, it does). The importance of placebos has long been recognized in both medicine and athletics. There are anecdotes of coaches administering "superpills" to athletes to improve performance. Even though the pills contained only sugar, because the athletes believed that their performance would be improved, it was.

The popularity of specific ergogenic aids usually stems from their use by top athletes. The successful Japanese swim teams of the 1930s used supplemental oxygen during competition, so the practice spread. Many champion weight-trained athletes use anabolic steroids, which encourages their use by younger athletes. Testimonials for vitamin and protein supplements by Mr. America or Mr. Universe in a body building magazine perpetuate the use of sometimes dubious products, even in the face of conflicting evidence presented in prestigious research journals.

Research on ergogenic aids is sometimes fraught with contradiction and uncertainty stemming from poor experimental controls and the use of few subjects. Often, because the only information available on a specific agent is from studies using animal models or untrained subjects (who show wide variability in response to training), it is difficult to extrapolate the results to highly competitive athletes.

The most popular ergogenic aids used to improve athletic performance are listed in Table 14-1. Although most of these have been shown to be worthless, the mystique of ergogenic aids continues to captivate almost everyone associated with sport. This chapter will explore the most popular ergogenic aids as well as discuss possible side effects.

Banned Substances

The International Olympic Committee (IOC) has banned the use of substances taken for the purpose of unfairly and artificially improving performance in competition (Table 14-2). The banned list appears to be based on

TABLE 14-1 Some Substances or Techniques Used as Ergogenic Aids

Alcohol
Alkalies
Amino acids
Amphetamines
Anabolic steroids
Aspartates
β-blockers
Bee pollen
Caffeine
Camphor
Cocaine
Cold
Digitalis
Electrical stimulation
Epinephrine
Gelatin
Growth hormone
Heat
Human chorionic gonadotrophin
Hypnosis
Marijuana
Massage
Mineral supplements
Negatively ionized air
Nicotine
Nitroglycerine
Norepinephrine
Organ extracts
Oxygen
Periactin
Protein supplements
Sulfa drugs
Strychnine
Vitamin supplements
Wheat germ oil
Yeast

SOURCE: G. A. Brooks and T. D. Fahey. Exercise Physiology: Human Bioenergetics and Its Applications. New York: Macmillan, 1984, p. 613.

the attempt to discourage any pretext of unfair competition, since the beneficial effects of many of these substances have not been demonstrated. Banned substance classifications include psychomotor stimulants, sympathomimetic amines, miscellaneous central nervous system stimulants, narcotic analgesics, and anabolic steroids. Caffeine (>15 $\mu g \cdot ml^{-1}$—this blood level of caf-

TABLE 14-2 **Substances Banned by the International Olympic Committee**

Psychomotor Stimulant Drugs
Amphetamine
Benzphetamine
Cocaine
Ethylamphetamine
Fencamfamin
Fenproporex and related compounds
Methylamphetamine
Methylphenidate
Norpseudoephedrine
Pemoline
Phenmetrazine
Phentermine
Pipradol
Prolintane

Sympathomimetic Amines
Ephedrine
Methylephedrine
Methoxyphenamine and related compounds

Miscellaneous CNS Stimulants
Amiphenazole
Bemegride
Caffeine ($>15\ \mu g\cdot ml^{-1}$)
Leptazole
Nikethamide
Strychnine and related compounds

Narcotic Analgesics
Dextromoramide
Dipipanone
Heroin
Methadone
Morphine
Pethidine and related compounds

Anabolic Steroids
Methandrostenolone (Dianabol)
Nandrolone phenpropionate (Durabolin)
Nandrolone decanoate (Deca-Durabolin)
Oxandrolone (Anavar)
Oxymesterone (Oranabol)
Oxymetholone (Anadrol)
Stanozolol (Winstrol) and related compounds
Testosterone

feine would result from drinking about five cups of coffee) and testosterone were added to the banned list just prior to the 1984 Olympics.

Attempts at detecting the use of banned substances in international sport have escalated from relatively modest efforts at the 1960 Olympics in Rome to the multimillion-dollar project at the 1984 Olympics in Los Angeles. Testing procedures involve collecting urine specimens from medal winners or randomly selected athletes and determining if any of the banned substances are present in the samples. A strict protocol for sample collection ensures fairness for all the competitors (Figures 14-1 and 14-2). Samples are analyzed at one of several laboratories designated by the IOC.

Unfortunately, many banned substances are found in a variety of over-the-counter and prescribed medications. For example, banned substances are contained in some nonprescription medications such as decongestants, throat lozenges, topical nasal decongestants, and eye drops. This is a tremendous problem for athletic coaches and administrators. Accidental consumption of substances found on the list in one instance resulted in the disqualification of an Olympic gold medal winner. Consequently, many of the larger countries involved in international sports competition have engaged pharmacology consultants to help them sift through the complications involved in the consumption and detection of drugs.

Anabolic–Androgenic Steroids

Anabolic steroids are drugs that resemble androgenic hormones (sometimes called male hormones) such as testosterone (Figure 14-3). Athletes consume them in the hope of gaining weight, strength, power, speed, endurance, and aggressiveness. They are widely used by athletes involved in such sports as track and field (mostly the throwing events), weight lifting, and American football. However, in spite of their tremendous popularity, their effectiveness is controversial. The research literature is divided on whether or not anabolic steroids enhance physical performance; yet almost all athletes who consume these substances extol their beneficial effects and feel that they would not have been as successful without them.

There are several possible reasons for the large differences between experimental findings and empirical observations. First, an incredible mystique has arisen around these substances, providing fertile ground for the placebo effect. Second, the use of anabolic steroids in the "real world" is considerably different from that in rigidly controlled, double-blind experiments (in a double-blind study, neither the subject nor the experimenter knows who is taking the drug). Most studies have not used the same drug dosage used by athletes, as institutional safeguards prohibit administration of high dosages of substances possibly dangerous to human subjects. In addition, subjects in

Los Angeles Olympic Organizing Committee
Los Angeles, California 90084 USA

Olympic Health Services
Doping Control Collection
Contrôle de Dopage

Winner / Vainqueur [ ]   No.

1 Last Name / Nom de Famille

2 First Name / Prénom

3 Country / Pays

4 Accreditation No. / No. de l'accreditation

5 Start No. / Numéro de départ

6 Sport/event / Sport/épreuve

7 Competition Site / Lieu de compétition

8 Time / Heure

9 Date / Date   Month / Mois   Day / Jour

10 The selected competitor must report to the doping control station at the above site as soon as possible, but not later than 60 minutes from the above specified time. The competitor may be accompanied by a team official, coach or doctor. If he/she fails to report for doping control within the given time limit, he/she will have to face sanctions in accordance with the rules for doping control specified by the IOC.

Le concurrent choisi doit se présenter le plus tôt possible au poste de contrôle de dopage, situé sur le lieu de competition indiqué ci-dessus, dès dessus. Le concurrent peut être accompagné d'un officiel de l'équipe, de l'entraîneur ou du médecin. Si il/elle ne se présente pas au contrôle de dopage dans les délais précisés, il/elle sera soumis/e aux sanctions prévues par les règlements du contrôle de dopage spécifié par le CIO.

I hereby acknowledge receipt of this notice at the time indicated above.
J'accuse réception de cet avis à l'heure indiquée ci-dessus.

Competitor's signature / Signature du concurrent

Random / Au Hasard [ ]   No.

11 International Federation representative / Représentant de la Fédération Internationale
Signature / Signature

12 Doping Control escort / Escorte de contrôle de dopage
Signature / Signature

13 Time arrived at station / Heure d'arrivée au poste

14 Time completed sampling procedure / Heure à la fin du prélèvement

15 I declare that I am satisfied with the manner in which the sample taking procedure was carried out
Je certifie être satisfait de la façon dont le prélèvement d'échantillon a été fait
Competitor's signature / Signature du concurrent

16 Comments / Commentaires

17 Accompanying person (if any) / L'Accompagnateur (le cas échéant)
Signature / Signature

18 Medication / Medicaments	Dosage / Dose	Taken Today / Pris Ajourd'hui YES/NO	Taken Yesterday / Pris Hier YES/NO
1			
2			
3			

Gender / Sexe [ ]M [ ]F

19 Code Number / Numéro de code

20 International Federation representative (if any) / Représentant de la Fédération International (le cas échéant)
Signature / Signature

21 IOC Medical Commission representative (if any) / Représentant de la commission médicale du CIO (le cas échéant)
Signature / Signature

22 Doping control laboratory technician / Technicien du laboratoire de contrôle de dopage
Signature / Signature

23 Doping control coordinator / Chef du poste de contrôle de dopage
Signature / Signature

Green Copy–Competitor's Copy
Copie verte–Copie du Concurrent

Yellow Copy–IOC Medical Commission
Copie jaune–Copie de la Commission Médicale du CIO

Pink Copy–IOC Medical Commission
Copie rose–Copie de la Commission Médicale du CIO

Figure 14-1
Doping control collection form used at the 1984 Olympics held at Los Angeles.

Figure 14-2
Collecting urine samples at the 1984 Olympics.

research experiments seldom resemble accomplished weight-trained athletes. Under these conditions, we must assess the results of sound research studies, as well as clinical and empirical field observations, to obtain a realistic profile of the use, effects on performance, and side effects of these substances.

How Anabolic Steroids Work

Male hormones, principally testosterone, are partially responsible for the tremendous developmental changes that occur during puberty and adolescence. Male hormones exert both androgenic and anabolic effects. Androgenic effects are characterized by changes in primary and secondary sexual characteristics such as enlargement of the penis and testes, changes in the voice, hair growth on the face, axilla, and genital areas, and increased aggressiveness. The anabolic effects of androgens are characterized by accelerated growth of muscle, bone, and red blood cells, and enhanced neural conduction.

Anabolic steroids have been manufactured to enhance the anabolic properties (tissue building) of the androgens and minimize the androgenic (sex-linked) properties. However, no steroid has completely eliminated the androgenic effects because the so-called androgenic effects are really anabolic ef-

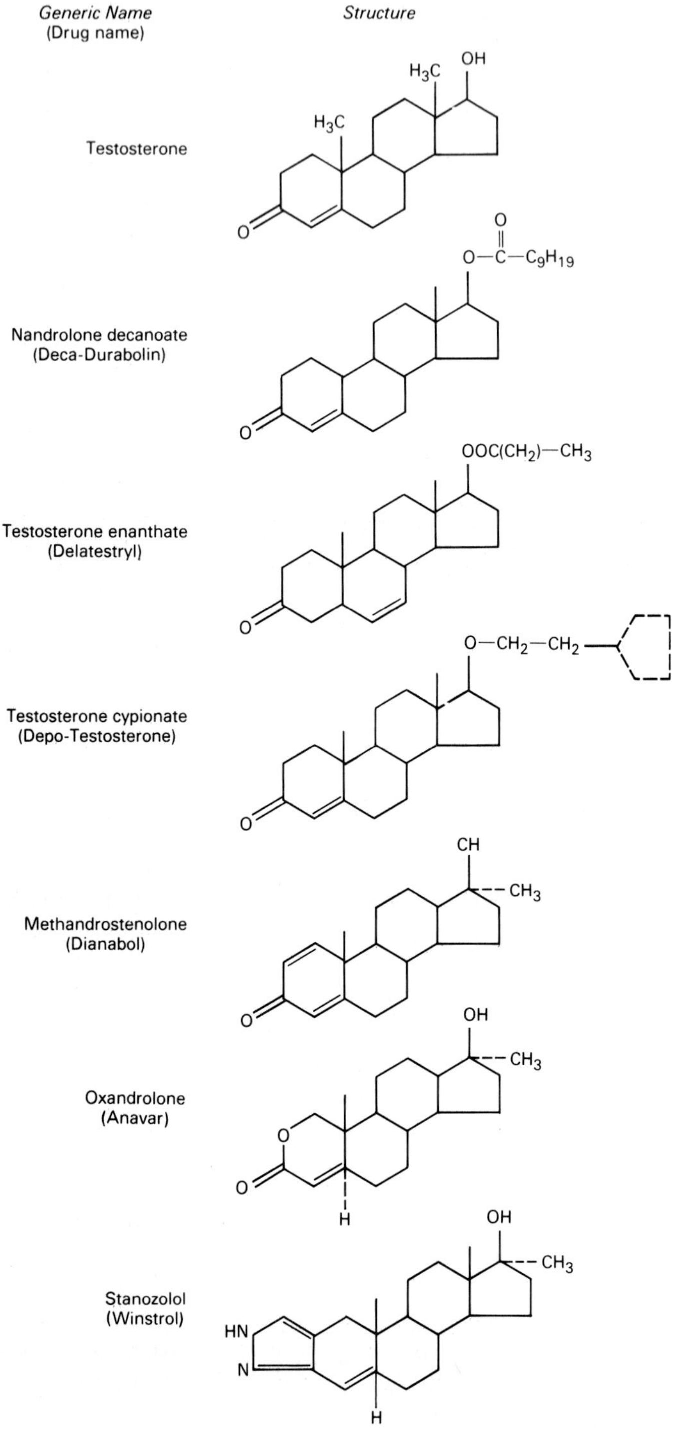
Generic Name
(Drug name)
Structure
Testosterone
H3C
OH
Nandrolone decanoate
(Deca-Durabolin)
O—C—C9H19
Testosterone enanthate
(Delatestryl)
OOC(CH2)—CH3
Testosterone cypionate
(Depo-Testosterone)
O—CH2—CH2
Methandrostenolone
(Dianabol)
CH
CH3
Oxandrolone
(Anavar)
OH
CH3
H
Stanozolol
(Winstrol)
HN
N
H

Figure 14-3
Structure of testosterone and the principal anabolic steroids used by athletes.

fects in sex-linked tissues; that is, the effects of male hormones on accessory sex glands, genital hair growth, and oiliness of the skin are a reflection of protein anabolism in those specific tissues. The steroids with the most potent anabolic effect are also those with the greatest androgenic effect.

Although the process is not completely understood, male hormones work by stimulating receptor molecules in muscle cells, which activate specific genes to produce proteins (Figure 14-4). They also affect the activation rate of enzyme systems involved in protein metabolism, thus enhancing protein synthesis. They may also block the action of corticosteroid hormones, which has the effect of preventing degradation (called an anticatabolic effect).

Heavy resistance training seems to be necessary for anabolic steroids to exert any beneficial effect on physical performance. Most research studies that have demonstrated improved performance with anabolic steroids used experienced weight lifters who were capable of training with heavier weights and producing relatively greater muscle tension during exercise than novice subjects. Some researchers have speculated that the real effect of anabolic steroids is the creation of a "psychosomatic state" characterized by sensations of well-being, euphoria, increased aggressiveness, and tolerance of stress, allowing the athlete to train harder. Such a psychosomatic state would be most beneficial to experienced weight lifters, who have developed the motor skills to exert maximal force during strength training. A high-protein diet may also be important in maximizing the effectiveness of anabolic steroids.

The effects of anabolic steroids on factors important to physical perfor-

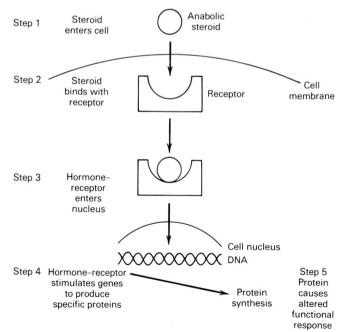

Figure 14-4

Theoretical model of how steroid hormones affect cell growth. Steroid hormone enters the cell and binds to a receptor molecule. The bound hormone can then enter the nucleus and activate specific genes to produce proteins. These proteins in turn bring about the cellular changes triggered by the hormone.

(SOURCE: Adapted from J. Wright. *Anabolic Steroids and Sports.* Natick, Mass.: Sports Science Consultants, 1978.)

mance are unclear, as the well-controlled, double-blind studies have rendered conflicting results. In studies showing beneficial effects, body weight increased by about 4 lb, lean body weight by about 6 lb (fat loss accounts for the discrepancy between gains in lean mass and body weight), bench press increased by about 15 lb, and squats by about 30 lb (these values represent the average gains for all studies showing a beneficial effect). Almost all studies have failed to demonstrate a beneficial effect on maximal oxygen consumption or endurance capacity. Anabolic steroid studies have typically lasted 6 to 8 weeks and have usually used relatively untrained subjects.

The gains made by athletes in uncontrolled observations have been much more impressive. Weight gains of 30 or 40 lb, coupled with 30% increases in strength, are not unusual. Such case studies lack credibility because of the absence of scientific controls. It would be foolish, however, to completely disregard such observations because the "subjects" have been highly trained and motivated athletes.

Side Effects of Anabolic Steroids

The principal side effects of anabolic steroids can be subdivided into those attributable to (1) the normal physiological actions of male hormones that are inappropriate in the recipient and (2) toxic effects caused by the chemical structure of the drug (principally oral "C-17 alpha-alkylated" oral anabolic steroid) (Table 14-3).

"Physiological" side effects include reduced production of endogenous testosterone, pituitary gonadotropin hormones, and hypothalamic-releasing factors (all of which control testicular function and sperm cell production). Libido may be increased or decreased. The structural similarity of anabolic steroids to aldosterone causes them to increase fluid retention. Steroid use by women and immature children may cause masculinizing effects such as hair growth on the face and body, deepening of the voice, oily skin, increased activity of the approcrine sweat glands, acne, and baldness. In women, some of these masculine changes are irreversible. Children will initially experience accelerated maturation followed by premature closure of the epiphyseal growth centers in the long bones. Women may also experience clitoral enlargement and menstrual irregularity.

Anabolic steroids have been shown to affect the regulation of the hypothalamic–gonadotropin–testicular axis, which controls normal reproductive processes (Figure 14-5). The anabolic steroids suppress luteinizing hormone (LH) and follicle-stimulating hormone (FSH), resulting in a decreased production of testosterone by the testes. This process can result in testicular atrophy and decreased sperm production. These changes also reverse themselves after withdrawal from the medication; however, the possibility exists that prolonged use of these substances may permanently disturb this delicate regulatory system. During periods when they are not taking anabolic ste-

TABLE 14-3　**Major Side Effects of Anabolic Steroids**

Liver toxicity
   Elevated levels of SGOT, SGPT, alkaline phosphatase, and bilirubin
   Increased bromsulphalein (BSP) retention
   Hepatocellular carcinoma
   Peliosis hepatitis
   Cholestasis
Elevated CPK and LDH
Elevated blood pressure
Edema
Alterations in clotting factors
Elevated cholesterol and triglycerides
Decreased HDL
Elevated blood glucose
Increased nervous tension
Altered electrolyte balance
Depressed spermatogenesis
Lowered testosterone production
Reduced gonadotrophin production (LH and FSH)
Increased urine volume
Premature closure of epiphyses in children
Masculinization
Increased or decreased libido
Sore nipples
Acne
Lowered voice in women and children
Clitoral enlargement in women
Increased aggressiveness
Nosebleeds
Muscle cramps and spasms
GI distress
Dizziness
Disturbed thyroid function
Wilms' tumor
Prostatic hypertrophy
Prostatic cancer
Increased activity of apocrine sweat glands

SOURCE: G. A. Brooks and T. D. Fahey. Exercise Physiology: Human Bioenergetics and Its Applications. New York: Macmillan, 1984, p. 619.

roids, some athletes use drugs (i.e., human chorionic gonadotropin, HCG) that stimulates the natural production of testosterone.

Oral anabolic steroids, such as methandrostenolone (Dianabol), present the greatest risk of biological toxicity, particularly to the liver, because their structure has been altered to make them more biologically active (Table 14-4). This causes the steroid to become concentrated in the liver much earlier

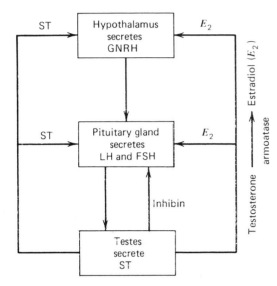

Figure 14-5
The feedback control system of the hypothalamic–pituitary–gonadal axis. Testosterone (ST) exerts independent control over the hypothalamus, which secretes gonadotrophin-releasing hormone (GNRH), and pituitary, which secretes luteinizing hormone (LH) and follicle-stimulating hormone (FSH). The aromatization of testosterone to estradiol provides additional regulation of the hypothalamus and pituitary. Inhibin, which is produced in the testes, also controls the production of FSH.

(SOURCE: G. A. Brooks and T. D. Fahey. Human Bioenergetics and Its Applications. New York: Macmillan, 1984, p. 620.)

and in greater quantity than the injectable varieties. Athletes using anabolic steroids typically exhibit elevated blood levels of liver enzymes such as glutamic-oxalacetic transaminase (SGOT), glutamic-pyruvic transaminase (SGPT), and alkaline phosphatase, which indicate liver toxicity. Elevated levels of blood glucose, CPK, and bilirubin have also been noted. These changes are usually reversible upon withdrawal from the drug. Prolonged administration in some groups of patients has been linked to severe liver disorders such as peliosis hepatis, hepatocellular carcinoma, and cholestasis.

A particularly disturbing observation occurs in several factors that are linked to increased risk of coronary heart disease. These are high levels of cholesterol, and triglycerides, elevated blood pressure, and decreased levels of high-density lipoproteins (HDL) (Figure 14-6). Cholesterol and triglyceride levels above 300 mg% and HDL levels of less than 10 mg% have been noted in athletes taking large doses of anabolic steroids (respective ideal levels for cholesterol, triglycerides, and HDL in males are 180, 100, and 60 mg%.) Al-

TABLE 14-4 **The Effects of 17-Alpha-Alkylated (Oral) Anabolic Steroids on Liver Function**

Anabolic steroids may cause:
- Intrahepatic cholestasis (impairment of bile flow)
- Ultrastructural changes in liver canaliculi, microvilli, and mitochondria
- Biochemical changes resulting in reduced hepatic excretory function
- Vascular complications: peliosis hepatis (blood-filled cysts in the liver)
- Benign and malignant liver tumors
- Focal nodal hyperplasia

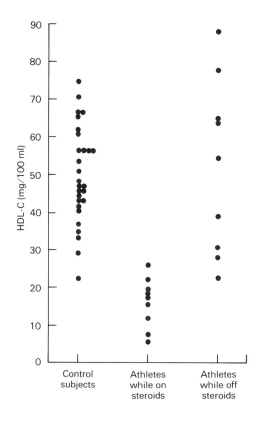

Figure 14-6

The effects of anabolic steroids on HDL-cholesterol in five world-class weight-trained athletes. HDL-C, a substance that is thought to provide protection against heart disease, is greatly suppressed when the athlete is taking anabolic steroids. HDL-C rebounds toward normal levels when the drug is withdrawn.

(SOURCE: G. E. Peterson and T. D. Fahey. HDL-C in five elete athletes using anabolic-androgenic steroids. Physician Sportsmed. 12(6):120–130, 1984.)

though it appears that high cholesterol and triglyceride levels may be partially related to diet (many weight-trained athletes consume high-fat, high-cholesterol diets), the low HDL level seems to be directly related to the anabolic steroids. Many weight-trained athletes compete for 10 to more than 20 years, subjecting themselves to the real possibility of premature death from atherosclerosis. Hypertension is also a common observation, probably because of the fluid-retention properties of these drugs.

A variety of miscellaneous side effects have been reported, including muscle cramps, gastrointestinal distress, headache, dizziness, sore nipples, and abnormal thyroid functions. Some of these side effects have become manifest in individuals who took low doses for short periods of time. To summarize, anabolic steroids are probably effective for increasing strength and lean body mass in trained athletes, but they present possible grave health risks that could be life threatening.

Use of Anabolic Steroids by Athletes

In some sports, anabolic steroids are used by the majority of accomplished athletes. Unfortunately, the administration of these dangerous substances is often accomplished without medical supervision. Self-administration has re-

TABLE 14-5 Anabolic–Androgenic Steroids Used by Athletes Listed in Order of Androgenicity[a]

Orals	Injectables
Maxibolin (ethyloestrenol)	Deca-Durabolin (nandrolone decanoate)
Anavar (oxandrolone)	Durabolin 50 (nandrolone phenpropionate)
Winstrol (stanozolol)	Delatestryl (testosterone enanthate)
Dianabol (methandrostenolone)	Testosterone propionate
Anadrol (oxymetholone)	Depo-Testosterone (testosterone cypionate)
	Aqueous testosterone

[a]Trade names are given with generic names in parentheses, except that testosterone propionate and aqueous testosterone are generic names.
SOURCE: G. A. Brooks and T. D. Fahey. Exercise Physiology: Human Bioenergetics and Its Applications. New York: Macmillan, 1984, p. 622.

sulted in sometimes ridiculously high doses. A report in a body building magazine mentioned an individual who was taking 100 times the recommended dosage and was spending $150 a week on anabolic steroids.

Table 14-5 presents the most popular oral and injectable anabolic steroids, listed in order of androgenicity. In general, athletes tend to take the less androgenic steroids during building periods (off-season conditioning) and the more androgenic substances during competitive periods. They will also often take combinations of steroids (a practice called stacking) to obtain the most beneficial effects. Table 14-6 presents an example of the anabolic steroids taken by a world-class athlete during a transition period between conditioning and competition.

Growth Hormone

Growth hormone (GH), a polypeptide hormone produced by the adenohypophysis (anterior pituitary gland), has been used by some power lifters, body builders, and throwers to increase muscle mass and strength. To date, no large-scale research has been done of its effect on athletic performance. Table 14-7 summarizes measurements made on a world-class power lifter who was on a 6-week, self-administered growth hormone regimen. This athlete experienced a large increase in lean body mass and a decrease in fat. This observation is consistent with testimonials from athletes who have claimed weight gains of 30 to 40 lb in 10 weeks accompanied by equally remarkable gains in strength. Nitrogen balance becomes highly positive when GH is administered to adult humans, which lends some credence to these claims. It must be stressed that uncontrolled observations and testimonials from athletes are not acceptable substitutes for well-structured scientific studies. We must therefore wait

Week	Injectable Steroid	Daily Oral Steroid	Training Program
1–2	100 mg Deca-Durabolin every 5 days	8 mg Winstrol	Heavy weight training— high volume, medium intensity
3–4	100 mg Deca-Durabolin every 5 days	10 mg Winstrol 10 mg Dianabol	Heavy weight training— high volume, medium intensity
5	100 mg Deca-Durabolin every 5 days	10 mg Winstrol 20 mg Dianabol	Heavy weight training— high volume, medium intensity
6	100 mg Deca-Durabolin every 5 days	Decreasing dosage	Low volume, low intensity—rest week
7–8	No injectables	No orals	Low volume, high intensity
9	No injectables	10 mg Dianabol	Low volume, high intensity Lift heavy once during week
10	200 mg Delatestryl every 5 days	15 mg Dianabol	Low volume, high intensity Lift heavy once during week
11	200 mg Delatestryl every 5 days	20 mg Dianabol	Low-volume, low-intensity weight training
12	200 mg Delatestryl every 5 days 100 mg testosterone propionate day before meet	25 mg Dianabol	Competition, no lifting

[a]This table should not be considered an endorsement for use of anabolic steroids. It is merely intended to demonstrate use patterns in strength-trained athletes.

SOURCE: G. A. Brooks and T. D. Fahey. Exercise Physiology: Human Bioenergetics and Its Applications. New York: Macmillan, 1984, p. 623.

until such studies are accomplished before evaluating the effects of this substance on performance or body composition.

Growth hormone is a potent anabolic agent that facilitates the transport of amino acids into cells. An increased rate of amino acid transport into muscle cells is associated with muscle hypertrophy. Growth hormone is also involved in the formation of connective tissue and exerts a stimulatory effect on somatomedin, which is an important hormone in chondrocyte metabolism. Growth hormone is also involved in carbohydrate and fat metabolism.

The use of this substance may have severe consequences. Growth hor-

TABLE 14-7 Effects of 6-Week Administration of Human Growth Hormone to a World-Class Power Lifter on Body Composition and Left Ventricular (LV) Wall Thicknesses of the Heart[a]

Week	Weight (lb)	% Fat	Lean Body Mass (lb)	LV Septal Thickness (mm)	Posterior Wall Thickness (mm)
Pre	272.1	20.0	217.7	11.0	12.0
4	279.6	17.4	230.9	———	———
6	280.3	16.5	234.1	13.0	12.0
8	277.9	15.7	234.1	———	———

[a]Body composition measured by underwater weighing and left ventricular wall thicknesses determined by M-mode echocardiography. Human growth hormone was administered during weeks 1–6.

mone is known to cause diabetes, which could become permanent if large doses are administered. Because of its general anabolic effect, growth hormone could cause cardiomegally (enlarged heart walls, see Table 14-7), which could result in increased myocardial oxygen demand. Combining an enlarged heart induced by administration of growth hormone with the possibility of accelerated atherosclerosis resulting from administration of anabolic steroids could drastically increase the risk of heart disease. It could also cause symptoms of acromegaly, characterized by enlarged bones in the head, face, and hands, osteoporosis, arthritis, and heart disease. The skeletal changes are irreversible.

In the past, growth hormone has been very expensive and in short supply because it was obtained only from cadavers or rhesus monkeys. Recent advances in genetic engineering, however, have made this substance more widely available. Even with such severe side effects, the possibility that growth hormone may allow dramatic increases in performance in a short time may render its use irresistible to some athletes.

Amphetamines

Amphetamines are perhaps the most abused drugs in sports; they are particularly popular in football, basketball, track and field, and cycling. Athletes use them to prevent fatigue and to increase confidence, cardiovascular endurance, muscle endurance, speed, power, and reaction time. Generic examples of amphetamines include benzedrine, dexedrine, dexamyl, and methedrine.

These drugs act as both central nervous system and sympathomimetic stimulants (sympathomimetic effects mimic the action of the sympathetic nervous system). Amphetamines stimulate the central nervous system by directly affecting the reticular activating system and postganglionic nerves. CNS effects include increased arousal, wakefulness, confidence, and the feeling of an enhanced capability to make decisions. Sympathomimetic effects include increased blood pressure, heart rate, oxygen consumption in the brain, and glycolysis in muscle and liver, vasoconstriction in the arterioles of the skin and spleen, and vasodilation in muscle arterioles.

The effectiveness of amphetamines in improving athletic performance is controversial. Many studies were poorly controlled, used low dosages, and did not allow enough time for absorption of the drug. Although approximately 15 to 50 mg of d-amphetamine is a common dose in athletics, some studies used a dose as low as 5 mg. These drugs are readily absorbed orally, however, they take $1\frac{1}{2}$ to 2 hr to reach peak levels in the body (peak levels are reached in 30 min if the amphetamine is administered by injection). Yet some studies began performance testing within a half hour of administration. Also, amphetamines create a euphoric sensation that is easily identifiable, which makes a true double-blind study almost impossible.

Amphetamines became popular during World War II with soldiers who used them to ward off fatigue. Studies have generally supported the effectiveness of amphetamine as a psychotropic drug that masks fatigue but have been equivocal on their ability to improve endurance performance. Many studies have demonstrated enhanced feelings of well-being and improved exercise capacity in fatigued subjects. Fatigued animal and human subjects have been shown to improve endurance (time to fatigue) in marching, cycling, swimming, and treadmill exercise and improved simple reaction time. Amphetamines have no effect on reaction time in rested subjects.

Most studies have failed to demonstrate an effect on cardiovascular function, even though exercise time to exhaustion and peak lactate often increased. Maximal values for oxygen consumption, heart rate, minute volume, respiratory exchange ratio, respiratory rate, oxygen pulse, CO_2 production, and ventilatory equivalent were unaffected by amphetamines. The bulk of evidence indicates that amphetamines act as a potent psychotropic agent.

The effects of amphetamines on strength and power seem to depend on the number of motor units recruited. For example, substantial increases in knee extension strength have been demonstrated without corresponding increases in elbow flexion strength. In sprinting, acceleration but not top speed is enhanced by the drug. This points to an increased excitability of the muscles but no increase in their maximal capacity. Most studies show increases in static strength but mixed results in muscle endurance.

The effects of amphetamines on sports performance are also unclear. They appear to aid power-oriented movement skills in activities that employ constant motor patterns, such as shot putting and hammer throwing. They are probably less effective in sports requiring the execution of motor skills in an unpredictable order, such as football, basketball, and tennis. In these sports, amphetamines may be deleterious because they may interfere with the body's fatigue alarm system, cause confusion, impair judgment, and, in high concentrations, cause neuromuscular blockade and loss of effective motor control.

Amphetamines can cause a variety of severe side effects. They increase the risk of hyperthermia because of their vasoconstriction effect on the arterioles of the skin. Numerous deaths in endurance sports have been reported among athletes competing in the heat while under the influence of these drugs. In addition to being addictive, these drugs can also cause tremulousness, psychic distress, insomnia, dry mouth, and cardiac arrhythmias.

Cocaine

Cocaine is an alkaloid derived from the leaves of the coca plant and acts as a central nervous system stimulant. It has become very popular with certain segments of the population. Cocaine has also become popular with some athletes, with reports often surfacing in the news media of its rampant use by professional football and basketball players. The use of cocaine as a stimulant has a long history beginning with the Incas in Peru. Its use was advocated by Sigmund Freud and was an important ingredient in Coca-Cola during the early days of the product.

The drug produces a feeling of exhilaration and an enhanced sense of well-being, and it depresses fatigue. It works by inhibiting the reuptake of norepinephrine in sympathetic neurons and has a direct sympathomimetic effect. Cocaine has been shown to increase work capacity in several poorly controlled studies. However, in rats, cocaine had no effect on swim time to exhaustion. Cocaine is an extremely dangerous drug, particularly when it is administered intravenously or converted to the free base and smoked.

Caffeine

Caffeine is a xanthine that acts as a cerebrocortical stimulator and may stimulate the adrenal medulla to release epinephrine. It also stimulates the heart (stimulating both rate and contractility of the heart at rest), causes peripheral vasodilation, and acts as a diuretic by blocking renal tubular reabsorption of sodium. In athletics, caffeine is used as a stimulant and as a fatty acid mobilizer. It is found in a variety of food products such as coffee, tea, and chocolate.

Caffeine is a much weaker stimulant than amphetamine, yet it is widely used by weight lifters and throwers (discus, shot, javelin, and hammer) to enhance strength and power. These athletes take the caffeine in the form of strong coffee or through over-the-counter medications such as Vivarin or No-doze. Although some older, poorly controlled studies found improvements in strength and power from this substance, these findings have not been replicated by well-controlled studies.

Caffeine appears to enhance performance in prolonged endurance exercise by mobilizing free fatty acids and sparing muscle glycogen. Ivy et al. found that a total of 500 mg of caffeine, administered before and during a 2-hr ride on an isokinetic bicycle ergometer, resulted in 7.4% greater work production. Caffeine appears to be an effective ergogenic aid in events such as marathon running.

The use of caffeine as an ergogenic aid is not without danger. The diuretic and cardiac stimulatory properties of this substance can combine to increase the risk of ECG arrhythmias, such as ventricular ectopic beats and paroxysmal atrial tachycardia. This is particularly alarming for older, less well-conditioned individuals. Caffeine can also caused delayed or lightened sleep and is addicting.

Nutritional Supplements

Athletes spend an absolute fortune on an endless variety of dietary supplements such as protein, vitamins, and weight gain products. An overwhelming body of literature has demonstrated that as long as an athlete is receiving a balanced diet, dietary supplements have no effect on performance. If the diet is deficient in any essential nutrient, however, then supplementation may very well be beneficial. Diet and performance are discussed in Chapter 13, so this section will focus on those nutritional supplements that are specifically used as ergogenic aids.

Carbohydrate (CHO) feeding, often in the form of glucose, dextrose, or honey, has long been used as an ergogenic aid to increase strength, speed, and endurance. CHO feeding has no effect on strength, power, or high-intensity short-term exercise and has been shown to decrease performance in endurance activity, but delays fatigue if taken during exercise.

Endurance performance decreases following preexercise glucose feeding. CHO feeding causes an initial rise in blood sugar and then a reflex increase in the secretion of insulin from the pancreas, which also inhibits free fatty acid mobilization. Thus, CHO feeding prior to endurance exercise results in an accelerated depletion in muscle glycogen and a reduced exercise capacity. An added problem is that the ingestion of carbohydrate slows gastic emptying, which could increase the risk of hyperthermia in endurance exercise, particularly if conducted in the heat.

Wheat germ oil has been highly touted as an ergogenic aid that increases endurance. The beneficial constituents of this product are purported to be vitamin E (alpha-tocopherol) and octacosanol. The proposed mechanism of its beneficial effect is that it reduces the oxygen requirement of the tissues and improves coronary collateral circulation. Early studies that demonstrated improvements in endurance performance have not been consistently replicated. Neither wheat germ nor vitamin E has been shown to increase maximal oxygen consumption, although one study found that vitamin E increased $\dot{V}_{O_2,max}$ by 9% at an altitude of 1524 m (5000 ft) and 14% at 4572 m (15,000 ft).

A variety of vitamins have been used as ergogenic aids. These substances, though essential, are required in extremely small quantities. It has been hypothesized that since mitochondrial mass increases as a result of endurance training, more vitamins may be needed to support the increased metabolic activity. However, vitamin deficiency in athletes has not been consistently demonstrated. In fact, most athletes take many times the minimum daily requirement for these substances.

Vitamin C has been used to improve both cardiovascular and muscle endurance. Although vitamin C has been shown to speed up the process of acclimatization to heat, most studies have not demonstrated any effect on factors important to endurance performance. B vitamins, such as thiamine, riboflavin, and niacin have become extremely popular with athletes for improving endurance, strength, and recovery from fatigue. Most studies have failed to find any beneficial effects.

Pangamic acid, sometimes called vitamin B_{15}, has been hailed as a miracle substance that improves endurance and fights off fatigue. This product has come under increasing criticism from the Food and Drug Administration because it is not an identifiable substance (not a vitamin or provitamin) and has no established medical or nutritional usefulness. The active ingredient in this product is thought to be N, N-dimethylglycine (DMG), which is said to increase oxygen utilization. Although some studies support the claims of improved endurance, the most stringently controlled investigations have not. The use of this substance may be dangerous because of its potential for mutagenesis.

The administration of buffering substances such as sodium bicarbonates has been suggested as an ergogenic aid in preventing fatigue during endurance exercise. This stemmed from the belief that inducement of alkalosis would prevent the accumulation of blood lactate and thus fatigue. Research studies have been equivocal on the effects of alkaline salts on performance. Although one study found that infusion of bicarbonate and Tris-buffer had no effect on performance in a 400-m run, another study reported that alkalyzing agents improve bicycle ergometer exercise performance. Two mechanisms may be involved in improving high-intensity exercise performance with these agents. First, alkalyzing agents buffer the effects of metabolic acids (mainly lactic acid) in the blood. Second, and perhaps more important, lactic acid efflux (movement) from muscle may be promoted by keeping blood pH higher than muscle pH. In this way bicarbonates and other bases in the circulation may help to minimize the effect of exercise on reducing muscle pH and, perhaps, prevent fatigue.

Marconi and co-workers have reported decreased blood lactate concentration during exercise and increased maximal oxygen consumption following administration of an α-ketoglutarate-pyridoxine complex (PAK). The possible mechanism of action of this substance is unclear, and more research is needed before it can be accepted as an effective ergogenic aid.

Aspartate, which is potassium and magnesium salts of aspartic acid, has been used to reduce fatigue. It has been hypothesized that its ingredients work by accelerating the resynthesis of ATP and CP in muscle and by sparing glycogen. As with many so-called ergogenic aids, beneficial effects have been demonstrated only in poorly controlled studies that used few subjects.

A variety of other nutritional substances have been proposed as ergogenic aids including bee pollen, gelatin, lecithin, phosphates, and organ extracts. Although little research is available concerning them, there is little reason to support their effectiveness. The case for organ extracts seems to almost be a throwback to the times when warriors ate the hearts or livers of brave adversaries to obtain some of their prowess in battle.

Blood Doping

Blood doping, or induced erythrocythemia, consists of increasing blood volume by transfusion of packed red blood cells for the purpose of increasing oxygen transport capacity. The transfusion can use blood from a matched donor, however, it is typically accomplished by the removal, storage, and subsequent reinfusion of the subject's own blood. This procedure received considerable publicity with the publication of a paper by Ekblom, Goldbarg, and Gullbring, who reported increases in work capacity and $\dot{V}_{O_2 max}$ of 23% and 9%, respectively. It also caught the interest of the media when several long-distance runners were suspected of using this technique in the 1972 and 1976 Olympics.

The majority of studies show improvements in maximal oxygen consumption (ranging from a 1 to 26% increase) and endurance exercise capacity (ranging from a 2.5 to 37% increase) following induced erythrocythemia. The increase in blood volume induces a decreased heart rate and cardiac output, with no change in stroke volume during submaximal exercise, and an increase in stroke volume and cardiac output, with no increase in maximal heart rate, during maximal exercise. In addition, arterial oxygen tension (P_{aO_2}) is increased during submaximal and maximal exercise (Figure 14-7). The development of the freeze technique of storing blood has enabled blood to be

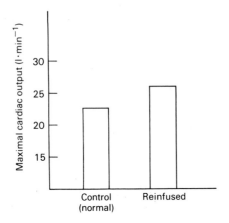

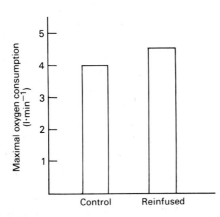

Figure 14-7

The effects of "blood doping" on cardiac output and maximal oxygen consumption. Blood doping increases cardiac output by increasing blood volume, which enhances venous return of blood to the heart. Arterial oxygen content is enhanced because more red blood cells are available to transport oxygen. Maximal oxygen consumption increases because of enhanced arterial oxygen content and a higher cardiac output.

(SOURCE: Adapted from data of J. M. Thomson, J. A. Stone, A. D. Ginsburg, and P. Hamilton, O_2 transport during exercise following blood reinfusion. J. Appl. Physiol. 53:1213–1219, 1982.)

stored longer with less damage to the red blood cells, which make this technique more effective.

Training may be an important prerequisite for the beneficial effects of blood doping to manifest themselves. In untrained rats, maximal oxygen consumption increases with hematocrit until the hematocrit reaches 40%. After that, further increases in hemoconcentration do not result in increased $\dot{V}_{O_2 max}$ because of the increase in blood viscosity.

Blood doping appears to be a relatively safe procedure in normal, healthy individuals. Reinfusion of autologous blood caused no abnormal changes in the exercise electrocardiogram or in blood pressure. However, homologous transfusions carry with them the risk of hepatitis, AIDS, bacterial communication, and blood type incompatibility.

Presently there is no test to detect blood doping. The changes in hemoconcentration are very similar to those induced by altitude acclimatization.

Although this practice clearly falls within the spirit of the antidoping regulations of the International Olympic Committee, there is no effective means for enforcing a ban against this procedure.

Oxygen

Supplemental oxygen has been used before and during exercise in an attempt to enhance performance, and after exercise to hasten recovery. The first use of this technique was by the Japanese in the 1932 Olympic Games held in Los Angeles. Because they were successful, the practice became institutionalized in several sports. The sight of a gasping football player on the sidelines with an oxygen mask over his face has become common.

Oxygen breathing *immediately* prior to exercise will increase the oxygen content of the total blood volume by 80 to 100 ml. In exercise lasting less than 2 min, supplemental oxygen will improve maximal work capacity by approximately 1% and decrease the submaximal exercise heart rate. Most studies (but not all) have shown that oxygen can be beneficial in short-term maximal efforts in swimming and running. This is not a very practical ergogenic aid because of the time lag between the administration of oxygen and the start of performance. Runners and swimmers must take the time to prepare themselves in the starting blocks, and football players must align themselves in formation. During this time, the increase in blood oxygen content dissipates.

Although supplemental oxygen could theoretically be of benefit in recovery from repeated maximal efforts, several studies have been unable to demonstrate that oxygen breathing affected the characteristic changes in ventilation, heart rate, blood pressure, or power output.

Oxygen breathing during exercise improves work capacity, increases maximal oxygen consumption, and decreases submaximal heart rate. Supplemental oxygen effectively increases oxygen transport capacity by increasing the oxygen dissolved in the blood, and perhaps by increasing maximal myocardial oxygen consumption. With the exception of mountain climbing, supplemental oxygen breathing during exercise is of little practical significance, as few sports allow an athlete to carry an oxygen tank on the field.

Interocclusal Splints

Interocclusal splints, or mandibular orthopedic repositioning appliances (MORAs), are corrective mouth orthotics designed to correct malocclusion and temporomandibular joint (TMJ) imbalance. The theory behind this device is that TMJ dysfunction causes muscle tension, which impairs muscle strength. It has been hypothesized that the splint changes the position of the TMJ, which relieves pressure on the auriculotemporal nerve, thus relieving tension in the neck and shoulder muscles.

Although numerous personal testimonials and clinical observations testify to the beneficial effects of this device, there is scant experimental evidence. Recent well-controlled investigations found that MORAs had no effect on strength and muscular endurance.

Proponents of this device claim that 90% of the population has some degree of TMJ imbalance; however, critics point out that every joint has a normal range of deviation and that few people experience TMJ pain when clinching their teeth. Some people have a vested interest in supporting these devices because of their income-generating potential, so their clinical enthusiasm has to be viewed with a jaundiced eye. Further, it is difficult to run a double-blind investigation with the splint, which makes the placebo effect a prominent factor in any result. It appears that the interocclusal splint is another possible ergogenic aid that requires considerable investigation before it becomes an accepted part of the athletic cornucopia.

Electrical Stimulation

Electrical stimulation has been used for many years as a treatment modality in the rehabilitation of injured muscle, and to prevent denervation atrophy, decrease spasticity and muscle spasm, reduce contractures, and prevent deep vein thrombosis. Healthy athletes have recently begun using this technique to increase strength and power.

There is little evidence that electrical muscle stimulation is a beneficial supplement to traditional strength-training techniques in healthy subjects. Romero et al., using untrained females as subjects, demonstrated substantial increases in isometric knee extension strength (31% in the nondominant leg) but were unable to demonstrate such changes isokinetically. In a subsequent study of this group, however, Fahey demonstrated increases in isokinetic strength when the muscle was stimulated in a stretched position. Nevertheless, the strength increases did not exceed those that could be attained through resistive exercise training techniques.

Although studies of the effects of electrical stimulation on athletes have generally been negative, they have usually been conducted during a 6-week experimental period, which may not be enough time to render statistically significant results.

Psychological and Mechanical Ergogenic Aids

The techniques and devices of psychological and mechanical aids are largely beyond the scope of this discussion because they largely lie within the domains of psychology of sport and biomechanics, but they will be mentioned briefly. Psychological ergogenic aids are practiced to reduce mental restraints to maximum performance. They include hypnosis, rehearsal strategies (sometimes called imaging), and stress management techniques. Although these techniques are widely practiced and popular, their effectiveness is very difficult to demonstrate experimentally.

Mechanical ergogenic aids have had a tremendous effect in some sports. Perhaps the best examples are pole vaulting (fiberglass pole), skiing (metal and fiberglass skis and plastic boots), and running (all-weather tracks). Advanced technology is having a significant effect on improving designs in clothing (lighter, better fitting clothes that reduce drag), shoes (better support, fit, and shock absorption), and equipment (e.g., disks with weight centered on the outside for more lift, golf balls with more dimples for greater distance, larger tennis rackets that make it easier to hit the ball).

It appears that ergogenic aids will continue to be of interest to athletes and people participating in sports as long as there is the slim chance of getting a slight edge over the competition.

Summary

Ergogenic aids are substances or techniques that are used to improve athletic performance. The majority of so-called ergogenic aids are ineffective, are sometimes dangerous, and rely on the power of suggestion for their beneficial effects to manifest themselves. However, some do improve performance and provide the athlete with a definitive competitive advantage. The International Olympic Committee (IOC) has banned the use of many such substances and initiated an extensive, sophisticated testing program to discourage their use. Popular ergogenic aids include anabolic steroids, blood doping, nutritional supplements, growth hormone, bicarbonate, amphetamines, and caffeine.

Anabolic steroids are synthetic male hormones that are used to improve strength, power, endurance, and muscle size. They work by stimulating protein synthesis and inhibiting protein breakdown. The drugs seem to be most effective in experienced weight trainers involved in high intensity strength training programs. Numerous, sometimes catastrophic side effects have been reported in athletes and patients using these drugs including liver toxicity, coronary heart disease, cancer, masculinization in women, and premature closure of the bone growth centers in children.

Amphetamines act as both CNS and sympathomimetic stimulants. Athletes use them to prevent fatigue and to increase confidence, cardiovascular endurance, muscle endurance, speed, power, and reaction time. They appear to aid power-oriented movement skills such as shotputting but probably hamper the execution of motor skills requiring sensory integration in sports such as football or basketball. The use of amphetamines are accompanied by serious physiological and psychological side-effects including impaired temperature regulation, cardiac arrhythmias, psychic distress, insomnia, and addiction.

Caffeine stimulates the CNS and stimulates the release of epinephrine. Athletes use caffeine as a stimulant and as a fatty acid mobilizer (which spares muscle glycogen and improves endurance performance). Caffeine has recently been added to the IOC's banned substance list.

Blood doping is the practice of increasing blood volume by transfusion of packed red blood cells for the purpose of increasing oxygen transport capacity. It has been shown to increase $\dot{V}_{O_2max}$ by as much as 26%. While prohibited by the IOC, there is presently no effective test to detect its use.

Numerous mechanical and psychological ergogenic aids are widely and enthusiastically used by novice sportspersons and professional athletes. Some of them, such as the fiberglass pole vaulting pole and metal skis, have revolutionized their sport. Others, such as rehearsal strategies (imaging), are widely practiced but their effectiveness has yet to be proven.

Selected Readings

BROOKS, R.V., G. JEREMIAH, W.A. WEBB, and M. WHEELER. Detection of anabolic steroid administration to athletes. J. Steroid Biochemistry 11:913–917, 1979.

BURKETT, L.N., and A.K. BERNSTEIN. Strength testing after jaw repositioning with a mandibular orthopedic appliance. Physician Sportsmed. 10:101–107, 1982.

BUSKIRK, E.R. Some nutritional considerations in the conditioning of athletes. Annu. Rev. Nutr. 1:319–350, 1981.

CELEJOWA, I., and M. HOMA. Food intake, nitrogen, and energy balance in Polish weight lifters, during a training camp. Nutrition Metabol. 2:259–274, 1970.

CHANDLER, J.V., and S.N. BLAIR. The effect of amphetamines on selected physiological components related to athletic success. Med. Sci. Sports Exercise 12:65–69, 1980.

CURRIER, D., J. LEHMAN, and P. LIGHTFOOT. Electrical stimulation in exercise of the quadriceps femoris muscle. Phys. Ther. 59:1508–1512, 1979.

FAHEY, T.D., and C.H. BROWN. The effects of an anabolic steroid on the strength, body composition, and endurance of college males when accompanied by weight training program. Med. Sci. Sports 5:272–276, 1973.

FAHEY, T.D., M. HARVEY, R.V. SCHROEDER, and F. FERGUSON. The effects of sex differences and knee joint position on electrical stimulation modulated strength increases. Med. Sci. Sports Exercise 17:144–147, 1985.

FOSTER, C., D.L. COSTILL, and W. J. FINK. Effects of pre-exercise feedings on endurance performance. Med. Sci. Sports 11:1–5, 1979.

FRISCHKORN, C.G.B. and H.E. FRISCHKORN. Investigations of anabolic drug abuse in athletics and cattle feed. J. Chromatography 151:331–338, 1978.

GLEDHILL, N. "Bicarbonate ingestion and anabolic performance." *Sports Medicine* 1:177–180, 1984.

GLEDHILL, N. Blood doping and related issues: a brief review. Med. Sci. Sports Exercise 14:183–189, 1982.

IVY, J.L., D.L. COSTILL, W.J. FINK, and R.W. LOWER. Influence of caffeine and carbohydrate feedings on endurance performance. Med. Sci. Sports. 11:6–11, 1979.

KINDERMANN, W., J. KEUL, and G. HUBER. Physical exercise after induced alkalosis (bicarbonate or tris-buffer). Eur. J. Appl. Physiol. 37:197–204, 1977.

LOPES, J.M., M. AUBIER, J. JARDIM, J.V. ARANDA, and P.T. MACKLEM. Effect of caffeine on skeletal muscle function before and after fatigue. J. Appl. Physiol. 54:1303–1305, 1983.

MARCONI, C., G. SASSI, and P. ARRETTELLI. "The effect of an α-hetoglutarate-pyridoxine complex on human maximal aerobic and anabolic performance." *Eur. J. Appl. Physiol.* 49:307–317, 1982.

MEYERS, F.H., E. JAWETZ, and A. GOLDFIEN. Review of Medical Pharmacology. Los Altos, Calif.: Lange Medical, 1980.

MOORE, M. Corrective mouth guards: performance aids or expensive placebos? Physician Sportsmed. 9:127–132, 1981.

MORGAN, W. (ed.). Ergogenic Aids and Muscular Performance. New York: Academic Press, 1972.

O'SHEA, J.P. Anabolic steroids in sport: a biophysiological evaluation. In: Schriber, K., and E.J. Burke. Relevant Topics in Athletic Training. Ithaca, N.Y.: Mouvement Publications, 1978.

PERCY, E.C. Ergogenic aids in athletics. Med. Sci. Sports 10:298–303, 1978.

PETERSON, G.E., and T.D. FAHEY. HDL-C in five elite athletes using anabolic-androgenic steroids. Physician Sportsmed. 12(6):120–130, 1984.

RICHARDSON, J.H. A comparison of two drugs on strength increase in monkeys. J. Sports Med. 17:251–254, 1977.

ROGOZKIN, V., and B. FELDKOREN. The effect of retabolil and training on activity of RNA polymerase in skeletal muscles. Med. Sci. Sports 11:345–347, 1979.

ROMERO, J.A., T.L. SANFORD, R.V. SCHROEDER, and T.D. FAHEY. The effects of electrical stimulation of normal quadriceps on strength and girth. Med. Sci. Sports Exercise 14:194–197, 1982.

SCHUBERT, M.M., R.L. GUTTU, L.H. HUNTER, R. HALL, and R. THOMAS. Changes in shoulder and leg strength in athletes wearing mandibular orthopedic repositioning appliances. J. Am. Dent. Assoc. 108:334–337, 1984.

SMITH, G.M. and H.K. BEECHER. Amphetamine sulfate and athletic performance. JAMA 170:542–557, 1959.

SMITH, G.M. and H.K. BEECHER. Amphetamine, secobarbital and athletic performance. JAMA 172:1502–1514, 1623–1629, 1960.

SOUCCAR, C., A.J. LAPA, and R.B. doVALLE. The influence of testosterone on neuromuscular transmission in hormone sensitive mammalian skeletal muscles. Muscle Nerve 5:232–237, 1982.

TAYLOR, W.N. Anabolic Steroids and the Athlete. Jefferson, N.C.: McFarland & Co., 1982.

THOMSON, J.M. O_2 transport during exercise following blood transfusion. J. Appl. Physiol. 53:1213–1219, 1982.

WILLIAMS, M.H. Drugs and Athletic Performance. Springfield, Ill.: Charles C Thomas, 1974.

WILLIAMS, M.H. (ed.) Ergogenic Aids in Sport. Champaign, Ill.: Human Kinetics Publishers, 1983.

WILLIAMS, M.H. Nutritional Aspects of Human Physical and Athletic Performance. Springfield, Ill.: Charles C Thomas, 1976.

WRIGHT, J. Anabolic Steroids and Sports. Natick, Mass.: Sports Science Consultants, 1978.

WRIGHT, J. Anabolic Steroids and Sports. Vol. 2. Natick, Mass.: Sports Science Consultants, 1982.

WRIGHT, J. Anabolic steroids and athletics. Exercise Sports Sci. Rev. 8:149–202, 1980.

15

Exercise, Growth, and Aging

People involved in the understanding and prescription of exercise are working increasingly with children and older adults. Children's sports programs are very popular throughout the world. It is important for the administrators of these programs to be familiar with the characteristics and exercise responses of growing children. Likewise, large numbers of older people are participating in exercise programs. Older adults constitute a significant portion of the population of the industrialized nations, and their proportion will continue to grow with the aging of the post-World War II "baby-boom" generation. An understanding of the aging process, disease, and the benefits and limitations of exercise in aging humans is essential to all students of exercise physiology.

The challenges presented by exercise to growing children and aging adults may appear to be similar to each other, but they are based on fundamentally different mechanisms. The child's immature temperature regulatory, skeletal, and nervous systems are often unable to tolerate the same level of physical stress as the mature adult. In general, young children cannot learn motor skills as rapidly as adults or achieve the same degrees of physical fitness. However, during adolescence, potential improvements in exercise capacity may exceed those of any other time of life. Older people, on the other hand, are unable to perform at the same level as young adults because their physiological systems are deteriorating. Although older adults can improve physical fitness, they do not have the same capacity for physical adaptability they had when they were younger.

Exercise is important during aging and growth. Physical training in older people has been shown to slow deterioration of many physiological processes. For example, $\dot{V}_{O_2max}$, an important measure of vitality and physical performance capacity, can be significantly improved in older people. Without exercise, this important factor generally deteriorates and contributes to the common ambulatory problems of the aged. Exercising during growth will contribute to a better developed functional capacity, and may result in qualitative improvements in neural and musculoskeletal development.

Physical performance in children and adolescents must always be assessed in light of the growth process. Growth involves a series of developmental stages that are remarkably similar in all people. Individual differences in diet, exercise, and health may affect these stages to a certain extent, but the basic pattern remains the same. Each of these stages has a profound influence on individual capability for physical performance. Attempts to rush the developmental process are futile and may lead to physical and emotional harm.

It is extremely difficult to fully quantify the effects of aging on physiological function and physical performance. Individual outlooks and expectations can greatly affect life style, which can appear to either accelerate or delay the aging process. Disease can further obscure the relationship between aging and exercise performance. Various systemic disorders, such as osteoarthritis and atherosclerosis, are so common in the aged that they are sometimes considered a normal part of the aging process. Although it is readily apparent that age has a deteriorating affect on physiological capacity, its effect is extremely difficult to separate from those of deconditioning and disease.

The purpose of this chapter is to examine the relationship between growth, aging, exercise capacity, and physical training. Emphasis will be placed on the importance of exercise during growth and aging and the relative importance of environmental and genetic factors in determining physical performance.

Exercise and Growth

An understanding of exercise and growth requires a basic knowledge of the growth process. Children gradually develop a readiness (learning capability based on physiological maturation) for specific motor skills and types of exercise. This readiness depends on factors such as neurological, cardiovascular, and psychosocial development. This discussion will focus on the physiological aspects of development that affect physical performance.

The Nature of the Growth Process

Growth involves the transformation of nutrients into living tissue. It implies the development of the organism in an orderly fashion and represents a predominance of anabolic (building) over catabolic (breakdown) processes. Growth is characterized by the progressive transformation of the organism into the adult form.

Growth proceeds along an irregularly shaped curve. During the first 2 years of life, height and weight increase rapidly. This is followed by a progressively declining growth rate during childhood. At puberty, there is an abrupt increase in the growth rate, called the adolescent growth spurt (Figure 15-1). All people adhere to the basic growth curve, but individual differences in environment can affect the rate of change in height, weight, and physiological development.

Growth during Childhood During childhood, the period between about 2 years and the onset of puberty, there is a steady but gradual increase in height and weight, with height increasing faster than weight. Males tend to be taller and heavier than females; however, females have relatively longer legs, which indicates a greater level of maturity (the focus of growth progresses from head to feet, so greater leg length indicates further progression on the growth curve). Although the growth rate is faster in males, the relative changes are similar in both sexes. The skeletal age of girls is more advanced throughout childhood. Between the ages of 6 and 10 years, girls gain

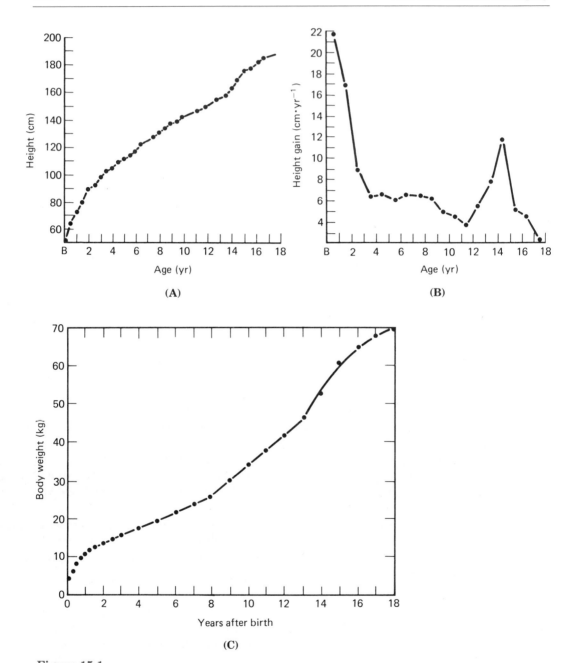

Figure 15-1
Increases in height (a), height gain (b), body weight (c), and percent of adult weight (d) with age in males. The growth rate is rapid during the first 2 years of life, levels off somewhat during childhood, and then accelerates again during adolescence.

(SOURCE: Laird, A. K. Evolution of the human growth curve. Growth 31:345–355, 1967. In: G. A. Brooks and T. D. Fahey. Exercise Physiology: Human Bioenergetics and Its Applications. New York: Macmillan, 1984, p. 663, Figure 30-1c.)

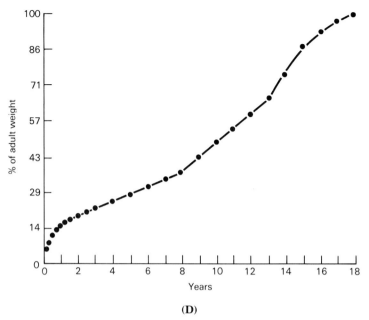

Figure 15-1 (Continued)

in pelvic width faster than boys, while boys tend to have larger thoraxes and forearms. Although there are some sex differences in growth during childhood, the anthropometric characteristics are almost the same until puberty.

The gradual growth rate during childhood is conducive to learning motor skills (Figure 15-2). The relatively constant ratio between height and lean body mass provides a stable environment for developing coordination and neuromuscular skill. This is an important period for the introduction and development of gross motor activities such as running, jumping, hopping, and throwing. However, the limited muscle mass and the fragile skeletal epiphyseal growth centers make vigorous strength training less appropriate (except physical skills that require the use of body weight as the resistance).

Growth at Puberty and Adolescence   Adolescence is the final period in the growth process leading to maturity. It is a time of rapid increases in height and weight accompanied by puberty, the time when the sex organs become fully developed (Figure 15-3). The adolescent growth spurt generally begins at about 10½ to 13 years in girls and 12½ to 15 years in boys. Ten- to 13-year-old girls will often be taller than males of the same age, but when the boys' growth spurt occurs they generally catch up and then surpass the girls.

Because puberty and the growth spurt occur at the same time, the degree of sexual maturation is often used to assess the position on the growth curve (Table 15-1). In girls, the growth spurt generally occurs when the breasts and

Figure 15-2
Childhood is a good time to develop gross motor skill because of the relatively slow growth rate during this period of development.

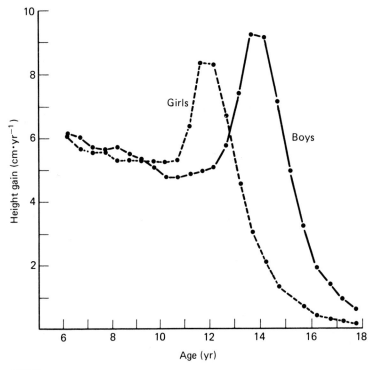

Figure 15-3

The adolescent growth spurt for boys and girls.

(SOURCE: J. M. Tanner. Growth at Adolescence. Oxford: Blackwell Publications, Ltd., 1962. In: G. A. Brooks and T. D. Fahey. Exercise Physiology: Human Bioenergetics and Its Applications. New York: Macmillan, 1984, p. 666.

TABLE 15-1 Pubertal Stage Ratings for Boys and Girls[a]

Pubertal Stage	Pubic Hair	Genital Development	Breast Development
1	None	Testes, scrotum about same size and proportions as in early childhood	Elevation of papilla only
2	Sparse growth of long, slightly pigmented downy hair, straight or only slightly curled, appearing chiefly at base of penis or along labia	Enlargement of scrotum and testes; skin of scrotum reddens and changes in texture; little or no enlargement of penis at this stage	Breast bud stage; elevation of breast and papilla as small mound; enlargement of areolar diameter
3	Considerably darker, coarser, and more curled; hair spreads sparsely over junction of pubes	Enlargement of penis, which occurs at first mainly in length; further growth of testes and scrotum	Further enlargement and elevation of breast and areola, with no separation of their contours
4	Hair now resembles adult in type, but area covered is still considerably smaller than in adult; no spread to medial surface of thighs	Increased size of penis with growth in breadth and development of glans; further enlargement of testes and scrotum; increased darkening of scrotal skin	Projection of areola and papilla to form a secondary mound above the level of the breast
5	Adult in quantity and type with distribution of horizontal (or classically "feminine" pattern); spread to medial surface of thighs but not up the linea alba or elsewhere above the base of the inverse triangle. In about 80% of Caucasian men and 10% of women, pubic hair spreads further, but this takes some time to occur after stage 5 is reached. This may not be completed until the midtwenties or later	Genitalia adult in size and shape; no further enlargement after stage 5 is reached	The mature stage; projection of papilla only, due to recession of areola to general contour of breast

[a] Pubertal stage is rated on a scale of 1 to 5. Stage 1 represents prepubertal development, whereas stage 5 represents the characteristics of the adult. Stages are determined by the degree of development of pubic hair in both sexes, genital development in boys, and breast development in girls.

SOURCE: Adapted from L. Larson. Fitness, Health, and Work Capacity. New York: Macmillan, 1974. pp. 516–517.

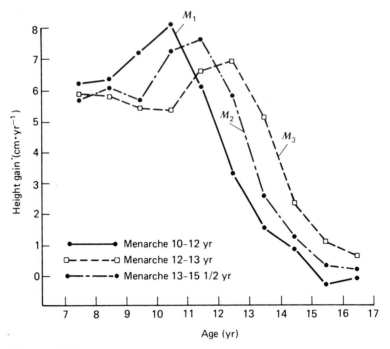

Figure 15-4

Peak velocities in height for early-, average-, and late-maturing girls. M_1, M_2, M_3: average time of menarche for each group.

(SOURCE: J. M. Tanner. Growth at Adolescence. Oxford: Blackwell Publications, Ltd., 1962. In: G. A. Brooks and T. D. Fahey. Exercise Physiology: Human Bioenergetics and Its Applications. New York: Macmillan, 1984, p. 667, Figure 30-4.

pubic hair first appear. This is followed by menarche, the first menstruation. Menarche provides a definite landmark for the assessment of maturation that is not available in boys. The closest indicators of maturity in boys, in addition to pubic hair, are the appearance of facial hair and the change in voice.

Adolescent growth characteristics are different in late and early maturers. The rate of growth is more intense the earlier the growth spurt occurs (Figure 15-4). Boys who mature earlier tend to be more muscular, with shorter legs and broader hips. Girls who mature earlier have shorter legs and narrower shoulders than those who mature later. Additionally, late maturers tend to become slightly taller adults. Even though the growth spurt is less in late maturers, they are growing over a longer period of time.

The characteristic sexual differences in anthropometric measures arise during puberty. Males develop greater height and weight with larger musculature and broader shoulders, while females develop larger hips. The growth spurt is slightly more than 3 in. a year in girls and about 4 in. a year in boys.

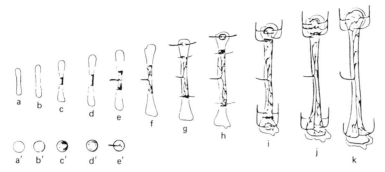

Figure 15-5

Diagram of the development of a typical long bone and its blood supply: (a) cartilage model; (b) development of the bone collar; (c) development of calcified cartilage in primary center; (d) extension of the bone collar; (e, f) the invasion of the cartilage by vascular sprouts and mesenchyme with formation of two areas of bone formation toward the bone ends; (g, h, i) secondary centers develop in the bone ends as the central area expands; (j, k) epiphyseal plates disappear, and the blood vessels of the diaphysis and epiphysis intercommunicate.

(SOURCE: W. Bloom and D. W. Fawcett. Textbook of Histology. Philadelphia; W. B. Saunders, 1975. In: G. A. Brooks and T. D. Fahey. Exercise Physiology: Human Bioenergetics and Its Applications. New York: Macmillan, 1984, p. 670, Figure 30-5.)

The adolescent growth spurt has a profound effect on physical performance. Males make marked improvements in endurance, strength, speed, power, and various motor skills. Females, on the other hand, often experience a leveling off in skills.

Skeletal Changes during Growth   Increases in height occur because of skeletal growth, principally in the long bones. Bone growth occurs at the epiphyseal growth plates. These are located at both ends of long bones between the articular epiphysis and the central diaphysis (Figure 15-5). The process of bone formation, called ossification, continues until the growth plates themselves are finally closed. Linear growth can continue as long as the ossification centers are open. The union of bone growth centers begins at puberty in some bones but is not completed until the age of 18 years or later.

Exercise, which stresses bones and stimulates bone growth, does not seem to enhance linear bone growth but does increase bone density and width. In general, therefore, exercise during growth creates a skeleton composed of denser, stronger bone that is better able to withstand stress. Disease or trauma can cause injury to the growth plates, which could affect growth. For this reason, it is extremely important to avoid situations that could adversely damage these areas. Studies have shown, for example, that excessive baseball pitching by youngsters can cause epiphyseal damage. It is possible that heavy weight lifting could have the same effect (although this has not been demonstrated).

Changes in Body Composition

The ratio of fat to fat-free weight is particularly important during growth because overweight children tend to become overweight adults. Physical activity is vitally important in the maintenance of ideal body composition. Obese youngsters tend to be less active than lean children, and these activity patterns tend to persist throughout life. However, programs of vigorous physical activity have been shown to reverse the process.

Increases in body fat occur because of increases in fat cell size, cell number, or both. Fat cells increase in number until early adolescence. After that, increased body fat occurs mainly by increasing cell size. Once developed, fat cells can only decrease in size, not in number. This may be a reason for the dismal prognosis for long-term weight control in obese adults. It may be possible to affect the development of fat cells during growth by means of diet and physical activity. Failure to do this could result in a lifelong weight problem (see Chapter 14).

During childhood, females have slightly more fat than males. Typically, body fat percentages are about 16% for 8-year-old boys and 18% for 8-year-old girls. At puberty, marked changes in body composition occur. Boys make rapid increases in lean weight and decreases in percentage of fat. Percentage of fat typically drops 3 to 5% between ages 12 and 17. Females also experience increases in lean mass, although less than boys, and increases in body fat. An untrained 17-year-old female is typically around 25% fat. However, an athlete will often have less than 16 to 18% fat (Figure 15-6).

Physical activity will not change the essence of these growth-related stages of body composition. In females, for example, vigorous training will not prevent the increase in fat that occurs during adolescence; but the gains will be less than in sedentary girls. Studies comparing active and inactive young-

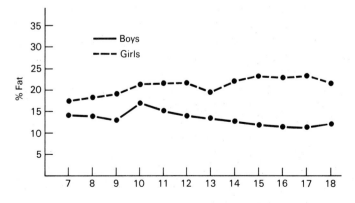

Figure 15-6

Body composition during growth and aging in males (bottom line) and females (top line).

(SOURCE: From data of Parizkova. In: G. L. Rarick (ed.). Physical Activity: Human Growth and Development. New York: Academic Press, 1972.)

sters show that training consistently results in higher lean body mass and lower body fat. These advantages do not persist into adulthood, however, unless the training is continued. Inactivity will result in decreased muscle mass and increased fat.

Body composition is an important consideration in the development of motor skills. The relatively slow growth period is an important period for learning gross motor skills. These efforts may be compromised if the child is overweight. The relatively weak muscles could have considerable difficulty overcoming the burden of excess body mass.

Muscle Growth and Physical Performance

Muscle growth accounts for a considerable portion of weight gains during growth. There is a steady growth of muscle tissue during the first 7 years of life, followed by a slowing trend in the years immediately preceding puberty. In the normal child, muscle and skeletal growth keep pace with one another. During the pubertal growth spurt, muscle grows at a rapid rate, particularly in boys. The increase in muscle tissue typically occurs slightly after the greatest increases in height. This explains the awkward gangliness in children of that age.

In boys, the increases in muscle size are related to improvements in strength. On the average, rapid increases occur at about 14 years and continue throughout adolescence. However, there are considerable individual differences that can be attributed to such factors as maturational level, body build, and amount of physical activity. Muscle strength and size are of considerable concern to children because they are the most important predictors of athletic success.

The extent of the development and performance of muscle is dependent, in large part, on the relative maturation of the nervous system. High levels of strength, power, and skill are impossible if the child has not reached neural maturity. Myelination of nerves is not complete until sexual maturity has been achieved, so an immature child cannot be expected to respond to training or reach the same level of skill as adults.

Significant training-induced muscle hypertrophy does not occur until adolescence in boys. This is because of the low levels of male hormones (principally testosterone) found in sexually immature children. Male hormones, called androgens, are important regulators of protein synthesis (see Chapter 12). Adult males have about ten times the amount of androgens as prepubertal children and adult women. Maximal strength-gaining potential in males is not possible until adult levels of androgens are achieved. However, prepubertal children can improve strength considerably by weight training. Such practices are safe and beneficial as long as the training sessions are supervised and no maximum lifting is allowed. Sex differences in strength may also be partially attributed to the higher number of muscle cell nuclei in males. Males probably have a greater capacity for muscle hypertrophy (and thus strength) because of the critical role that the muscle cell nuclei play in protein synthesis.

Cardiovascular and Metabolic Function during Growth

There is a progressive decline in resting and maximum heart rate during childhood and adolescence. Heart rates tend to be the same in girls and boys during childhood but are about three to four beats higher in females during and after adolescence. At puberty in boys, there is a tendency for submaximal exercise and recovery heart rates to be lower, even in the absence of vigorous training. The decreased heart rate is accompanied and perhaps caused by a greater resting and exercise stroke volume resulting from an increased heart size and blood volume.

Resting and exercise systolic blood pressure rise progressively, particularly during puberty. Blood pressure assumes adult values shortly after the adolescent growth spurt. The pubertal acceleration in blood pressure occurs in females before males, but the boys quickly catch up and surpass the girls.

Exercise capacity and maximal oxygen consumption (in liters $\cdot$ min^{-1}) increase gradually throughout childhood. During puberty, there is a dramatic increase in boys and a leveling off in girls. The improvements in endurance capacity occur because of enhanced oxygen transport and metabolic capacities and increased muscle mass.

Prepubertal youngsters do not seem to respond to endurance training as well as adolescents and adults. Some studies show no improvement in $\dot{V}_{O_2max}$ from training beyond that expected in normal growth. There may even be a difference between children and adults in the way they adapt to training. For example, studies using interval training as the exercise stimulus have usually failed to significantly improve $\dot{V}_{O_2max}$; however, studies using prolonged endurance exercise, such as cross-country running, have resulted in gains.

It appears that the training threshold may be higher in immature children. Prepubertal youngsters have a limited ability for cardiac hypertrophy and metabolic enzyme synthesis, both important factors in improving endurance performance. This may be due to their low androgen levels. Androgens are potent stimulators of muscle hypertrophy, protein synthesis, and red blood cell production. These factors have far-reaching effects on oxygen transport and the production of ATP.

The pubertal increase in $\dot{V}_{O_2max}$ corresponds to the time of the greatest increase in height (Figure 15-7). At the same time, androgen secretion in boys increases dramatically, which results in hypertrophy of cardiac muscle, stimulation of red cell and hemoglobin production, and proliferation of metabolic enzymes. These maturationally induced changes make possible large induced increases in endurance, which are even greater with involvement in a vigorous endurance training program.

Some researchers have called the adolescent growth period a critical time for the development of maximal aerobic power (a controversial viewpoint).

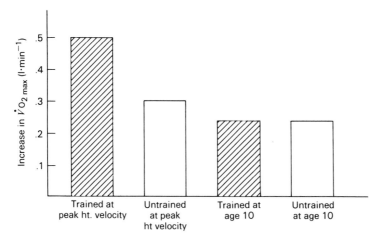

Figure 15-7

Increase in $\dot{V}_{O_2\,max}$ in trained and untrained boys at peak height velocity (period of greatest growth rate) and during prepuberty. These data suggest that large improvements in fitness are possible during "critical" growth periods.

(SOURCE: From the data of Miriwald et al., 1981.)

The reasons for this are probably as much sociological as physiological. Adolescence provides the first opportunity for large increases in physical capacity. Those who take advantage of this may develop a superior capacity for exercise that may persist into adulthood. Successful participation in sports may result in a habit of exercise training that is continued throughout life; however, the benefits of adolescent exercise are clearly not maintained, unless training is continued. A sedentary 40-year-old man will likely have a low capacity for exercise regardless of his activity level as an adolescent.

Genetic Considerations

The question of the relative contribution of environment and genetics has been highly controversial for more than 40 years. Are champions made or born? If children are subjected to proper training at a young age, will they reach a higher level of performance than they would if they began later in life? Researchers are beginning to find the answers to these questions.

Determination of the genetic component of performance usually involves comparison of identical and nonidentical twins. Because identical twins have the same genetic material, variability in performance will be due solely to

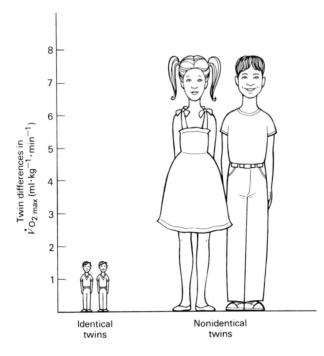

Figure 15-8

Interpair differences in $\dot{V}_{O_2 max}$ between groups of identical and nonidentical twins. The smaller differences in identical twins indicates the strong genetic component in this important physiological measure.

(SOURCE: From the data of V. Klissouras. Prediction of athletic performance: genetic considerations. Can. J. Appl. Physiol. 1:195–200, 1976.)

environmental considerations. Variability in the nonidentical twins is due to a combination of genetic and environmental factors.

Most of these studies indicate that, in the absence of physical training, the genetic component is the most important factor determining individual differences in performance (Figure 15-8). In relatively sedentary populations, there is little if any difference in $\dot{V}_{O_2 max}$ between identical twins, while the differences in nonidentical twins are often considerable. Genetic studies are important for emphasizing the trained state as a temporary level of adaptation. Training studies with identical twins do demonstrate that the active twin improves while the sedentary twin does not. But, when the levels of activity are similar, heredity asserts itself and physiological characteristics in the genetically identical individuals move closer together.

The adaptability of the human body is limited. Maximal oxygen consumption, for example, can be improved by only about 20%. Thus, an athlete must start out with a high oxygen transport capacity if he or she is ever to reach Olympic levels of performance. Studies of the characteristics of athletes seem to reinforce this.

Can champion athletes be selected at a young age? The top few athletes during childhood do tend to become top athletes in adolescence and adulthood. However, except for these, prediction of superior athletic prowess becomes tenuous at best. The best approach seems to be to provide a wide range of activities to all and provide extra help for those who show interest and talent.

Exercise and the Aging Process

The fitness boom has captured the imagination of all segments of the population, most notably people over 50 years of age. Is exercise good for them or are these people better off "taking it easy"? As we shall see in Chapter 17, exercise is not for everyone. In some medical conditions, many of which are more prevalent to older people, exercise may be dangerous or unwise. However, there is good evidence that exercise is important in older people in promoting vitality and preventing premature death or disability from a variety of degenerative diseases.

The Nature of the Aging Process

Aging can be defined as the progressive reduction in the capacity to regulate the body's internal physiology (homeostasis), resulting in an increased risk of death. Simply stated, the physiological control mechanisms do not work as well in old people. Reaction time is slowed, resistance to disease is impaired, work capacity is diminished, recovery from effort is prolonged, and body structures are less resilient.

Most of the body's biological systems possess a large capacity and tolerance for emergency output. For example, in the heart the maintenance of cardiac output is possible even in the face of extreme vascular disease and drastically impaired cardiac function. Likewise, the pulmonary system has a large reserve capacity for ventilating the alveoli. Its function is limited only by extreme environmental conditions or disease. Unfortunately, the margin of safety in these systems diminishes with age (Table 15-2).

It appears that no matter how well people take care of themselves, their physiological processes will eventually lay prey to the ravages of old age. This fact is consistent across all animal species. Obviously, all animals of a species do not live to precisely the same age; there are individual differences. Likewise, the quality of life can be considerably different. In humans, some can be fit and alert at 100 years, while others are invalids in their 60s.

Genetic considerations seem to be the most important factor dictating the length of life, while a combination of environmental and genetic factors govern the quality of life. The maximum life-span in humans is slightly over 110 years, a figure that has remained unchanged for 300 years in spite of tremendous advances in public health. Genetic research reinforces this. Studies of identical and nonidentical twins show that the life-span of the latter is remarkably similar. The identical twins usually die within 2 to 4 years of each other, while the interval in the nonidentical twins averaged 7 to 9 years.

TABLE 15-2 Physiological Effects of Aging

Effect	Functional Significance
Cardiovascular	
Capillary/fiber ratio ↓	Decreased muscle blood flow
Cardiac muscle and heart volume ↓	Decreased maximal stroke volume and cardiac output
Elasticity of blood vessels ↓	Increased peripheral resistance, blood pressure, and cardiac afterload
Elasticity of blood vessels ↓	Increased peripheral resistance, blood pressure, and cardiac afterload
Myocardial myosin-ATPase ↓	Decreased myocardial contractility
Sympathetic stimulation of SA node ↓	Decreased maximum heart rate
Respiration	
Condition of elastic lung support structures ↓	Increased work of breathing
Elasticity of support structures ↓	Decreased lung elastic recoil
Size of alveoli ↑	Decreased diffusion capacity and increased dead space
Number of pulmonary capillaries ↓	Decreased ventilation/perfusion equality
Muscle and joints	
Muscle mass ↓	
Number of Type II a and b fibers ↓	
Size of motor units ↓	
Action potential threshold ↓	Loss of strength and power
$(Ca^{++}$, myosin)-ATPase ↓	
Total protein and N_2 concentration ↓	
Size and number of mitochondria ↓	Decreased muscle respiratory capacity
Oxidative enzymes: SDH, cytochrome oxidase, and MDH ↓	Decreased muscle respiratory capacity
Lactate dehydrogenase ↓	Slowed glycolysis
Stiffness of connective tissue in joints ↑	Decreased joint stability and mobility
Accumulated mechanical stress in joints ↑	Stiffness, loss of flexibility, and osteoarthritis
Water content in intervertebral cartilage ↓	Atrophy and increased chance of compression fractures in spine
Bone	
Bone minerals ↓	Osteoporosis—increased risk of fracture
Body composition and stature	
Body fat ↑	Impaired mobility and increased risk of disease
Kyphosis ↑	Loss of height

SOURCE: G. A. Brooks and T. D. Fahey. Exercise Physiology: Human Bioenergetics and Its Applications. New York: Macmillan, 1984, pp. 685–686, Table 31-1.

366

Although little is known of the process, aging seems to be caused by aberrations in the genetic functions of cells. With time there is a progressive buildup of abnormal genetic material, which gradually impairs the ability of the cells to reproduce and function normally. This process undoubtedly affects the cellular communications systems, which control metabolic processes such as protein synthesis. This can result in the formation of tissues that do not function as well, such as stiff and brittle cartilage and inactive enzymes. This process can result in autoimmune syndromes that can cause the body to destroy its own tissues.

The aging process also seems to represent an accumulation of insults and wear-and-tear, which results in the gradual loss of the ability to adapt to stress. As we have seen, most physiological control mechanism are highly adaptable (see Chapter 1). Joints, for example, adapt to mobilization by maximizing their range of motion to the extent of the stress. If the joint is injured repeatedly over a lifetime, the joint capsule thickens resulting in a gradual loss of range of motion. Likewise, microtrauma in the circulation leads to the proliferation of smooth muscle and the formation of plaque and calcification that eventually impairs the ability of the vessels to vasodilate and thus adequately supply the tissues with blood (see Chapter 16). Theoretically, lifelong endurance training that reduces resting and submaximal exercise heart rate might decrease the degree of arterial microtrauma, thus resulting in less extensive development of coronary artery disease.

Although the maximum life span is finite, the quality of life is extremely variable. Exercise seems to be an important factor in maximizing physiological functions throughout life. Research has shown that physical activity has significant effects on many biological activities. In fact, for some processes, it almost appears to make "time stand still."

The Aging Process and the Effects of Exercise

The effects of aging touches both cellular function and systemic regulation (Table 15-2). Peak physiological function, for the most part, occurs at about 30 years of age. After that, most factors decline at a rate of about 0.75 to 1% a year. The decline in physical capacity is characterized by a decrease in $\dot{V}_{O_2max}$, maximal cardiac output, muscle strength and power, neural function, flexibility, and increased body fat. All of these factors can be positively affected by training. In fact, remarkable levels of performance are possible, particularly if physical training has been maintained throughout life.

Exercise training does not retard the aging process, it just allows the individual to perform at a higher level. Comparisons of trained and sedentary individuals indicate a similar decrease in work capacity with age. Of course, the trained subjects achieved a higher level of performance at all ages. In some cases the decrease in performance is greater in the trained than the untrained individual, indicating the difficulty of maintaining a high physical capacity with advancing age (Figure 15-9).

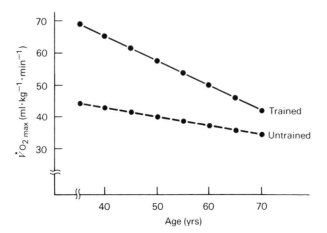

Figure 15-9
The effects of age on $\dot{V}_{O_2max}$ ($ml \cdot kg^{-1} \cdot min^{-1}$) in trained and sedentary men. With age, trained men lose a relatively higher percentage of functional capacity than sedentary men. This may reflect a difficulty in maintaining a trained state with increasing age, or perhaps decreased training volume and intensity with time.

Cardiovascular Capacity $\dot{V}_{O_2max}$ decreases approximately 30% between the ages of 20 and 65 (Figure 15-9). This occurs because of decreases in maximal heart rate, stroke volume, and arteriovenous oxygen difference. Thus, aging produces decreases in both oxygen transport and oxygen extraction capacities.

During submaximal exercise, heart rate is higher at any given work rate. Maximum heart rate decreases progressively with age (Figure 15-10). Also, cardiovascular drift is greater in the aged. Cardiovascular drift is the tendency of physiological factors such as heart rate, core temperature, and ventilation to rise at a constant work rate. There is also a longer recovery rate for both submaximal and maximal exercise. The effects of aging on functional capacity are summarized in Table 15-3.

Aging impairs the heart's capacity to pump blood. There is a gradual loss of contractile strength caused, in part, by a decrease in Ca^{++}-myosin ATPase activity. The heart wall stiffens, which delays ventricular filling. This delay decreases maximum heart rate and perhaps stroke volume. The impairments in maximal heart rate and stroke volume result in substantial decreases in cardiac output.

Numerous cellular changes occur in the cardiovascular system that help explain its diminished capacity to transport gases and substrates (see Table 15-2). There is a decreased elasticity in the major blood vessels and in the heart. This is usually accompanied by narrowing of the blood vessels in the muscles, heart, and other organs. Heart mass usually decreases, and fibrotic changes sometimes occur in the heart valves. The fiber/capillary ratio is reduced, which impairs the blood flow to the muscles. Also, the venous valves deteriorate. These valves serve to keep blood flowing toward the heart (see Chapter 7).

These changes have several consequences for cardiovascular perfor-

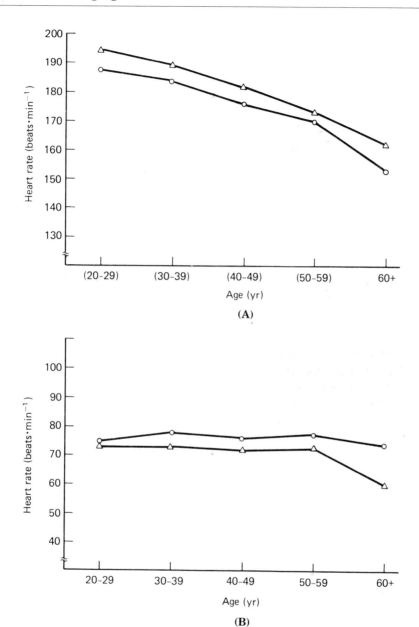

Figure 15-10

Fiftieth percentile of maximal *(A)* and resting *(B)* heart rate with age. Triangle = males; circles = females.

(SOURCE: Data from M. Pollock, J. H. Wilmore, and S. M. Fox. Health and Fitness Through Physical Activity. New York: John Wiley, 1978. In: G. A. Brooks and T. D. Fahey. Exercise Physiology: Human Bioenergetics and Its Applications. New York: Macmillan, 1984, p. 689, Table 31-2.)

TABLE 15-3 Changes in Functional Capacity and Body Composition with Age in Males

Effect	Age (year)	
	20	**60**
$\dot{V}_{O_2max}$ (ml·kg^{-1}·min^{-1})	39	29
Maximal heart rate (beats·min^{-1})	194	162
Resting heart rate (beats·min^{-1})	63	62
Maximal stroke volume (ml)	115	100
Maximal (a − v) O$_2$ difference (ml·liter^{-1})	150	140
Maximal cardiac output (liters·min^{-1})	22	16
Resting systolic blood pressure (mm Hg)	121	131
Resting diastolic blood pressure (mm Hg)	80	81
Total lung capacity (liters)	6.7	6.5
Vital capacity (liters)	5.1	4.4
Residual lung volume (liters)	1.5	2.0
Percentage fat	20.1	22.3

SOURCE: G. A. Brooks and T. D. Fahey. Exercise Physiology: Human Bioenergetics and Its Applications. New York: Macmillan, 1984, p. 690, Table 31-2.

mance. Vascular stiffness increases the peripheral resistance to blood flow, which forces the heart to work harder to push blood into the circulation and increases myocardial oxygen consumption at a given intensity of effort. Cardiac hypoxia can ensue because of atherosclerotic changes in the coronary arteries. The higher peripheral resistance also raises systolic blood pressure at rest and during maximal exercise.

Arteriovenous oxygen difference decreases, which contributes to the diminished aerobic capacity. This occurs because of a reduction in the fiber/capillary ratio, total hemoglobin, and the respiratory capacity of muscle. Muscle mitochondria decrease in size and number along with decreases in several oxidative enzymes.

There also seems to be a diminished capacity of autonomic reflexes that control blood flow. At rest, circulation to the skin is often poor, which can make peripheral body parts uncomfortably cold. During physical activity, a disproportionate amount of blood is directed to the skin, which can further hamper oxygen extraction. Additionally, the elderly are more subject to orthostatic intolerance; they sometimes have difficulty maintaining blood pressure when going from a horizontal to a vertical posture.

Endurance training induces improvements in aerobic capacity in the aged that are similar to those in young people. Most studies indicate that gains of about 20% in $\dot{V}_{O_2max}$ can be expected in a 6-month endurance exercise program. As in the young, individual differences can be accounted for by initial fitness, motivation, intensity and duration of the program, and genetic characteristics.

Endurance training results in a decrease in submaximal heart rate at a given work load, decreased resting and exercise systolic blood pressure, and faster recovery heart rate. Abnormal electrocardiographic findings, such as ST segment depression, have also been shown to improve (this finding has not been replicated by the majority of investigators). Although the reason for this is unclear, it could be due to reduced oxygen consumption in the heart, or perhaps (less likely) to the development of coronary collateral circulation.

Pulmonary Function The normal lung enjoys a large reserve capacity that can meet ventilatory requirements even during maximal exercise. The reserve capacity begins to deteriorate gradually between 30 and 60 years of age, with an acceleration after that. This process may be faster if the individual is a smoker or is chronically subjected to significant amounts of airborne contaminants.

The three most important changes that occur in this system with aging are a gradual increase in the size of the alveoli, the disintegration of the elastic support structure of the lungs, and a weakening of the respiratory muscles. These changes can interfere with the ventilation and perfusion of the lung, both of which can impair the oxygen transport capacity (see Chapters 5 and 6).

Enlargement of alveoli also occurs in chronic obstructive pulmonary disease (see Chapter 16). Thus, it is difficult to separate the effects of disease from those of aging. Alveolar enlargement is accompanied by a decrease in pulmonary vascularization. Both of these changes decrease the effective area available for diffusion.

The loss of pulmonary elasticity and the weakening of respiratory muscles can have a marked affect during exercise. Both of these changes make expiration more difficult and increase the work of breathing (the oxygen cost of moving air in and out of the lungs). The loss of elastic recoil results in premature closing of airways, which impairs ventilation in some of the alveoli. Because of the restrictions of flow, there is an increased dependence on breathing frequency, rather than tidal volume, for ventilation during increasing intensities of exercise.

The deterioration of pulmonary function is similar in magnitude to those in the cardiovascular system. So, unless the decline in pulmonary function is accentuated by disease, ventilation remains adequate during exercise in the aged. Ventilation does not seem to limit endurance performance in the young or old. Rather, cardiac output is probably the most important limiting factor.

Training will increase maximum ventilation, but the improvements parallel those of cardiac output. Although the breathing muscles can be strengthened through exercise, most of the changes are irreversible. Because of the large reserve capacity of the lungs, however, the changes can be tolerated quite well.

Skeletal System Bone loss is a serious problem in older people, particularly in women. Women begin to lose bone mineral at about 30 and men at about 50 years of age. Bone loss, called osteoporosis, results in bone with less density and strength. Osteoporosis increases the risk of fracture, which drastically increases the short-term mortality rate. One study found a 50% death rate within 1 year after hip fractures.

Although the cause of bone loss in the aged is not completely understood, it seems to be related to a combination of factors including inactivity, diet, skeletal blood flow, and endocrine function. These factors may induce a negative calcium balance that steadily saps the bones of this important mineral.

Exercise has been shown to be important in the prevention and treatment of osteoporosis. Bones, like other tissues, adapt to stresses placed on them. They become stronger when stressed and weaker when not stressed. Even extremely fit astronauts show some bone loss when their bones are not subjected to the stresses of gravity. Bone mineral content can be maintained by exercise, even in people more than 80 years of age.

Joints   Joints become less stable and less mobile with age. Aging is often associated with degradation of collagen fibers, fibrous synovial membranes, joint surface deterioration, and decreased viscosity of synovial fluid. Joint stiffness and loss of flexibility are common in the elderly. In fact, some researchers feel that osteoarthritis is a natural result of the aging process. It is interesting to note that articular cartilage, which is avascular, is supplied with nutrients only when it is bathed in synovial fluid, a process associated with compression and decompression during movement.

It is difficult to separate aging from accumulated wear and tear. Trauma to joint cartilage results in the formation of scar tissue, characterized by the buildup of fibrous material that makes the connective tissue stiffer and less responsive to stress. This can result in a thickened joint capsule, often containing debris, which impairs range of motion. Osteoarthritis in the elderly is located principally in areas receiving the most mechanical stress. It is unclear, therefore, if the restricted range of motion found in the joints is primarily the result of aging or of repeated trauma. Range of motion exercises have been shown to dramatically increase flexibility in a relatively short time. It is improbable, however, that exercise can significantly undo damage to joints that have undergone extensive degeneration.

Skeletal Muscle   Marked deterioration in muscle mass occurs with aging. It is characterized by decreases in the size and number of muscle fibers, decreases in the muscles' respiratory capacity, and increases in connective tissue and fat. These changes can have severe consequences in the elderly: mobility may be hampered, incidents of soft tissue pain are more common, and work capacity is impaired. Aging results in decreases in isometric and dynamic strength and in speed of movement.

There is a loss of fibers from individual motor units. This results in less available contractile force when a motor unit is recruited. The nature of the motor units also changes: there is a selective loss of Type II fibers (fast twitch muscles), which diminishes available strength and power.

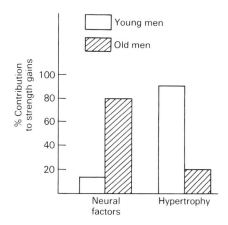

Figure 5-11

Relative contribution of neural factors and hypertrophy toward strength gains in young and old men following 8 weeks of training. Note that while the relative strength gains were equal, hypertrophy contributes most to strength in the young, while neural factors are most important in the old.

(SOURCE: Data from T. Moritani and H. A. DeVries.)

The loss of the muscle's biochemical capacity is characterized by decreased activity of oxidative and glycolytic enzymes. In very old age, there is evidence of the formation of incomplete or inactive enzymes. Some researchers have found decreases in the size and number of mitochondria (size of the mitochondrial reticulum). All of these changes will affect ATP production and thus impair physical working capacity.

The mechanisms involved in muscle contraction are also impaired, which contributes to the loss of strength and power. Aging muscle is less excitable and has a greater refractory period. Thus, a greater stimulus is needed for contraction and a longer period of time is required before the muscle can respond to another stimulus. Myosin ATPase activity, ATP, and CP are also reduced, particularly in fast twitch muscle, which further impairs muscle function.

Relative strength changes from training are similar in the young and old, at least in short-term programs. Because of the difficulty conducting such research, available data are restricted to observations of a few months. These studies indicate a fundamental difference in the way the elderly increase strength. Young men increase strength primarily by hypertrophy, whereas old people (and young women) increase strength by increased neural stimulation. Thus, the young improve the contractile capacity of the fibers, while the elderly rely on improved motor unit recruitment (Figure 15-11). The diminished capacity for hypertrophy in older males may be related to decreases in testosterone.

It is extremely doubtful that the parity in strength gains between young and old would continue for more than a few months. As the elderly have a limited ability for muscle hypertrophy, they would probably quickly reach their maximum strength potential because of the finite number of motor units available for recruitment.

Body Composition and Stature   There are marked changes in body composition and stature with age. Body weight increases steadily beginning in the 20s and continues to increase until about 55 or 60 years, and then begins to decline. Height decreases gradually. Weight gain is accompanied by increased body fat and decreased lean body mass. Males advance from an average of 15% fat at 17 years to about 28% at 60. Women change from about 25% at 17 years to about 39% at 60 years. These values are highly variable and tend to be much less in the trained individual. The distribution of fat tends to change in aging. There is tendency for a greater proportion of the total body fat to be located internally rather than subcutaneously.

Increased body fat with age is of concern because of its possible relationship with disease and premature mortality. Exercise is extremely important in managing body composition in the elderly. Metabolic rate slows with age, which necessitates a low caloric diet to maintain a normal body composition (This decrease in BMR is probably largely caused by a decrease in lean body mass and an increase in fat). The low-calorie diet of many elderly people is often low in the necessary vitamins and minerals. Regular exercise enables the elderly to consume more calories, which allows them to satisfy their nutritional requirements.

Stature decreases with age as a result of an increased kyphosis, or rounding of the back, compression of intravertebral disks, and deterioration of vertabrae. A cross-sectional study by Durin and Womersley showed a 6-cm decrease in height between 17-and 60-year-olds. This, of course, may represent modern trends of increased height; however, loss of height with age is well documented.

Neural Function   Many neurophysiological changes occur with aging. Again, it is often difficult to separate the changes resulting from aging from those caused by disease. The principal changes include decreased visual acuity, hearing loss, deterioration of short-term memory, inability to handle several pieces of information simultaneously, and decreased reaction time.

Physical training seems to have little effect on the deterioration of neural function. A study by Heikkninen and coworkers could find no difference in neurobiological factors between extremely fit elderly endurance athletes and sedentary men. They concluded that the effects of endurance training in the elderly are largely limited to functions that are apparently relevant to physical performance. In other words, exercise training will improve performance in the elderly, but it will not prevent aging.

Exercise Prescription for the Elderly

The principles of exercise prescription (see Chapter 17) apply to people of all ages. However, because of the increased risk of exercise for the elderly, caution is required. Electrocardiographic abnormalities, particularly during exercise, are regular findings in the elderly. Aberrations such as ST segment depression, heart blocks, and arrhythmias are common enough to warrant routine exercise stress testing for any elderly person wishing to undertake an exercise program.

Great care must be taken when determining the type and intensity of exercise. In a sedentary person the exercise should be one that minimizes soft tissue injuries. Good choices are walking and swimming. More vigorous exercise, such as running and racquetball, should be attempted only when the person has achieved sufficient fitness.

Ideally, the intensity of exercise should coincide with the target heart rate. As discussed in Chapter 17, this is calculated from the maximal heart rate, which is often predicted from the formula: $HR_{max} = 220 - age$. This method may be particularly inaccurate in the elderly, however, and may lead to problems with their exercise prescription. Although this method is fairly accurate for estimating maximal heart rate at the 50th percentile of the population, it does not take into consideration the tremendous variability observed in the older age group. Maximal heart rates in people over 60 can range from highs of over 200 to lows of 105 beats per minute. Thus, target heart rates predicted on the basis of age can often either underestimate or overestimate the ideal exercise intensity. An accurate measurement of maximal heart rate is preferable to a predicted one.

Very often older people have misperceptions about physical conditioning. They sometimes underestimate their stamina and, consequently, exercise at extremely low intensities. In some elderly persons, it is important to increase the frequency of exercise until sufficient fitness is developed to also increase the intensity.

Summary

The growth process is similar in all people and must be considered when assessing exercise capacity and designing training programs. The growth curve follows an S shape, with rapid increases in height and weight occurring during the first 2 years, followed by a declining growth rate during childhood, and an accelerated rate during puberty. During childhood, the relative changes are similar in both sexes, although girls tend to be more mature than boys. The gradual growth rate during childhood is conducive to learning gross motor skills.

Adolescence is a period of rapid growth during which the child attains sexual maturity. Males, who attain puberty later than females, develop greater height and weight with larger musculature and broader shoulders, while females develop larger hips. Males experience large improvements in all areas of physical performance, while females tend to level off in most areas. The reasons for these sex differences in performance seem to be based as much in sociology as physiology. Adolescence may be a critical period for the development of many types of physical abilities.

Exercise appears to be important for optimal skeletal development. Trauma can cause injury to the bone growth centers, which could affect growth. Caution should be exercised when prescribing activities that are potentially dangerous to these bone growth centers.

The prevention of obesity is particularly important during periods of rapid growth because fat cells are proliferating during these times. It may be that regular exercise and proper diet during growth may prevent the development of some fat cells and thus be a factor in lifelong weight control.

The effects of aging are difficult to separate from those of degenerative diseases and deconditioning. However, it is clear that aging takes its toll on almost every facet of physiological function. Although the life span of any species is identifiable within relatively narrow limits, the quality of life can be extremely variable. Clearly, regular exercise training can improve the quality of life by increasing physical capacity or at least slowing its deterioration.

After 30 years of age, most physiological functions decline at a rate of approximately 0.75 to 1% a year. The decline in physical capacity is characterized by a decrease in $\dot{V}_{O_2,max}$, maximal cardiac output, muscle strength and power, neural function, flexibility, and increased body fat.

Although exercise does not appear to retard the aging process, it does improve functional capacity. Older people cannot reach the same absolute physical capacity as the young, but they can improve by about the same relative percentage.

Selected Readings

ADAMS, G., and H. DEVRIES. Physiological effects of an exercise training regimen upon women aged 52–79. J. Gerontol. 28:50–55, 1973.

ALBINSON, J.G., and G.M. ANDREW. Child in Sport and Physical Activity. Baltimore: University Park Press, 1976.

ÅSTRAND, P.-O. Human physical fitness with special reference to sex and age. Physiol. Rev. 36:307–335, 1956.

BARNARD, J., G. GRIMDITCH, and J. WILMORE. Physiological characteristics of sprint and endurance runners. Med. Sci. Sports 11:167–171, 1979.

BAR-OR, O. Pediatric Sports Medicine. New York: Academic Press, 1984.

BAR-OR, O., R. SHEPARD, and C.L. ALLEN. Cardiac output of 10- to 13-year-old boys and girls during submaximal exercise. J. Appl. Physiol. 30:219–223, 1971.

BORTZ, W.M. Effect of exercise on aging—effect of aging on exercise. J. Am. Geriat. Soc. 28:49–51, 1980.

DALLMAN, P.R. and M.A. SIMES. Percentile curves for hemoglobin and red cell volume in infancy and childhood. J. Pediatr. 94:26–31, 1979.

DANIELS, J., N. OLDRIDGE, F. NAGLE, and B. WHITE. Differences and changes in VO_{2max} among young runners 10 to 18 years of age. Med. Sci. Sports 10:200–203, 1978.

DEHN, M.M. and R.A. BRUCE. Longitudinal variations in maximal oxygen uptake with age and activity. J. Appl. Physiol. 33:805–807, 1972.

DEVRIES, H. Physiological effects of an exercise training program regimen upon men aged 52 to 88. J. Gerontol. 25:325–336, 1970.

DEVRIES, H. Tips on prescribing exercise regimens for your older patient. Geriatrics 35:75–81, 1979.

DUDA, M. "Prepubertal strength training gains support." Physician Sports Med. 14(2):157–161, 1986.

DURIN, J., and J. WOMERSLEY. Body fat assessed from total body density and its estimation from skinfold thicknesses: measurement on 481 men and women aged from 16 to 72 years. Br. J. Nutr. 32:77–97, 1974.

EKBLOM, B. Effect of physical training in adolescent boys. J. Appl. Physiol. 27:350–355, 1969.

ERIKSSON, B. Muscle metabolism in children—a review. Acta Paediatr. Scand. (Suppl.) 283:20–28, 1980.

ERIKSSON, B., I. ENGSTROM, P. KARLBERG, A. LUNDIN, B. SALTIN, and C. THOREN. Long-term effect of previous swim training in girls. A 10-year-follow-up of the "girl swimmers." Acta Paediatr. Scand. 67:285–292, 1978.

ERIKSSON, O., and B. SALTIN. Muscle metabolism during exercise in boys aged 11 to 16 years compared to adults. Acta Paediatr. Belg. 28 (Suppl.): 257–265, 1974.

FAHEY, T.D., A. DELVALLE-ZURIS, G. OEHLSEN, M. TRIEB, and J. SEYMOUR. Pubertal stage differences in hormonal and hematological responses to maximal exercise in males. J. Appl. Physiol. 46:823–827, 1979.

GORDON, T., W.B. KANNEL, M.C. HJORTLAND, and P.M. MCNAMARA. Menopause and coronary heart disease, the Framingham study. Ann. Int. Med. 89:157–161, 1978.

KLISSOURAS, V. Prediction of Athletic Performance: Genetic Considerations. Can. J. Appl. Sport Sci. 1:195–200, 1976.

KLISSOURAS, V., F. PIRNAY, and J. PETIT. Adaptation to maximal effort: genetics and age. J. Appl. Physiol. 35:288–293, 1973.

LARSON, L. (ed.). Fitness, Health, and Work Capacity. New York: Macmillan, 1974, pp. 435–450, 516–524.

MACEK, M., J. VAVRA, and J. NOVOSADOVA. Prolonged exercise in prepubertal boys. Cardiovascular and metabolic adjustment. Eur. J. App. Physiol. 35:291–298, 1976.

MALINA, R.M. Growth and Development: The First Twenty Years in Man. Minneapolis: Burgess, 1975.

MALINA, R.M. Growth, maturation, and human performance. In: G.A. Brooks. Perspectives on the Academic Discipline of Physical Education. Champaign, Ill.: Human Kinetics, 1981, pp. 190–210.

MEEN, H.D., and S. OSEID. Physical activity in children and adolescents in relation to growth and development. Scand. J. Soc. Med. 29 (Suppl.): 121–134, 1982.

MIRWALD, R., D.A. BAILEY, N. CAMERON, and R.L. RASMUSSEN. Longitudinal comparison of aerobic power in active and inactive boys aged 7 to 17 years. Ann. Human Biol. 8:405–414, 1981.

MURASE, Y., K. KOBAYASHI, S. KAMEI, and H. MATSUI. Longitudinal study of aerobic power in superior junior athletes. Med. Sci. Sports Exercise 13:180–184, 1981.

NIINIMAA, V., and R. J. SHEPHARD. Training and oxygen conductance in the elderly. J. Gerontology 33:354–367, 1978.

ORLANDER, J., and A. ANIANSSON. Effects of physical training on skeletal muscle metabolism and ultrastructure. Acta Physiol. Scand. 109:149–154, 1980.

PARIZKOVA, J. Longitudinal study of the development of body composition and body build in boys of various physical activity. Human Biol. 40:212–223, 1968.

RARICK, G.L. (ed.). Physical Activity: Human Growth and Development. New York: Academic Press, 1973.

RARICK, G.L. The emergence of the study of human motor development. In: G.A. Brooks. Perspectives on the Academic Discipline of Physical Education. Champaign, Ill.: Human Kinetics, 1981, pp. 163–184.

ROCHE, A.F. and R.M. MALINA. Manual of Physical Status and Performance in Childhood. New York: Plenum Press, 1983.

RUTENFRANZ, J., K. ANDERSEN, V. SELIGER, F. KLIMMER, I. BERNDT, and M. RUPPEL. Maximum aerobic power and body composition during the puberty growth period: similarities and differences between children of two European countries. Eur. J. Pediatr. 136:123–133, 1981.

SALTIN, B., and G. GRIMBY. Physiological analysis of middle-aged and former athletes. Circulation 38:1104–1115, 1968.

SALTIN, B., L. HARTLEY, A. KILBOM, and I. ASTRAND. Physical training in sedentary middle-aged and older men. Scand. J. Clin. Lab. Invest. 24:323–334, 1969.

SHEPARD, R. Physical Activity and Aging. Chicago: Year Book Publishers, 1978.

SIDNEY, K., and R.J. SHEPARD. Frequency and intensity of exercise training for elderly subjects. Med. Sci. Sports 10:125–131, 1978.

SMITH, E., and R. SERFASS (eds.). Exercise and Aging. Hillside, N.J.: Enslow Publishers, 1981.

STAMFORD, B.A. Physiological effects of training upon institutionalized geriatric men. J. Gerontology 27:451–455, 1972.

STERN, J., and M. GREENWOOD. A review of development of adipose cellularity in man and animals. Fed. Proc. 33:1952–1955, 1974.

SUOMINEN, H., E. HEIKKINEN, T. PARKATTI, S. FORSBERG, and A. KIISKINEN. Effects of lifelong physical training on functional aging in men. Scand. J. Soc. Med. (Suppl.) 14:225–240, 1980.

TIMIRAS, P.S. Developmental Physiology and Aging. New York: Macmillan, 1972.

VACCARO, P., C.W. ZAUNER, and W.F. UPDYKE. Resting and exercise respiratory function in well trained child swimmers. J. Sports Med. Phys. Fitness 17:297–306, 1977.

WEBER, G., W. KARTODIHARDJO, and V. KLISSOURAS. Growth and physical training with reference to heredity. J. Appl. Physiol. 40:211–215, 1976.

16

Exercise and Disease

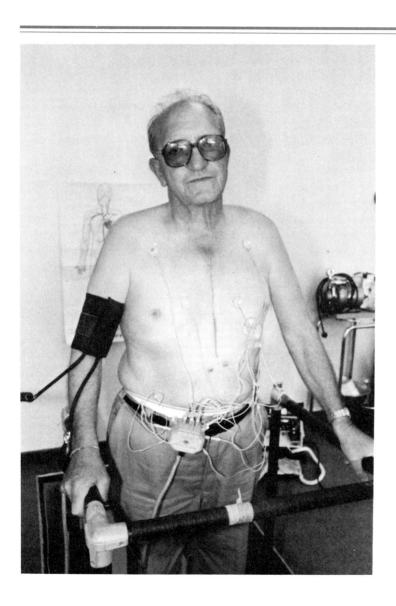

Exercise is currently being used as an adjunct treatment for many diseases such as coronary heart disease, hypertension, diabetes, asthma, and arthritis. Exercise training increases functional capacity (improving the quality of life), and can often positively affect the disease process. For example, exercise has been shown to lessen the risk of heart disease, reduce the insulin requirement in Type I diabetics (insulin-dependent diabetics), and improve pulmonary function in asthmatics. Because exercise training is potentially dangerous in people with various diseases, however, physical activity programs must be applied judiciously.

People in various diseased states are notoriously inactive. During the past 10 years, many medical experts have recognized that inactivity and bed rest contribute to the debilitation that usually accompanies most diseases. Just as training results in improvement in physical working capacity, inactivity leads to deterioration. For example, until quite recently, treatment for cardiac and postoperative patients involved prolonged bed rest. However, the forced inactivity resulted in additional difficulties that were sometimes worse than the original problem.

The influence of exercise on many diseases and the susceptibility to illness is only beginning to be understood. For example, little is known of the effect of training on the immune system. Although the few published studies indicate that moderate exercise (e.g., 8-mile run) has no effect on immune responses in healthy people, more chronic, severe exercise might have negative consequences. Certainly, people who are involved in exercise prescription should realize that exercise is potentially destructive if the duration or intensity of training is excessive for the individual.

This chapter will present an overview of the indications and contraindications of exercise in selected diseases.

The Dangers of Bed Rest and Deconditioning

As shown in Table 16-1, bed rest has far-reaching effects on most aspects of physiological function. Studies overwhelmingly show that decreased function or inactivity of an organ results in serious functional and histochemical changes. In many instances, disease can be made worse by prolonged bed rest, and sometimes irreversible problems can develop. It is little wonder that current treatment for the postoperative patient and for most diseases calls for early ambulation and physical activity.

The negative effects of bed rest seem to be due primarily to the decrease in hydrostatic pressure (fluid pressure within the body, mainly influenced by gravity) within the cardiovascular system, lower energy expenditure due to inactivity, decreased pressure on the skeleton, and psychological stress. These negative effects are also seen in healthy astronauts exposed to hypogravity.

TABLE 16-1 Effects of Prolonged Bed Rest on Physiological Function

Decreases	Increases	No Effect
Maximum stroke volume	Maximum heart rate	Mean corpuscular hemoglobin concentration
Orthostatic tolerance	Diastolic blood pressure	Forced vital capacity
Arterial vasomotor tone	Resting heart rate	Resting or exercise arteriovenous O_2 difference
Systolic time interval	Extra vascular and intravascular IgG[a]	
Coronary blood flow	Submaximal exercise heart rate	Vital capacity
Maximal O_2 consumption		Maximum voluntary ventilation
Pulmonary capillary blood volume	Submaximal exercise cardiac output	Total lung capacity
Plasma volume	Sleep disturbances	Proprioceptive reflexes
Skin blood flow	Diuresis	
Total diffusing capacity	Incidence of urinary infection	
Cerebrovascular tone	Incidence of deep vein thrombosis	
Sweating threshold temperature	Urinary excretion of calcium and phosphorus	
Vasomotor heat loss capacity	Nitrogen excretion	
Red blood cell production	Serum corticosteroids	
Red cell mass	Cultured staphylococci in nasal mucosa	
Hemoglobin	Extracellular fluid	
Serum proteins	Tendency to faint	
Serum albumin	Incidence of constipation	
Intracellular fluid volume	Cholesterol	
Serum electrolytes	Low-density lipoproteins	
Coagulating capacity of blood	Growth hormone	
Bone calcium	Electrocardiographic ST-segment depression	
Bone density	Renal diurnal rhythms	
Insulin sensitivity		
Acceleration tolerance		
Blood flow to extremities		
Catecholamines		
Serum androgens in males		
Muscular strength and mass		
Muscle tone		
Leukocyte phagocytic function		
Visual acuity		
Resistance to infection		
Systolic blood pressure		
Balance		

[a] Immunoglobulin G.

The most profound changes from bed rest occur in the cardiovascular system. Impairments include diminished capacity of the heart, reduced plasma and blood volumes, and impaired control of the blood vessels. Maximal oxygen uptake and work capacity decrease from as little as 1% to as much as 26%, depending on the type and duration of confinement. For example, the effects of bed rest are much less devastating if the patient is allowed to sit during confinement. In the seated posture, hydrostatic pressure is greater in most blood vessels, so that the deconditioning effects are less severe.

Bed rest also produces orthostatic intolerance, the inability of the circulation to adjust to the upright posture. The reduction in hydrostatic pressure in the horizontal position seems to be the primary stimulus for this phenomenon. When a bedridden patient assumes an upright posture, there is a sudden decrease in venous return of blood to the heart resulting from reduced cardiovascular tone, blood volume, and muscle tone. The heart rate increases rapidly in an attempt to increase cardiac output. However, blood pressure falls and cerebral blood flow is impaired, leading to dizziness and fainting. Orthostatic intolerance is a good example of how bed rest can worsen a disease state. In a heart patient, the decreased stroke volume, blood pressure, coronary blood flow, and myocardial contractility can sometimes lead to heart failure or reinfarction.

Bed rest also affects muscle and bone. There is a marked decrease in muscle tone that is accompanied by a loss of muscular strength and endurance. Little change occurs in body weight, however, because the loss of lean body mass is usually accompanied by an increase in fat. Bone demineralization occurs at a rapid rate during bed rest. This is due to reduced longitudinal stress on the bones rather than to inactivity. The dissolution occurs at different rates in the various parts of the skeleton. The weight-bearing bones are particularly vulnerable: because they are under the most stress, they have the most to lose during deconditioning.

The effects of prolonged bed rest are usually reversible with adequate ambulation. The physiological effects, if not too advanced, can be reversed with an appropriate training program. One problem is that the negative effects of bed rest lead to a vicious circle, particularly in the elderly: disuse leads to debilitation, which leads to a further desire to stay in bed or remain inactive.

The negative adaptability resulting from inactivity certainly has implications for the athlete or individual interested in a high level of fitness. Although the atrophy in muscles of a casted leg or the debilitation experienced by the postoperative patient are extreme examples of physiological deterioration, the essence is similar in a highly conditioned individual who suddenly assumes a sedentary life-style—physiological processes adapt to the lower stresses with reduced functional capacity.

Coronary Heart Disease

Coronary heart disease (CHD) involves a steady buildup of atherosclerotic plaque in the coronary arteries, leading to diminished myocardial blood flow.

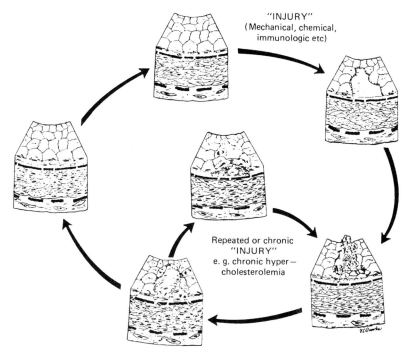

Figure 16-1

The response-to-injury hypothesis of the production of atheroma. The figure illustrates the response to a single *(outer cycle)* and repeated *(inner cycle)* injury. Endothelial injury results in smooth muscle proliferation and connective tissue formation. In the single event, the lesion heals and regresses. During chronic insult, the process accelerates and is accompanied by lipid deposition in the lesion..

(SOURCE: R. Ross and J. A. Glomset. The pathogenesis of atherosclerosis. N. Engl. J. Med. 295:369–377, 420–425, 1976. In: Brooks and Fahey, p. 505.)

The effect on the heart depends on the degree of ischemia (impaired blood flow). If blood flow is not totally blocked, but is insufficient to satisfy the myocardial oxygen demand, then angina (heart pain) or arrhythmias (abnormal electrical conduction patterns) can develop. If, however, blood flow is totally cut off, or reaches a critical level of ischemia, the damage is irreparable because anoxia does not merely hamper cardiac function, it leads to necrosis of cells. The death of a portion of the myocardium is commonly called a heart attack (clinically, a myocardial infarction or MI). Survivability, or the degree of impairment, depends largely on the amount of tissue destroyed.

Atherosclerosis, a form of arteriosclerosis, refers to the development of fibrotic, lipid-filled plaques in the walls of the larger arteries (Figure 16-1). The process involves smooth muscle proliferation from the media of the artery, lipid and mineral accumulation, and connective tissue formation in the inner lining of the arteries (arterial intima). Although the deadly effects of atherosclerosis are often centered in the heart, it can impair blood flow to all vital organs, including the brain, kidneys, and liver. Arteriosclerosis can result in extensive circulatory damage that is ultimately impervious to medical intervention. The most logical approach is to prevent the disease before it becomes life-threatening.

Current research indicates that prevention is possible. Some researchers believe that the process may be reversible, but the bulk of evidence does not support this contention. Although there is still much to be learned, the incidence of heart disease can be decreased by a systematic reduction in factors that increase the risk of heart disease (Table 16-2).

The Risk Factors of Coronary Heart Disease

Heart disease is the number one killer in countries such as the United States and Great Britain, while it is practically unknown in more than half the world. In most Western countries, heart disease begins to manifest itself during childhood. By age 20, it is estimated that 75% of white males have heart disease to a significant degree. Although females are less likely to suffer from coronary heart disease, they are experiencing an increase in incidence.

There has been a reduction in heart disease in the United States in recent years (Figure 16-2). The mechanisms of this decrease are unclear, but the increased awareness of CHD risk factors and the blossoming interest in preventive medicine may have played a role.

The three most important risk factors of coronary heart disease appear to be hyperlipidemia, hypertension, and cigarette smoking. Each of these can increase the chances of developing heart disease by 300%. A person who smokes two packs of cigarettes a day, or who has cholesterolemia above 260 mg $\cdot$ dl^{-1} (versus 180), or has a blood pressure greater than 150/90 mm Hg (versus less than 120/80) is three times more likely to develop the disease.

Other risk factors, such as sex (male gender), diabetes, type A behavior, stress, diet, age, family history, and inactivity, also increase the risk of heart disease, particularly when they are combined with other factors. Factors such as lack of physical fitness and obesity are considered particularly important, because they often directly affect other risk factors as well as exert an independent effect. Any program to reduce the risk of heart disease should include efforts to improve the diet, stop smoking, reduce stress, control diseases such as diabetes and hypertension, and exercise regularly.

Physical Activity and the Risk of Heart Disease

Until recently, lack of physical activity was classified as a minor risk factor in the development of coronary heart disease. However, recent evidence suggests that regular physical exercise is extremely important in reducing the

TABLE 16-2 Risk of Developing CHD

| Risk Factor | Relative Level of Risk | | | | |
	Very Low	Low	Moderate	High	Very High
Blood pressure (mm Hg)					
Systolic	<110	120	130–140	150–160	170>
Diastolic	<70	76	82–88	94–100	106>
Cigarettes (per day)	Never None in 1 yr	5	10–20	30–40	50>
Cholesterol (mg · 100 ml^{-1})	<180	200	220–240	260–280	300>
Triglycerides (mg · 100 ml^{-1})	<80	100	150	200	300>
Glucose (mg · 100 ml^{-1})	<80	90	100–110	120–130	140>
Body fat (%)					
Men	<12	16	22	25	30>
Women	<15	20	25	33	40>
Stress and tension	Almost never	Occasional	Frequent	Nearly constant	
Physical activity minutes above 6 cal · min^{-1} (5 METS)[a] per week	240	180–120	100	80–60	30<
ECG stress test abnormality (ST depression, mm)[b]	0	0	0.5	1	2>
Family history of premature heart attack[c] (blood relative)	0	1	2	3	4>
Age	<30	35	40	50	60>

[a] A MET is equal to the oxygen cost at rest. One MET is generally equal to 3.5 ml · kg^{-1} of body weight per minute of oxygen uptake or 1.2 cal · min^{-1}.

[b] Other ECG anormalities are also potentially dangerous and are not listed here.

[c] Premature heart attack refers to <60 years of age.

SOURCE: From M. L. Pollock, J. H. Wilmore, and S. M. Fox. Health and Fitness Through Physical Activity. New York: John Wiley, 1978, p. 78.

risk of the disease and the magnitude of other risk factors such as hypertension, obesity, and hyperlipidemia.

Since the early 1950s, epidemiological studies have demonstrated the relationship between physical activity and a reduced risk of heart disease. A number of studies compared active and sedentary populations: London bus drivers (sedentary) and bus conductors (active), postal clerks (sedentary) and postal deliverers (active), and active versus sedentary longshoremen (Figure 16-3). These studies have been criticized for being ex post facto (after the fact) investigations. It is possible that less coronary-prone individuals self-selected

385

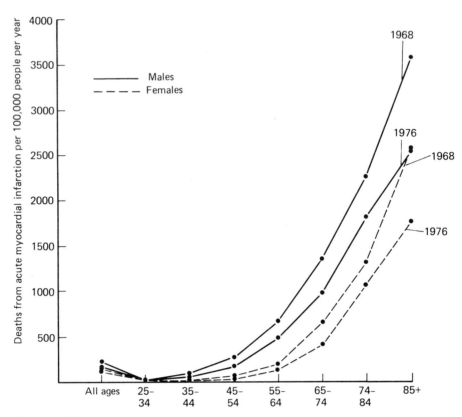

Figure 16-2

The chances in 100,000 of dying from acute myocardial infarction in 1968 and 1976 (all races). The decrease in mortality may be due to educational efforts to alter life-styles that increase the risk of coronary heart disease.

(SOURCE: G. A. Brooks and T. D. Fahey. Exercise Physiology: Human Bioenergetics and Its Applications. New York: Macmillan, 1984, p. 511.)

themselves into more active occupations. In addition, not all epidemiological studies demonstrated the reduced risk of CHD in more active occupations.

A fundamental problem in all of these population profile studies is the failure to adequately define the level of physical activity in the active and sedentary groups and to truly differentiate between the fit and unfit. A study by Cooper demonstrated an inverse relationship between the level of physical fitness, as measured on a treadmill test, and the risk of heart disease. Extremely fit people tended to be less fat, with lower blood pressure, cholesterol, triglycerides, uric acid, and glucose. Morris and coworkers showed that vigorous exercise during leisure time resulted in a substantial reduction in the risk of heart disease.

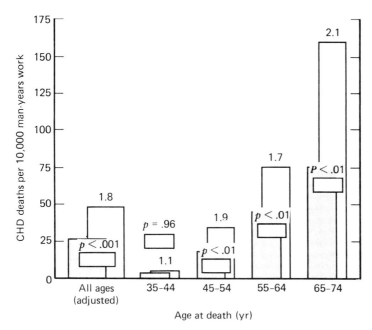

Figure 16-3
Deaths from CHD in long-shoremen according to physical activity of work (range in kcal · min^{-1}) and age at death: shaded bars = heavy activity (5.2–7.5); un-shaded bars = moderate and light activity (1.5–5.0); the relative risk (moderate and light/heavy) is given above the bars.

(SOURCE: R. S. Paffenbarger and W. E. Hale. Work activity and coronary heart disease. N. Engl. J. Med. 292:545–550, 1975. In: G. A. Brooks and T. D. Fahey. Exercise Physiology: Human Bioenergetics and Its Applica-tion: New York, Macmillan, 1984, p. 515.)

Recent studies using animals provide direct experimental evidence that moderate endurance exercise can result in a reduction of coronary atheroscle-rosis. Kramsch et al. demonstrated that exercising monkeys who were fed an atherogenic diet had substantially reduced overall atherosclerotic involve-ment, lesion size, and collagen accumulation than did sedentary controls. Further, the trained monkeys had larger hearts and wider coronary arteries (Figure 16-4). In contrast, the control animals, who were fed the same diet, suffered significant narrowing of the coronary arteries and, in one case, sud-den death.

Autopsies on marathon runners, who died from causes other than coro-nary heart disease, consistently find enlarged and widely patent coronary arteries. This does not actually prove that endurance training provides a measure of protection against the disease. It does, however, add to existing evidence pointing in that direction. Unfortunately, intensive endurance training does not appear to provide immunity from heart disease as was hypothesized by some researchers. There are well-documented reports of severe three- and four-vessel coronary artery disease in serious marathon runners.

A summary of the mechanisms by which physical activity may reduce the occurrence or severity of coronary heart disease appears in Table 16-3. Endurance training aids in a reduced risk of CHD by improving the meta-bolic capacity and affecting factors involved in the development of the dis-ease. Metabolic function is improved by such adaptations as increased elec-tron transport capacity, thyroid function, myocardial efficiency, efficiency of

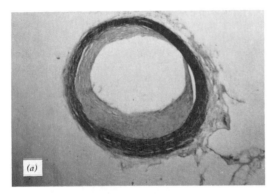

Figure 16-4
Micrographs of comparable sections of the left main coronary artery in sedentary *(a)* and active *(b)* monkeys on an atherogenic diet.

(SOURCE: D. M. Kramsch, A. J. Aspen, B. M. Abramowitz, T. Kreimendahl, and W. B. Hood. Reduction of coronary atherosclerosis by moderate conditioning exercise in monkeys on an atherogenic diet. N. Engl. J. Med. 305:1483–1489, 1981. In: G. A. Brooks and T. D. Fahey, Exercise Physiology: Human Bioenergetics and Its Applications: New York: Macmillan, 1984, p. 516.)

peripheral blood distribution and return, and decreased resting heart rate, submaximal exercise heart rate, arterial blood pressure (although exercise training increases blood pressure in some patients), and obesity. These factors lessen the load on the heart, thus decreasing the chance of developing ischemia. Other changes, such as decreased LDL, triglycerides, glucose intolerance, and platelet stickiness, may retard or reverse the process of atherosclerosis.

An effective exercise program instituted for the purpose of reducing the risk of coronary heart disease must be integrated with efforts to control other risk factors such as diet, stress, smoking, and hypertension. The exercise program must be appropriate for the individual and consider factors such as age, functional capacity, and existing diseases and physical limitations. Exercise prescription is discussed extensively in Chapter 17.

Cardiac Rehabilitation

Exercise therapy represents a radical change in philosophy and treatment of the cardiac and cardiac-prone patient. It has gained widespread acceptance

TABLE 16-3 Mechanics by Which Physical Activity May Reduce Occurrence or Severity of CHD

Increase	Decrease
Vessel size	Serum lipid levels:
HDL cholesterol	Triglycerides
Myocardial efficiency (ejection fraction and stroke volume at rest and during exercise)	LDL cholesterol
	HDL-C/LDL-C ratio
Efficiency of peripheral blood distribution and return	Glucose intolerance
	Obesity–adiposity
Electron-transport capacity	Platelet stickiness
Fibrinolytic capability	Arterial blood pressure
Red blood cell mass and blood volume	Heart rate
Thyroid function	Vulnerability to dysrhythmias
Tolerance to stress	Neurohormonal overreaction
Prudent living habits	"Strain" associated with psychic "stress"
"Joie de vivre"	Regional myocardial ischemia
Width of coronary artery lumina	Circulating catecholamines (rest)
Metabolic turnover of collagen in the heart	Reduction of size of atheroma
	Collagen accumulation in coronary arteries
Ventricular fibrillation threshold	

ᵃ Abbreviations: HDL-C high density lipoprotein cholesterol, LDL-C Low density lipoprotein cholesterol.

SOURCE: Adapted from S. M. Fox, J. P. Naughton, and W. L. Haskell. Physical activity and the prevention of coronary disease. Ann. Clin. Res. 3: 404–432, 1971; and W. L. Haskell. Cardiovascular benefits and risks of exercise: the scientific evidence. In: R. H. Strauss (ed.). *Sports Medicine*. Philadelphia: W. B. Saunders, 1984, p. 65.

as an important tool in returning these individuals to physiological and psychological competence. Myocardial infarction patients involved in a rehabilitation program have been found to experience an improved sense of well-being, reduced anxiety and depression, improved exercise capacity, reduced ST-segment depression on the electrocardiogram (this has not been consistently demonstrated), reduction in blood pressure, reduced heart rate at rest, reduced serum cholesterol and triglycerides, elevated high-density lipoprotein cholesterol, and perhaps reduced mortality rate.

Candidates for the program include people with documented myocardial infarction or stable angina pectoris, postoperative cardiovascular surgery patients following procedures such as myocardial revascularization (bypass surgery and angioplasty), peripheral arterial obstructive surgery, valve replacement, and repair of congenital heart defects, and those who are at high risk to develop heart disease because of significant predisposing factors. Patients with unstable conditions, such as those described in Table 17-1, are generally excluded from the program.

The heart patient suffers both physical and emotional distress. After a myocardial infarction or heart surgery, there is a loss of cardiac function due to injury and a loss of working capacity (fitness) because of deconditioning. In addition, the patient is faced with psychological difficulties stemming from fear of death or disability, and the perception of a changing life-style that could affect family, friends, economic well-being, and employment.

A primary goal of the cardiac rehabilitation program is to help the patient return to his or her quality of life before onset of the event and to develop optimal physiological function. Initially, this consists of doing simple tasks such as dressing and showering; ultimately, it may include resumption of physically demanding occupations and recreational activities. Ideally, rehabilitation will return the individual to an acceptable level physiologically, mentally, socially, vocationally, and economically.

Exercise training has been shown to play an important role in the rehabilitation of most coronary patients. Physical activity should be integrated with a total program that includes cessation of cigarette smoking, weight control, proper diet, and return to work and a normal social life. Interestingly, some heart patients actually improve their fitness from before their heart attack. The cardiac event provides potent motivation to become more active and increase awareness of coronary risk factors.

The ideal cardiac rehabilitation program consists of three phases: the inpatient program (Phase I), the outpatient therapeutic program (Phase II), and the exercise maintenance program (Phase III). Exercise prescription for cardiac patients is discussed in Chapter 17.

The inpatient program is conducted in the hospital during the early period following the myocardial infarction or cardiovascular surgery. Early activity has been shown to reduce anxiety and depression and to prevent some of the adverse effects of bed rest. In addition, the program helps to provide both the physiological and psychological climate for resumption of normal activities. The inpatient program includes appropriate medical treatment, patient and family education, and graded physical activity. By the end of this phase the patient should be able to meet low-level demands of daily activity such as dressing, showering, toilet, and walking up a flight of stairs.

The outpatient therapeutic program is also usually conducted in the hospital and includes supervised exercise, vocational rehabilitation, and behavioral counseling. The exercise program is typically held at least 3 days a week and is closely monitored (ECG is observed during exercise) by a nurse, physical therapist, or exercise physiologist (who are physician supervised). Occupational task simulation is conducted to ensure that the individual is physiologically prepared to resume work.

Symptom-limited treadmill testing is important in exercise prescription in early exercise programs and is typically administered prior to discharge from the hospital. In addition, patients should be retested periodically to detect late-occurring ischemia and arrhythmias and to reassess the exercise prescription.

A principal goal of the high-level outpatient program is to develop a functional capacity of 8 METS or 28 to 30 ml $O_2 \cdot kg^{-1} \cdot min^{-1}$. This will produce a fitness that will serve the needs of a sedentary life-style and act as a minimum criteria for discharge from the outpatient program. A person typically remains in most outpatient programs for about 3 months after a myocardial infarction.

The outpatient program allows the physician to ensure satisfactory medical status by reviewing resting and exercise ECG, blood pressure response to various stimuli, and symptoms. Additionally, patients can obtain the necessary education about the nature of heart disease and the signs and symptoms associated with their problem.

The exercise maintenance program is ideally conducted in an environment especially organized for cardiac and risk-prone individuals. Many fine programs have been established through hospitals, the YMCA, university physical education departments, medical schools, and private clinics. The purpose of this phase of the cardiac rehabilitation program is to prevent recurrence and to improve physical working capacity. This program can be used to evaluate the status and effectiveness of treatment regimens in the patient, maintain patient compliance with life-style changes, and provide a safer environment for the exercise program. Exercises may include endurance exercise, such as walking, jogging, cycling, swimming, resistive exercise, and arm exercise. The design of the exercise program should reflect the physical requirements of the patient's job.

Hypertension

Hypertension is high arterial blood pressure, usually defined as systolic blood pressure above 140 mm Hg or diastolic blood pressure above 90 mm Hg (this figure is flexible and varies somewhat with age and sex). It is considered a major health hazard, with approximately 12% of the population dying from associated complications such as stroke, congestive heart failure, kidney failure, and heart attack. It is sometimes called the silent killer because it usually has no apparent symptoms and accounts for more than 1.5 million deaths a year in the United States alone. Blood pressure above 150/90 increases the risk of heart disease by three times in men of all ages and by six times in 40 to 60-year-old women.

Hypertension affects the development of atherosclerosis, increases myocardial oxygen consumption at rest and with exercise, and causes cellular changes in the heart and blood vessels. Hypertension has two principal effects on the development of atherosclerosis: (1) it is thought to be directly involved in the process of damage to the vascular endothelial cells by increasing shear forces, torsion, and lateral wall pressure; (2) the higher pressure is thought to increase the filtration of lipids into the intimal cells.

Although the cause of most cases of hypertension is unknown, the disease is among the most treated conditions in medicine. Treatment methods include surgery, weight control, electrolytes restriction, drugs, psychological stress management, and exercise. Although drugs (principally beta-blockers and diuretics) are the most common method of treatment, recent evidence suggests that weight control and exercise may be just as effective and safer than pharmacological intervention in treating borderline cases of the disease. However, as stated previously, exercise training may increase resting blood pressure in some patients with hypertention.

Endurance exercise training reduces resting systolic blood pressure by 5 to 25 mm Hg and diastolic blood pressure by 3 to 15 mm Hg. The reduction in blood pressure depends on the age and weight (percentage fat) of the patient, the nature of the exercise program, the use of other blood pressure–reducing techniques, and the resting blood pressure. Exercise is most effective in reducing blood pressure when the patient is older (over 35 years of age), obese, and has a resting blood pressure in excess of 125/85 mm Hg. The exercise must be aerobic (endurance) and of sufficient duration, intensity, and frequency to train the oxygen transport system (see Chapter 17). Exercise alone will not reduce blood pressure to normal levels without pharmacological intervention when the pressure is above 155/100 mm Hg.

The causes of reduced blood pressure with endurance exercise training are not clearly understood. Possible mechanisms include reduced cardiac output at rest, decreased activity of the sympathetic nervous system (including decreased catecholamine synthesis by the adrenal gland), changes in insulin metabolism (possibly affecting sodium reabsorption by the kidney), loss of body fat (in obese persons), modification of the peripheral baroreceptors, and reduced activity of the renin–angiotensin system (important in regulating blood pressure). These mechanisms affect both of the component factors of blood pressure: cardiac output and peripheral resistance.

Exercise for People with Hypertension

Care must be taken when prescribing exercise and administering exercise stress tests to hypertensives. Even though exercise is sometimes used as an adjunct treatment of the disease, the utmost caution should be used in its application: although exercise training tends to lower resting blood pressure, exercise itself raises systolic blood pressure. During or immediately after exercise these individuals may be more susceptible to heart failure, coronary ischemia, angina, claudication, and possibly stroke. Heart failure can occur as a result of an increased load on the heart resulting from hypertension and from the effects of coronary disease. During exercise stress tests, it is particularly important to take frequent measurements so that falling systolic blood pressure can be detected immediately.

Unaccustomed exercise such as shoveling snow, water skiing, or carrying heavy suitcases that induce Valsalva's maneuver (expiring against a closed glottis) are particularly dangerous for hypertensive individuals. The combination of isotonic and isometric exercise, especially in the cold, raises blood pressure and produces an imbalance between the oxygen supply and oxygen demand of the myocardium. In addition, local release of K^+ resulting from the muscle contraction elicits a pressor response that also raises blood pressure. Activities involving upper body work above shoulder level will also raise the blood pressure because the blood vessels in the arms do not dilate to the same extent as the leg muscles during exercise. Inverted positions, such as "standing on your head," are also not recommended.

During exercise stress testing, care should be taken to prevent patients from tightly grasping the supports of the treadmill or bicycle ergometer. Because this introduces an isometric contraction it may increase systolic and diastolic blood pressure.

Persons with hypertension should avoid high-intensity, low-repetition weight lifting. However, moderate resistive exercise using relatively high repetitions could be beneficial. If strength can be improved, then the blood pressure response to possibly dangerous situations may be reduced. During strength-building exercises, the hypertensive should be particularly careful to breath normally rather than hold his breath.

Warm-up is very important for this group. Sudden, high-intensity exercise can result in explosive increases in blood pressure that compromise coronary artery blood flow. Hypertensives should increase the intensity of exercise very gradually. They should stress low-intensity, long-duration endurance activities rather than short-term, high-intensity exercise. Walking, jogging, or swimming is more appropriate than interval sprint training or start-and-stop sports such as racquetball.

Drug side effects should be considered in the exercise prescription and the patient warned of possible symptoms (see Appendix III). The diuretics can cause hypovolemia and muscle cramps and could conceivably precipitate or augment heat injury during heavy exercise in hot environments. Certainly, if the diuretics cause significant dehydration, they could hamper work capacity and increase the incidence of arrhythmias. Adrenergic inhibitors, depending on the drug, produce side effects such as orthostatic intolerance, bradycardia, asthma, fatigue, and drowsiness. Propranolol (a commonly prescribed beta-blocker), for example, reduces heart rate at rest and during exercise, and its effects should be taken into consideration in the exercise prescription. Vasodilators, again depending on the drug, can produce hypotension, tachycardia, and postural weakness. With all hypertension medication, particular attention should be directed toward warm-down or continued low-level exercise after the workout because of the dangers of hypotension, which can produce dizziness or fainting.

Diabetes

Diabetes mellitus is a disease caused by a lack of production of the hormone insulin, which is produced by the beta cells of the pancreas. There are two types of diabetes: type I and type II. Type I is insulin dependent, which requires injections of insulin. Type II is insulin independent, caused not by a lack of insulin production but insulin receptor loss or receptor insensitivity. Type II diabetes can usually be controlled by diet alone, or by diet and oral hypoglycemic drugs.

Insulin plays a pivotal role in fuel homeostasis. Many tissues require insulin for the uptake of glucose. In the normal individual when more glucose is available in the blood than is needed, insulin is secreted and acts to store glucose in muscle tissue and the liver as glycogen. Glycogen can later be broken down in the liver when blood levels are low. This process of glycogen breakdown becomes very important during exercise when a lot of glucose is needed for optimum performance.

High blood sugar (hyperglycemia) is a prominent characteristic of diabetes. High blood sugar results from a lack of insulin in type I diabetics, or from tissue insensitivity to insulin in type II diabetics. A major problem in type I diabetics is an increase in the breakdown of fats and protein in an effort to meet the body's energy need.

Diseases of large and small blood vessels are common in diabetics. In fact, diabetes is considered a major risk factor of cardiovascular disease. Diabetes is typically accompanied by arteriosclerosis, which greatly increases the risk of heart attack and stroke. Diabetes also produces abnormalities in the capillaries. The disease seems to make the blood platelets more adhesive or sticky, causing them to occlude the small capillary openings. Diabetes also often causes nerve damage (neuropathy) and deterioration of myelin, an important covering of the axons of myelinated nerve fibers. The specific effects of the disease includes heart attack, gangrene, kidney failure, blindness, cataracts, muscle weakness, and ulceration of the skin.

Control of the disease involves maintaining normal or near-normal levels of blood glucose by injecting insulin. Depending on the type of diabetes being treated, therapy may include insulin, oral hypoglycemic agents, diet, and exercise. It is also important to regulate the metabolism of fats and proteins. Diet is very important for the diabetic. Food intake must be enough to satisfy the needs of growth (in children) and metabolism, but not enough to produce obesity. The American Diabetic Association recommends that diabetics eat a balanced diet composed of about 50% complex carbohydrates, 35% fat, and 15% proteins. It is recommended that dietary cholesterol and saturated fats be curtailed to reduce the risk of heart disease.

A fundamental problem in the treatment of diabetes is that an injection of insulin is not the same, physiologically, as the natural secretion of insulin by the pancreas. Normally, insulin is released both continuously (basal secretion) and in larger amounts in response to increases in blood glucose. For example, after a meal, blood sugar rises and insulin is secreted to utilize the fuel effectively. In the diabetic, insulin is administered all at once. Many of the side effects of the disease manifest themselves when there is a chronic imbalance between insulin levels and glucose; in other words, diabetes becomes very dangerous when it is not well controlled. Acute dangers are insulin shock and diabetic coma, while chronic dangers include vascular and neural pathology.

Exercise seems to be very effective in reducing the side effects of the disease. Exercise provides three major benefits for the diabetic: (1) Endurance exercise reduces the diabetic's need for insulin. The lower the insulin dosage, the closer to normal physiology; this results in less of a metabolic roller coaster, allowing for easier control of the disease. (2) Endurance exercise reduces platelet adhesiveness. The blood platelets, which are stickier in diabetics, achieve normal adhesiveness for about 24 hr after exercise such as running, swimming, or cycling. (3) Regular endurance exercise reduces the severity of the risk factors of coronary artery disease such as hypertension, obesity, blood lipids, and serum uric acid.

Exercise is not recommended unless the diabetes is under control, that is, the blood sugar levels can be predictably regulated. Participation in physical activity presents control problems that have to be worked out on a trial-and-error basis. The most immediate problem is hypoglycemia—low blood glucose. Glucose utilization is much greater during exercise than at rest. The diabetic who is taking insulin is involved in a daily and often hourly juggling act trying to balance energy intake (food), energy output (exercise and resting metabolism), and insulin (energy regulator). A variation in any one of these three factors requires adjustment in the others.

Many active diabetics choose to counterbalance the increased glucose requirements of exercise by consuming extra food just before exercise, usually a high-sugar type such as candy, orange juice, or graham crackers. This works particularly well if the time or amount of exercise is irregular. If exercise habits are more predictable, then a change in the amount of insulin injected each day might help prevent hypoglycemia. The body works a lot like a machine: exercise at a given intensity for a given amount of time has a predictable fuel requirement. Regular, predictable exercise habits make the control of diabetes much easier.

It is very important to protect against hypoglycemia—particularly for the athletically active diabetic. Hypoglycemia can result in a severe impairment of judgment and loss of coordination, which could lead to injury. A person in a state of hypoglycemia can easily overestimate his or her capacity, with potentially tragic results.

When a diabetic is in poor control of the disease and has hyperglycemia, he or she may also be in a state of ketosis. Ketosis is a condition characterized by the accumulation of large amounts of acetoacetic acid, beta-hydroxybutyric acid, and acetone (collectively called ketones) in the blood. Ketosis occurs when the availability of carbohydrates is severely diminished and fats must be used as the predominant substrate. The blood concentration of ace-toacetic acid can rise to as high as 30 times above normal, leading to extreme acidosis. If left to progress, ketosis can lead to diabetic coma. Exercise is not recommended when a person has ketosis or hypoglycemia. Under certain conditions exercise can make the problem worse by increasing blood sugar levels even higher. Diabetes should therefore be controlled before undertaking an exercise program.

Another problem that occurs when a poorly controlled diabetic exercises is an excessive release of growth hormone. Growth hormone is very important in the regulation of blood lipids, in addition to its roll in the growth processes during childhood and adolescence. Excessive secretion of growth hormone in uncontrolled diabetes may contribute to arteriosclerosis. Again, the solution is to get diabetes well under control and then begin exercising.

Diabetics who take insulin have a choice of where to inject it. Injections are usually given beneath the skin covering the thigh, upper arms, abdomen, or buttocks. The site of injection is not terribly important unless exercise is to follow. It then becomes critically important. If insulin is injected in an area of a muscle involved in exercise, then the insulin goes into the bloodstream much more rapidly, because of increased blood flow to that area, and may lead to hypoglycemia (Table 16-4). For example, if a runner injected insulin into a leg and then went out to run, the insulin would begin to act more quickly and more powerfully than normal. The problem can be avoided by injecting the insulin in the abdomen or arm. In addition, the timing of the injection and the timing of the preexercise glucose load (candy, juice, etc.) should be considered.

Because of their increased risk of heart disease, diabetics of any age should

TABLE 16-4 The Effects of Site of Injection of Insulin in a Diabetic on Glucose Metabolism during Exercise[a]

Route of Glucose Injection	Site of Injection	Liver Glucose Production	Muscle Glucose Utilization	Blood Level
IV	Any	+ +	+ +	0
SC	Nonexercising limb	+ +	+ +	0 - *
SC	Exercising limb	+	+ +	-

[a] Key to symbols and abbreviations: IV = intravenous; SC = subcutaneous; + = increase; + + = large increase; − = decrease; * = a mild reduction; 0 = no change in glucose may occur.
SOURCE: Adapted from O. Bar-Or. Pediatric Sports Medicine. New York: Springer-Verlag, 1983.

get a treadmill test before starting an exercise program. Heart disease, which most frequently manifests itself in the nondiabetic population beginning at about 35 to 45 years of age, appears sooner among diabetics. Diabetics should therefore be thoroughly evaluated so that they can safely participate in their exercise program.

Chronic Obstructive Lung Disease

Chronic obstructive lung disease (COPD) is progressive and is characterized by airway destruction of alveoli, retention of mucous secretions, narrowed airways, and respiratory muscle weakness. Categories of this disease include emphysema, asthma, and bronchitis, although they are seldom distinct.

Emphysema is characterized by a loss of alveoli and their related vasculature. In addition to the loss of functional lung tissue, the hypoxia created by the reduction of blood supply results in pulmonary vasoconstriction that tends to further reduce the surface area for gas exchange. The disease increases pulmonary artery pressure, first during exercise and then at rest, which leads to structural hypertrophy and hyperplasia of the smooth muscle pulmonary vascular bed, followed by fibrosis and atherosclerosis. Ultimately, the pulmonary hypertension leads to right heart failure.

Emphysema patients often exhibit chest deformities because of their use of accessory muscles for ventilation. Their diaphragm is fixed in an inspiratory position, their chest is overexpanded, and their breathing muscles, as a whole, are weakened. There is a decrease in adenosine triphosphate and phosphocreatine in the intercostal muscles, which seems to be related to increasing airway obstruction. Patients show a higher than normal residual lung volume and have difficulty expiring rapidly.

Chronic bronchitis is described as a persistent productive cough, with episodes of infected sputum and shortness of breath (dyspnea). Bronchitis patients typically show blood gas abnormalities caused by aberrations in ventilation and perfusion of the lungs. At the later stages of the disease, extensive peripheral edema often results from pulmonary hypertension and right heart failure.

Ventilation and diffusion of respiratory gases are limiting in obstructive lung disease due to weak respiratory muscles, narrowed obstructive airways, and destroyed or compromised alveoli. Physical work capacity is usually low, and patients often complain of dyspnea (labored breathing) at rest (Table 16–5).

Because of the overriding effects of the work of breathing during exercise to exhaustion, the COPD patients will exhibit low maximal heart rates, maximal respiratory exchange ratios of less than 1.0, and lower blood lactates than healthy individuals. All of these factors indicate that the person is lim-

TABLE 16-5 Principal Changes in Oxygen Transport Capacity in Chronic Obstructive Pulmonary Disease

Factor	Effect
Maximal heart rate	Decreased
$\dot{V}_{O_2 max}$	Decreased
Maximal cardiac output	Decreased
Alveolar oxygen tension ($P_{A_{O_2}}$)	Increased
Arterial oxygen tension ($P_{a_{O_2}}$)	Decreased
Pulmonary artery blood pressure	Increased
Ventilatory reserve	Decreased

ited by breathing capacity rather than metabolic capacity. These people are also often unable to push themselves during exercise because of anxiety produced by shortness of breath. Maximal exercise ventilation will often reach or exceed that of the measured maximal voluntary ventilation (MVV), which causes dyspnea and fatigue at low exercise intensities. People with normal lung function normally ventilate about 60% of MVV.

Unfortunately, lung function does not seem to improve with training in these individuals. There is evidence, however, that endurance training may delay the deterioration of pulmonary function. Maximal oxygen consumption and work capacity improve, provided the patients are motivated and the exercise prescription is very moderate.

Exercise prescription for these individuals should include progressive endurance exercise, such as walking or stationary cycling. Breathing exercises are also an important part of the program. Ideally, the exercise pace should be determined by monitoring arterial PO_2. Noninvasive instruments, such as the transcutaneous ear oximeter, make this practical for most pulmonary laboratories. Breathing exercises are aimed at increasing airflow to obstructed and restricted areas, improving respiratory muscle endurance, decreasing the use of accessory breathing muscles, facilitating mucus removal, and maintaining chest mobility.

Asthma

Asthma is technically an obstructive lung disease. However, because it is frequently experienced without emphysema or bronchitis, particularly in the young, it will be treated independently. Asthma is a lung disorder characterized by edema in the walls of the small bronchioles, secretion of thick mucus into their lumens, and spasm of their smooth muscle walls. Symptoms include choking, the sensation of shortness of breath, wheezing, tightness in the chest, increased mucus production, and fatigue. When an asthma attack occurs, breathing becomes labored, particularly during expiration, due to a reduction in bronchiolar diameter. An attack can be caused by such things as emotional upset, dust, pollen, cold and damp weather, smoke, and exercise.

Because exercise is one factor that precipitates an asthma attack, it is understandable that many asthmatics shun physical activity. However, medications developed for asthma not only make exercise possible but actually decrease the incidence and severity of asthmatic attack. Asthmatics involved in exercise programs have improved lung function, muscle coordination, and emotional adjustment. Usually, there is a decrease in the frequency and severity of asthmatic attacks.

Although exercise can be beneficial, it is not without risk to the asthmatic as overexertion is a prominent precipitator of asthma. It is particularly important that these individuals increase the intensity of their programs gradually and avoid environmental conditions (such as air pollution and extreme cold) that will complicate their asthma. Exercise should be modified or curtailed if the asthmatic is too tired, under emotional stress, or if it is too cold, humid, or smoggy. Under adverse environmental conditions, exercise bouts should be kept short, less than about 3 min at a time (or as tolerated). These people should avoid swimming in excessively cold water because this can induce an asthma attack. Swimming in water with a comfortable temperature is an ideal exercise because the increased pressure on the thorax facilitates expiration.

Asthma is often associated with allergies. Some degree of allergic control is desirable before beginning a vigorous endurance program. One possible suggestion is to undergo a series of allergy shots to desensitize against aggravating substances. At the very least, the asthmatic can prevent allergic reactions by avoiding dusty areas, pollen, and smoke.

An asthmatic should take a treadmill test before beginning an exercise program. Ideally, this test should include arterial blood–gas analysis. In people with normal lung function, the lungs are capable of almost completely oxygenating the blood during even the heaviest levels of exercise. However, asthmatics may not be able to supply enough oxygen to the blood at the heavier levels of exertion; diffusion becomes a limiting factor. The treadmill and blood gas measurements make it possible to select a safe upper limit of exercise.

If exercise seems to bring on an attack, the asthmatic should make sure to take his or her medication before the workout. Modern medications have enabled asthmatics to participate in even the most vigorous sports, including endurance events in the Olympic Games. In the 1972 Games, an asthmatic won a gold medal in swimming, only to be disqualified for taking his asthma medication. An excellent prescription drug available in aerosol that is acceptable for international competition is albuterol. Asthmatic drugs can prevent exercise-induced asthma or reduce the effects once they have occurred.

The control of chronic recurrent wheezing is usually accomplished using sympathomimetic drugs such as ephedrine or epinephrine in the form of an aerosol inhalant.

Asthmatics should be encouraged to drink a lot of water when they participate in endurance exercise. Ingesting water reduces the thickness of lung secretions and thus facilitates breathing.

These individuals should participate in self-paced activities and avoid overly competitive situations when they are beginning their exercise programs. Endurance-interval training, 30-sec to 3-min bouts of exercise followed by short rests, is well tolerated by most asthmatics and is recommended as a conditioning method during the early stages of physical training. Beginners should ideally exercise in a supervised environment. An inhaler and 100% oxygen should be available, along with somebody to assist if a difficulty develops. The asthmatic should be instructed in relaxation positions and breathing exercises in the event of shortness of breath or distress.

Arthritis

Arthritis is an inflammatory joint disease. The Arthritis Foundation estimates that more than 31 million people in the United States have this disorder to some extent and that the economic impact exceeds $13 billion a year. The most common forms of the disease include osteoarthritis, rheumatoid arthritis, juvenile rheumatoid arthritis, ankylosing spondylitis, systemic lupus erythematosus, and gout. Arthritis is chronic but may go into remission periodically.

Osteoarthritis

Osteoarthritis is the most common form of arthritis. It is caused by wear and tear of the joints and is a common effect of the aging process. Individual differences in the presence of arthritis can be accounted for by such factors as age, previous injury or trauma, heredity, previous joint disease, and metabolic diseases. This type of arthritis is specific to individual joints, rather than spreading to other joints. Pain can vary from none at all to debilitating.

Osteoarthritis damages the articular cartilage of joints. This is often accompanied by bone spurs and adhesions in the membranes and ligaments of the joint. The associated pain usually results in decreased range of motion and disuse atrophy caused by the person's avoidance of any motion that is uncomfortable. The limitation of activity results in the formation of further adhesions, which further limits motion.

Exercise prescription for people with osteoarthritis includes range of motion and strength exercises and activities that minimize weight bearing, such as swimming. Often a reduction of body fat is recommended to help take pressure from joints. Analgesics will often help relieve pain so that the necessary exercises can be accomplished.

Rheumatoid Arthritis

Arthritis is a common manifestation of rheumatoid diseases such as rheumatoid arthritis, lupus erythematosus, and polyarteritis nodosa. These are autoimmune diseases in which aberrant immunoglobulins combine to form anti-immunoglobulin antibodies called rheumatoid factor. The rheumatoid factor binds with antigens and immune complexes in tissue and produces an inflammatory response. Scar tissue is eventually formed with repeated inflammatory episodes, so the inflammation itself is a potent precipitator of tissue damage.

Exercise is contraindicated during an inflammatory period because it increases the severity of the inflammation and the tissue damage. Because excessive bed rest and deconditioning can also lead to deterioration, the right balance of rest and exercise is needed. Researchers recently studied 23 patients with rheumatoid arthritis who were involved in physical training for 4 to 8 years. They found less pronounced degenerative changes, improved exercise tolerance, and fewer sick days from work in the active patients. They concluded that although there is a risk of overuse during physical activity in rheumatoid arthritis patients, it is better to be overactive than the reverse.

Range of motion exercises and minimal weight-bearing endurance exercises such as swimming or walking may be practiced when appropriate. Drugs such as aspirin, fenoprofen, indomethacin, tolmetin, corticosteroids, and phenylbutazone are usually used to relieve pain and facilitate mobilization exercises.

Another potentially serious problem associated with rheumatoid diseases is cardiopulmonary involvement. Sixty percent of patients with systemic lupus erythematosis will have pleuritis or pericarditis, or both. Inflammation of small- or medium-sized blood vessels is relatively common in all rheumatoid diseases. Caution should be used as excessive exercise could be destructive to the heart.

Summary

Exercise is currently being used as an adjunct treatment for many diseases such as coronary heart disease, hypertension, diabetes, asthma, and arthritis. While exercise can be helpful in helping the patient cope with a variety of health disorders, it must be applied judiciously because of the possible dangers involved. However, it is widely recognized that the dangers of bedrest and deconditioning can sometimes be more devastating than the primary disease process.

Bedrest has a profound and wide-spread effect on the body. It diminishes the capacity of the heart, produces orthostatic intolerance, reduces plasma and blood volumes, impairs circulatory control, and results in muscle atrophy and loss of bone minerals. The effects of bedrest are usually reversible with adequate ambulation.

Coronary heart disease is the number one killer in Western countries. The disease involves a steady buildup of atherosclerotic plaque in the coronary arteries leading to diminished myocardial blood flow and myocardial infarction. Factors that increase the risk of CHD include hypertension, hyperlipidemia, smoking, genetics, male sex, lack of physical activity, obesity, diabetes, and psychological stress. Human and animal studies strongly suggest that exercise training reduces the incidence of CHD.

Cardiac rehabilitation programs stress improvement in diet, exercise, and smoking habits have become an accepted part of the treatment of many cardiac patients. There are three phases of cardiac rehabilitation. Phase I is the in-patient program conducted in the hospital shortly after surgery or myocardial infarction and attempts to prepare the patient for resumption of normal activities. Phase II is the outpatient therapeutic program and includes supervised exercise, vocational rehabilitation, and behavioral counseling. Phase III is the exercise maintenance program that is conducted to help the patient continue the modified, healthier life-style.

Hypertension is often called the silent killer because of the absence of overt symptoms. Exercise training tends to reduce resting blood pressure in patients with moderate hypertension but may increase blood pressure in some patients. Patients with hypertension should avoid heavy upperbody exercise, particularly in cold weather. Moderate strength training may reduce the pressor response when the patient performs upper body exercise. Drug side-effects should be considered when monitoring the exercise programs of people with hypertension.

Exercise is beneficial for people with type I and type II diabetes provided the disease is in control (blood sugar can be regulated predictably). Exercise is beneficial for these patients because it reduces the risk of heart disease, decreases platelet adhesiveness, and increases insulin sensitivity. An exercise program requires that the diabetic adjust the factors that determine diabetic control: insulin, diet, and exercise. Great care must be taken to avoid insulin shock that can easily result if these three factors are not considered and balanced properly. Exercise in the uncontrolled diabetic will exacerbate hyperglycemia and may lead to ketoacidosis and diabetic coma.

Exercise is an important part of the treatment of patients with chronic obstructive lung disease. Although exercise can improve the quality of life in these people by increasing cellular respiratory capacity and cardiovascular function, it has not been shown to improve the course of the disease itself. Asthmatics can benefit from an endurance exercise program provided that the intensity of the program is increased gradually and they avoid adverse environmental conditions.

Exercise can help patients with both osteo- and rheumatoid arthritis. Patients with rheumatoid arthritis should avoid strenuous exercise during the active phase of the disease. Exercise prescription should stress range of motion and nonweight bearing activities.

Selected Readings

BAR-OR, O. Pediatric Sports Medicine. New York: Springer-Verlag, 1983.

BROWN, H.V., and K. WASSERMAN. Exercise performance in chronic obstructive pulmonary diseases. Med. Clin. N. Am. 65:525–547, 1981.

DEBUSK, R., N. HOUSTON, W. HASKELL, G. FRY, and M. PARKER. Exerise training soon after myocardial infarction. Am. J. Cardiol. 44:1223–1229, 1979.

FAHEY, T.D. Athletic Training: Principles and Practice. Palo Alto: Mayfield Publishing Co, 1986.

FARDY, P.S., J.L. BENNETT, N.L. REITZ, and M.A. WILLIAMS. Cardiac Rehabilitation. St. Louis: C.V. Mosby, 1980.

GREENLEAF, J., and S. KOZLOWSKI. Physiological consequences of reduced physical activity during bed rest. Exercise Sport Sci. Rev. 10:84–119, 1982.

HANSON, P.G., and D.K. FLAHERTY. Immunologic responses to training in conditioned runners. Ann. Allergy 47:73–75, 1981.

HANSON, P., M.D. GIESE, and R.J. CORLISS. Clinical guidelines for exercise training. Postgrad. Med. 67:120–138, 1980.

HANSON, P., and R. KOCHAN. Exercise and diabetes. Primary Care 10:653–662, 1983.

KAVANAGH, T., R.J. SHEPHARD, A.W. CHISOLM, S. QURESHI, and J. KENNEDY. Prognostic indexes for patients with ischemic heart disease enrolled in an exercise-centered rehabilitation program. Am. J. Cardiol. 44:1230–1240, 1979.

KEMMER, F.W., and M. BERGER. Exercise and diabetes mellitus: physical activity as part of daily life and its role in the treatment of diabetic patients. Int. J. Sports Med. 4:77–88, 1983.

KOFFLER, D. The immunology of rheumatoid diseases. Clinical Symposia 31:2–36, 1980.

KOIVISTO, V., and R.S. SHERWIN. Exercise in diabetes. Postgrad. Med. 66:87–96, 1979.

KONIG, K. Changes in physical capacity, heart size and function in patients after myocardial infarction, who underwent a 4-to-6-week physical training program. Cardiology 62:232–246, 1977.

NICKERSON, B.G., D.B. BAUTISTA, M.A. NAMEY, W. RICHARDS, and T.G. KEENS. Distance running improves fitness in asthmatic children without pulmonary complications or changes in exercise-induced bronchospasm. Pediatrics 71:147–152, 1983.

NORDEMAR, R., B. EKBLOM, L. ZACHRISSON, and K. LUNDQVIST. Physical training in rheumatoid arthritis: a controlled long-term study. (I and II). Scand J. Rheumatol. 10:17–30, 1981.

SANDLER, H. Effects of bed rest and weightlessness on the heart. In: Hearts and Heartlike Organs. New York: Academic Press, 1980, pp. 435–523.

TIPTON, C.M. Exercise, training, and hypertension. Exercise Sport Sci. Rev. 12:245–306, 1984.

WILSON, P.K., P.S. FARDY, and V.F. FROELICHER. Cardiac Rehabilitation, Adult Fitness, and Exercise Testing. Philadelphia: Lea & Febiger, 1981.

17

Exercise Testing and Prescription

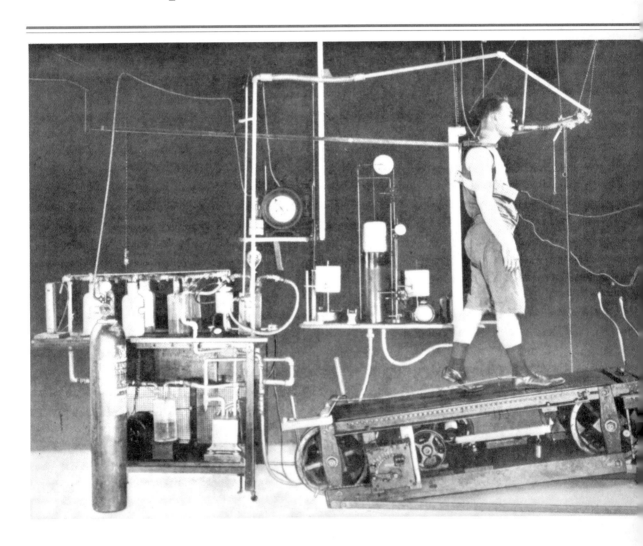

The purpose of exercise training is to stress the body's physiological systems so that they adapt and increase their capacity (see Chapter 1). People who are physically fit have repeatedly adapted to a series of exercise stresses and have subsequently developed an improved ability to meet the demands of physical effort. Depending on the nature of the exercise training program, physically fit people tend to have greater cardiac output, strength, flexibility, power, muscle capillary density, and muscle oxidative capacity than sedentary people.

The exercise training program must stress the body at a level appropriate for the individual, or injury will occur. On the other hand, the body will fail to adapt if the exercise stresses are insufficient. The ideal exercise prescription is one that stimulates the body to adapt at the fastest rate with the lowest risk of injury.

Optimal progression in an exercise program occurs when the intensity reaches a threshold percentage of maximal capacity rather than at any specific exercise training load. For example, running a mile in 10 min would probably be an excessive exercise intensity for a person with a recent myocardial infarction but would represent a subthreshold training stimulus for an accomplished runner. Optimal exercise intensity occurs between 50 and 85% of $\dot{V}_{O_2max}$, which allows for the fastest rate of development in endurance capacity while affording an acceptable risk of injury.

Individualized exercise prescription can be only accomplished if the maximum capacity is known. A number of laboratory and field tests have been devised to measure physical fitness. These tests may be conducted on a running track, treadmill, bicycle ergometer, stepping bench, arm ergometer, swimming flume, wheelchair ergometer, or other similar devices. Fitness tests vary in their safety, accuracy, and specificity to particular forms of exercise (e.g., swimming tests have little applicability to the fitness required in running).

This chapter will discuss the principles of measuring cardiovascular fitness and prescribing exercise programs. Cardiovascular exercise is stressed because it is most important for the health and well-being of the typical adult. Other topics that will be discussed include contraindications to exercise, principles of ergometry, and exercise stress testing.

Medical Screening for Persons Wishing to Begin an Exercise Program

Exercise training will be safe and enjoyable for most people; however, there are those with medical conditions that make exercise dangerous (Table 17-1). For these people, the exercise program should be either modified, medically supervised, or not undertaken at all.

Anyone older than 35 or anyone under 35 years old with significant health problems should receive a medical examination before beginning an exercise program. This examination should include a medical history and appropriate procedures (blood chemistry, blood pressure, resting electrocardiogram, etc.) to identify conditions that might make an exercise program dangerous. In addition, persons of any age who experience any unusual symptoms, such as chest pain, viral infections, irregular heart beats, shortness of breath, or severe pain emanating from muscles, joints, or the skeleton, should also consult a physician before continuing with the exercise program.

A detailed discussion of medical contraindications to exercise is beyond the scope of this book. However, from Table 17-1 we can see that medical conditions that significantly limit the body's ability to adapt to physiological challenges make exercise dangerous. For example, congestive heart failure (failure of the heart to adequately empty during systole) and unstable angina (heart-related chest pain) indicate that the heart is being stressed at a high

TABLE 17-1 Contraindications to Exercise and Exercise Stress Tests

Congestive heart failure (moderate to severe)
Unstable angina
Hypertrophic–cardiomyopathy
Severe aortic stenosis
Pulmonary hypertension
Myocarditis, pericarditis, bacterial endocarditis, acute rheumatic fever or cardiomy-
  opathy within the past year
Uncontrolled hypertension
Serious arrhythmias
  Second- and third-degree AV blocks
  Uncontrolled atrial fibrillation
  Excessive or complex PVCs
  Ventricular tachycardia
Marked bradycardia (other than in endurance-trained individuals)
Fixed-rate artificial pacemaker
Significant cardiac enlargement
Valvular disease, moderate to severe
Recent pulmonary embolism
Severe anemia
Uncontrolled metabolic disease (diabetes mellitus, thyrotoxicosis, myxedema)
Transient illness accompanied by fever
Certain orthopedic disabilities
Inappropriate blood pressure response to exercise testing
Overdose of cardiac drugs such as digitalis, quinidine, lidocaine, procainamide,
  propranolol, and verapamil
Mental instability

percentage of its diminished capacity. Further stress induced by exercise could only lead to a deterioration in the medical condition. Uncontrolled diabetes (blood sugar cannot be predictably regulated) can be made much worse by exercise, possibly resulting in ketoacidosis (high levels of ketones) or diabetic coma. It is clear that while exercise training will be beneficial for most people, it is not for everyone.

Functional Capacity

Functional capacity, the maximum ability to convert chemical energy into mechanical energy, is largely determined by cardiovascular fitness. Maximal oxygen consumption ($\dot{V}_{O_2max}$) is considered the best measure of cardiovascular fitness and is often used synonymously with functional capacity. The limiting factors of maximal oxygen consumption and the physiology of the heart and circulation were discussed in Chapters 5 and 8. The reader should thoroughly review the basic concepts presented in these chapters in order to better understand the role of functional capacity in exercise testing and prescription.

Functional capacity is typically expressed as METs (Eq. 17-1), $\dot{V}_{O_2max}$ (ml $\cdot$ kg^{-1} $\cdot$ min^{-1}), or $\dot{V}_{O_2max}$ (liters $\cdot$ min^{-1}).

$$1 \text{ MET} = 3.5 \text{ ml} \cdot \text{kg}^{-1} \cdot \text{min}^{-1} \qquad (17\text{-}1)$$

or

$$1 \text{ MET} = 300 \text{ ml } O_2 \cdot \text{min-}^1$$

or

$$1 \text{ MET} = 1 \text{ kcal} \cdot \text{kg}^{-1} \cdot \text{hr}^{-1}$$

$\dot{V}_{O_2}$ (ml $\cdot$ kg^{-1} $\cdot$ min^{-1}) is the relative maximal oxygen consumption, derived by dividing gross oxygen consumption measurements (ml $\cdot$ min^{-1}) by body weight. $\dot{V}_{O_2}$ (liters $\cdot$ min^{-1}) is the absolute oxygen consumption measured for the individual. All of these measures are largely reflected and limited by the capacity of the cardiovascular system.

A MET is the resting metabolic rate (resting $\dot{V}_{O_2}$ measured in a sitting position). One MET is approximately equal to an oxygen consumption of 3.5 ml $\cdot$ kg^{-1} $\cdot$ min^{-}1. When using METs, exercise intensity is expressed in multiples of the resting metabolic rate (see Table 17-2). For example, an exercise intensity of 2 METs indicates that the individual is exercising at a level that is two times the resting metabolic rate. METs is a good means of expressing exercise intensity because it is easier for people to remember and understand.

Most sports scientists use relative oxygen consumption expressed in milliliters per kilogram per minute to describe functional capacity. METs are

TABLE 17-2 Energy Cost of Various Activities[a]

Activity	Calories[b] (cal/min)	METs[c]	Oxygen Cost (ml/kg/min)
Archery	3.7–5	3–4	10.5–14
Backpacking	6–13.5	5–11	17.5–38.5
Badminton	5–11	4–9	14–31.5
Basketball			
Nongame	3.7–11	3–9	10.5–31.5
Game	8.5–15	7–12	24.5–42
Bed exercise (arm movement, supine or sitting)	1.1–2.5	1–2	3.5–7
Bicycling (pleasure or to work)	3.7–10	3–8	10.5–28
Bowling	2.5–5	2–4	7–14
Canoeing (rowing and kayaking)	3.7–10	3–8	10.5–28
Calisthenics	3.7–10	3–8	10.5–28
Dancing (social and square)	3.7–8.5	3–7	10.5–24.5
Fencing	7.5–12	6–10	21–35
Fishing			
(bank, boat, or ice)	2.5–5	2–4	7–14
(stream, wading)	6–7.5	5–6	17.5–21
Football (touch)	7.5–12	6–10	21–35
Golf			
(using power cart)	2.5–3.7	2–3	7–10.5
(walking, carrying bag, or pulling cart)	5–8.5	4–7	14–24.5
Handball	10–15	8–12	28–42
Hiking (cross-country)	3.7–8.5	3–7	10.5–24.5
Horseback riding	3.7–10	3–8	10.5–28
Horseshoe pitching	2.5–3.7	2–3	7–10.5
Hunting, walking			
Small game	3.7–8.5	3–7	10.5–24.5
Big game	3.7–17	3–14	10.5–49
Jogging	10–15	8–12	28–42
Mountain climbing	6–12	5–10	17.5–35
Paddleball (racquet)	10–15	8–12	28–42
Sailing	2.5–6	2–5	7–17.5
Scuba diving	6–12	5–10	17.5–35
Shuffleboard	2.5–3.7	2–3	7–10.5
Skating (ice or roller)	6–10	5–8	17.5–28
Skiing (snow)			
Downhill	6–10	5–8	17.5–28
Cross-country	7.5–15	6–12	21–42
Skiing (water)	6–8.5	5–7	17.5–24.5
Snow shoeing	8.5–17	7–14	24.5–49
Squash	10–15	8–12	28–42

TABLE 17-2 Energy Cost of Various Activities[a] (Continued)

Activity	Calories[b] (cal/min)	METs[c]	Oxygen Cost (ml/kg/min)
Soccer	6–15	5–12	17.5–42
Softball	3.7–7.5	3–6	10.5–21
Stair climbing	5–10	4–8	14–28
Swimming	5–10	4–8	14–28
Table tennis	3.7–6	3–5	10.5–17.5
Tennis	5–11	4–9	14–31.5
Volleyball	3.7–7.5	3–6	10.5–21
Walking (see Table 4.4)			

[a] Energy cost values based on an individual of 154 lb of body weight (70 kg).

[b] Calorie = a unit of measure based on heat production. One calorie equals approximately 200 ml of oxygen consumed.

[c] MET = basal oxygen requirement of the body sitting quietly. One MET equals 3.5 ml of oxygen per kilogram of body weight per minute.

SOURCE: Pollock M., J. Wilmore, and S. Fox. *Health and Fitness Through Physical Activity.* New York: Wiley, 1978, p. 124.

calculated from $\dot{V}_{O_2}$ ($ml \cdot kg^{-1} \cdot min^{-1}$), so the terms are synonymous (see Table 17-3). The use of METs and $\dot{V}_{O_2}$ per unit body weight is useful because it facilitates the comparison of people with different body weights. Larger people tend to consume more oxygen because they have more tissue; there-

TABLE 17-3 Cardiorespiratory Fitness Classification[a]

Age (years)	*Maximal Oxygen Uptake (ml/kg/min)*				
	Low	**Fair**	**Average**	**Good**	**High**
Women					
20–29	<24	24–30	31–37	38–48	49+
30–39	<20	20–27	28–33	34–44	45+
40–49	<17	17–23	24–30	31–41	42+
50–59	<15	15–20	21–27	28–37	38+
60–69	<13	13–17	18–23	24–34	35+
Men					
20–29	<25	25–33	34–42	43–52	53+
30–39	<23	23–30	31–38	39–48	49+
40–49	<20	20–26	27–35	36–44	45+
50–59	<18	18–24	25–33	34–42	43+
60–69	<16	16–22	23–30	31–40	41+

[a] Data from Preventive Medicine Center, Palo Alto, Calif., and from a survey of published sources.

fore, it is possible for a large, sedentary person to have a considerably larger absolute $\dot{V}_{O_2max}$ (liters $\cdot$ min^{-1}) than a more physically fit, but smaller person. The use of functional capacity expressed per unit body weight factors out the effects of body mass and allows for the comparison of people on the basis of cardiovascular capacity.

Several theoretical problems are associated with the use of maximal oxygen consumption divided by body weight. It is assumed that body weight accounts for all the differences in $\dot{V}_{O_2max}$ observed among people; however, only about 50% of $\dot{V}_{O_2max}$ is determined by body weight, and other components such as training and genetics account for the remainder. This problem is more than theoretical nitpicking. The use of $\dot{V}_{O_2}$ expressed per unit body weight can occasionally create confusion when attempting to assess a person's physical fitness. For example, rapid weight loss will result in an apparent increase in functional capacity expressed as maximum METs or $\dot{V}_{O_2max}$ (ml $\cdot$ kg^{-1} $\cdot$ min^{-1}), with no actual improvement in oxygen transport capacity. In this circumstance, functional capacity would be better expressed in liters per minute. In most instances, however, expressing functional capacity per kilogram of body weight is useful and practical.

Measuring Maximal Oxygen Consumption

Oxygen consumption is typically measured in most laboratories by indirect, open circuit calorimetry. This technique involves obtaining expiratory volume (minute volume) and gas composition measurements of a resting or exercising subject (expiratory volume can also be determined by measuring inspired volume). Required laboratory instruments include a flow meter or spirometer to measure expiratory volume, gas analyzers to measure oxygen and carbon dioxide, a thermistor to measure the temperature of the expired gases, and a barometer to measure barometric pressure.

The most common ventilatory measurement instruments include the pneumotachograph, gasometer, and spirometer (Tissot) (Figure 17-1). Ventilation is measured directly by one of these instruments (expired gases flow from the subject's mouth directly into the ventilation meter) or by collecting the gases in large bags or balloons and then measuring the ventilatory volumes at the end of the test.

Temperature and barometric pressure are measured so that gas volumes can be expressed at standard conditions (i.e., BTPS and STPD). The temperature of the expired gases must be measured continuously because it changes rapidly during progressive intensity exercise tests. Barometric pressure needs to be measured only at the beginning of a test because it remains relatively stable.

The composition of the expired gases are measured either continuously, from a mixing chamber, from aliquots (small rubber bags containing a portion of the expired air), or from a large collection bag. The selection of a technique depends on available equipment, budget, and expertise.

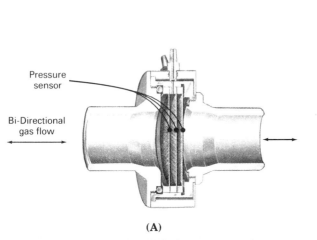

Pressure sensor

Bi-Directional gas flow

(A)

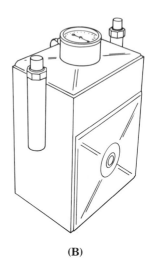

(B)

(C)

Figure 17-1

Three devices for measuring pulmonary minute volume: *(A)* pneumotachometer, *(B)* Parkinson-Cowan gasometer, and *(C)* chain-compensated (Tissot) spirometer.

(SOURCE: Tissot spirometer courtesy of W. E. Collins, Inc., Braintree, Mass.)

Continuous measurements are usually unnecessary unless breath-by-breath oxygen consumption measurements are required. The problem with continuous measurements lies in the characteristics of an expired breath. The beginning of a breath is higher in oxygen and lower in carbon dioxide than the end of a breath (and vice versa). High-speed gas analyzers, computers, and sophisticated computer programs are necessary for continuous gas analysis because the composition of each expired breath changes so quickly.

Mixing chambers are used in most laboratories for gas sampling during oxygen consumption measurements (Figure 17-2). The mixing chamber is a plastic box with baffles that helps to mix the expired breaths. The mixing chamber allows for continuous gas sampling without the technological problems presented by continuous breath-by-breath sampling. This method works best when measurements are made during "steady state" (when the metabolism has reached a relative equilibrium). Some error is introduced when the composition of expired gases is changing rapidly, which occurs at the end of a maximal oxygen consumption test. However, these errors are small and, for most applications (i.e., those that do not require extreme accuracy), of minor significance.

Aliquot sampling techniques have many of the same benefits and problems of mixing chambers. This technique involves continuous sampling of a small portion of expired air that has been collected in a small rubber bag (aliquot). Three bags are usually attached to a three-way valve, with one bag collecting gas, while another bag is being analyzed, and a third bag is emptied with a vacuum pump (Figure 17-3).

Large bag collection techniques involve collecting and analyzing all the expired gases during a particular time interval. These techniques typically use either Douglas bags, weather balloons, or a large Tissot spirometer. Although previously widely used, large bag techniques have been replaced by

Figure 17-2

Example of a mixing chamber. This device mixes expired air during the open circuit measurement of oxygen consumption.

(SOURCE: Courtesy of Vacumed, Inc., Ventura, Calif.)

Figure 17-3
Wilmore-Costill valve. This
valve is used as part of a semi-
automated procedure to measure oxygen consumption.

(SOURCE: Courtesy of Jack Wilmore.)

the aforementioned techniques. They are awkward and not very adaptable to
rapid and repeated measurements. They were necessary when gas analysis
was accomplished with manual chemical analyzers such as the Scholander
and Haldane apparatuses. However, they are accurate and do serve a purpose
when other systems are unavailable or extreme accuracy is needed (e.g., with
100% O_2 breathing experiments).

Low-cost microcomputers and instrument interfaces have enabled the
widespread use of on-line oxygen consumption systems, in both research laboratories and clinical settings (Figure 17-4). On-line systems automatically
measure gas volume and composition, calculate oxygen consumption, display
information, and store data. These systems can be constructed from commercially available components including a computer, analog-to-digital converter
(translates information from the analyzers to the computer), ventilation meter, oxygen analyzer, carbon dioxide analyzer, mixing chamber, respiratory
valve (Daniels, Hans-Rudolf, triple J, etc.), tubing, thermistor, and nose clip.
These systems can be expanded to include computer disk drives (floppy and
hard disks), printer, plotter, and even a human voice simulator. Commer-

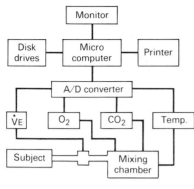

On-line $\dot{V}O_2$ System

(A)

Figure 17-4

(A) A schematic diagram of an on-line oxygen consumption system using a low-cost microcomputer. The output from gas analyzers and other physiological equipment is automatically translated to the computer through an analog-to-digital converter. Oxygen consumption is calculated, displayed, and stored.

(B) A commercially constructed system for measuring $\dot{V}_{O_2}$.

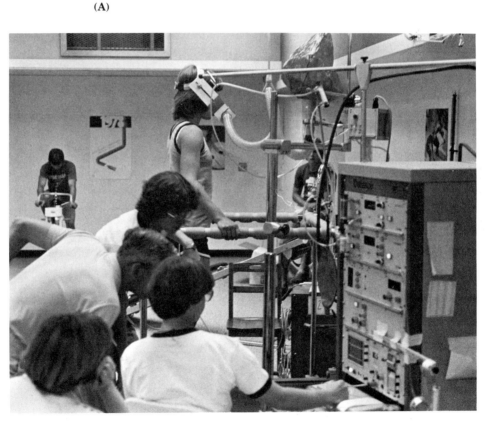

(B)

cially constructed systems are also available, but at considerably greater expense.

Tests of Functional Capacity

Functional capacity tests can be subdivided into laboratory tests and field tests. Laboratory tests are more accurate and reliable than field tests but tend to be considerably more expensive and technologically difficult to perform. Laboratory tests involve the measurement of maximal oxygen consumption while the subject exercises on devises such as a treadmill, bicycle ergometer, arm ergometer, or swimming flume. Field tests estimate maximal oxygen consumption from established formulas based on individual performance of running, bench stepping, cycling, or swimming tasks.

Tests can be either maximal or submaximal. The advantages of submaximal tests are that they are physically less demanding of the subject, take less time, and may be safer (this point is controversial). Maximal tests are more accurate and provide a better physiological profile of the subject. Safety procedures should be the same for both types of test (physician supervision, ECG monitoring, defibrillator, emergency medications, etc.). Although unmonitored submaximal tests are appropriate in young subjects, they could be dangerous in older or symptomatic populations. Older or symptomatic subjects often have extremely low levels of functional capacity or develop problems at submaximal levels of exercise. Submaximal tests may unwittingly become supramaximal tests in some subjects. In addition, problems that develop during unmonitored submaximal tests may develop into medical emergencies if left to progress.

Exercise Test Measurements

A variety of physiological measurements are possible during an exercise tolerance test including the electrocardiogram (heart rate obtained from the ECG), blood pressure, rate pressure product (heart rate $\times$ systolic blood pressure), ventilation (volume and rate), oxygen consumption, perceived exertion (Table 17-4), myocardial perfusion (thallium-201), left ventricular performance (radionuclide cineangiography, blood pool labeling studies), core and skin temperature, cardiac output, substrates (glucose, lactate, etc.), and visualization of the heart walls (echocardiography).

Clinically, the most common stress test measurements are the ECG, blood pressure, oxygen consumption, and test duration. Test duration (treadmill stage, power, etc.) is an adequate predictor of maximal oxygen consumption in untrained subjects (but not heart patients).

All laboratories should follow established guidelines (American College

TABLE 17-4 Borg Rated Perceived Exertion Scale (RPE)

6
7 Very, very light
8
9 Very light
10
11 Fairly light
12
13 Somewhat hard
14
15 Hard
16
17 Very hard
18
19 Very, very hard
20

SOURCE: G. Borg. The perception of physical performance. In: R.J. Shephard (ed.). Frontiers of Fitness. Springfield, Ill.: Charles C. Thomas, 1971, p. 287.

of Sports Medicine, American Heart Association, etc.) for conducting graded exercise testing. These guidelines specify requirements for physician supervision, safety equipment (defibrillator, emergency medication, etc.), and criteria for stopping a test (fatigue, critical levels of ST-segment depression, arrhythmias, angina, etc.).

The test administrator should be aware of signs that place the subject at increased risk during the test. These include indications of "power failure" (decrease in central blood volume), ischemia (the heart muscle is not getting enough blood), and arrhythmia (aberrant ECG rhythm). Indications of power failure include a falling systolic blood pressure during exercise, central nervous system distress (weaving or dizziness), and diaphoresis (cold sweat). Ischemia is indicated by ST-segment depression, arrhythmias, and angina (chest pain; see Figures 17-5 and 17-6). Arrhythmias are abnormal electrocardiograms that can result in decreases or total interruption in cardiac output (see Figure 17-7). Each laboratory should have written criteria for stopping functional capacity tests. These should be based on a sound rationale such as those presented in the American College of Sports Medicine's *Guidelines for Graded Exercise Testing and Exercise Prescription*.

Precise methods are necessities for ensuring accuracy and subject safety. All instruments must be regularly calibrated and serviced (including the bicycle ergometer and treadmill). Skin electrode preparation must be meticulous in order to obtain artifact-free ECGs. Tests should be stopped if a good ECG tracing cannot be obtained while the subject is exercising.

417

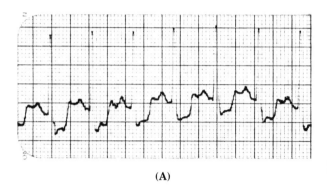

(A)

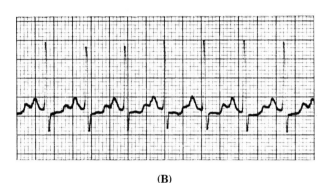

(B)

Figure 17-5

ST-segment depression before and after coronary artery bypass surgery. Coronary artery disease may result in coronary ischemia (inadequate blood flow) that is often detected by ST-segment depression on the electrocardiogram. In this patient, bypassing the obstructed coronary artery resulted in relief of ischemia and a marked reduction in ST-segment depression.

(SOURCE: G. A. Brooks and T. D. Fahey. *Exercise Physiology: Human Bioenergetics and Its Applications.* New York: Macmillan, 1984, p. 521.

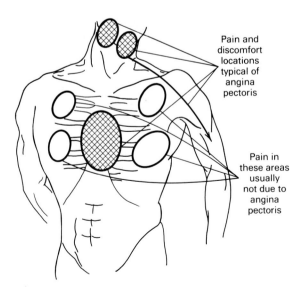

Pain and discomfort locations typical of angina pectoris

Pain in these areas usually not due to angina pectoris

Figure 17-6

Angina pectoris is pain caused by coronary artery ischemia. Pain in the center of the chest, neck, or radiating down the left arm may be angina pectoris *(dark ovals)*. Pain in the more lateral aspects of the chest *(light ovals)* is more typical of a "stitch" (exercise or gastrointestinally related side pain) and is not usually due to coronary ischemia.

(SOURCE: Adapted from L. T. Sheffield. The meaning of exercise test findings. In: S. M. Fox (ed.). Coronary Heart Disease: Prevention, Detection, Rehabilitation with Emphasis on Exercise Testing. Denver: International Medical Corporation, Department of Professional Education, 1974, p. 9.)

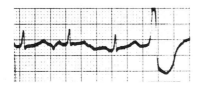

Figure 17-7
Example of a premature ventricular contraction (PVC). PVCs arise from ventricular ectopic foci (emergency pacemakers).

Physical Preparation for Exercise Tolerance Testing

A number of physical factors must be considered to ensure test standardization and consistency including pretest diet and exercise, clothing, room temperature, and medication. Failure to consider these factors can decrease the reliability of the measurements and may even place the subject at risk of injury. In addition, factors such as informed consent, human rights, and documentation should be given serious thought to protect the examiner and to reduce anxiety in the subject.

Subjects should report to the laboratory in a postabsorptive state. However, a light carbohydrate meal 3 to 4 hr prior to the test may be permitted. Cigarettes and caffeine products should be avoided because they could affect the results of the test by increasing heart rate, blood pressure, and the incidence of arrhythmias.

Proper clothing is important for comfort, safety, and artifact-free electrocardiograms. Subjects should wear running shoes and shorts. Women should also wear a tight-fitting bra that provides support but does not interfere with the ECG electrodes.

Tests should be conducted in a comfortable environmental temperature between 16 and 25°C. (62–77°F.) and at a relative humidity of 60% or lower. True tests of functional capacity should be conducted as close to sea level elevation as possible. $\dot{V}_{O_2max}$ is decreased by approximately 3% at an altitude of 5500 ft (see Chapter 12).

Warm-up is important during the test to prevent abnormalities in the electrocardiogram, avoid musculoskeletal injury, and facilitate the redirection of blood to the working muscles. The warm-up stage also gives the subject time to become familiar and comfortable with the exercise and allows the metabolic instruments time to achieve a degree of equilibrium before the more important maximal measurements are required. A monitored cool-down is important to prevent venous pooling and minimize stress on the heart.

Informed consent and human rights are important considerations during exercise stress testing. Subjects must always be treated courteously and with respect. Noise and distractions must be minimized and all attention should be focused on the subjects and the measurement instruments. Subjects should fully understand what is expected of them and the possible risks of taking a maximal exercise test. An informed consent declaration should be signed and witnessed.

All aspects of an exercise tolerance test should be documented. Any abnormal symptoms or physiological responses should be recorded on a standardized form. This precaution is important for both the subject and test administrator.

The use of medications is dependent on the purpose of the test. Tests of functional capacity instituted for the purpose of exercise prescription should be conducted while the subject is on typical medication (see appendix III for a list of classification of cardiac drugs and their effects). Medication schedules for subjects taking diagnostic treadmills will vary depending on the physician's objective for the test.

The Treadmill Test

The treadmill is the most common apparatus for determining functional capacity. This device allows the application of precise exercise intensities using types of exercise familiar to the vast majority of people (walking and running). This device is preferred by most researchers and clinicians because it renders a higher peak oxygen consumption than can be obtained with other techniques (see Table 17-5). Disadvantages include high cost, size, inability to directly measure power output, subject anxiety, and difficulty making measurements such as blood pressure (and, to a certain extent, electrocardiograms). Additionally, the treadmill cannot be used for people who are unable to walk (i.e., paraplegics, people with severe fractures or advanced neurological disease, etc.)

A variety of treadmill test protocols are used to measure functional capacity. The most common include the Bruce, Naughton, Balke, and Ellestad, and various modifications of these tests (Table 17-6). Although these protocols vary in their use of speed and slope, they have several factors in common—they are all continuous, standardized, include a warm-up, and involve a minimum to moderate metabolic transition between stages. Tests should be selected on the basis of subject population and the desired measurements.

Continuous treadmill tests involve the introduction of increasing intensities of exercise without a rest period between stages (a stage is an individual

TABLE 17-5 Comparison of Functional Capacity Achieved on a Treadmill and Other Devices (Treadmill = 100%)

	Males (%)	Females (%)
Bicycle ergometer (seated)	93	91
Bicycle ergometer (reclining)	90	88
Arm ergometer	88	85
Step test	96	98

TABLE 17-6 Principle Treadmill Protocols

Min	Bruce Test Speed (mph)	Bruce Test % Grade	Modified Bruce Test Speed (mph)	Modified Bruce Test % Grade	Balke Test Speed (mph)	Balke Test % Grade	Naughton Test Speed (mph)	Naughton Test % Grade	Ellestad Test Speed (mph)	Ellestad Test % Grade	Modified Åstrand Test Speed (mph)	Modified Åstrand Test % Grade
1	1.7 →	10 →	1.5 →	5 →	3.3	0	1.2 →	0 →	1.7 →	10 →	5–8.5	0 →
2						2						
3						3	2.0 →	3.5 →				
4	2.5 →	12 →	1.7 →	10 →		4			3.0 →			2.5 →
5						5	2.0 →	7.0 →				
6						6			4.0 →			
7	3.4 →	14 →	2.5 →	12 →		7	2.0 →	10.5 →				5.0 →
8						8			5.0 →			
9						9	2.0 →	14.0 →				
10	4.2 →	16 →	3.4 →	14 →		10			6.0 →	15 →		7.5 →
11						11	2.0 →	17.5 →				
12						12			7.0 →			
13	5.0 →	18 →	4.2 →	16 →		13	3.0 →	12.5 →				10.0 →
14						14			8.0 →			
15						15	3.0 →	15.0 →				
16	5.5 →	20 →	5.0 →	18 →		16						
17						17	3.0 →	17.5 →				
18						18						
19	6.0 →	22 →				19	3.0 →	20.0 →				
20						20						
21						21						
22						22						
23						23						
24						24						
25						25						

421

segment of the exercise test characterized by a specific speed and grade). Continuous tests are the method of choice because they are less time-consuming and are as effective as discontinuous tests (discontinuous tests employ a rest interval between stages).

Standardization is an extremely important consideration in exercise testing, as in all experimental research. The treadmill test is an example of the common stimulus–response technique of experimental inquiry. A stimulus is introduced (i.e., a precise, standardized exercise intensity) and the response is measured (heart rate, ECG, $\dot{V}_{O_2}$, blood pressure, perceived exertion, etc.). It is important that each subject take the test in the same manner as other subjects. All subjects must walk and run at the appointed time during the test. For example, it is inappropriate for a subject to run during stage 3 of a Bruce test because the test protocol requires subjects to walk during that stage. Running would increase the O_2 cost of the stage. Subjects must not be allowed to hold onto the railing of the treadmill during the test because it makes the tests irreplicable. Lack of standardization leads to increased variability of the metabolic requirement of the test (see Figure 17-8). Devices such as treadmill programmers that automatically change the speed and elevation of the treadmill during the test at specific time intervals facilitate the standardization of treadmill tests.

The metabolic increment between stages (increase in speed and grade) should not exceed 3 METs in healthy subjects and 0.5 to 1.0 MET in cardiac patients. Most exercise tests use 2- to 3-min stages. Tests should be chosen that are appropriate for the subject. For example, a modified Bruce test with a lower exercise intensity during the warm-up stage may be more appropriate for a recent myocardial infarction patient than the more strenuous standard Bruce test. Walking tests, such as the Balke, tend to render lower values for $\dot{V}_{O_2max}$, maximal heart rate, and are less reliable in young fit in-

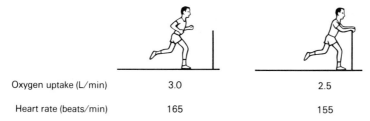

| Oxygen uptake (L/min) | 3.0 | 2.5 |
| Heart rate (beats/min) | 165 | 155 |

Figure 17-8
The effects of holding the railing during treadmill running on oxygen consumption and heart rate. It is important that treadmill tests be standardized, particularly when oxygen consumption is predicted on the basis of test duration.

(SOURCE: Adapted from P. O. Åstrand. Principles in ergometry and their implications in sports practice. Sports Med. 1:1–5, 1984.)

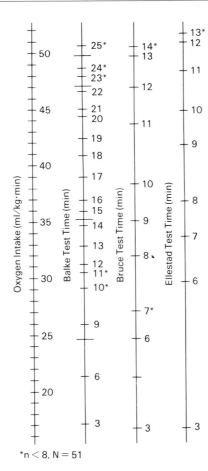

Figure 17-9

A nomogram to predict oxygen consumption from exercise duration during the Balke, Bruce, and Ellestad maximal treadmill stress test protocols.

(SOURCE: Modified from M. L. Pollock. A comparison of four protocols. Am. Heart J. 92:39–46, 1976.)

dividuals. However, the Balke might be the method of choice if blood pressure measurements were particularly critical (i.e., subjects with hypertension).

A variety of equations and nomograms have been established to predict oxygen uptake from exercise intensity on the treadmill (Eqs. 17-2 and 17-3, Source: American College of Sports Medicine, 1986, Figure 17-9, and Table 17-7). Energy cost of walking at speeds between 50 and 100 m·min^{-1} (1.9 and 3.7 mph):

$$\dot{V}_{O_2} \, (\text{ml} \cdot \text{kg}^{-1} \cdot \text{min}^{-1}) = \text{Horizontal component} + \text{Vertical component}.$$

Horizontal component: $\dot{V}_{O_2} \, (\text{ml} \cdot \text{kg}^{-1} \cdot \text{min}) = [\text{Speed} \cdot 0.1] + 3.5$ (17-2)

where: speed is expressed in meters per minute (1 m · min^{-1} = 0.0373 mph), 0.1 (ml · kg^{-1} · min^{-1}) is the oxygen cost of walking at 1 m · min^{-1}, and 3.5 (ml · kg^{-1} · min^{-1}) is the resting oxygen consumption or 1 MET.

Vertical component: $\dot{V}_{O_2} \, (\text{ml} \cdot \text{kg}^{-1} \cdot \text{min}^{-1}) = \%$ grade · speed · 1.8

TABLE 17-7A   Approximate Oxygen Cost of Walking (ml·kg^{-1}·min^{-1})

Speed		Grade					
m·min^{-1}	mph	0%	5%	10%	15%	20%	25%
50	1.87	8.5	13.0	17.5	22.0	26.5	31.0
55	2.05	9.0	14.0	18.9	23.9	28.8	33.8
60	2.24	9.5	14.9	20.3	25.7	31.1	36.5
65	2.43	10.0	15.9	21.7	27.6	33.4	39.3
70	2.61	10.5	16.8	23.1	29.4	35.7	42.0
75	2.80	11.0	17.8	24.5	31.3	38.0	44.8
80	2.99	11.5	18.7	25.9	33.1	40.3	47.5
85	3.17	12.0	19.7	27.3	35.0	42.6	50.3
90	3.36	12.5	20.6	28.7	36.8	44.9	53.0
95	3.54	13.0	21.6	30.1	38.7	47.2	55.8
100	3.73	13.5	22.5	31.5	40.5	49.5	58.5

TABLE 17-7b   Approximate Oxygen Cost of Running (ml·kg^{-1}·min^{-1}) at a 0% Grade

Speed			
m·min^{-1}	mph	$\dot{V}_{O_2}$	METs
140	5.2	31.5	9.0
145	5.4	32.5	9.3
150	5.6	33.5	9.6
155	5.8	34.5	9.9
160	6.0	35.5	10.1
165	6.2	36.5	10.4
170	6.3	37.5	10.7
175	6.5	38.5	11.0
180	6.7	39.5	11.3
185	6.9	40.5	11.6
190	7.1	41.5	11.9
195	7.3	42.5	12.1
200	7.5	43.5	12.4
205	7.6	44.5	12.7
210	7.8	45.5	13.0
215	8.0	46.5	13.3
220	8.2	47.5	13.6
225	8.4	48.5	13.9
230	8.6	49.5	14.1
235	8.8	50.5	14.4
240	9.0	51.5	14.7

where: % grade is the slope of the treadmill expressed as a fraction (vertical distance climbed/belt speed), speed is expressed in meters per minute, and 1.8 is the oxygen cost of a power output of 1 kgm.

Energy cost of running at speeds greater than 134 m $\cdot$ min^{-1} (5 mph):

$$\dot{V}_{O_2}\ (ml \cdot kg^{-1} \cdot min^{-1}) = \text{Horizontal component} + \text{Vertical component.} \quad (17\text{-}3)$$

Horizontal component: $\dot{V}_{O_2}\ (ml \cdot kg^{-1} \cdot min^{-1}) = [\text{Speed} \cdot 0.2] + 3.5$

where: speed is expressed in meters per minute, 0.2 (ml $\cdot$ kg^{-1} $\cdot$ min^{-1}) is the oxygen cost of running per meter per minute, and 3.5 (ml $\cdot$ kg^{-1} $\cdot$ min^{-1}) is the resting oxygen consumption, or 1 MET.

Vertical component: $\dot{V}_{O_2}\ (ml \cdot kg^{-1} \cdot min^{-1}) = \%\ \text{grade} \cdot \text{speed} \cdot 1.8 \cdot 0.5$

where: % grade is the slope of the treadmill expressed as a fraction, speed is expressed in meters per minute, 1.8 is the oxygen cost of a power output of 1 kgm, and 0.5 is the factor used to correct for the difference in O_2 cost of the vertical component of treadmill and outdoor running. (Note: the factor 0.5 should not be used if this equation is to be used for outdoor running.)

These equations, nomograms, and tables are not as accurate as direct measurements. Subjects will vary in efficiency and the oxygen cost of their running or walking style. For example, some people exhibit more up-and-down motions when walking than others, which increases the metabolic cost of the activity. However, the equations are useful when direct measurements are not possible.

Bicycle Ergometer (Cycle Ergometer)

The bicycle ergometer is the preferred instrument for stress testing in some laboratories, particularly in Europe. This device has the advantage of being relatively inexpensive, portable, and less intimidating than a treadmill. Physiological measurements are easier to obtain because the upper body is more stationary than on a treadmill or bench step. Power output can be measured directly, which makes the instrument attractive for energetic studies. Bicycle ergometry can be conducted in either an upright or a supine position.

Its disadvantages are many, particularly when testing women, elderly subjects, and people unfamiliar with cycling. Cycling places a considerable load on the quadriceps, which can lead to local muscle fatigue and limit performance before the capacity of the cardiovascular system is maximized (the purpose of a functional capacity test is to test the capacity of the cardiovascular system rather than the endurance capacity of particular muscle groups). Functional capacity measured on a bicycle ergometer is typically 8 to 15% lower than on a treadmill. Bicycle ergometer performance is largely dependent on the motivation of the subject. If the pedal revolutions decrease, then oxygen uptake decreases. Fatiguing subjects can volitionally and prematurely slow down when they begin to tire, resulting in an underestimation of functional capacity.

There are three basic types of bicycle ergometers: electrically braked, mechanically braked, and isokinetic. Electrically and mechanically braked ergometers place a known load on a flywheel (rotating mass analogous to the front wheel on a bicycle). These ergometers depend on the subject to pedal the ergometer at a set rate to obtain a given power output. In the isokinetic dynamometer, the pedal revolution is constant but the resistance is variable. Braked ergometers are by far the most commonly used for functional capacity testing.

Power is the term used to define the intensity of exercise performed on a bicycle ergometer. Power is work per unit of time (Eq. 17-4)

$$Power = Work/Time \qquad\qquad (17\text{-}4)$$

where:

Work   = Force × Distance,
Force   = frictional resistance to pedaling, and
Distance = revolutions per minute (rpm) and distance that the flywheel travels per revolution.

The watt is the accepted unit of measurement for power output (SI unit). Previously, the most common unit of measurement was the kilopond-meter per minute (kpm · min^{-1}; also called kilogram-meter per minute, kgm · min^{-1}). A kilopond-meter is the force required to move a mass of 1 kg a distance of 1 m at the normal acceleration of gravity. One watt is equal to 6.12 kpm · min^{-1}.

A bicycle ergometer that is to be used for testing should include indicators of frictional resistance and revolutions per minute. Rpm must be measured exactly with a device such as a microswitch and counter, rather than estimated from a speedometer because deviations in specified rpm will affect the total power output. The ergometer should be regularly calibrated to ensure accuracy. This is a simple matter in a friction-braked ergometer, but electrically braked ergometers typically require calibration by the manufacturer.

No specific test protocols are universally used by the majority of laboratories, but there are a few basic principles that should be used when designing a bicycle test. Basic considerations include starting power output, power increments, subject population, and standardization.

Exercise loads are administered in fixed increments or determined on the basis of heart rate response (Figure 17-10). In healthy subjects, starting power is 50 to 100 W (typically, 50 W in women and 100 W in men) and increased

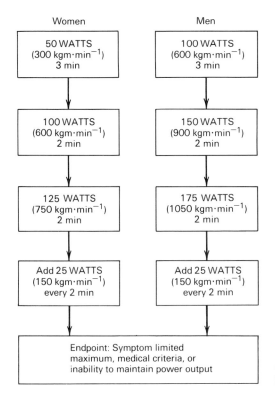

Figure 17-10

Sample bicycle ergometer protocols for men and women.

by 25 to 50 W every 2 to 3 min. Patient populations typically begin at 25 to 50 W with power increments of 5 to 25 W per stage.

Bicycle ergometer tests are usually conducted at 50 to 70 rpm in both healthy and patient populations. Subjects should be prompted to maintain the specified cadence with a metronome set at twice the rpm (i.e., if the cadence is 60 rpm, then the metronome should be set for 120 beats per minute). Trained cyclists are often tested at 90 rpm to simulate the pedaling cadence typically used in the sport. (In addition, when testing cyclists, the seat, pedals, and handlebars may be modified to assist the athletes in reaching a higher functional capacity.)

Oxygen consumption can be measured directly or estimated during bicycle ergometry from a predictive equation (Eq. 17-5 Source: American College of Sports Medicine 1986, Table 17-8).

$$\dot{V}_{O_2} \text{ (ml} \cdot \text{min}^{-1}) = [\text{Power output (W)} \cdot 12.2] + 300 \tag{17-5}$$

or

$$\dot{V}_{O_2} \text{ (ml} \cdot \text{min}^{-1}) = [\text{Power output (kgm} \cdot \text{min}^{-1}) \cdot 2.0] + 300$$

TABLE 17-8 Approximate $\dot{V}_{O_2}$ and METs on Bicycle Ergometer for Subjects with Different Body Weights

Power Output		$\dot{V}_{O_2}$	METs[b]					
W[a]	kgm·min⁻¹	(liters·min⁻¹)	50 kg	60 kg	70 kg	80 kg	90 kg	100 kg
25	150	0.6	3.4	2.8	2.4	2.1	1.9	1.7
50	300	0.9	5.1	4.2	3.6	3.2	2.8	2.5
75	450	1.2	6.8	5.7	4.8	4.2	3.8	3.4
100	600	1.5	8.5	7.1	6.1	5.3	4.7	4.2
125	750	1.8	10.2	8.5	7.3	6.4	5.7	5.1
150	900	2.1	12	10	8.5	7.5	6.6	6
175	1050	2.4	13.7	11.4	9.7	8.5	7.6	6.8
200	1200	2.7	15.4	12.8	11	9.6	8.5	7.7
225	1350	3	17.1	14.2	12.2	10.7	9.5	8.5
250	1500	3.3	18.8	15.7	13.4	11.7	10.4	9.4
275	1650	3.6	20.5	17.1	14.6	12.8	11.4	10.2
300	1800	3.9	22.2	18.5	15.9	13.9	12.3	11.1
325	1950	4.2	24	20	17.1	15	13.3	12
350	2100	4.5	25.7	21.4	18.3	16	14.2	12.8

[a]The equivalency of watts and kilogram-meter per minute is approximate.
[b]1 MET is approximately equal to $3.5 \text{ ml·kg}^{-1}\text{·min}^{-1}$.

where: 12.2 and 2.0 is the oxygen cost (ml · min⁻¹) of 1 W or 1 kgm · min⁻¹, respectively, and 300 (ml) is the resting oxygen consumption.

The equations predict the gross amount of oxygen consumed in liters per minute. These values must be divided by body weight to calculate oxygen consumption in milliliters per kilogram per minute, or METs. Standardization is critical when predicting $\dot{V}_{O_2}$. Factors that must be considered include seat height, rpm, static exercise performed while gripping the handlebars, and ambient environment.

Step Tests

Step tests are among the oldest techniques for measuring functional capacity. Popular procedures, such as the Harvard step test, involve completion of an exercise protocol and the measurement of recovery heart rate. Recovery heart rate was used in these tests because it was technically difficult to measure exercise pulse rates, and accurate equations to predict oxygen consumption during bench stepping were unavailable. However, recovery pulse rate is only moderately related to maximal oxygen consumption, so these types of tests are less appropriate than current procedures for measuring physical fitness.

Step tests have the advantage of being inexpensive, portable, and technically simple to perform. They can be adapted to field situations such as physical education classes and can be administered to large numbers of people in a relatively short time. The disadvantages make this test inappropriate for the laboratory. Physiological measurements are difficult to perform, and there is a danger of tripping, which makes this type of test inappropriate for the elderly and certain types of medically impaired subjects (particularly the orthopedically and neurologically impaired). Large step heights must be used when testing young, healthy subjects, which can lead to local muscle fatigue and an underestimation of functional capacity. Functional capacity measured on a step test is typically 5 to 7% less than that measured on a treadmill. To be accurate, the subjects must stand upright and not lean over as they step up.

As discussed, step tests are typically used in field situations, so oxygen consumption is usually estimated rather than directly measured. Predicting oxygen consumption during bench stepping requires a knowledge of the bench height and the number of lifts per minute. Oxygen consumption is predicted in milliliters per kilogram per minute (Eq. 17-6 Source: American College of Sports Medicine, 1986; Table 17-9).

Predicting $\dot{V}_{O_2}$ during bench stepping:

$$\dot{V}_{O_2} \ (\text{ml} \cdot \text{kg}^{-1} \cdot \text{min}^{-1}) = (O_2 \text{ cost of positive and negative work}) + (O_2 \text{ cost of horizontal movement}) \tag{17-6}$$

TABLE 17-9 **Oxygen Cost of Bench Stepping (ml·kg^{-1}·min^{-1})**

Step Height		Step Frequency (Steps·min^{-1})				
cm	in	15	20	25	30	35
4	1.6	6.7	8.9	11.1	13.4	15.6
6	2.4	7.4	9.9	12.3	14.8	17.3
8	3.1	8.1	10.8	13.5	16.2	19
10	3.9	8.8	11.8	14.7	17.7	20.6
12	4.7	9.6	12.7	15.9	19.1	22.3
14	5.5	10.3	13.7	17.1	20.6	24
16	6.3	11	14.7	18.3	22	25.7
18	7.1	11.7	15.6	19.5	23.4	27.3
20	7.9	12.4	16.6	20.7	24.9	29
22	8.7	13.2	17.5	21.9	26.3	30.7
24	9.4	13.9	18.5	23.1	27.7	32.4
26	10.2	14.6	19.4	24.3	29.2	34
28	11	15.3	20.4	25.5	30.6	35.7
30	11.8	16	21.4	26.7	32	37.4
32	12.6	16.7	22.3	27.9	33.5	39.1
34	13.4	17.5	23.3	29.1	34.9	40.7
36	14.2	18.2	24.2	30.3	36.4	42.4
38	15	18.9	25.2	31.5	37.8	44.1
40	15.7	19.6	26.2	32.7	39.2	45.8
42	16.5	20.3	27.1	33.9	40.7	47.4

The oxygen cost of the positive and negative work of bench stepping:

$$\dot{V}_{O_2} \text{ (ml} \cdot \text{kg}^{-1} \cdot \text{min}^{-1}) = \text{Bench height (m)} \cdot \text{Step rate (per min}^{-1}) \cdot 1.8 \cdot 1.33$$

where 1.8 is the oxygen cost (ml) of a power output of 1 kgm and 1.33 is the factor used to calculate the oxygen cost of the total work (positive work + negative work, where the oxygen cost of negative work is one-third that of the positive work).

The oxygen cost of horizontal movements (moving back and forth while stepping on and off the step):

1. Divide step rate by 10 to estimate the MET cost of the horizontal movements.
2. Multiply the MET cost of horizontal movements by 3.5 to get the oxygen cost of horizontal movements.
3. Add the oxygen cost of horizontal movements to the oxygen cost of positive and negative work to get the total oxygen cost of the bench stepping exercise.

Bench stepping and bicycle ergometer test protocols are similar. Step tests require a variable height bench and a metronome to maintain cadence. The most common procedure is to begin with a step height of 2 cm and a stepping cadence of 30 repetitions per minute. One repetition consists of the subject standing in front of the step bench, placing one foot and then the other on the step bench, then returning to the starting position, one step at a time (the metronome should be adjusted to make four sounds per repetition). The step height is increased 2 to 4 cm every 1 to 2 min. Another variation is to use a bench with a fixed height, but increase the number of repetitions per exercise stage. This method is less desirable than the adjustable step bench technique because it requires greater cooperation from the subject and subjects him or her to a greater risk of injury (a subject has to move faster when fatigued).

Exercise-Specific Tests

As discussed in Chapter 7, the determination of maximal oxygen consumption requires that the test endpoint be determined by the cardiovascular system rather than by local muscle fatigue. Using this criterion, tests involving arm ergometry, wheelchair ergometry, and swimming will not render true measurements of functional capacity (Figures 17-11 and 8-6).

Field Tests The Cooper 12-min run, the Balke 15-min run, and the 1½-mile run are among the most popular exercise-specific tests. These tests have a relatively good relationship to $\dot{V}_{O_2\text{max}}$ in young, healthy subjects but are less precise in other populations. They may be dangerous for some people because the electrocardiogram is not monitored during the test. Cooper recommends a low-level conditioning period before taking the test.

Swimming tests performed on a heterogeneous population measure skill

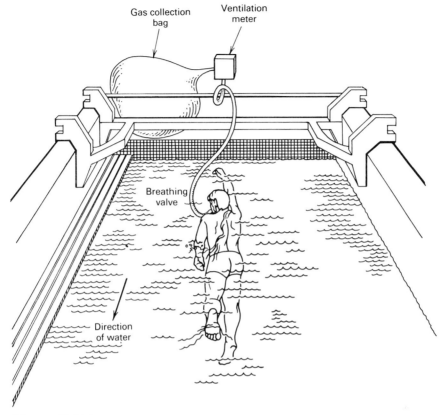

Figure 17-11A

Swimming flume for measuring exercise capacities during swimming: b)
Field measurement of $\dot{V}O_2$ during wheel chair propulsion.

(SOURCE: Adapted from I. Holmer, Physiology of swimming man *Acta Physiologica Scand.*
(Suppl 407), 1974)

rather than functional capacity. The energy cost in swimming is dictated by
the metabolic requirements of forward propulsion and body drag (resistance
provided by a body in water). Propulsion can be increased and drag decreased
by improving technique. Swimming tests are valuable in developing an exercise prescription for swimming and measuring functional capacity in well-
trained swimmers.

Upper Body Endurance Tests Wheelchair and arm ergometers stress
the relatively small upper body muscles. Maximal exercise on these devices
results in local muscle fatigue rather than a cardiovascular limitation of exercise. Decrements of 25% or more between these upper body tests and a
treadmill are not uncommon. However, in subjects, such as paraplegics, who

Figure 17-11B.
Field test measurement of V_{O_2} during wheel chair propulsion.

(SOURCE: T. D. Fahey.)

are unable to use their legs, these tests are all that is available for assessing functional capacity.

Submaximal Tests

Submaximal exercise tests attempt to predict functional capacity from the heart rate response during a submaximal bout of exercise. Procedures such as the Åstrand bicycle ergometer test rely on the nearly linear relationship between oxygen consumption and heart rate and an assumed maximal heart rate (i.e., $HR_{max} = 220 - age$).

A simple procedure that requires one or two five-min exercise bouts is shown in Figure 17-12. This technique involves the prediction of maximal power output derived from the assumed linear relationship between heart rate and power output. $\dot{V}_{O_2max}$ is predicted using the equation presented on page 427. The accuracy of this technique is based on a series of assumptions

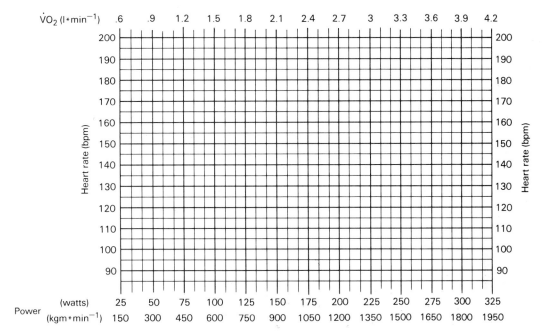

Figure 17-12
Predicting $\dot{V}_{O_2max}$ from submaximal power output and heart rate. Note that this technique may be subject to considerable error and should be used with caution. Instructions: (1) Estimate maximal heart rate (subtract age from 220). (2) Plot heart rate response during two to three different 5-min exercise bouts on a bicycle ergometer. The power output for the first exercise bout should be approximately 50 W for men and 25 W for women. Subsequent power outputs should not raise the heart rate above 75% of predicted maximum heart rate. (3) Extend power-heart rate line to predicted maximum heart rate. (4) Read predicted V_{O_2max} from the top of the chart.

(age predicted maximum heart rate, linear relationship between HR and power output, and the accuracy of the $\dot{V}_{O_2}$–bicycle ergometry equation). Small errors in any one of these assumed values can lead to considerable error.

The pulse working capacity 170 (PWC_{170}) is a popular submaximal test of cardiovascular capacity that is similar to the procedure just mentioned. PWC_{170} involves plotting the relationship of heart rate and power output on two to five repetitions of 2- to 3-min exercise bouts of increasing intensity. The power output at a heart rate of 170 beats per minute is predicted from the power–heart rate relationship.

As discussed, it should not be assumed that unmonitored submaximal exercise tests are acceptable for testing older or symptomatic patients. Problems can and do occur at any level of exercise. In addition, these deceptively simple unmonitored tests can unwittingly become supramaximal exercise tests for older or deconditioned subjects.

Exercise Prescription to Develop Functional Capacity

The ideal, well-rounded physical activity program might consist of running, weight training, stretching, swimming, calisthenics, and relaxation exercises. In addition, sports requiring a high degree of skill might be added, such as golf, tennis, skiing, badminton, basketball, racquetball, and handball. Most people do not have the luxury of participating in such a program. They have a limited amount of time and require a program that will render the maximum benefits in a relatively short time.

How Much Exercise Is Necessary?

As discussed in Chapter 11, a high functional capacity is important in reducing the risk of coronary heart disease. The goal of the health-oriented program should be to increase the functional capacity to at least the "good" level of physical fitness (relative to age and sex) shown in Table 17-3. Essential factors in achieving this goal are the type, frequency, duration, and intensity of exercise (Table 17-10).

Type The health-directed exercise program should emphasize rhythmic, continuous endurance activities such as walking, running, cycling, swimming, and cross-country skiing. "Stop-and-start" activities, such as tennis and racquetball, are acceptable if the skill level is high enough for the activity to be continuous and the intensity is vigorous. However, the personality of the individual should be considered when prescribing competitive sports as exercise. Some health experts have suggested that excessive competition by a

---

TABLE 17-10 Recommended Quantity and Quality of Exercise for Developing and Maintaining Fitness in Healthy Adults

Mode of activity
Aerobic or endurance exercises, such as running-jogging, walking-hiking, swimming, skating, bicycling, rowing, cross-country skiing, rope skipping, and various game activities

Frequency of training
3 to 5 days per week

Intensity of training
At least 60% of heart rate reserve plus resting heart rate, or 50 to 85% of maximum oxygen uptake. Heart rate reserve = HR max − HR rest.

Duration of training
15 to 60 min of continuous aerobic activity. Duration is dependent on the intensity of the activity.

SOURCE: Adapted from a position statement of the American College of Sports Medicine.

"type A" person may actually negate the positive effects of physical activity and increase the risk of coronary heart disease.

The choice of an activity depends on the individual's functional capacity and factors such as body fat percentage, previous musculoskeletal injuries, and individual preference. Running is inappropriate if the physical fitness is low because the stress of running will probably result in injury. A person who dislikes swimming will be unlikely to continue the program if that type of exercise is prescribed.

Planning is an important ingredient in making progressive improvements in fitness. People should have several activity options available to them. For example, if a person is injured while running, he should switch to swimming or cycling. A "fair-weather" walker should have an alternative activity for rainy days.

Frequency   For most people, the ideal exercise frequency varies from 3 to 6 days per week. However, in sedentary people or heart patients who are just beginning a program, more frequent, shorter exercise training sessions are often appropriate. For example, in these types of subjects, daily or twice-daily exercise sessions of 5 min in duration may be easily tolerated and lead to the most rapid rate of physiological adapation. As fitness improves, the person can extend the time of each session until a longer and more beneficial exercise training session can be tolerated. However, excessive exercise frequency should be avoided by most people beginning a program because they will rarely adhere to the prescription of a high-frequency–short-duration exercise training program (they tend to overtrain and consequently develop overuse injuries). In general, deconditioned persons should be advised to begin with three to four sessions of moderate activity per week and should progress to more frequent sessions only as fitness improves. Research has shown that people sustain more musculoskeletal injuries as the frequency of exercise increases. People must realize that their bodies will not adapt at a faster rate than they are capable. Overtraining usually results in injury rather than accelerated training gains.

Inflexible training schedules are inadvisable. People should avoid exercising when ill, in extreme heat or cold, or when overly tired, even if they have not completed the number of workout sessions they have planned for the week.

Duration   The ideal duration of a training session for a healthy adult is between 20 and 60 min. Low-intensity exercise, such as walking, and "stop-and-start" sports, such as tennis and racquetball, should be practiced at least 45 min. As with frequency, no exercise duration is appropriate for everyone. People should be instructed to stop when they are overly tired or experience symptoms such as leg cramps, chest pains, dyspnea, or irregular heart rhythms.

Intensity This is perhaps the most critical aspect of the exercise prescription. If the intensity is insufficient, there will be little improvement in fitness. If the intensity is excessive, however, then injury may occur. For example, in a study of people who sustained a nonfatal heart attack, excessive exercise intensity was cited as a precipitating factor. More frequently, excessive exercise intensity leads to a variety of overuse musculoskeletal injuries that necessitates a drastic reduction or cessation of their training activities.

As discussed, the ideal exercise intensity for healthy adults is between 50 and 80% of $\dot{V}_{O_2max}$, or approximately 70 to 90% of maximum heart rate. This intensity can be estimated from the heart rate. From Figure 17-13, it can be seen that a given percentage of maximum heart rate does not correspond to the same percentage of $\dot{V}_{O_2max}$ (e.g., 60% HR_{max} = 43% $\dot{V}_{O_2max}$). An accurate assessment of proper training intensity can be obtained using the heart rate reserve (HR_{max} − HR_{rest}) and the Karvonen formula (Eq. 17-7).

$$THR = 0.6 \text{ to } 0.8 \cdot (HR_{max} - HR_{rest}) + HR_{rest} \qquad (17\text{-}7)$$

where 0.6 to 0.8 is a range of percentages of HR reserve (choose one for each calculation), HR_{max} is the measured or predicted maximum heart rate, and HR_{rest} is a typical resting value for the resting heart rate.

Maximum heart rate can be measured or estimated. Measurement during a monitored exercise stress test is preferred because it is safer. In young, fit, asymptomatic people, however, HR_{max} can be measured after a maximum field test such as a 300 to 400-m sprint. This is a dangerous procedure in older, sedentary, or symptomatic populations. HR_{max} can also be estimated by subtracting the person's age from 220.

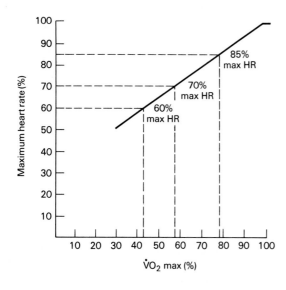

Figure 17-13

The relationship between V_{O_2} and heart rate. Notice that a given percentage of maximal heart rate is not equal to the same percentage of V_{O_2max}. In addition, note that the relationship is curvilinear during heavy exercise, which introduces error when one tries to estimate metabolic rate and functional capacity from heart rate.

(SOURCE: Adapted from M. L. Pollock, J. H. Wilmore, and S. M. Fox. Health and Fitness Through Physical Activity. New York: John Wiley, 1978.)

"Fine-Tuning" the Program These exercise prescription principles should be used only as rough guidelines. People will vary in the way they feel on a particular day. If they feel ill, they should not exercise. If they feel particularly good, then they can sometimes exceed the exercise prescription with few adverse side effects (provided they are healthy and reasonably fit).

People should be told about other indicators of intensity and fatigue, such as sweating, ventilation, and perceived exertion. The basic exercise prescription should cause people to sweat during the training session. People should understand that this is normal and desirable. The "talk test" is a rough indicator of proper exercise intensity. People should exercise at the faster rate at which they can carry on a conversation. This places them at an intensity of approximately 60 to 70% of $\dot{V}_{O_2max}$. Finally, people should learn to associate a particular level of perceived exertion with the target heart rate. This will enable them to exercise more consistently at the proper intensity.

Exercise Prescription for the Cardiac Patient

The exercise training program should be based on an exercise test that includes measurement of heart rate, blood pressure, and, ideally, oxygen consumption during graded exercise. Patients should be evaluated for ischemia, arrhythmias, and adequate blood flow to the extremities (leg pains, or intolerable claudication, in these patients are sometimes caused by vascular disease in the lower extremities). Medications such as beta-blocking agents, digitalis, diuretics, vasodilators, and antiarrhythmics should be considered in the exercise prescription (Appendix III). Exercise tests designed to aid in the exercise prescription should be conducted while the patient is taking normal medications.

Exercise testing can begin as early as 1 to 2 days prior to discharge from the hospital. The exercise prescription should be evaluated regularly. A training diary, ideally kept by the exercise leader, should be used to record the nature, intensity, and duration of each exercise session. Clinical studies have shown that consideration of intensity of the exercise is vital to improved capacity. Training above 50 to 60% of maximum will result in improved work capacity and lowered resting and submaximal exercise heart rates, whereas recreational activities generally will not.

Myocardial oxygen consumption ($M\dot{V}_{O_2}$) is an important consideration when prescribing calisthenic and resistive exercises to cardiac patients. As discussed in Chapter 7, an acceptable indirect index of myocardial oxygen consumption is *heart rate* × *systolic blood pressure* (i.e., rate-pressure product, RPP). Exercises of the same metabolic cost can vary considerably in $M\dot{V}_{O_2}$. Exercises that require use of the upper extremities, or those that induce Valsalva's maneuver, should be administered with care. Likewise, exercise should be prescribed with discretion in the presence of angina. An exercise that might be easily tolerated by one patient may produce an ischemic response in another.

The amount of improvement in cardiovascular capacity in the cardiac rehabilitation program depends on adherence to the program over months and years. Adherence to the program depends on program design, attitude of the spouse, nature of the activities, and the accessibility of facilities and personnel. Reinforcers such as knowledge of reduction in percentage fat, body weight, reduced heart rate and blood pressure at rest and during exercise, decreased angina, and improved working capacity are potent motivators. Realistic short-term goals can also be very effective in maximizing adherence to the program.

There has been considerable interest in marathon training for the postcardiac patient. It has even been suggested that such training may offer immunity from coronary disease (a theory that is not taken seriously by most experts). However, marathon training has definite limitations, as the vast majority of postcardiacs simply do not have the aerobic capacity to run a marathon safely. In addition, most occupations require training in the upper extremities, rather that the legs. There are minimal cross-over benefits between lower and upper body exercise. Muscle specificity must be considered in the exercise prescription of the cardiac patient who will return to vocational and avocational activities.

Cardiac patients involved in heavy exercise should take precautions and avoid unnecessary risks—more than 60% of coronary patients who die do so before they get to the hospital. Care should be taken to avoid competition and exercising in adverse environments. Patients should run with a group of people trained in cardiopulmonary resuscitation (CPR) and ideally in a supervised, monitored environment.

Summary

The exercise training program should stress the body at a level appropriate for the individual or injury may occur. Exercise training is not appropriate for everyone. Some medical conditions make exercise dangerous. People with significant disease risk factors should engage in an exercise program only after seeking medical advice.

Maximal oxygen consumption ($\dot{V}_{O_2max}$) is considered the best measure of cardiovascular fitness. It is measured in a laboratory but can be estimated with various field tests. Oxygen consumption at various exercise intensities during walking, running, cycling, and bench stepping can be estimated using established equations.

The minimum exercise program for health promotion has been determined to be participation in endurance-type exercise (walking, running, cycling, swimming, etc.), 3 to 5 days a week, for 20 to 60 min, at 60 to 80% of $\dot{V}_{O_2max}$. Heart rate can be used as an aid to selecting the proper exercise intensity.

Selected Readings

AMERICAN COLLEGE OF SPORTS MEDICINE. Guidelines for Graded Exercise Testing and Exercise Prescription. Philadelphia: Lea & Febiger, 1986.

AMERICAN HEART ASSOCIATION. Exercise Testing and Training of Individuals with Heart Disease or at High Risk for Its Development: A Handbook for Physicians. Dallas: American Heart Association, 1975.

ÅSTRAND, P.-O. Principles in ergometry and their implications in sports practice. Sports Med.:1–5, 1984.

BARNARD, R.J., G.W. GARDNER, N.V. DIACO, R.N. McALPIN, and A.A. KATUS. Cardiovascular responses to sudden strenuous exercise: heart rate, blood pressure, and ECG. J. Appl. Physiol. 34:833–837, 1973.

BROOKS, G.A., and T.D. FAHEY. Exercise Physiology: Human Bioenergetics and Its Applications. New York: MacMillan, 1984.

BRUCE, R.A., and T.A. DeROUEN. Exercise testing as a predictor of heart disease and sudden death. Hosp. Pract. 14:69–75, 1978.

CONSOLAZIO, C.F., R.E. JOHNSON, and L.J. PECORA. Physiological Measurements of Metabolic Functions in Man. New York: McGraw-Hill, 1963.

DONOVAN, C.M., and G.A. BROOKS. Muscular efficiency during steady-rate exercise II: effects of walking speed on work rate. J. Appl. Physiol. 43:431–439, 1977.

FROELICHER, V.F. Exercise Testing and Training. New York: Le Jacq Publishing Co., 1983.

GAESSER, G.A., and G.A. BROOKS. Muscular efficiency during steady-rate exercise: effects of speed and work rate. J. Appl. Physiol. 38:1132–1139, 1975.

HANSON, P., M.D. GIESE, and R.J. CORLISS. Clinical guidelines for exercise training. Postgrad. Med. 67:120–138, 1980.

KAIJSER, L. Limiting factors for aerobic muscle performance. Acta Physiol. Scand. 346 (Suppl.):1–96, 1970.

KATCH, F.I., F.N. GIRANDOLA, and V.L. KATCH. The relationship of body weight on maximum oxygen uptake and heavy work endurance capacity on the bicycle ergometer. Med. Sci. Sports 3:101–106, 1971.

KEUL, J. Limiting Actors of Physical Performance. Stuttgart: Georg Thieme, 1973.

McHENRY, P.L. The risks of graded exercise testing. Am. J. Cardiol. 39:935–937, 1977.

MELLEROWICZ, H., and V.N. SMODLAKA. Ergometry: Basics of Medical Exercise Testing. Baltimore: Urban & Schwarzenberg, 1981.

NAUGHTON, J.P., and H.K. HELLERSTEIN (eds.). Exercise Testing and Exercise Training in Coronary Heart Disease. New York: Academic Press, 1973.

POLLOCK, M.L. A comparison of four protocols for maximal treadmill stress testing. Am. Heart J. 92:39–46, 1976.

POLLOCK, M.L., J.H. WILMORE, and S.M. FOX. Health and Fitness Through Physical Activity. New York: John Wiley, 1978.

ROWELL, L.B., H.L. TAYLOR, and Y. WANG. Limitations to prediction of maximal oxygen intake. J. Appl. Physiol. 19:919–927, 1964.

SALTIN, B., and P.-O. ÅSTRAND. Maximal oxygen uptake in athletes. J. Appl. Physiol. 23:353–358, 1967.

SHEPHARD, R.J. Can we identify those for whom exercise is hazardous? Sports Med. 1:75–86, 1984.

SHEPHARD, R.J. Human Physiological Work Capacity. London: Cambridge University Press, 1978.

SHEPHARD, R.J. Tests of maximum oxygen intake, a critical review. Sports Med. 1:99–124, 1984.

STROMME, S.B., H. FREY, O.K. HARLEM, O. STOKKE, O.D. VELLAR, L.E. AARO, and J.E. JOHNSON. Physical activity and health. Social Med. 29 (Suppl.):9–36, 1982.

TAYLOR, H.L., E.R. BUSKIRK, and A. HENSCHEL. Maximal oxygen intake as an objective measure of cardiorespiratory performance. J. Appl. Physiol. 8:73–80, 1955.

TAYLOR, H.L., W.L. HASKELL, S.M. FOX, and H. BLACKBURN. Exercise tests: a summary of procedures and concepts of stress testing for cardiovascular diagnosis and function evaluation. In: Blackburn, H. (ed.). Measurement in Exercise Electrocardiography. Springfield, Ill.: Charles C Thomas, 1969.

THOMPSON, P.D. Cardiovascular hazards of physical activity. Exercise Sport Sci. Rev. 10:208–235, 1982.

WILMORE, J.H., and D.L. COSTILL. Semi-automated systems approach to the assessment of oxygen uptake during exercise. J. Appl. Physicol. 36:618–620, 1974.

WILMORE, J.H., J.A. DAVIS, and A.C. NORTON. An automated system for assessing metabolic and respiratory function during exercise. J. Appl. Physiol. 40:619–624, 1976.

WYNDHAM, C.H., N.B. STRYDOM, W.P. LEARY, and C.G. WILLIAMS. A comparison of methods of assessing the maximum oxygen intake. Int. Z. Angew. Physiol. Arbets 22:285–295, 1966.

Appendix I

List of Symbols and Abbreviations

Note: A dash over any symbol indicates a mean value (e.g., $\bar{x}$); a dot above any symbol indicates time derivate (e.g., $\dot{V}$).

Respiratory and Hemodynamic Notations

V	gas volume
$\dot{V}$	gas volume/unit time (usually liters/min)
R	ventilatory respiratory exchange ratio (volume CO_2/volume O_2 $= \dot{V}_{CO_2}/\dot{V}_{O_2}$)
RQ	cellular respiratory quotient ($\dot{V}_{CO_2}/\dot{V}_{O_2}$)
I	inspired gas
E	expired gas
A	alveolar gas
F	fractional concentration in dry gas phase
f	respiratory frequency (breath/unit time)
TLC	total lung capacity
VC	vital capacity
FRC	functional residual capacity
RV	residual volume
T	tidal gas
D	dead space
FEV	forced expiratory volume
$FEV_{1.0}$	forced expiratory volume in 1 sec
MET	multiple of the resting metabolic rate, approximately equal to 3.5 ml O_2/kg body weight/min

MVV	maximal voluntary ventilation (maximum breathing capacity, MBC)
D_L	diffusing capacity of the lungs (ml/min $\times$ mm Hg)
P	gas pressure
B or Bar	barometric
STPD	0°C, 760 mm Hg, dry
BTPS	body temperature and pressure, saturated with water vapor
ATPD	ambient temperature and pressure, dry
ATPS	ambient temperature and pressure, saturated with water vapor
Q	blood flow or volume
$\dot{Q}$	blood flow/unit time (without other notation, cardiac output; usually liters/min)
SV or V_S	stroke volume
HR or f_H	heart rate (usually beats/min)
BV	blood volume
Hb	hemoglobin concentration (g/100 ml)
HbO_2	oxyhemoglobin
Hct	hematocrit
BP	blood pressure
TPR	total peripheral resistance
C	concentration in blood phase
S	percentage saturation of Hb
a	arterial
c	capillary
v	venous

Temperature Notations

T	temperature
r	rectal
s	skin
e	esophageal
m	muscle
ty	tympanic
M	metabolic energy yield
C	convective heat exchange
R	radiation heat exchange
E	evaporative heat loss
S	storage of body heat
°C	temperature in degrees celsius
°F	temperature in degrees Fahrenheit

Body Dimensions

W	weight
H	height
L	length
LBM	lean body mass
BSA	body surface area

Statistical Notations

M, $\bar{X}$	arithmetic mean
SD or S.D.	standard deviation
SE or S.E.	standard error of the mean
n	number of observations
r	correlation coefficient
range	smallest and largest observed value
Σ	summation
P	probability
*	denotes a (probably) significant difference; $P < 0.05$

Examples

V_A	volume of alveolar gas
$\dot{V}_E$	expiratory gas volume/minute
$\dot{V}_{O_2}$	volume of oxygen/minute (oxygen uptake/min)
$\dot{V}_{O_2 max}$	maximal volume of O_2 consumed/min
V_T	tidal volume
P_A	alveolar gas pressure
P_B	barometric pressure
F_{IO2}	fractional concentration of O_2 in inspired gas
P_{AO2}	alveolar oxygen pressure
pH_a	arterial pH
Ca_{O2}	oxygen content in arterial blood
$Ca_{O2} - C\bar{v}_{O2}$	difference in oxygen content between arterial and mixed venous blood, often written $(a-v)O_2$
T_r	rectal temperature
$(a-v)_{O2}$	arterial venous O_2 difference

Chemical and Physical Notations

ADP	adenosine diphosphate
AMP	adenosine monophosphate
ATP	adenosine triphosphate
Ca^{++}	calcium ion
Cl^-	chloride ion
CO_2	carbon dioxide
CP	creatine phosphate
e^-	electron
FFA	free fatty acids
H	hydrogen atom
H^+	hydrogen ion
$H^.$	hydride ion
HCO_3^-	bicarbonate ion
Hg	mercury
H_2CO_3	carbonic acid
H_2O	water
K^+	potassium ion
kcal	kilocalorie
kcal/min	kilocalories per minute
kg	kilogram
m	meter
meq	milliequivalent
min	minute
ml	milliliter
mm	millimeter
mmol	millimole
mM	millimolar
Na^+	sodium ion
O_2	oxygen
P	power
PC	phosphocreatine
P_i	inorganic phosphate
PP_i	pyrophosphate
sec	second

Based on Federation Proceedings 9:602–605, 1960.

Appendix II

Units and Measures

Note: The basic unit of measurement adopted by the System International D'Unites will be denoted as the basic SI unit.

Acceleration

Basic SI unit: meter per second squared ($m \cdot sec^{-2}$)
1 centimeter per second squared ($cm \cdot sec^{-2}$) $= 10^2 m \cdot sec^2$
1 kilometer per hour per second ($km \cdot hr^{-1} \cdot sec^{-1}$) $= 2.7 \times 10^{-1} m \cdot sec^{-2}$
Common Anglo-Saxon units of acceleration:
1 foot per second squared ($ft \cdot sec^{-2}$) $= 3.048t \times 10^{-1} m \cdot sec^{-2}$
1 mile per hour per second ($mile \cdot hr^{-1} \cdot sec^{-1}$) $= 4.470 \times 10^{-1} m \cdot sec^{-2}$

Angle

Basic SI unit: radian (rad)
1 degree (°) $= 1.754 \times 10^{-2} rad$
1 minute (') $= 2.908 \times 10^{-4} rad$
1 second (") $= 4.848 \times 10^{-6} rad$
1 grade (g) $= 1.570 \times 10^{-2} rad$

Angular Velocity

Basic SI unit: radian per second (rad·sec^{-1})
1 degree per minute (°min^{-1}) $= 2.908 \times 10^4$rads·sec^{-1}
1 radian per minute (rad min^{-1} $= 1.6 \times 10^{-2}$rad·sec^{-1}
1 degree per second (°sec^{-1}) $= 1.745 \times 10^{-2}$rad·sec^{-1}

Area

Basic SI unit: square meter (m^2)
1 square micrometer (m^2) $= 10^{-12}$m^2
1 square millimeter (mm^2) $= 10^{-6}$m^2
1 square centimeter (cm^2) $= 10^{-4}$m^2
1 square decameter (dm^2) $= 10^2$m^2
1 square hectometer (hm^2) $= 10^2$m^2
1 square kilometer (km^2) $= 10^6$m^2
Common Anglo-Saxon units of area:
1 square inch (in.^{2}) $= 6.451 \times 10^{-4}$m^2
1 square foot (ft^2) $= 9.290 \times 10^{-2}$m^2
1 square yard (yd^2) $= 8.361 \times 10^{-1}$m^2
1 acre (ac^2) $= 4.046 \times 10^3$m^2
1 square mile (mi^2) $= 2.589 \times 10^6$m^2

Density

Basic SI unit: kilogram per cubic meter (kg·m^{-3})
1 microgram per cubic centimeter (μg·cm^{-3}) $= 10^{-3}$kg·m^{-3}
1 milligram per cubic centimeter (mg·cm^{-3}) $= 1$ kg·m^{-3}
1 gram per cubic centimeter (g·cm^{-3}) $= 10^3$ kg·m^{-3}
Common Anglo-Saxon unit of density:
1 pound per cubic foot $= 1.601 \times 10$kg·m^{-3}

Force

Basic SI unit: newton (N)
1 pond (p) $= 9.80665 \times 10^{-3}$ N
1 kilopond (kp) $= 9.80665$ N
1 dyne (dyn) $= 10^{-5}$ N

446

Common Anglo-Saxon unit of force:
1 foot-pound (ft lb · sec^{-2}) = 0.13825495437 N

Frequency

Basic SI unit: hertz (Hz)
1 kilohertz (kHz) = 1000 Hz
Common Anglo-Saxon unit of frequency:
1 cycle per second (c/sec) = 1 Hz

Length

Basic SI unit: meter (m):
1 angstrom (Å) = 10^{-10} m
1 nanometer (nm) = 10^{-9} m
1 micrometer (μm) = 10^{-6} m
1 millimeter (mm) = 10^{-3} m
1 centimeter (cm) = 10^{-2} m
1 decimeter (dm) = 10^{-1} m
1 decameter (dam) = 10 m
1 hectometer (hm) = 10^2 m
1 kilometer (km) = 10^3 m
Common Anglo-Saxon units of length:
1 inch (in.) = 2.540×10^{-2} m
1 foot (ft) = 3.048×10^{-1} m
1 yard (yd) = 9.144×10^{-1} m
1 fathom (fath) = 1.828 m
1 furlong (fur) = 2.011×10^2 m
1 statute mile (mi) = 1.609×10^3

Linear Velocity

Basic SI unit: meter per second (m·sec^{-1})
1 centimeter per sec (cm·s^{-1}) = 10^{-2}m·sec^{-2}
1 kilometer per hour (km·hr^{-1}) = 2.7×10^{-1}m·sec^{-1}
Common Anglo-Saxon units of linear velocity:
1 foot per second (ft·sec^{-1}) = $3.048 \times ^{-1}$m·sec^{-1}
1 mile per hour (mile·hr^{-1}) = 4.470×10^{-1}m·sec^{-1}

Mass

Basic SI unit: kilogram (kg)
1 picogram (pg) $= 10^{-15}$ kg
1 nanogram (ng) $= 10^{-12}$ kg
1 microgram (μg) $= 10^{-9}$ kg
1 milligram (mg) $= 10^{-6}$ kg
1 gram (g) $= 10^{-3}$ kg
1 metric ton (t) $= 10^3$ kg
Common Anglo-Saxon units of mass:
1 ounce (oz) $= 2.834 \times 10^{-2}$ kg
1 pound (lb) $= 4.535 \times 10^{-1}$ kg
1 short ton (sh tn) $= 9.071 \times 10^2$ kg

Power

Basic SI unit: watt (W)
1 joule per second (j·sec^{-1}) $= 1$ W
1 erg per second (erg sec^{-1}) $= 10^7$ W
1 kilopond meter per minute (kpm·min^{-1}) $= 0.1635$ W
Common Anglo-Saxon units of power:
1 British thermal unit per hour (Btu·hr^{-1}) $= 2.931 \times 10^{-1}$ W
1 horsepower (hp) $= 7.457 \times 10^2$ W

Pressure

Basic SI unit: newton per square meter (N·m^{-2})
Common laboratory unit: millimeters of mercury (mm Hg)
1 mm Hg $= 133.322$ N·m^{-2}
1 atomsphere (atm) $= 101325$ N·m^{-2}
1 torr (torr) $= 133.322368$ N·m^{-2}

Temperature

Basic SI unit: Kelvin (K)
Common laboratory unit: degrees Celsius (°C). Note: The Celsius scale is subdivided into the same intervals as the Kelvin scale but has its zero point displaced by 273.15 K.

1 degree Celsius (°C) = 1 K
1 degree Celsius (°C) = 9/5 °Fahrenheit
Common Anglo-Saxon units of temperature:
1 degree Fahrenheit (°F) = 5/9 K
1 degree Rankine (°R) = 5/9 K

Time

Basic SI unit: second (sec)
1 minute (min) = 6×10 sec
1 hour (hr) = 3.6×10^3 sec
1 day (d) = 8.64×10^4 sec
1 year (y, 365 d) = 3.1536×10^7 sec

Volume

Basic SI Unit: cubic meter (m^3)
Common laboratory unit: liter (1)
1 cubic nanometer (nm^3) = 10^{-27} m^3
1 cubic micrometer (μm^3) 10^{-18} m^3
1 cubic millimeter (mm^3) = 10^{-9} m^3 = 1 microliter (μl)
1 cubic centimeter (cc^3) = 10^{-6} m^3 = 1 milliliter (ml)
1 cubic decimeter (dm^3) = 10^{-3} m^3 = 1 liter (l)
1 cubic kilometer (km^3) = 10^9 m^3 = 1 hectoliter (hl)
Common Anglo-Saxon units of volume:
1 cubic inch (in.^{3}) = 1.638×10^{-5} m^3
1 cubic foot (ft^3) = 2.831×10^{-2} m^3
1 cubic yard (yd^3) = 7.645×10^{-1} m^3
1 fluid ounce (fl oz) = 2.957×10^{-2} l
1 liquid quart (liq qt) = 9.463×10^{-1} l
1 gallon (gal) = 3.785 l

Work and Energy

Basic SI unit: joule (J)
1 kilocalorie (kcal) = 4186 J
1 kilopond meter (kpm) = 9.807 J

1 Newton meter (Nm) = 1 J
Common Anglo-Saxon units of power:
1 British thermal unit (Btu) = 1.055×10^3 J
1 horsepower-hour (hph) = 2.685×10^6 J
1 foot pound-force (ft lbf) = 1.356 J

Appendix III

Cardiac Drugs and Their Effects[a]

Digitalis (cardiac) Glycosides

Examples:

Oral: digitalis, digitoxin, digoxin, lanatoside C, acetyldigitoxin, gitalin.

Parenteral: ouabain, deslanoside, digitoxin, digoxin

Use: In heart failure—slows heart rate, increases cardiac contractility (inotropic effect), suppresses supraventricular antiarrhythmias, and reduces ventricular rate during atrial flutter or atrial fibrillation by increasing the automaticity of the secondary pacemakers in the atrioventricular node.

Mechanism of action: (1) CNS autonomic activity (2) Inhibition of (Na^+, K^+)-ATPase exchange pump

Effects on exercise or ECG: May increase work capacity and produce ST-segment depression on ECG.

[a]Note: This chart is a generalization. Particular drugs within a group may have different effects, particularly in abnormal physiological states, or when other drugs are taken concurrently.

Source: Brooks G. A. and T. D. Fahey Exercise Physiology: Human Bioenergetics and Its Applications. New York: Macmillan, 1984.

Diuretics

Examples:

High-potency diuretics (site of action is the ascending limb of the loop of Henli): organomercurials, ethacrynic acid, furosemide, bumetamide

Moderately potent (site of action is the proximal portion of the distal convoluted tubule): chlorothiazide, thiazides, phthalimidines, quinazolinones, benzene disulfonamides, and chlorobenzamides

Potassium-sparing diuretics (site of action is the distal portion of the distal convoluted tubule): spironolactone, triamterene, and amiloride

Use: Hypertension, heart failure, fluid retention, pulmonary edema

Mechanism: Generally work by inducing sodium diuresis (increased sodium excretion)

Effects on exercise and the ECG: May induce hypotension, ST-segment depression on ECG (if there is potassium depletion), and hyperglycemia. Will increase the frequency of arrhythmias in digitalis toxicity.

Catecholamines (sympathomimetic amines)

Examples: epinephrine, norepinephrine, isoproterenol, dopamine, and dobutaimine—administered intravenously or intramuscularly, or in aerosol (epinephrine or isoproterenol)

Use: To regulate heart rate and rhythm, arterial blood pressure; to increase cardiac contractility and peripheral organ perfusion (particularly in the lungs). Clinically, used in treatment of chronic obstructive pulmonary disease, allergic reactions (anaphylaxis), low cardiac output, and cardiac arrest.

Mechanism of action: Acts directly on α and β receptors of various tissues (smooth muscle, gland, or heart), which can produce mixed results. Stimulated α receptors cause vasoconstriction, whereas β receptors result in vasodilation, stimulation of heart rate and myocardial contractility, and relaxation of nonvascular smooth muscle.

Effects on exercise or ECG: May improve work capacity by increasing cardiac output and myocardial contractility, decrease the work of breathing in asthmatics, cause arrhythmias and electromechanical dissociation.

Vasodilators

Examples: Nitroglycerin, isosorbide dinitrate, hydralazine, isordil, prazocin, phentolamine, phenoxybenzamine, and trimethaphan—administered intravenously, sublingually, orally, or typically

Use: Angina, chronic congestive heart failure, hypertension, valvular heart disease, congenital heart diseases, chronic pulmonary hypertension

Mechanism: Some exert a direct and general effect on smooth muscle (nitroglycerine), whereas others act as an α-adrenergic blockade (phenoxybenzamine). Work principally by reducing the afterload of the heart, thus lowering myocardial O_2 consumption.

Effects on exercise and the ECG: Nitrites increase work capacity by raising the angina threshold. May cause hypotension and fainting. May increase orthostatic intolerance in bed rest.

β-Adrenergic Blocking Drugs

Examples: propranolol, alprenolol, lopressor, tenformin, metoprolol, atenolol

Use: Hypertension, angina, hypertrophic cardiomyopathy, congestive cardiomyopathy, cardiac arrhythmias, and thyrotoxicosis. Reduces heart rate and blood pressure.

Mechanism: β-adrenergic blocker

Effects on exercise and ECG: Decreases heart rate and blood pressure at rest and during exercise, decreases cardiac contractility, decreases work capacity, and may cause false negative on ECG.

Antiarrhythmic Drugs

Examples: Quinidine, procainamide, lidocaine, phenytoin, mexiletine, tocainide, and aprindine—administered orally or intravenously

Use: Suppression of arrhythmias; type of arrhythmia will dictate type of drug.

Mechanism: Individual drugs in this category have different mechanisms, including decreased automaticity, decreased membrane conductance to sodium, increased membrane conductance to potassium, decreased membrane conductance to calcium, and antisympathetic activity.

Effect on exercise or ECG: May cause false negative on ECG and may increase submaximal exercise heart rates (dose dependent)

Calcium Channel Blockers

Examples: Nifedipine, verapamil, diltiazem.

Use: Variant angina, classic angina, unstable angina, coronary spasm, reentrant supraventricular tachycardia, idiopathic hypertrophic subaortic stenosis.

Mechanism of action: Inhibits calcium ion influx from sarcoplasmic reticulum and T-tubules into myocardial cells, preventing contraction of calcium-dependent muscle.

Effects on exercise or ECG: Increases exercise tolerance by raising angina threshold and decreasing peripheral vascular resistance. ECG effects include: increased atrial refractory period, reduced A-V node conduction velocity, decreased automaticity and excitability of Purkinje fibers, and decreased ventricular conduction rate resulting in a broadened QRS complex.

Index